GOC

# Making Judicial Decisions

*Good Judgment*, based upon Robert J. Sharpe's experience as a lawyer, law professor, and judge, explores the role of the judge and the art of judging. Engaging with the American, English, and Commonwealth literature on the role of the judge in the common law tradition, *Good Judgment* addresses key questions: What exactly do judges do? What is properly within their role, and what falls outside? How do judges approach their decision-making task?

In an attempt to explain and reconcile two central features of judging – namely, judicial choice and judicial discipline – this book explores the nature and extent of judicial choice in the common law legal tradition and the structural features of that tradition that control and constrain the element of choice. As Sharpe explains, the law does not always provide clear answers, and judges are often left with difficult choices to make; on the other hand, the power of judicial choice is disciplined and constrained, and judges are not free to decide cases according to their own personal sense of justice. Accessibly written to appeal to the non-specialist reader with an interest in the judicial process, *Good Judgment* also tackles fundamental issues about the nature of law and the role of the judge and will be of particular interest to lawyers, judges, law students, and legal academics.

ROBERT J. SHARPE is a judge of the Court of Appeal for Ontario. He taught at the Faculty of Law, University of Toronto, from 1976 to 1988 and served under Chief Justice Brian Dickson as Executive Legal Officer at the Supreme Court of Canada from 1988 to 1990.

ROBERT J. SHARPE

# Good Judgment

## Making Judicial Decisions

UNIVERSITY OF TORONTO PRESS
Toronto   Buffalo   London

© University of Toronto Press 2018
Toronto Buffalo London
utorontopress.com
Printed in the U.S.A.

ISBN 978-1-4875-0306-2 (cloth)   ISBN 978-1-4875-2243-8 (paper)

---

**Library and Archives Canada Cataloguing in Publication**

Sharpe, Robert J., author
Good judgment : making judicial decisions / Robert J. Sharpe.

Includes bibliographical references and index.
ISBN 978-1-4875-0306-2 (hardcover).   ISBN 978-1-4875-2243-8 (softcover)

1. Judges.   2. Judges – Canada.   3. Judicial process.   4. Judicial
process – Canada.   I. Title.

K2146.S53 2018   347'.014   C2018-902369-4

---

This book has been published with the help of a grant from the Federation
for the Humanities and Social Sciences, through the Awards to Scholarly
Publications Program, using funds provided by the Social Sciences and
Humanities Research Council of Canada.

University of Toronto Press acknowledges the financial assistance to its
publishing program of the Canada Council for the Arts and the Ontario
Arts Council, an agency of the Government of Ontario.

**Canada Council   Conseil des Arts
for the Arts    du Canada**

# Contents

*Preface*   vii

1 Introduction   3

2 A Judge's Work   18

3 Is the Law Uncertain?   53

4 Do Judges Make Law?   77

5 Rules, Principles, and Policies   98

6 Disciplined Judicial Decision-Making   125

7 Working with Precedent   146

8 Authority: What Counts?   170

9 Judicial Decision-Making: A Case Study   188

10 Standard of Review and Discretion   203

11 Role of the Judge in a Constitutional Democracy   228

12 A Judicial State of Mind   249

Conclusion   270

*Glossary*   275

*Notes*   279

*Index*   333

# Preface

This book, based upon my experience as a lawyer, law professor, and judge, explores the role of the judge and the art of judging. What exactly do judges do? What is properly within their role, and what falls outside? How do judges approach their decision-making task? The central theme of the book is an attempt to explain and reconcile two fundamental features of judging: judicial choice and judicial discipline. The law does not always provide clear answers, and judges are left with difficult choices to make. On the other hand, the power of judicial choice is disciplined and constrained, and judges are not free to decide cases according to their own personal sense of justice. This book explores the nature and extent of judicial choice in the common law legal tradition and the structural features of that tradition that control and constrain that element of choice.

I decided to write the book after participating in the National Judicial Institute's *Good Judgment: Judicial Method and Decision-Making* seminar in December 2012. I owe a debt of thanks to the primary organizers, Justice Georgina Jackson and Professor Brettel Dawson, for involving me in that seminar and for planting the seed for this book.

For the past four years, I taught a seminar at the Faculty of Law, University of Toronto, based on various drafts of this book. I have benefited greatly from the contributions of my students and my judicial, professional, and academic colleagues who participated in the seminar by discussing draft chapters.

I also benefited from the contributions of several student research assistants. I thank Will Main and Spencer Robinson for their help. I owe a special thanks to Scarlett Smith, who assisted me in the final stages of preparation and who provided me with countless suggestions for improvement both in style and in substance.

I thank several friends and colleagues who read the manuscript at various stages and who offered valuable comments and insights. I list them in alphabetical order: Bryan Finlay, Helena Likwornik, James MacPherson, Caroline Mandell, Jason Nyers, Guy Pratte, Kent Roach, Stephen Waddams, and Alison Warner.

I thank the Honourable R. Roy McMurtry, my former Chief Justice, who kindly gave me permission to use the image of his painting "Osgoode Hall" on the cover.

I thank Ian MacKenzie for his copy editing as well as my law clerk Veenu Goswami and my assistant Adriana Urtubey for their help with proofreading.

Finally, I thank Len Husband, Wayne Herrington, and the team at the University of Toronto Press for their care and attention in the publication of this book.

Robert J. Sharpe
June 2018

# GOOD JUDGMENT

## Making Judicial Decisions

## Chapter 1

# Introduction

In this book, I explore the role of an appellate judge in Canada. I write it with some trepidation. Many of the issues I discuss are difficult and controversial. I am a judge, not a legal philosopher. No doubt many judges, lawyers, academics, non-lawyers, and politicians will disagree with some of the views I express. But I decided to write the book anyway. The process would force me to clarify my own thinking on the judicial function, and it seems to me that there is something to be said for setting out the views of an experienced Canadian appellate judge in the early years of the twenty-first century.

My goal is to explore the role of the judge and the art of judging. What exactly do judges do? What is properly within their role, and what falls outside? How do judges approach their decision-making task? I can only speak for myself, but I will speak as frankly as I can. I will do my best to provide insight into the mind of one working judge. I hope that my account will be of interest and accessible not only to judges, lawyers, and law students, but also to non-specialist readers who are interested in the legal process.

The book is based on my experience of fifty years in the law. In this chapter I will briefly describe my path to provide some context for my views on the role of the judge. I will outline the experiences that have been formative for my legal career: my intellectual formation as a student at the Faculty of Law, University of Toronto, and a graduate student at Oxford; my experience in practice with MacKinnon, McTaggart; my academic career as a professor of law; my work with Chief Justice Brian Dickson at the Supreme Court of Canada; and finally my experience as a trial and appellate judge in Ontario.

## Law School

I entered first year at the Faculty of Law, University of Toronto, in 1966, and I immediately knew I had found my calling. It was the subject I had been looking for. I had studied political science and history at the University of Western Ontario, and to this day I remain very interested in both subjects. I had seriously considered doing graduate work in political science but, in the end, I was not convinced that I was suited for a career in that realm – whether it be in academe or in some form of public service.

I quickly learned that the study of law had an astonishingly wide theoretical dimension. My professors, it seemed, could not even agree on a basic definition of law. In the late 1960s, there was (I should add – there still is and probably always will be!) a lively debate about the very nature of law. For example, some professors seemed aligned with English legal philosopher H.L.A. Hart, who propounded a compelling positivist account of law.[1] Hart conceived of law as a self-contained, integral discipline, the validity and force of which did not depend upon external moral values. Any reassurance I could glean from Hart's crystal-clear and pure vision of the law was challenged by other professors who sided with American theoretician Lon Fuller. Fuller took a fundamentally different view of the relationship between law and morality.[2] Fuller argued that there are "principles of legality" that express the inner morality of law. These standards are integral to the concept of law and ensure that law embodies the moral values of respect, fairness, and predictability. According to Fuller, nothing that fails to meet these standards can qualify as law.

While Hart and Fuller debated whether the law was dependent upon external moral values,[3] Hart also debated Patrick Devlin, a prominent English judge, about the role of the criminal law in the enforcement of morality.[4] Legal realists were arguing, rather cynically I thought, that the law as expounded by the courts was nothing more than a product of the personal and political views of the judges.[5]

I was interested in these theoretical debates, but in the late 1960s legal theory was not the focus of our legal education. I have to admit as well that if there had been nothing more to law than legal theory, the study of law would not have captured me as it did. What I found truly compelling, and what our legal education stressed, was that law combined the theoretical dimension with the need for hard-nosed, practical reasoning to resolve the multitude of real-world problems that profoundly affect individuals and our society. I found the combination of a challenging intellectual discipline directly related to problems that matter in the real world to be compelling.

As I went from one class to another, I was exposed to the first-class minds of my professors and my fellow students, struggling to sort out the intricacies of crimes, torts, contracts, and property. I studied law in the era of the case method. We were assigned cases to read before each class. Most of the cases were leading decisions that stood as precedents, but some were relatively obscure cases that captured the professor's attention because they raised novel and intriguing points. We were expected to have identified the facts that mattered and to have disregarded the facts that did not count, to have identified the key issues, and to be ready with our own critical assessment of the court's decision. Most professors proceeded by asking questions, only grudgingly giving any indication of what they thought the answer should be. We were told that there were textbooks that purported to state the law. Some of our professors had written these books, but reliance on texts was discouraged. There was no substitute, we were told, for struggling through the mess of experience revealed by the cases, to build our own capacity to "think like a lawyer."

The study of law, unlike other disciplines, and certainly unlike the sciences, is not incremental. First-year students do not start with the basics and work their way up. Law students hone their skills by immediately focusing on tough cases and cutting-edge issues. This is both bewildering and exhilarating. Bewildering because most of us come to the law with the belief that the law is clear and definite. We think that once we learn the rules, we simply have to apply them to the facts. The first-year law student quickly learns that the law is often less than clear. Difficult cases arise and there is no obvious answer. Those were the cases upon which as fledgling lawyers we cut our teeth. Our professors were not interested in the easy cases at the shallow end of the pool. We were forced to plunge immediately into the deep end. We had not yet learned to swim, but we discovered that, with considerable effort and application, we could make it back to the edge of the pool.

I recall, as a first-year law student, being astonished to discover how uncertain the law is. The professors had lots of questions but very few answers. I thought they were playing games with us. But

now, fifty years later, the game still goes on. What was once a curios-
ity has now become a responsibility. As a judge, I have the responsibility to decide cases. Often the decision is anything but clear.

Where should the judge deciding the case look for guidance? Is
the point at issue governed by a common law precedent? If yes, does
the judge have to follow the precedent, or should it be distinguished,
ignored, or overruled? What policies did Parliament intend to implement when it enacted that statute? Is the result that seems to follow from applying the precedent or the statute fair and just? If not,
is there anything the judge can or should do to reach a just result?
What are the broader implications for society when deciding a case
this way or that? How should the law be changed to achieve the goal
of justice for all in a free and democratic society? Is this a change the
court can make, or must the problem be left to Parliament? There
were no easy answers, and the law school debates about these questions bear remarkable similarity to the discussions my colleagues
and I have as we work out how to decide the cases that come before
the court.

In this book I will do my best to explain, on the basis of my own
experience, how I think judges should resolve these issues.

### France

After my first year of law school, I took a year away from law to live
and study in France at the University of Caen. I took a French language and civilization course designed for foreign students. I sat in
on a few law classes, but I cannot claim that I was a diligent student.
I did spend a lot of time conversing with my fellow foreign students
in fractured French, and, by the end of the year, I had acquired a reasonable level of proficiency. The defining moment occurred towards
the end of my year in the spring of 1968 when an uprising of French
students provoked a near revolution. As an innocent observer, I had
my one and only encounter with tear gas. I was glued to the radio
and to debates over the political crisis that ensued.

The experience of living in France had a lasting effect upon my
outlook. I learned what it was like to live as a foreigner, completely
immersed in another language and culture. I did my best to understand what was happening and to explain my own views, but, like
many of the litigants I now see in court, I had barriers of culture
and language to overcome. I learned a lot about a great nation with

a rich cultural and intellectual tradition that had experienced both revolution and war. I lived through a dramatic political crisis that shook France to the core. I saw how a powerful government could be threatened by a popular uprising of rowdy and disorganized students. I learned that one should never simply assume the justice of the status quo or think that things might not change. I also saw that, from the perspective of distance and different experience, one gains a richer appreciation of home.

## Articling

I graduated in 1970 with a law degree from the University of Toronto and articled with a small Toronto law firm, MacKinnon, McTaggart. It was a truly formative year. I was able to connect my interest in the intellectual and academic side of law with the practical side and learn how the law actually affects people. I had the privilege of working with a remarkable group of lawyers who shared that fascination. Bert MacKinnon, a brilliant advocate who would later become the first Associate Chief Justice of Ontario, was the leader of the firm. For reasons unclear to me, Bert often worked in the firm's small library rather than in his office. As an articling student, I regularly found myself in the library working on a memo. Bert had his calls directed to a phone in the library, and from my corner I watched and listened to a great lawyer carrying on his daily practice. I worked on many of the cases Bert was arguing, and he invariably took his articling students along when the case came before the court. Bert was a Rhodes Scholar and Oxford graduate, but a man of humble beginnings. He was determined to avoid any of the manners or trappings of the typical Bay Street lawyer, save one – he was a superb and fearless advocate.

I also worked very closely with, and learned a great deal from, Arthur Stone, a future member of the Federal Court of Appeal. Arthur was a generalist. He had an unusual practice that combined corporate-commercial work with a maritime law litigation. He was also counsel to the Institute of Chartered Accountants of Ontario. Like Bert, Arthur had a graduate degree in law, in his case a Harvard LLM.

Arthur and Bert personified the spirit of the firm. They had a vision of what it means to be a lawyer, a vision that Arthur conveyed to me when I first met him at my articling interview. It was a vision

that attracted me to the firm, and that has stayed with me ever since.
They saw the practice of law as much more than a money-making
exercise. For them, the practice of law was an intellectual pursuit
and a form of public service. They aspired not to maximize profit but
to attain professional integrity and excellence. They taught me by
their example that a lawyer's role is to offer wise and candid advice –
even if the advice is not what the client wants to hear. Advice that
is based upon a thorough and principled understanding of the law
and how it operates in society. They took enormous pride in delivering the best possible service to their clients, and they seemed uncon-
cerned that there might be someone down the street doing things
differently and making more money.

There were several other outstanding lawyers at MacKinnon,
McTaggart: Edgar Sexton, another future Federal Court of Appeal
judge, William Herridge, another Harvard graduate, and Joe Potts,
a Cambridge graduate and future member of the Supreme Court of
Ontario. Ian Binnie, a Cambridge graduate and brilliant advocate
who would later serve with great distinction for more than ten years
as a member of the Supreme Court of Canada, had taken the year
away from the firm to work in Tanzania, but I had the privilege of
working with Ian two years later after my Oxford interlude. Bert
MacKinnon and Ian Binnie, two of the finest legal minds I have encountered, had a remarkable ability to cut quickly through complex
and apparently unfavourable facts to uncover a compelling argument to advance their client's case. George Strathy, a brilliant young
lawyer who articled and joined the firm shortly after I did, is now
Chief Justice of Ontario.

### Oxford

During my articling year, I decided that much as I liked the look of
what it would be to practise law, I wanted to broaden my experience.
I was accepted at Oxford to study for the BCL, the Oxford equivalent
of an LLM, and my mentors at the firm encouraged me to go.

When I got to Oxford, I attended a few BCL classes and quickly
realized that excellent though they were, I had spent enough time
in the classroom and that I wanted a different experience. I was able
to transfer to the research-based DPhil program, the Oxford equivalent of a PhD, to write a thesis on the law of *habeas corpus* under
the supervision of Professor H.W.R. Wade. Despite its fundamental

importance, little had been written on *habeas corpus*. That was a gap that Professor Wade thought should be filled, and it seemed to me to be an ideal thesis topic. It was an important subject, easy to define, and the material was there to be mined in the case reports. When Professor Wade left for a sabbatical, Ian Brownlie became my supervisor. Brownlie was a distinguished international lawyer who would later hold the Chichele Chair in International Law at Oxford and argue many significant cases before the International Court of Justice. *Habeas corpus* was only barely within his realm of expertise, but he was a superb supervisor. As an Oxford law tutor he had taught subjects across the entire legal spectrum, and he provided the generalist's capacity to see the connections between my specific subject and other areas of the law. Brownlie was also a dedicated and highly accomplished legal scholar. He taught me how to attack and successfully complete a major writing project.

The Oxford experience strengthened my commitment, first acquired at the University of Toronto, to take an intellectually rigorous approach to law. Everywhere I looked, people were exploring and pushing ideas to the limit. The college structure, where faculty and students from across all disciplines mingle, encourages interdisciplinary debate. I was exposed to the finest lecturer I have ever heard when I attended a series given by Ronald Dworkin on what was then a work in progress, *Taking Rights Seriously*.[6] As will be apparent from the pages that follow, I have certainly been influenced by Dworkin's views.

In the early 1970s, there were relatively few DPhil students at Oxford, and many members of the faculty were dubious about what the DPhil offered. Supervision was spotty, and many students languished for years without completing the degree. Brownlie was determined that a successful thesis could be written in two years. I had planned to be in Oxford for no longer than that, so we formed a useful alliance. I left Oxford after two years with a complete draft of my thesis. I polished it during my time at the Bar Admission Course and graduated with the DPhil in 1974.

## Legal Practice

I returned to MacKinnon, McTaggart to practise law. My work was mostly civil litigation. Although I was a very junior lawyer, I was regularly in court arguing procedural motions, conducting short

trials, both civil and criminal, and I appeared on my own in the
Court of Appeal on a few cases. I also worked closely with the more
senior members of the firm on major files, interviewing witnesses,
working on legal opinions and memoranda, drafting pleadings
and affidavits, and conducting oral examinations for discovery and
out-of-court cross-examinations. I drafted written arguments or
factums for the Court of Appeal and the Supreme Court of Canada
and always attended as junior counsel when the case was argued.
It was an exceptional exposure to the real world of lawyering and
litigation.

### Academic Life and the University of Toronto

I enjoyed practice and likely would have remained at the firm had it
not been for a casual conversation with Martin Friedland. Marty had
been my first-year criminal law professor and after I graduated had
been appointed as the Dean of the Faculty of Law. Marty became a
life-long friend and mentor to whom I have always been able to turn
for advice. Horace Krever, my Civil Procedure professor, had just
been appointed to the bench, and Marty needed someone to teach
the subject. I mentioned to him that I would be interested in doing
some part-time teaching. That evoked little interest, but when I also
mentioned that I had converted my thesis into a book[7] and was just
reviewing the page proofs, Marty made me an offer: rather than just
teach a course, why not give academic life a serious try and come for
a year as a full-time faculty member. I thought I had nothing to lose
and I accepted.

I never regretted my decision to embark upon an academic career. It suited my abilities and my temperament. I enjoyed the teaching and I was enthusiastic about research and writing. I started out
teaching Civil Procedure and Criminal Law in the first-year program, as well as Remedies, an upper-year course that I designed. My
time in practice gave me a level of confidence I would have lacked
had I embarked on an academic career immediately after Oxford. It
allowed me to offer my students an academic approach imbued with
some real-life experience. It also influenced my research and writing.
I always saw my audience as including judges and practising lawyers as well as fellow members of the academy.

As a faculty member, I was permitted to do a limited amount of
outside work, and it was in that capacity that I remained on the

letterhead of my old law firm. I valued the connection with the firm, and I thought that my teaching and scholarly work benefited from my continued exposure to practice.

After a few years at the law school, and after the enactment of the *Canadian Charter of Rights and Freedoms*,[8] I moved away from criminal law and started to teach constitutional law. My combined interest in constitutional law and civil litigation led me to start the Constitutional Litigation Program, the modest predecessor of the David Asper Centre for Constitutional Rights. The idea was to take on *Charter* cases, almost always on a pro bono basis, and to involve the students in the preparation and argument. To my amazement the idea worked, and some very interesting cases came my way – no doubt in large part because the price was right! My usual role was to appear on behalf of a public interest litigant as an intervener in litigation started by other parties. In one case, I represented the Women's Legal Action Fund (LEAF),[9] and in another, an association of private schools,[10] and the Canadian Civil Liberties Association in several cases.[11] I was involved in some great cases, and I thoroughly enjoyed the challenge of arguing them before the courts at all levels.

I think that my years of teaching had made me a better advocate. My approach in the classroom had never been very theoretical or abstract. I was used to identifying and exploring the basic underlying principles and explaining complex ideas in simple terms that my students could absorb. To the extent that my approach as counsel was academic, it helped that I was arguing these cases in the early years of the *Charter* when the judges were treading new ground and were probably more open to a scholarly approach than they might have been in other areas.

## Executive Legal Officer at the Supreme Court of Canada

After twelve years of teaching I accepted Chief Justice Brian Dickson's offer to serve as the Executive Legal Officer at the Supreme Court of Canada. This gave me the opportunity to work very closely for almost three years with one of Canada's greatest judges. I did not have a clear job description, but I was involved in virtually all aspects of his work. I also got to know the other judges and to observe first-hand the workings of the court. It was an enormous privilege to work closely with Brian Dickson and to witness first-hand his

qualities of wisdom, decency, courage, and compassion. He enriched
my outlook on life and my approach to the law. I could have had no
finer role model.[12] I was committed to returning to the law school
after completing my work at the Supreme Court. At the same time,
the experience of working with a great judge certainly made me
think that at some point I would welcome a judicial appointment.

## Law School Dean

In 1990, I returned to the university as the Dean of the Faculty of
Law. I took enormous pride in being a member of the faculty. To
be selected as its leader was a great honour. I enjoyed my work
as Dean, working with a very strong faculty and with the exceptional group of enthusiastic and talented students it attracted. As
Dean, I was also involved in the general administration of the
university. That opened my eyes to the diversity and strength of
the University of Toronto, one of the world's great institutions of
higher learning.

As I approached the end of my term as Dean, I had no aspiration
for more university administration. I would have been content to
return to the professorial ranks, but I had a lingering feeling that
my time as a legal academic had run its course. I admired the new
wave of legal scholarship that was sweeping the academy. I thought
that the law school's emphasis on legal theory and interdisciplinary work was appropriate and in keeping with its academic mission.
But I could see that I was not as well suited to that style of scholarship as the fresh young PhDs in philosophy, economics, history,
and political science who had also acquired law degrees and who
would transform legal scholarship. My interest in law had always
tilted towards the academic side, but my scholarly work was largely
aimed at helping lawyers and judges solve practical and immediate
day-to-day problems. While I strongly believe that university law
faculties should encourage that type of scholarship, it seemed to me
that whatever knowledge and skills I had acquired would be better
deployed if I were a judge. So when the chance came, I opted for a
judicial career.

In February 1995, I began my judicial career as a trial judge on the
Ontario Court of Justice, General Division, since renamed the Superior Court of Justice. Four and a half years later, I was appointed to
the Court of Appeal for Ontario.

## Legal Theory: Another View of the Cathedral

I am interested in legal theory, because almost every legal theory book or article I read sheds some light on my work as a judge. I believe that academic and theoretical inquiry enriches one's appreciation and understanding of legal principles, and that a judge who is aware of theoretical issues and debates will be a better judge.

However, as anyone who has entered a courtroom will know, the daily task of deciding cases is anything but theoretical. As this book is based on the experience that I have just outlined, it should come as no surprise that my approach will be more practical than theoretical. The task of the judge is to decide specific cases that arise from actual disputes. I will argue in this book that the judge should always strive to decide cases in a manner that comports with the fundamental principles of justice that sustain our legal regime. At the same time, when deciding cases, the judge will necessarily focus upon the specific facts and circumstances of the case. The judge is acutely aware that the decision will directly affect the lives of the litigants, and the immediate objective will be to achieve practical justice.

My task as a judge is not to propound theory but to listen to the evidence and the legal arguments and to decide cases. The impartial judge does not come to that task with an agenda or with a theory to advance. I admire the efforts of scholars who develop and propound theories of justice with rigorous consistency. But as a judge, I am expected to keep an open mind.

To engage in theoretical and philosophical inquiry is to enter a dialogue that will continue for a long time and may never end. To be a judge is to decide a case once and for all, right now. Francis Bacon, the seventeenth-century philosopher and judge, observed, the discourses of philosophers "are as the stars, which give little light, because they are so high."[13] Or, to use a more modern saying, "[I]n theory there is no difference between theory and practice but in practice there is."[14] As a judge, I am confronted with the mess and confusion of the human condition. I must do my best to make sense of it all, decide the case, and then get on to the next one. I am neither equipped nor suited for the luxury of open-ended philosophical inquiry. The elusive pursuit of such a theory would be dangerous. It is likely to lead to the paralysis of indecision or to the application of a standard that appeals to me but that lacks sufficient legal pedigree.

I am also sceptical of an overly theoretical approach because I do not think that any single author or theory can completely or adequately explain the task of adjudication.[15] The law touches virtually every area of human activity and all manner of social interaction. The judge will confront a remarkably diverse range of human problems involving a wide range of subjects. I have not yet encountered any single theory that I thought was capable of responding to all those problems and subjects, and I doubt that I ever will. As Israeli Justice Aharon Barak puts it, "[H]uman experience is too rich to be imprisoned in a single legal theory."[16] And even if I did discover a theory that persuaded me that it was the answer to all problems, I doubt that such a theory would attract sufficiently widespread acceptance to count as a basis for deciding cases. A hallmark of modern liberal democracy is the acceptance that within a single society there will be differing views about the good. Justice is achieved not by selecting once and for all one view of the good over another but by mediating the differences through open and fair procedures that allow conflicting views to be heard.[17]

I will not consciously advocate or advance any particular theory of justice in this book. By theory of justice, I mean the kind of meta or high-level theory that expounds on a grand scale the way a polity should be ordered to achieve justice for all. I include in the category of meta-theory a school of thought that attempts to explain significant aspects of the legal system on the basis of some external discipline or philosophy (e.g., "law and economics").

However, as will be evident from the pages that follow, I do believe that judges should aspire to respect and maintain a rational and coherent legal regime based upon fundamental principles of justice. To achieve that objective, the judge must engage in the type of inquiry that has variously been described as "mid-level theory,"[18] "operative theory,"[19] or "interpretive theory."[20] The judge must be willing to look below the surface of the black-letter rules that apply to the case at hand. The judge must dig down to the underlying general legal principles that structure the legal regime as a whole. The judge has an obligation to ensure that each individual decision comports with the overall integrity of the legal order. While engaging with "the messiness of real-world judicial reasoning," the judge aspires to identify and apply principles that take into account not just the details but also the "broad landscape of precedents," to "expose inconsistencies," and to "formulate underlying rational principles" that will serve to guide decisions and to allow the courts to develop the law in a coherent manner.[21]

The metaphor I use to explain how I think a judge should use legal theory is borrowed from the great American legal scholar and judge Guido Calabresi. He titled his very influential article on the economic analysis of law "Property Rules, Liability Rules and Inalienability: One View of the Cathedral" and explained: "This article concerns only one possible way of looking at and analyzing legal problems … [W]e are merely interested in the light that a different legal approach may shed on legal problems frequently looked at from a legal process perspective … [T]his article is meant to be only *one* of Monet's paintings of the Cathedral at Rouen."[22]

Calabresi is referring to approximately thirty paintings by the great French impressionist painter Claude Monet depicting Notre Dame Cathedral at Rouen at various times of day and with different light and shadow. Each work shows a different aspect of the cathedral. We might prefer one to the others, but no single painting captures the cathedral to our complete satisfaction. It is only by looking at them all that we gain a deeper appreciation of the cathedral's beauty and majesty.

I suggest that "one view of the cathedral" offers a useful metaphor to explain how a judge might use legal theory. Each theory, like each painting, offers some insight into the legal process. Some theories offer more than others, but, like Monet's paintings, no single theory is capable of revealing or explaining to our complete satisfaction the full beauty and majesty of the cathedral to which we aspire: the goal of achieving justice under law.

### Outline of the Book

In chapter 2, "A Judge's Work," I describe the process for judicial appointments and suggest how the process for judicial appointments should be improved. I explain some of the day to day features of the work of trial and appellate judges. I consider the role of judges in guiding parties to pretrial settlement and as mediators. I consider the advantages and disadvantages of specialist and generalist judges. How do judges prepare for hearings and what resources do they have to draw upon? What is the relative importance of written and oral argument and how do judges engage with counsel? What is the process for actually deciding cases in an appellate court and what is the purpose of a dissenting judgment?

In chapters 3 to 5, I explore general issues about the nature of law
and the challenges of judging.

Chapter 3 considers the question of legal uncertainty. Why do I
say that the law is necessarily uncertain, and what are the implications of legal uncertainty for the judicial process? What is the extent
of legal uncertainty? Does legal uncertainty leave me free to decide
cases according to my own personal sense of justice? If not, what
prevents me from doing so? Are there "right answers" to every legal
question, and if not, what disciplines the choices I make?

In chapter 4, "Do Judges Make Law?," I turn to the issue of judicial
law-making. I will argue that elements of judicial law-making are an
inherent, inevitable, and desirable part of our common law tradition.
I will explain why I think that to be the case and consider the reach
and limits of the judicial law-making role.

In chapter 5, "Rules, Principles, and Policies," I examine the types
of legal norms or standards with which I work as a judge: specific
rules, general standards, overarching principles, and general policies. I consider how these types of legal norms relate to each other
and how judges can use them to create a rational and coherent
scheme of law. I consider the increasing tendency to cast the law in
terms of broad principles rather than specific rules and examine the
advantages and disadvantages of that approach.

In chapters 6 to 10, I consider the constraints that structure and
discipline judicial decision-making.

Chapter 6, "Disciplined Judicial Decision-Making," looks at the
nature of reasoning used by lawyers and judges and examines its
distinctive features. I examine certain institutional factors that structure judicial reasoning and limit the capacity of judges to decide
cases on the basis of their personal or political views. I argue that the
obligation to give reasoned decisions is fundamental to transparent,
accountable, and disciplined judicial decision-making.

In chapter 7, I turn to the idea of precedent. Why does the common
law insist on faithfulness to prior decisions? I consider the judicial
hierarchy and the distinctive roles played by trial, appellate, and
apex courts. When is a prior decision controlling? How do we deal
with our mistakes, and when can we depart from a prior ruling? I
explore the ways in which the law's adherence to precedent has soft-
ened in recent years and consider the implications of that tendency.

Chapter 8, "Authority: What Counts?," considers the use of non-
binding authority in judicial decision-making. When can a court

consider foreign law, academic writing, and non-traditional schol-arly sources? How should a judge use such sources when deciding a case?

In chapter 9, I pause to offer a case study of judicial decision-mak-ing, a case that identified a new civil wrong for invasion of personal privacy. This chapter provides a concrete example of many of the more general points that I discuss in the earlier chapters, and some readers might find it useful to read this chapter first as an introduc-tion to what follows.

Chapter 10 considers the related issues of "the standard of review" and "discretion" that define the roles of first-instance decision-mak-ers and appellate judges. What are the respective roles of trial and appellate courts when it comes to determining facts? Standard of review has become a judicial preoccupation. It limits the powers of reviewing and appellate courts to interfere with first-instance deci-sions. Is this consistent with the ideal of legality and respect for the law's general standards? What do we mean when we say a decision-maker has "discretion"? Does limiting review of discretionary deci-sions leave decision-makers free to decide as they please rather than according to some general legal standard?

Chapter 11, "Role of the Judge in a Constitutional Democracy," explores the rationale for judicial decision-making in constitutional cases. The chapter focuses on the legitimacy of judicial review to strike down laws that infringe upon the *Charter of Rights and Freedoms.*

Chapter 12, "A Judicial State of Mind," examines the essential attributes of judicial independence and impartiality. How do we ensure that judges display those qualities? Are judges expected or allowed to be compassionate, or must they always follow the letter of the law?

The book ends with a brief conclusion drawing together the main themes of the book.

I have tried to write this book in a style that will be accessible to readers without formal legal training, but I realize that my primary audience is likely to be law students, lawyers, and judges. While many of the issues I discuss are difficult and perplexing, they are issues that we all must be willing to confront and debate in a society that aspires to justice under law. I do not pretend to have provided answers that will end the debate, but I hope that my views will con-tribute something to it.

## Chapter 2

# A Judge's Work

In this chapter, I will describe the day-to-day work of trial and appellate judges as a prelude to my discussion of the decision-making process in later chapters. I begin with a brief discussion about how judges are appointed.

## The Appointment Process

The federal process for the appointment of Canadian judges can best be described as murky. The legal requirements for appointment are minimal, and the process is more vulnerable than it should be to the influence of politics, cronyism, and personal favouritism.

The *Constitution Act, 1867*, provides that "[t]he Governor General shall appoint the Judges of the Superior, District, and County Courts in each Province."[1] A judge so appointed has tenure of office, removable only by a joint address of the Senate and House of Commons, until the judge reaches the mandatory retirement age of seventy-five.[2] After fifteen years of service, provided the judge's combined age and years of service equal eighty, a judge has the option of carrying on as a full-time judge, retiring with the statutory pension or annuity,[3] or continuing in office as a "supernumerary" judge with reduced duties.[4] Many judges who reach the age of eligible retirement continue on with full-time duties. Some retire and join a law firm or become arbitrators and mediators. While I have no statistics, it is my impression that most elect supernumerary status. A supernumerary judge receives the same salary and benefits as a full-time judge. This is a good deal for the taxpayer, as the judge could simply retire and collect the statutory annuity of two-thirds salary. A supernumerary judge continues to work, usually half-time but sometimes more and, for working half-time, is paid one third of a judge's salary in addition to the annuity. It is also a good deal for the court, as the judge is replaced with a new appointment, and the court continues to benefit from the supernumerary judge's expertise. This is particularly important for busy courts, where it would be difficult for the regular full-time complement to keep up with the work.

By convention, judicial appointments are made by the Cabinet on the recommendation of the Minister of Justice. The federal *Judges Act* provides the minimum requirement for appointment, namely, being a member of the bar with ten years standing.[5] Most judges are at least in their mid-forties with fifteen to twenty years of legal experience. Most will have some experience as trial counsel in civil, family, or criminal cases; however, the number of judges appointed without litigation experience has grown in recent years. Some judges come from a commercial law background,[6] and there is a small but growing number of law professors appointed to the bench. The Court of Appeal for Ontario currently has seven former academics,[7] and all but one came to the court having sat as trial judges. Although I am obviously biased on the point, I support the appointment of academics to the bench. Academics are usually adept at discerning the principles that shape the law and accustomed to writing – skills that are very important for judges, particularly at the appellate level.

There is no statutory process for making appointments. Until fairly recently, there was no formal application process, and appointments were entirely within the discretion of the Minister of Justice and the government of the day. The process has gradually been improved but, in my view, it remains far from ideal. The first improvement came in 1966 when the Minister of Justice agreed to consult with the Canadian Bar Association's National Committee on the Judiciary prior to making judicial appointments. In the mid-1970s, the Minister of Justice appointed a special adviser for judicial appointments, someone who assumed responsibility for gathering information on prospective candidates for judicial office.

The process was significantly improved in 1988 when a new practice was adopted.[8] A candidate for judicial office must submit a written application indicating experience and interest and the names of individuals who could be contacted as references.[9] The application is considered by a Judicial Advisory Committee ("JAC") comprising a judge nominated by the Chief Justice of the province, lawyers nominated by the provincial law society, the bar association, and the provincial Attorney General, and lay persons nominated by the Minister of Justice.[10] The JAC does not interview candidates but does review their qualifications and is at liberty to contact the named referees and others to assess the candidate's suitability for judicial office.

Until 2007, the JAC assessed the candidates using the categories "highly qualified," "qualified," or "not suitable for judicial office" and sent the names of those highly qualified or qualified to the Minister of Justice. That was changed in 2007 when the committees were instructed to drop the highly qualified category and simply forward the names of all qualified candidates. Another change was to take away the voting rights of judges serving on the JACs. It is difficult to see any reason for those changes other than to restrict the capacity of the advisory committees to ensure high-quality appointments and to give the Minister greater control.

In 2016, the government announced a number of positive changes to the process. The "highly recommended" category has been restored, as have the voting rights of judicial JAC members. Members of the public are invited to apply for appointment to the JACs, and measures have been introduced to encourage diversity in judicial appointments. Entities responsible for nominating individuals to serve as members of JACs will be asked to take into account the need to ensure that JACs are representative of the diversity of Canada, and JAC members are to be provided with training on diversity, unconscious bias, and assessment of merit.

This process does weed out candidates who are clearly not suited to judicial office, but it falls well short of assuring that only the best candidates get appointed. The pool of qualified candidates is large and of varying quality, and there is nothing in place to discipline the Minister's selection of who gets appointed. It is also notorious that at times in the past, other Ministers who control the government's patronage agenda have been heavily involved in the process. There is a very long list of candidates who were approved by the advisory committee and who would have been excellent judges but, for reasons of politics and patronage, were passed over for inferior candidates. While the quality of judicial appointments in Canada is, generally speaking, quite good, it could be much better. I will discuss how the process could be improved below.

## Supreme Court of Canada Appointments

Perhaps of greatest public concern is the manner in which appointments to the Supreme Court of Canada are made. I emphasize that in recent years all those appointed to the Supreme Court of Canada have been well qualified for the position. The problem with the process is that it has lacked transparency and appears to be vulnerable to political manipulation.

The statutory qualifications for appointment to the Supreme Court are minimal. Anyone who is a superior court judge or a member of the bar of ten years' standing is eligible.[11] Most Supreme Court judges have prior judicial experience, but there is ordinarily at least one member of the court appointed directly from the bar. Most recently, Justices John Sopinka and Ian Binnie filled that role with great distinction. Eight of the nine current members of the court previously served as appellate judges. The ninth judge, Justice Suzanne Côté, was appointed directly to the court from the bar of Quebec. While experience as a trial judge is important for appellate judges, there is much to be said for some direct appointments from the bar to both the Supreme and intermediate appellate courts.[12] Senior counsel bring a fresh perspective from practice and enhance the credibility of the court with the practising bar.

The *Supreme Court Act* requires that three of the nine judges be appointed from Quebec.[13] By convention, three judges are from Ontario, two are from Western Canada, and one is from the Atlantic provinces. Supreme Court judges serve until age seventy-five[14] but may retire after ten years on the court.[15]

Appointments to the Supreme Court of Canada fall within the prerogative of the Prime Minister.[16] Until 2006, the Prime Minister simply announced the appointment on the advice of the Minister of Justice following informal consultation with senior members of the bench and bar. The process was widely criticized for lacking transparency, and many argued that the public was entitled to have some knowledge of the background and abilities of the candidates before they were appointed. Provincial governments long complained that they should have some say in appointments.

Starting in 2006, there was an attempt to open the window on Supreme Court appointments. Initially, the Minister of Justice appeared before a committee of parliamentarians, judges, and lawyers to announce the appointment and to answer questions.[17] Subsequent

appointments were made after a similarly composed advisory committee provided a shortlist to the Prime Minister, who then made the
nomination from that list. The nominee appeared before the committee in a public hearing to respond to questions, and the appointment was confirmed shortly thereafter. In 2009, the composition of
the advisory committee was changed and consisted of members of
Parliament with no outside judicial or legal representation. Brent
Rathgeber, a disgruntled Conservative MP who served on the 2011
advisory committee, reported that the committee's "unofficial criteria" for recommending the shortlist included "judgments support-
ing the government's law and order agenda; and, most importantly,
judicial deference."[18]

This process was abandoned following the failed attempt to appoint Justice Nadon to the Supreme Court in 2013. For the following
two appointments, the government reverted to a process where the
Prime Minister simply announced the appointments with no visible
input from the public, the judiciary, or the legal profession.[19]

The lack of a steady or consistent process to discipline the appointment of Supreme Court judges has been a matter of concern, and
there is continuing pressure for a more rigorous approach. We clearly
need to find a method that enjoys public acceptance and that reflects
the need to ensure merit, transparency, diversity, non-partisanship,
and judicial independence.

A new process was implemented in 2016 that led to the appointments of Justices Malcolm Rowe and Sheila Martin in 2017.
Aspiring candidates were invited to apply for the appointment,
and a detailed list of qualifications and assessment criteria was
announced.[20] A seven-member Independent Advisory Board for
Supreme Court of Canada Judicial Appointments was established.
Chaired by a former Prime Minister, the committee consists of a
retired judge nominated by the Canadian Judicial Council; two
lawyers, one nominated by the Canadian Bar Association and
the other by the Federation of Law Societies of Canada; a legal
scholar nominated by the Council of Canadian Law Deans; and
two non-lawyers nominated by the Minister of Justice. Applicants
submitted detailed applications. The government emphasized the
need to diversify the judiciary and indicated that only judges who
were functionally bilingual would be considered. The Advisory
Committee reviewed the applications and interviewed a shortlist.
It then provided the Prime Minister with a non-prioritized list of

three to five recommended candidates. The Minister of Justice was directed to consult on the shortlist of candidates with the Chief Justice of Canada, relevant provincial and territorial attorneys general, relevant Cabinet ministers, opposition Justice Critics, as well as members of the House of Commons Standing Committee on Justice and Human Rights, and the Standing Senate Committee on Legal and Constitutional Affairs. Following these consultations, the Minister of Justice was asked to present a recommendation to the Prime Minister, who then chose the nominee. The Minister of Justice and the Chair of the Advisory Board then appeared before the House of Commons Standing Committee on Justice and Human Rights to explain how the chosen nominee met the statutory requirements and the criteria established by the government, following which Justices Rowe and Martin appeared to answer questions from members of that same committee, the membership of which was supplemented by representatives from the Senate and other opposition parties. Shortly thereafter, the Prime Minister formalized the appointments.

Like most judges, I am not persuaded that public confirmation hearings where members of Parliament vote to accept or reject a nominee would improve the quality of appointments. As demonstrated by the American experience, public hearings can give rise to undue politicization. On the other hand, I concede that the public hearings held following the nomination of Supreme Court of Canada justices in 2006, 2011, 2012, 2016, and 2017 did not descend into partisan political charades. Their principal achievement was to expose the nominees to the public and to show them to be intelligent, decent, and principled human beings. This helped demystify the judicial process and make it more understandable to the ordinary citizen.

## Improving the Appointments Process

I have been involved in various international initiatives concerning judicial education and judicial independence. I am generally very proud of the administration of justice in Canada, but the question I always dread is "How are judges appointed in Canada?" On that very important aspect of ensuring a strong and independent judiciary, I am afraid that at the level of federal judicial appointments we have nothing to teach the rest of the world and much to learn.[21]

We need only look to the provincial level for an example of how the federal process could be significantly improved. The provinces appoint judges who sit in provincial courts and hear criminal, family, and, in some provinces, small claims cases. Ontario's appointment process is much more rigorous than the federal appointment process. It began as a pilot project in 1988 and was formalized in legislation in 1994.[22] As with the federal process, candidates submit a written application with named referees to a Judicial Appointments Advisory Committee (the "Committee"). The Committee – comprising two provincial judges, three lawyers, seven lay persons, and one member of the Ontario Judicial Council[23] – reviews the written application and contacts the applicant's referees. The Committee then interviews the strongest candidates and finally provides Ontario's Attorney General with a ranked list of two names for each specific appointment to be made. The Attorney General can only appoint one of the two named candidates or reject the list and require the committee to provide a fresh one. The advantage of this process is that it more or less eliminates the capacity of the Attorney General to make appointments on the basis of politics or personal favouritism. Under this process, the quality of appointments to the provincial bench has been very high, certainly much higher than it had been in the past when the Attorney General had complete control.

There certainly have been improvements in the federal appointments process, but it is still far from ideal. The main weakness is that while the advisory committees have the power to eliminate unqualified candidates, they lack the power to ensure that only the most highly qualified candidates are appointed. It is an accepted international norm that an independent judicial appointments commission "will recommend a single selected candidate for a judicial vacancy, who must then be appointed to that position by the appointing authority."[24] The United Kingdom, Israel, and South Africa[25] operate under that principle. This stands in stark contrast with the situation in Canada, where there is a large province-wide pool of candidates for every appointment. Under the reformed process for appointments to the Supreme Court of Canada, the selection committee was asked to provide a non-prioritized list of three to five names. In my view, that represents an unnecessary and undesirable limitation on the committee's capacity to ensure a high-quality appointment. If limiting the choice to a single name is too restrictive, giving the advisory committee the power to limit the choice to a very short prioritized list would significantly reduce the risk that appointments are based on politics or patronage.

Another weakness in the existing process for federal appointments is that it does not apply when a superior court trial judge is appointed to the Court of Appeal (although sitting provincially appointed judges are required to go through the process). The decision is left entirely within the control of the Minister of Justice and the Cabinet. This allows for appointments to be made on political grounds and without adequate consultation with the Chief Justice and the members of the court to which the appointment is made. The appointment of Court of Appeal judges is crucially important to the administration of justice. It should not be left entirely in the hands of politicians. There should be a more open application process to allow aspiring trial judges to apply. Applicants should be vetted by an advisory or selection committee that includes representation from the bench and the bar to ensure that the best qualified are appointed. The Chief Justice should always be consulted before an appointment is made to ensure that adequate account is taken of the views and needs of the court.

There is no process to govern the appointment of Chief Justices and Associate Chief Justices – appointments that, by convention, fall within the prerogative of the Prime Minister. The United Kingdom has quite properly abandoned unconstrained choice in the selection of the most senior judges, and so should Canada. A system similar to what we have in place for the appointment of trial, appellate, and Supreme Court judges should be adopted to develop a very short list of candidates for these senior positions.

## Diversity

A more diverse court is a better court for two reasons. First, a diverse court is more likely to take into account all aspects of an issue and therefore to make better decisions. Second, a diverse court will reflect the diversity of the population, which tends to foster public respect and confidence.

I reject the contention that taking diversity into account threatens the quality of appointments. If the judiciary does not reflect the diversity of society, the claim that judicial appointments are made strictly on merit will simply ring hollow. If the judiciary is overwhelmingly white, disproportionately male, and drawn from the privileged social and economic class, it is difficult to believe that sufficient effort has been made to find the most qualified candidates.

Diversity also strengthens the quality of the judiciary. It is accepted that representation of certain perspectives is needed to ensure curial competence. Constitutional and statutory provisions or conventions commonly require the appointment of judges from specific communities. The requirement for three judges from Quebec serves "to ensure that Quebec's distinct legal traditions and social values are represented on the Court."[26] Convention requires that there be three judges from Ontario, two from Western Canada, and one from Atlantic Canada. In the United Kingdom, convention requires that the Supreme Court include one judge from Scotland to ensure the court has the expertise to decide points of Scottish law, and a judge from Northern Ireland to ensure its perspective is heard.[27] Appointments to the International Court of Justice[28] and the International Criminal Court must take into account the need for representation of "the principal legal systems of the world."[29] Requirements of this kind may well have the effect of bypassing a candidate of superior legal skill in favour of an inferior candidate who satisfies the representational need. But can it be doubted that these requirements are necessary to ensure that the court has the relevant expertise to inspire public confidence? Judgments made by a court that reflects an appropriate diversity of legal tradition and geography are likely to be better because they are based upon a wide range of thought and experience.

The merit-based justification for taking diversity into account in judicial appointments holds even where we are not dealing with different legal traditions. I argue in chapter 12 that judges are inevitably influenced by their life's experience. One's life experience is significantly shaped by one's linguistic, socio-economic, cultural, and ethnic background. It is for that reason that I believe a court will make better decisions if its membership reflects the diversity of society. As Bertha Wilson, the first female member of the Supreme Court of Canada, predicted, women judges have made a difference.[30] The same will apply when we achieve a more diverse judiciary, one that brings the widest possible range of life experience that will assist and enrich collective decision-making.[31] Diversity in the judiciary will enhance public confidence in the capacity of the courts to deliver fair and impartial justice[32] and help us "rout from the law the clichéd stereotypes which have, for too long and too often, distorted judging."[33]

## Trial Judge

I now turn to the working life of a judge. My account is based on my own experience as a trial judge for four and one-half years and as an appellate judge for almost twenty years.

The court to which I was first appointed, now called the Ontario Superior Court of Justice, exercises general and inherent, or residual, jurisdiction over civil and criminal matters. Provincial superior courts play a central and constitutionally guaranteed role in the administration of justice.[34] Unless jurisdiction has been assigned specifically to some other court, the Superior Court has jurisdiction over all matters, including *Charter* cases, matters governed by provincial and federal legislation, and judicial review of administrative agencies.[35]

Some of my academic colleagues could not understand why I wanted to be a trial judge. On that point my mentors Brian Dickson and Antonio Lamer, who encouraged me to apply for an appointment, were firm and clear. They had both started their careers as trial judges, and they both loved the job. They also thought that, especially for me as an academic, it would be important to have trial experience and to prove myself at the day-to-day work of judging "in the trenches" before aspiring to appellate work. They were right in their assessment. There is much to be said for direct appointments of accomplished senior counsel to appellate courts, but some experience as a trial judge is a definite asset. The experience of being a trial judge made me a better appellate judge and it gave me a level of credibility with the bar and the judiciary that I might otherwise have lacked.

I thoroughly enjoyed being a trial judge. As I will explain in subsequent chapters, the work of the trial judge lies at the very heart of our system of justice. It involves "hands-on" engagement with the parties, the witnesses, and the facts. Most cases turn on the facts, and relatively few cases get appealed, so, for most cases, the decision of the trial judge is final. The experience of listening to the litigants, endeavouring to make fair and accurate factual findings, and crafting principled and practical decisions is both challenging and exhilarating.

## Presiding in Court

Most of my work on the trial court was on the civil and commercial side. A significant part of this work consisted of conducting trials, sometimes with a six-person jury, but most often sitting alone. Most of the civil trials I conducted were relatively short, ranging from a day to two weeks. They involved a wide range of matters, including contractual disputes, personal injury and medical malpractice claims, property disputes, contested estate matters, mortgages and guarantees, and family law disputes. I also did some longer trials, which typically had more at stake and involved more senior and experienced counsel. However big or small the case, however eminent or unknown the counsel, I quickly saw that every case deserves scrupulous attention, for every case is critically important to the litigants.

When conducting a civil trial, there was little I could do to prepare. Before the case started, I would have only the trial record, which consists of the written pleadings where the parties have set out in a summary and formal manner the case they hope to prove. Given the volume of work and the uncertainties of scheduling, I would often receive the trial record shortly before going into court and would start to appreciate what the case was really about only when counsel made their opening submissions.

When it came to presiding in court, I did my best to follow the example of Brian Dickson, whom I had watched at the Supreme Court and whose work as a trial judge I had closely studied.[36] He was unfailingly courteous and attentive to counsel and litigants, and he presided in a dignified manner. While he was quite formal in the courtroom, never resorting to jokes or banter with counsel, he was not overbearing, and he avoided stuffiness or haughtiness. He insisted that proceedings be conducted in an efficient and business-like manner. He was patient and attentive, never berating or abusing counsel, but rather engaging them in genuine intellectual exchange. I learned from Dickson that presiding in a no-nonsense manner sets the right tone. This involved simple things like making sure to always start court on time, keeping breaks within defined limits, and making prompt rulings on contested points of procedure and evidence.

Presiding at trial court is a serious business, and running a fair and efficient trial is a challenge. Rules and decorum must be followed. But a trial is also a very human process, and the tone must be one of courtesy, respect, dignity, and fairness. If I had to sum up the Dickson approach, I would describe it as being "firm but fair."

The judge must assert control over the process but at the same time let counsel present the case as they see fit. Patience is required, because counsel do not always present the case in a way that seems best to the judge. But it is their case, not the judge's. I found that it was best to give counsel some leeway, provided they followed the applicable rules and procedures and treated the court, the witnesses, and their opponent with respect. It was almost always best to be very careful about injecting myself unduly into the fray. My motto was "If you are wondering whether you should say something now, the answer is likely that it would be best to remain silent." My other method of self-control was to imagine what Justice Peter Cory would do. Justice Cory sat first as an Ontario trial judge, then as a member of the Court of Appeal for Ontario, and finally as a judge of the Supreme Court of Canada. He was an extraordinarily polite and kind judge. He listened patiently and, so far as I am aware, never lost his calm judicial composure. But he also had a strong sense of propriety, and when the situation demanded it, he could be very firm. So I would ask myself, "What would Peter Cory do in this situation?," and only if I thought that he would intervene would I allow myself to do so.

Trial courts are extremely busy, and motion and trial lists are long. There is constant pressure to ensure that cases are dealt with in a timely fashion and that the backlog is kept to a minimum. I found that as soon as I completed one case, the trial coordinator was there with another matter waiting to be heard. Very often, cases settle shortly before the trial date, and this makes the life of a trial judge unpredictable. When I went to the office in the morning, I often had little idea what I would be hearing unless I was hearing motions or on a long trial. The work was always engaging, constantly changing, and frequently dramatic. It was a bit like going to the theatre every day, not knowing what was playing and getting paid to direct the production.

## Making Prompt Decisions

A trial judge has to be decisive. To run an effective and efficient trial, the trial judge must be prepared to make frequent rulings on evidence and procedure to keep the trial on the rails and then, of course, decide the result at the end. Trial judges must work very hard to get every decision right, but they also have to learn that they can only do their best and that it is important to make the decision at hand and move on to the next. All judges are human, and no judge is perfect. To survive on the bench, every judge must learn to cope with the awesome responsibility of deciding the fate of one's fellow citizens without being paralysed by the responsibility.

I believe that prompt decision-making is a cardinal judicial virtue for three reasons. First, for the litigants it is agony waiting for the result, and we owe it to them to decide their case as promptly as we reasonably can. Second, it is in the interest of the judge to be prompt. The judge will never know more about the case than the moment the judge walks out of the courtroom having heard closing argument. Some time to reflect upon the case and to ponder the outcome may be required, but every day that passes, the judge will remember less. The longer the delay, the more difficult it will be to resurrect the details of the case. Third, I believe that prompt reasons tend to be better in quality than delayed reasons. Judgments are not like wine: they do not improve with age. Judgments will almost always be better if they are delivered promptly, when the case is fresh in the mind of the judge. A common feature of problematic trial decisions, the ones that end up being reversed on appeal, is that the trial judge had the decision under reserve for a lengthy period.

## Motions and Applications

As a trial judge, I heard many motions or applications, which are determined on a paper record of affidavit evidence and documents. Motions typically involve pretrial procedural issues, but decisions on motions can often be decisive of the litigation. I heard many summary judgment motions where the moving party argues that the facts are not in serious dispute and that a full trial will not be required. The frequency and importance of summary judgment as a procedural device to screen out weak cases and provide expeditious justice in others has increased since my time on the Superior Court.[37] Other motions turn on pure questions of law. For example, a party can move to dismiss a claim or a defence on the basis that even if the facts as pleaded by the other party are true, there is no claim or defence in law.

Applications are used to decide cases that involve contested points of law but do not involve a serious dispute about the facts. Increasingly, applications are being used to bring *Charter* issues before the courts. In commercial matters, it has become common to conduct trials by using a kind of blended application-trial procedure in which much of the evidence is led by affidavit and cross-examination, and live evidence is restricted to truly contested issues of fact.

Motions and application work is challenging but in a very different way from trial work. Considerable pre-hearing preparation is required. The evidence is presented in writing, and, in most cases, counsel are expected to file written arguments or factums. Time for oral argument is limited, and the judge is expected to come to the hearing knowing what the case is about. On a typical day in motions court, I would hear and dispose of several matters. Reasons must be given, and often the motions raised contentious legal issues that had to be carefully thought through. One has to develop an instinct for knowing when to decide a case on the spot with short written or oral reasons, and when prudence requires reserving the decision and giving it more consideration and fuller written reasons.

I was also on a team of judges assigned to deal with class actions, which often raise significant legal issues involving the rights of a large number of individuals. They are procedurally complex and require active and ongoing case management by a judge to ensure they proceed in an orderly and expeditious stage.

Overall, although I was a relatively junior judge, I think that I got more than my share of interesting cases, as I always made it clear that I was prepared to take on cases that would require writing substantial judgments.

## Divisional Court

In addition to trial and motions work, I sat as a member of the three-judge Divisional Court that primarily deals with judicial review of administrative tribunals. This was my introduction to collegial decision-making. I found that it is very different to sit with two other judges, and, as I was relatively junior, not to be in control over the proceedings. I was inspired by some of my senior colleagues who presided with patience, efficiency, and dignity. I was also surprised by what I thought to be overly aggressive and unduly controlling behaviour of others. The only saving grace was that this behaviour often seemed to disturb me more than counsel who, I suppose, knew what was coming and were ready to face the fire.

## Criminal Trials and Sentencing

While I spent most of my time doing civil work, I did conduct several criminal jury trials. I had taught criminal law for several years, and I wanted to do more criminal work, but there were several senior judges ahead of me who had acquired considerable expertise sitting more or less exclusively on criminal matters, and they were allowed to continue. This left less room for newcomers like me to do criminal cases.

I enjoyed working with juries in both civil and criminal cases. I was struck by the wisdom of juries, even when the verdict they returned was not the one I was expecting. Almost always, with a little refection, I could see the common sense wisdom of their decisions.

Working with a jury is challenging. The law and the rules of evidence are complex, yet when sitting with a jury, the judge must be able to explain the law in terms that are understandable to a lay person. When I was a trial judge, there was no worse experience than to see the eyes of jurors glaze over when delivering an instruction that was required by law but incomprehensible to the ordinary person.[38] I felt that the content of my charge was determined not by what would assist the jury in deciding the case, but what a higher court would be looking for in the event of an appeal. While a serious effort has been made to promote standardized, plain-language jury charges, they remain lengthy and complex.

The law gives trial judges significant discretion in sentencing. Fashioning a sentence that is fit for the crime, delivers justice to the victims, and is also tailored to the rehabilitative potential of the offender is an art, not a science. Most judges who preside in criminal cases say that sentencing is the most difficult task they face. On a purely human level, I found that sending a fellow human being to prison was a necessary but very unpleasant task, and I cannot say that I ever took any joy in doing it, even though I knew that the punishment was deserved.

## Settlement and Case-Management Conferences

One aspect of a trial judge's work that has increased since my time on the trial court is conducting settlement and case-management conferences. A major theme of modern court reform has been a push for more pretrial conferencing to streamline cases for trial and encourage more cases to settle and thereby reduce cost and delay in civil litigation.[39]

There is certainly a place for case management, a process that allows a judge to work with the parties to narrow issues and resolve procedural matters in an efficient manner. Case management is most effective where a judge is assigned to take charge of the file and manage the case up to trial. The judge becomes familiar with the parties and the issues, and can work with the parties to develop an effective overall strategy that will move the case on to trial as quickly and efficiently as possible. Case management is less effective and, in my view, often less than helpful when the file is passed on from one judge to the next as it works its way towards trial. Without a firm and consistent hand to guide the process, case management is susceptible to merely adding another layer of procedure and swallowing up scarce resources.[40]

In Ontario, pretrial conferencing has dominated in family law, prompted by an understandable desire to control the cost and human strife of protracted litigation. Ontario has also experimented with mandatory mediation, requiring parties to go through a mediation process and attempt to resolve the case by mutual agreement as a prerequisite for being given a trial date.

Some judges relish settlement conferences and find it worthwhile and rewarding. I am sceptical about taking these initiatives too far. I saw my primary role as a trial judge to be trying cases on their merits. I fear that the dominant theme in civil litigation has become to push the litigants towards settlement rather than trial and, indeed, to treat cases that do not settle as systemic failures. While judges do have a role in encouraging settlement, I think we need to be careful about the effect of pushing too hard for settlement.[41]

I have nothing against mediation or other forms of alternative dispute resolution. They are effective, and it is often better for the parties to avoid the kind of winner-take-all justice that comes with a court decision. However, mediation services are readily available from private providers, and it seems to me that when disputes are brought before the court, the justice system should be premised on the proposition that the parties are entitled to ask for a judicial decision about who is right and who is wrong. We need to be wary of the culture of settlement taking too firm a hold and defining the way the courts administer justice.

While I am probably swimming against the judicial tide, I have particular concerns about judicial mediation. A judicial mediation usually involves the judge meeting or caucusing separately with the parties. To be an effective mediator, the judge must gain the confidence of the parties. To do so, the judge-mediator meets separately with the parties and obtains information (e.g., a "bottom-line" position) that the party is not prepared to reveal to his opponent. The mediator uses, but does not reveal, that confidential information to push for an agreement. This, in my view, is quite different from a judicial settlement conference at which all parties are present, and all parties hear everything that is said.

The role of a judge is to decide cases according to law in an open and public process. The role of a mediator is to deflect the parties from insistence on their legal rights towards a mutually acceptable accommodation. I think there are risks when these roles are mingled. Judges do not act on the basis of secret or confidential information, and I question whether the power and prestige of judicial office should be used to push parties to a non-rights-based resolution of their dispute. The judge who conducts a mediation remains, in the eyes of the litigants, a judge. The views the judge expresses will be perceived as reflecting the rights and wrongs of the situation. Yet that is precisely contrary to the role of the mediator-judge, namely to get an agreement based upon interests, not rights. At the end of a long day of mediation, there is often some serious arm-twisting. I am not persuaded that judges should be twisting arms.[42]

I also think we need to be cautious about unduly diverting our scarce judicial resources away from adjudication and towards settlement and mediation. The most effective settlement tool we can offer is the immediate availability of a courtroom and a judge to try the case. Many will argue that settlement at the courtroom door is too late and too costly. However, it is important not to overlook the fact that front-end loading civil litigation with elaborate case-management and settlement conferences also imposes costs and causes delay. Settlements do not come for free. Parties must devote considerable resources to the investigation of the factual and legal foundation for their own case, and that of their opponent, to be in a position to make an informed decision on settlement. Counsel have to prepare written briefs and be ready to present effective oral submissions in order to provide the information that the judge conducting the settlement conference requires. It is not uncommon, particularly in family matters, to find parties facing trial unrepresented because their resources have been swallowed up in elaborate case-management and unsuccessful settlement conferences.

## Private Alternative Dispute Resolution

Trial courts face serious competition from the alternative dispute resolution industry. Senior lawyers and retired judges work as arbitrators, and many cases that would otherwise be litigated in court are being siphoned away into private arbitration. Private arbitrations involve one or more arbitrators conducting a trial-like proceeding, usually behind closed doors, and deciding the case by rendering an "award" similar to reasons for judgment given by trial judges. There are also many lawyers, retired judges, and lay people who provide mediation services, bringing parties together to resolve disputes through compromise. The difference between arbitration and mediation is that the former, like a civil trial, results in an imposed, rights-based decision, while the latter involves a consensual resolution in which the parties' interests, rather than their strictly legal rights, are reflected.

Arbitration is similar to litigation, but it offers three advantages. First, the parties can avoid the open-court principle and litigate their dispute in private. Second, they can pick their judge and ensure that they have someone who has expertise in the subject matter of the dispute. Third, they can opt for a tailor-made procedure and have more control over the timing of the process than is allowed in the court system.

Like many judges, I worry that the court system is losing too many commercial disputes to arbitration.[43] The common law tradition depends upon a steady flow of current disputes so that the law can be kept current and relevant to contemporary commercial practices.

Can the court system compete effectively with private arbitration? The open-court principle requires that, subject to narrow exceptions, judicial proceedings be heard in public, and judicial decisions be available to all. The open-court principle precludes the court system from providing parties with a forum in which they can litigate their dispute in private. Many arbitrations involve situations where the parties do not wish to wash their dirty laundry in public. On that front, the courts cannot compete. However, the court system should be flexible enough to match the other two reasons for arbitration – picking the judge and controlling the procedure – by offering parties some measure of control over the selection of the judge and the design of the process. We have the example of commercial list courts in many jurisdictions where a relatively small group of commercial law specialists preside and where flexible, tailor-made procedures can be designed by the parties under the court's supervision.

## The Generalist Judge

In Ontario and in most Canadian provinces and other common law jurisdictions, superior court trial judges are expected to be generalists and to be ready for anything.

As I will explain below, I think there is much to be said in favour of the generalist model at the appellate level. The argument for a generalist trial court is much weaker. While the generalist trial judge model prevails in theory, there has been a gradual drift towards more specialization at the trial level in the urban areas of most Canadian jurisdictions.

Most of the criminal work is done by provincial court judges who sit full time in the criminal court. At the level of the superior courts, most homicide trials are assigned to judges with extensive criminal law experience. In some provincial superior courts, all criminal work is assigned to criminal specialists. Most jurisdictions have specialized family law judges who have the aptitudes and skills required for the resolution of matrimonial disputes and issues involving children. In Toronto and other financial centres there is a specialized commercial list made up of judges with expertise in the area who work with special procedural rules designed to facilitate the efficient resolution of commercial disputes. The Federal Court of Canada provides expertise in immigration, intellectual property, and federal administrative law. The Tax Court deals exclusively with federal taxation law.

So while superior court judges who sit or circuit to smaller towns and cities must still be ready for anything, there has been a significant drift away from the generalist model towards a more specialized trial bench.

## Court of Appeal

After four and a half years as a trial judge, I was appointed to the Court of Appeal for Ontario. As I had already been appointed as a Superior Court judge, I did not have to apply for the position. I think it was widely known that because of my academic background and the nature of the work I had done on the trial court, I would welcome an appointment to the Court of Appeal. When I received a call from the Minister of Justice's judicial affairs adviser asking me if I would be interested, I did not hesitate to say yes.

Perhaps the most unusual thing about my appointment is that it came on the same day as that of my friend and colleague Jim MacPherson, who, like me, had come to the bench after an academic career, worked as Executive Legal Officer under Chief Justice Brian Dickson, and served as a law school dean.

To some extent, the move reflected a shift back to my work as an academic. There is an enormous amount of reading and greater demand for writing of a more scholarly nature than at the trial level and a greater opportunity to shape the law.

The Court of Appeal comprises twenty-two full-time members, including the Chief Justice and the Associate Chief Justice and several supernumerary judges who sit half-time. Our jurisdiction is very wide and embraces civil, criminal, family, administrative, and constitutional cases. We are a generalist court, and all members of the court are expected to hear appeals in all areas of law.

We are the busiest appellate court in Canada. About 1,500 appeals are filed each year. Approximately two thirds of those appeals proceed to oral argument, so we hear and decide about 1,000 appeals each year. With a full-time complement of twenty-two and several supernumerary judges, and as we sit in panels of three, that means we each hear approximately 110 appeals each year. We reserve judgment in 400–600 cases a year, yielding a workload of about twenty reserve judgments per judge. Approximately half of our work is criminal, and half is civil (here I include commercial, family, administrative, and estates matters). We also deal with over 1,000 motions each year. These are heard by a single judge and include a wide variety of issues, including bail pending appeal, security for costs, stays pending appeal, and requests for extensions of time to comply with procedural requirements. We also decide about 150 applications for leave to appeal. These applications are made to a panel of three judges and are decided on the basis of written argument. Most involve applications for leave to appeal from the Divisional Court.

It is an unwritten rule of our system of justice that a party has a right to a trial and a right to one appeal. Most appeals come to us as of right; that is, the litigants have a statutory right to appeal the trial decision, and they do not have to get permission or leave to bring their case before us. Appeals that have no chance of success are processed in the same way that we deal with meritorious appeals. We do not have the practice used by some overburdened American courts of deciding a significant volume of appeals in writing without oral argument. However, appeals that appear to be hopeless will be given less time for oral argument and usually can be decided with very short reasons for judgment. The respondent can move to quash an appeal on the ground that it is frivolous, but as that is a matter that must be decided by a panel of three judges, most parties find the most cost-efficient practice is simply to wait and argue the appeal in the usual way.

After the first level of appeal, the general rule is that leave is required to bring a second appeal to a higher court. With the exception of appeals involving indictable criminal offences where there has been a dissent on a point of law or the reversal of an acquittal,[44] litigants require leave to appeal one of our decisions to the Supreme Court of Canada.[45]

As we are an appellate court, we decide cases primarily on the basis of the trial record.[46] The process begins with the appellant serving and filing a Notice of Appeal identifying the grounds of appeal, the relief sought, and the jurisdiction of the court to entertain the appeal.[47] To get the case listed for hearing, the appellant is required to take a number of steps. The appellant must order relevant portions of the transcript or the trial record. The appellant must then prepare and file an appeal book and compendium containing the Notice of Appeal, the formal judgment appealed from, the reasons for judgment, and the trial exhibits and transcript extracts that the appellant intends to rely on in argument.[48] Finally, the appellant is required to prepare and file a factum, or written argument, explaining what the case is about, identifying the central issues and summarizing the argument the appellant intends to make.[49] The respondent then files its compendium and factum. Shortly before the hearing, it is the practice for both parties to file books of authorities containing the cases and other legal authorities they intend to rely on.

We impose a thirty-page (double-spaced) limit on the length of factums. A party who thinks a longer factum is required can request permission to file an extended factum, but the proposed extended factum must be presented. A judge will review the proposed factum and decide the request. In my view, it is often a mistake to file an extended factum. We have an enormous amount of reading, and most cases can be boiled down to one or two crucial points. For me, a short, concise factum that zeroes in on those crucial points is almost always more effective.

Well before the beginning of each term (we have three: fall, winter/spring, and summer), judges are assigned to weekly panels of three judges to hear appeals. For full-time judges, the normal assignment is two weeks' sitting time per month. The other two weeks are required for reading the materials of forthcoming cases and writing reasons for decisions on cases already heard. Other assignments include sitting as a single judge in chambers to hear motions and being assigned as Duty Judge for a week to fill in for another judge in the event of illness or a conflict. Assignments to panels are made by the Associate Chief Justice on the basis of ensuring a variety of panel combinations, achieving an appropriate balance of junior and senior judges, and satisfying our obligation to hear appeals argued in French. Panels are designated to hear either civil or criminal cases for the week.

The decision about what cases are to be assigned to each panel is ultimately that of the Chief Justice and the Associate Chief Justice. However, in practice the cases are assigned to the panels by our court staff on a more or less random basis, and ordinarily no attempt is made to match cases to the expertise of the panel.

## A Generalist Court

Like most intermediate courts of appeal, the court on which I sit is a generalist court. Our jurisdiction is wide and corresponds to that of the Superior Court from which most of our work comes. All members of the court are expected to hear all types of cases. As noted, it is not our practice to have specialist judges or panels, and the work is assigned more or less randomly. However, when an appeal is expedited or requires five judges, a special panel may be struck, which would ordinarily include some judges with expertise in the area.

I am a strong believer in a generalist appellate court. Our job is to oversee the legal process as a whole and to ensure that it is delivering fair, efficient, and effective justice to the litigants. That requires a perspective that can get lost if one becomes too specialized and too preoccupied with the details in a certain area of law. Specialists have a tendency to become too familiar and too comfortable with the way things have always been done. An outside perspective can bring a breath of fresh air. I often find that a colleague who has a background in criminal law has insights on civil cases that would not have occurred to me. I like to think the same happens occasionally when I sit on criminal cases. I argue throughout this book that it is important for appellate judges to strive for coherence and integrity in the law. That requires expertise in specific areas of law but also a broad perspective on the legal system as a whole. A generalist judge has that perspective.

## Law Clerks and Legal Officers

Most Canadian judges enjoy the support provided by law clerks – outstanding recent law school graduates who typically work at the court for a year, although in some courts the period is longer. At the Court of Appeal for Ontario, we employ nineteen law clerks on one-year contracts. The typical arrangement is for two judges to share a clerk, although our numbers allow a few judges to have their own clerk. The clerks are reassigned after six months, so they ordinarily work for three or four different judges during the course of the year. The competition for these positions is fierce, and only those with outstanding records are hired. They are selected and assigned by a committee of judges with the assistance of one of our legal officers. Most of our clerks have graduated from Ontario law schools, but we always have several from other provinces or from American law schools. Some satisfy their articling requirement by working at the court, while others have already been called to the bar. Most have worked in law firms as either articling or summer students.

Law clerks have become a very prominent and important feature of appellate courts around the common law world. They assist judges in preparing for hearings and in the preparation of reasons for judgment.[50] Law clerks also frequently help judges prepare speeches or lectures. Law clerks are young, intelligent, enthusiastic, and fresh from the academy, where they have been exposed to new ideas about law, and they bring those ideas to the court. They serve an important role by helping judges keep up to date with contemporary thinking and attitudes.

Like most appellate courts, we also employ permanent legal officers to assist with administrative and legal work. At the Ontario Court of Appeal, we have eight legal officers, many of whom are former law clerks. We regularly have government lawyers seconded to the court as legal officers, often as short-term parental leave replacements. Our Senior Legal Officer supervises the scheduling of appeals, serves as a significant point of contact with the bar and in-person litigants, and assumes general responsibility for monitoring the court's procedures and day-to-day operations. The other legal officers assist us by reviewing and advising on applications for leave to appeal and reviewing upcoming appeals to recommend time lim-its for oral argument. They also assist us with administrative work that requires legal expertise, and they provide research, preparation, and editing assistance in relation to complex and jurisprudentially important appeals.

## Pre-hearing Preparation

We receive the written materials for our cases about two weeks be-fore the oral hearing. We spend considerable time preparing for the oral argument. Some judges ask their law clerks to prepare a written "bench memo" summarizing the facts and arguments and identify-ing the key issues. Some judges ask their clerks to include in the bench memo their own assessment of the merits of the appeal, but others do not. My practice, and that of a number of my colleagues, is to have my clerk review the materials and then give me an oral brief-ing before I read anything. I find this more helpful than a written bench memo, which is just one more thing for me to read. The oral briefing introduces me to the case, helps me plan how I will read the record, and allows the clerk and me to develop a tentative strategy about how I should approach the case.

After the clerk's oral briefing, I delve into my reading of the writ-ten materials. In civil matters, I usually like to start with the reasons of the trial judge. I do this because my job is to assess the legal integ-rity of the result reached by the trial judge. Thus, my starting point should be to understand how the trial judge dealt with the evidence and arguments. I then move to the factums to see how the case will be argued. Where I go from there will depend upon the nature of the case. In cases that raise purely legal issues, it may not be necessary to read the trial record in any detail. On the other hand, where there is an attack on the trial judge's factual findings or procedural or evi-dentiary rulings, I will have to immerse myself in the trial record. In other cases, say a contracts case, the issue may turn on the wording of one or more documents, and I will fasten my attention on those. I always look at the law cited by the parties, but again the level of detail will vary. If it is clear that our decision will turn on one or two leading cases, I will focus on those cases. Other cases may require reading a larger body of case law.

In criminal cases I follow more or less the same pattern when the appeal is from a judge-alone trial. If the case was tried by judge and jury, the adequacy of the trial judge's charge to the jury on the law to be applied will often be the focal point of the appeal, and I will read it carefully, usually after I have identified the specific issues the appellant has raised.

In some cases, it may seem that a potentially important issue has not been adequately dealt with by the parties, and I will ask my clerk or one of our legal officers to investigate it further. If it turns out that the parties have missed something I think is important, I confer with the other judges assigned to hear the case, and if we think it advisable, we will ask the Senior Legal Officer to advise the parties to be ready to address the issue in oral argument. We are reluctant to raise issues not identified by the parties, but sometimes we have to do so to ensure that the case is properly decided.[51] This often occurs when there is an issue about our jurisdiction to hear the appeal.

The three judges assigned to hear the appeal rarely discuss the case in detail before the oral hearing. The panel does not meet until a few minutes before oral argument, when we may exchange a few quick observations on the case we are about to hear. We do not follow the practice of some other provincial courts of appeal where primary responsibility for preparing reasons is assigned to a particular judge well in advance of oral argument, and the case is discussed in some detail at a conference before the case is heard.[52] Our practice is based on the idea that we each have an independent obligation to come to the appeal having read the material and with an open mind. While it is not possible to read the files in preparation for the oral hearing without forming a tentative opinion about how the case should be decided, there is a danger that views that should remain tentative will harden into firm opinions if we engage in detailed pre-hearing conferences.

## Oral Argument

Lawyers often ask me about the relative importance of written and oral argument. The written argument is very important. It is our introduction to the case, and first impressions are often difficult to shake. However, oral argument remains very important in our court, and cases are sometimes won or lost on the day of the hearing. Good counsel are able to discern from our questions the areas we find problematic, and if counsel can answer those concerns, a case that seemed doomed prior to oral argument may turn out to be a winner.

While oral argument is important on appeal, my own view is that the impact of oral argument diminishes as the case works its way up the judicial hierarchy. Effective advocacy is critical at trial. Cases are won or lost on how the case is framed, what evidence is introduced, how effectively the witnesses are cross-examined, and what legal arguments are made. Appeals tend to focus on a few crucial points. The factual record has been established, and the room for inventive argument is limited.

Most appeals in our court are heard in half a day or less, so that during a typical week, a panel of three judges will hear between eight and twelve appeals. We impose time limits for oral argument. Counsel are asked to estimate the time they require. One of our legal officers, under the supervision of a judge assigned to deal with time limits, assesses the appeal and the time requested and makes a time allocation. If counsel thinks more time is needed, they can make that request to one of our "list judges," assigned to deal with such requests, who will decide whether more time should be given.

Time limits were introduced shortly before I arrived at the court, in order to clear a backlog of appeals. There was some resistance to imposing time limits. A few of my senior colleagues thought time limits to be a radical and unwarranted departure from the traditions of oral advocacy. I think that all judges and experienced counsel now welcome time limits as a measure that tends to focus the argument on the crucial and decisive issues.

Another advantage, not often acknowledged, is that time limits make for a more patient bench. In the days before time limits, despite their stated belief in giving counsel free reign in oral argument, some judges became restless at the prospect of having to listen to lengthy losing arguments. They developed the unfortunate habit of jumping in to push their own view of the case in an attempt to shut down the argument almost before it began. Time limits give the bench the assurance that, however hopeless the appeal may seem, they have to listen for only a defined period of time.

We do, of course, engage counsel with questions, and good counsel are very adept at responding to questions and taking the cue about what concerns us. The cut and thrust of oral argument is one of the most interesting and rewarding aspects of our work, and it plays a crucial role in the disposition of our appeals. It brings the central issues into sharp focus and allows us to test arguments for legal and practical validity.

There are a variety of judicial styles and practices when it comes to oral argument. In my experience, overly aggressive "put-down" questioning is on the wane. We are there to listen, and while we do not have to accept everything we hear, parties and counsel should be treated with respect. I could never see the point of trying to beat a lawyer into submission, however far-fetched the argument. I think it is preferable for the judge to explain politely and clearly the problem with the submission and then give counsel a chance to respond. If the answer is not persuasive, enough said, move on to the next point.

Most of the time, we sit in panels of three. However, the Chief Justice can direct that an appeal be heard by a five-judge court. Most often, this is done where a party presents a plausible argument that we should reconsider one of our prior decisions. Occasionally, a five-judge court is established to hear an appeal involving a difficult or novel point of general importance that needs to be settled in a definitive manner.[53] Canadian intermediate appellate courts do not follow the American practice of convening *en banc*, where the case is heard by all members of the court to resolve certain contentious points of law.

## Deciding the Appeal

Following oral argument, we immediately retire to discuss the case. Starting with the most junior judge, we each state our assessment of the appeal. The discussion is very open, collegial, and informal, but we do not hesitate to put our position forcefully. The post-hearing conference usually lasts only for a few minutes, especially if we have another case to hear. If we are in doubt about the case, we reserve our decision and continue our deliberations later.

Responsibility for assigning the task of writing reasons ultimately falls on the senior judge who is sitting on the case, but in our court it is usually determined by consensus. We remain with the same panel of three for a week, and typically at the end of the week we divide up the work of preparing reasons for our reserved judgments. If we disagree on the result at conference, one of the judges in the majority will undertake the task of writing first reasons. The work is divided on the basis of interest, expertise, and workload. Occasionally we have a further formal conference to discuss the case, and we routinely have informal discussions about the case as the process of writing reasons unfolds.

We decide a high proportion of our appeals immediately after oral argument or within a day or so of the hearing. This is because most cases fall into what we describe as the "error-correction" category. These are cases that raise issues that concern only the immediate parties – did the trial judge make an error on a well-established point that calls for appellate intervention? Such cases do not require us to say anything that we think could have value as a precedent for the future. We decide these cases by delivering relatively short reasons, responding to the specific arguments advanced, but not attempting to provide a full account of all aspects of the case. The immediate parties to the appeal are the intended audience for this style of short reasons. However, as we operate under the open-court principle, all our reasons are published on our court website and available to the public at large. Although reasons of this kind are not intended to have precedential value, counsel are permitted to cite them to us in subsequent cases. They are decisions of the court and, unlike some American courts,[54] we have rejected the proposition that they are non-binding or not to be cited in future cases. This, I think, has a salutary effect. It means we cannot hide anything we do and thereby disciplines any inclination we might have to try to decide a case on a one-off basis "on the equities." We have to be prepared to live with the consequences of every decision we make.

In Ontario, until recently, we often labelled a short judgment "Endorsement." This label is derived from the practice of writing the reasons on the back of the appeal book, but it was routinely used for longer reasons released days or weeks after the hearing. To the extent that it conveys the impression that we do not always give reasons for judgment, the label is misleading. We take very seriously our obligation to respond to the arguments and to explain why we do or do not accept them, and we now label dispositions of this kind "Reasons for Decision," reserving the label "endorsement" for short reasons handwritten on the back of the appeal book. However, given the nature and volume of our work, it is neither necessary nor possible for us to deliver full reasons, setting out all the facts and details of every case. If our decision has no precedential value, we meet our duty to give a reasoned decision by responding to the arguments in a way that assures the parties that we have understood their position and so that they can understand why one has lost and the other has succeeded. That purpose can often be achieved in a few paragraphs or pages.

We deliver comprehensive reasons for judgment in about 15–20 per cent of the cases we hear. Full reasons for judgment typically include identification of the result in the court below, the essential facts, the issues to be resolved, an analysis of those issues explaining the basis for our decision, and the actual disposition of the appeal.

We are required by statute to render our decisions within six months of the oral hearing.[55] Most cases are decided in a shorter time but regrettably some judgments are released more than six months after argument. This should not happen. We have a court protocol to monitor reserved judgments. A list of cases under reserve is circulated monthly identifying the judge assigned to write reasons and briefly stating the issue. If reasons have not been circulated at the four-month point, the president of the panel is directed to ask for a conference to discuss progress. If reasons are not released within six months, the judge who has been assigned to write the reasons can be relieved from sitting to ensure that the judgment is released as soon as possible. We assume a collective responsibility to have judgments released in a timely fashion, and where a colleague has a particularly heavy burden of reserves, we are prepared to assist with temporary relief from sitting duties.

As I will argue in chapter 6, the need to justify the outcome with persuasive reasons is a centrally important discipline on judicial decision-making. My own practice is to start writing as soon as possible. Memory fades, particularly in an environment where one is faced with a steady stream of new cases to read, hear, and decide. The longer one waits, the more difficult writing becomes. I often start to write even when I am not certain how I will decide the case, as writing helps me clarify my thinking. Even if I know I will need more time to reflect or do further reading and research, I find it is very important immediately to write at least an outline of the facts and issues while the case is fresh in my mind. I go through several drafts of every judgment I write, but as I write on my computer, I engage in constant revision and rewriting, and I do not count how many drafts it takes to get to the final product. Like most judges, I have started to write a judgment thinking I would decide the appeal one way, only to find that the judgment I had in mind "won't write" and that it must go the other way.[56]

The factums the parties have filed serve as an important source when writing reasons, as they contain a clear statement of the facts, the issues, the arguments, and the relevant authorities. We also record oral argument and have ready access to the recordings from our office desktop.

I do not follow the practice of having a law clerk prepare a first draft of reasons for judgment. While that practice appears to be common in American courts,[57] I believe it to be the exception rather than the rule in Canada, except at the Supreme Court of Canada, where some judges have acknowledged that they have clerks prepare first drafts.[58] In my view, reasons for judgment should be written by judges, not by law clerks. I explain the discipline judgment-writing imposes on the decision-making process in chapter 6. If the task of writing the judgment is delegated by the judge, that discipline is lost. Ghostwritten reasons create a risk of unacceptably result-oriented decision-making, lacking the rigour derived from carefully working out in one's own mind a proper legal justification for the decision.

I do, however, rely heavily on my law clerk to comment on and edit my reasons. I look to the clerk for both substantive and technical support. On the substantive side, I welcome critical comments on my draft reasons and encourage the clerk to disagree with me if the clerk thinks I am wrong. I sometimes ask my clerk to research and prepare a memorandum on points that seem to need further investigation. On the more technical side, our clerks are trained to follow a court style guide to ensure consistency, and we rely on them to check the accuracy of facts and citations. The clerks note-up cases we have cited to ensure that we have not missed subsequent authority. Without the assistance of our law clerks, we would not be able to maintain the high standard we set for our work.

In some cases – relatively few – we come upon an important point that was not addressed in argument. This might be a relevant case on point that was decided after argument, or it may simply be a point the parties failed to deal with. We will not ordinarily decide an appeal on a point that was not argued. To do so infuriates the lawyers who lose the case and who may feel that, if given the chance, they could have answered the point. However, it is not unheard of for the Supreme Court of Canada to decide appeals on points not addressed by the parties.[59] In our court, if we think that an unaddressed point could be decisive, we will ask the parties for further written argument. On the other hand, if we come across an authority that was not mentioned in argument but that merely adds to or supplements the law we were given, we consider it appropriate to cite the authority in our reasons.

Once draft reasons have been written and edited by the law clerk, they are circulated to the other members of the panel. Our protocol for reserved judgments requires colleagues to respond to draft reasons promptly. I welcome comments and suggestions for improvement, both editorial and substantive. Our practice is to deal with comments and suggestions informally without elaborate memoranda, a practice that is quite manageable with three-judge panels. We circulate our judgments for comment in electronic form, and most of us give our comments and suggestions by way of track changes on the draft judgment. If a colleague has a substantive concern with my draft, we will discuss it, and I will do my best to accommodate the concerns expressed.

We do not follow the practice of some appellate courts of circulating our draft judgments to all members of the court for comment. We do, however, often ask colleagues who did not sit on the case to review draft reasons. We do this if the case falls within an area of the colleague's interest and expertise. In other cases, we may want to be sure that the judgment has the right tone and does not seem to be unduly critical of a party, counsel, or trial judge. We also routinely discuss our cases around the lunch table, and there is opportunity for informal vetting of our work by colleagues who did not sit on the case.

### Dissenting and Concurring Reasons[60]

Until recently, the norm in English appellate courts was for each judge to deliver an opinion without any apparent prior consultation with colleagues who sat on the case. The advantage of this practice is that it emphasizes the duty of each judge to form an independent view of every case. However, that advantage comes at a considerable cost. Multiple opinions often made it difficult to discern a precise rationale for the decision. Some common law appellate courts, including the United Kingdom Supreme Court, continue to follow that tradition, with each judge writing reasons, although that seems now to happen only after some discussion and with some effort to avoid lengthy multiple opinions.[61] On the other hand, the practice of the Judicial Committee of the Privy Council, until 1949 Canada's final court of appeal, was to issue a single judgment, on the theory that the opinion was to serve as advice to the Queen rather than as a judicial judgment.[62] Courts that operate in the codified civil law tradition typically do not allow for dissents, although that is not the practice in Quebec.

At the Supreme Court of Canada,[63] each judge wrote separate reasons, until the late 1920s, when Chief Justice Anglin tried to reduce the number of separate opinions. In the late 1960s, Chief Justice Cartwright initiated the practice of holding a post-hearing conference to encourage pre-judgment discussion, with a view to reducing the number of opinions. In recent years, the Supreme Court has endeavoured, with varying degrees of success, to reduce the number of separate opinions. However, in highly contentious cases, it is not uncommon to find several judges writing with concurring and dissenting reasons. These judgments are difficult to read, and lawyers and lower court judges struggle to discern the precedent the case establishes.[64] Most observers despair over complex judgments of this nature. However, there are a minority of observers who argue that multiple and varying opinions reflect the duty of each judge to come to an independent decision.[65] It has also been argued that it is better to confront the complexity and subtlety of the law in contentious areas rather than papering over the differences with compromised and sometimes opaque reasons.[66]

Dissents and separate concurring opinions are relatively rare in Canadian intermediate appellate courts. According to a recent study, the rate at the Ontario Court of Appeal is about 2 per cent.[67] In some cases, it is apparent from the oral hearing and the post-hearing conference that there is a fundamental difference of opinion and that the court will be divided in the result. But those cases are exceptional. Almost all of our judgments are unanimous.

We approach decision-making as a collegial exercise, and we are almost always able to settle on one set of reasons, usually authored by one member of the panel but sometimes released as an opinion "by the court." We are confusingly inconsistent in our use of "by the court." Sometimes we use it to reinforce the strength of our opinion on a high-profile case.[68] More common are cases where we render a short judgment immediately after argument to dispose of a case that has no jurisprudential significance.

There is much to be said in favour of collegial decision-making. The personal or idiosyncratic views of one judge are diluted, and an opinion that reflects the collective wisdom of three judges is usually sounder than one that is the product of one judge.[69] On the other hand, as we routinely assign the task of writing reasons to one member of the panel, the reasons usually bear the distinctive marks of the author. Even if I would have written the judgment differently, I will not dissent on peripheral or legally insignificant points of difference.

On the other hand, if I disagree with a colleague's reasons on a point of principle, I will write separate reasons explaining why I take a different view. In chapter 6, I argue that the obligation to give a reasoned opinion is central to judicial integrity, accountability, and transparency. It follows from that argument that if I disagree with the thrust of the reasoning, I have a professional duty to dissent.[70] A dissent in a contentious case reassures the litigants and the public that all sides of the case were fully considered.

However, as I rarely dissent and almost never write separate concurring opinions, some may regard my claim as hollow, and it requires me to reflect upon the reasons for the infrequency of dissent on my court. The spirit of collegiality tends to discourage dissents or concurring reasons. Few if any judges like to dissent,[71] perhaps for the reason expressed by the great American judge Learned Hand, who wrote that a dissent "cancels the monolithic solidarity on which the authority of the bench of judges so largely depends."[72] If we find that we disagree with some aspect of a colleague's reasons, we invariably discuss the difference and do our best to resolve it. The colleague may not regard the point as crucial and may be prepared to modify the reasons accordingly. If that does not happen, and if I regard the point as one of principle, I have found that a draft dissent or concurrence will often persuade the colleague to accommodate my concern.

A factor that discourages dissents is our inclination towards minimalism, or deciding cases on the narrowest possible grounds, a phenomenon I discuss in chapters 4 and 6. If we disagree on a point and the point does not have to be dealt with to decide the appeal, we find that it is often possible and better to write narrowly and unanimously.

Another significant reason for our low rate of dissent is the nature of the cases we decide. As I have explained, a very significant portion of our cases lie in the "error correction" category. In these appeals, the issue is simply whether the trial judge made a readily identifiable error of law. Such cases do not make new law but turn on settled jurisprudence. The issue is simply "right or wrong," and there is usually little room for disagreement. This is very different from the situation on national supreme courts, which decide only seventy or so cases per year selected for hearing because they raise contentious points of law having national importance.

Related to this is the fact that we sit in panels of three or sometimes five. Three people deciding predominantly error-correction appeals are almost certainly going to agree at a higher rate than nine people deciding highly contentious jurisprudential appeals. Even when three or five judges are deciding a contentious jurisprudential appeal, the risk of disagreement is lower than if there are nine judges. It is easier for three people to find common ground than for nine, especially where the three share a common experience of practising and judging in one jurisdiction, whereas the nine come from different parts of the country and from very different legal traditions. However, as an American judge has suggested, there may also be too few dissents from intermediate appellate courts and too many from supreme courts.[73]

It is sometimes suggested that the spirit of collegiality discourages dissents because the potential dissenter does not want to risk irritating a colleague or fraying the relationship. I do not consider that to be a good reason to remain silent. An important aspect of a sound collegial relationship is mutual respect and toleration. Judges tend to be accomplished lawyers who have an aptitude for acute legal analysis and the ability to express clear and forceful opinions. Working with people of that calibre is invigorating, but one has to expect that differences of opinion will occur. If a colleague takes a different view on a point of principle, I do not take that difference personally, and I have never felt that any of my colleagues did so when I was the one in disagreement. Collegiality should not be eroded by forceful dissents, although it is crucial to the maintenance of good collegial relations that the tone be respectful of the opposing viewpoint. Justice Antonin Scalia was famous for his biting dissents.[74] While some of his colleagues maintained that his barbs did not erode collegiality,[75] I am far from confident that collegiality would survive his invective on all courts. Perhaps more important is that intemperate dissents demean the integrity of the judicial process in the eyes of the public by suggesting that decisions are driven by personal factors extraneous to the law. It is one thing to disagree strongly and quite another to suggest that any divergence from one's own opinion can only be the product of bad faith or wilful violation of the judicial oath.

A well-written dissent serves many purposes. Dissents tell losing parties that they were heard and that their arguments were understood. A dissent may clarify the decision of the majority by putting into prominent focus the other side of the argument. If the panel disagrees, a patched up compromise designed to attract unanimous support will often lack clarity. Better to set out the difference in clear terms so that everyone can plainly see what the majority accepted and what it rejected.

A dissent holds one's colleagues' "feet to the fire."[76] They are forced to confront difficulties or weaknesses in their reasoning. As Justice Ruth Bader Ginsburg states, "[T]here is nothing better than an impressive dissent to lead the author of the majority opinion to refine and clarify her initial circulation."[77] Even if the majority refuse to narrow the decision, by pointing out flaws in the reasoning a dissent may limit the reach and future influence of a majority decision. As a prominent dissenter observed, a dissent indicates that the majority opinion was "at the very margin ... and that it would not be extended much further and may even someday be overruled."[78] And sometimes an opinion the author thought would be a dissent proves to be sufficiently persuasive to attract a majority.

Dissents may also affect rights of appeal to a higher court. In appeals involving indictable criminal offences, a dissent on a point of law gives the appellant an automatic right of appeal to the Supreme Court of Canada.[79] In cases where leave is required, a well-reasoned dissent may persuade the Supreme Court to grant leave to appeal.

Dissents also appeal "to the intelligence of a future day,"[80] and, in the words of Justice William Brennan, a frequent dissenter, "dissents seek to sow seeds for future harvest."[81] There is a long list of dissents that, over time, have prevailed in their persuasiveness over that of the majority. While that does not often happen at the level of intermediate appellate courts because of the relatively strict view we take on precedent, it is not uncommon at the Supreme Court of Canada[82] and other apex courts.[83]

## Chapter 3

# Is the Law Uncertain?

The very idea of law suggests the need for clear rules – rules that are capable of producing just and predictable results to govern society and social relations. Citizens need to know in advance what they can and cannot do so that they can govern their conduct and plan their affairs in an orderly fashion. Lawyers need clear rules to advise clients. The conduct of those who exercise public power, such as the police, has to be disciplined and controlled. Judges need settled legal doctrines to decide cases in a principled and consistent manner.

Yet a great judge, Benjamin Cardozo, wrote, "I was much troubled in spirit, in my first years on the bench, to find how trackless was the ocean on which I had embarked. I sought for certainty. I was oppressed and disheartened when I found the quest for it was futile."[1] The ideal system, said Cardozo, would be "a code at once so flexible and so minute, as to supply in advance for every conceivable situation the just and fitting rule."[2] But that level of perfection, Cardozo realized, is unattainable. Judges are confronted with the task of deciding cases for which the law seems to provide no clear answer. And where the law does provide a clear rule, the result it produces may seem unjust. Reconciling the need to provide stability and certainty in the law and at the same time to reach just results in particular cases is a constant challenge.

In this chapter, I explore the nature and extent of legal uncertainty. I begin with two features of law that make it, to some extent, uncertain. The first is the generality of law, the quality that makes law universal in application and objective in nature. The second is that all laws have to be applied in a factual context, and the context is constantly changing. I then turn to the extent of the law's uncertainty and argue that, as a practical matter, most of the time the law does provide adequate and appropriate guidance. Finally, I turn to "hard cases" where there is a significant element of uncertainty. I argue that when confronted with a "hard case," the judge's task remains to find the right or the best answer.

## The Generality of Law

I believe that an element of uncertainty in the law is inevitable. Laws are expressed in language, and the precise meaning of language is often a matter for debate. The same words mean different things to different people and in different contexts. Even if we can agree on the meaning of the words used to state the law, we confront the problem of generality, an essential characteristic of law itself. Laws must be framed in terms of norms or standards that have general application. The idea that law is of necessity general in nature is as old as Aristotle. He observed that "all law is universal."[3] Generality gives the law its objective, rational, and systematic quality. It is what distinguishes the law from the judicial decision applying it. A legal regime that consisted only of rules specific enough to decide every case without interpretation or judgment would be nothing more than a "wilderness of single instances."[4]

As the English legal philosopher H.L.A. Hart put it, the law has, by its very nature, an "open-texture."[5] Deciding cases requires the exercise of judgment. Someone must identify the relevant legal standard, determine the facts, and decide whether, and to what extent, the legal standard governs in the circumstances of the case. That is the role of the judge. The need for judicial fact-finding and legal interpretation injects a human element and a measure of uncertainty into the application of the law.

Aristotle also recognized that while generality and the universality of its application was an identifying feature of law, it could also be the source of injustice. "The law," he wrote, "takes account of the majority of cases, although not unaware that in this way errors are made." Errors are made because general legal standards cannot anticipate or account for all possible situations. Aristotle recognized this problem and argued, "[T]he law is none the less right; because the error lies not in the law nor in the legislator, but in the nature of the case; for the raw material of human behaviour is essentially of this kind."[6] In this passage, Aristotle identified a central dilemma in achieving justice under law. Universality of application is a necessary attribute of law. But because the "raw material of human behaviour" is variable, the universal legal norm will not yield just results in all cases. A well-conceived "one size fits all" rule will produce just results in most cases. However, there will almost always be some cases where there is a twist on the facts not contemplated by the rule, with the result that the rule seems to produce an unjust result.

### Precise Rules: Gaps and Exceptions

One apparent solution to the problem of uncertainty would be to frame legal rules and standards, created by either statute or common law precedent, narrowly and precisely so that the legal answer can be readily provided without the need for unpredictable human judgment. This approach may appear to reduce the level of uncertainty, but it gives rise to the twin problems of over- and under-inclusiveness.

The precisely drafted rule will almost inevitably fail to cover all possibilities. This is known as under-inclusiveness. The specific rule leaves gaps, in other words, situations where the narrow rules provide no answer. If there are gaps in the rules, there will be uncertainty in the law. The gaps have to be filled thorough the exercise of judicial interpretation and discretion. The narrow and specific rules do not articulate a general legal principle to guide judicial interpretation, and this may make it difficult to predict how cases falling into the gaps will be decided.

The problem of gaps is a frequently encountered feature of the common law tradition. Precedent-making decisions of the common law courts turn on their facts. The decision will govern future cases where the facts fall within the law as laid down in the prior decision. However, as the reasoning of common law judges is fact-driven and inductive rather than deductive, the precedents leave gaps, and there will be room for argument about how a new case presenting different facts should be decided.

The second problem with precisely framed rules is over-inclusiveness. The apparent certainty achieved by a more or less mechanical application of a specific rule comes with a price. Mechanical application may work in some or even most cases, but it will tend to produce unjust results in others. On its face, the rule applies, but the result seems to be wrong. It is overly inclusive as, according to its letter the rule applies, yet according to its spirit or the underlying value the rule is intended to promote, it does not. To take a familiar example, a municipal by-law provides that "no vehicles are permitted in public parks."[7] Does this apply to a child's tricycle? A teen's bicycle? An ambulance? The truck of a maintenance or gardening crew? Must the judge decide the case according to the letter of the law and ban all these means of conveyance, or is it acceptable for a conscientious judge to look to the purpose of the law in order to avoid what seems to be an unjust result?

Judges working in the common law tradition feel compelled by their sense of justice to resist unjust results. Their justification for departing from the accepted rule is usually that the result it yields does not align well with the underlying values that the rule seems to uphold.

Unable to stomach an apparently unjust result produced by a rule, judges craft exceptions to reach a just result. The exception allows the judge to advance the perceived reason behind the rule, but it weakens the clarity and certainty of the rule itself. Exceptions make it difficult to discern when the rule actually applies, whether an established exception applies, or whether a new exception will be created. If the list of exceptions continues to grow, the exceptions may overwhelm the rule and coalesce as a new rule or set of rules. Lord Mansfield, an eighteenth-century English judge, described this process as follows: "General rules are ... varied by change of circumstances. Cases arise within the letter, yet not within the reason, of the rule; and exceptions are introduced, which, grafted upon the rule, form a system of law."[8] This organic evolution of legal standards and the element of uncertainty it entails is a product of the common law's inductive approach and preoccupation with doing justice on the specific facts of each case.

The phenomenon of gaps and exceptions that arise from rigid rules is illustrated by the evolution of the modern law of negligence. Until the decision of the House of Lords in *Donoghue v Stevenson* in 1932,[9] there was no general principle defining when an injured party could recover damages for injury to person or property caused by the negligent act of another party. The precedent cases established that if the injured party could show that the defendant had breached a legal duty of care, the injured party could recover. There was, however, no principled or general definition of when a duty of care would arise. In the case of an injury caused by defective goods, liability based on contract, where the injured party had dealt directly with the negligent vendor or manufacturer, was well established. The direct dealings with the vendor or manufacturer gave rise to a relationship of "privity" of contract upon which the injured party could base the claim. But if the injured party had no direct contractual relationship with the negligent manufacturer or vendor, there was no "privity" between the parties, and liability for negligence was problematic.

In most cases, judges felt bound by the privity of contract doctrine to deny recovery where the injured party had not dealt directly with the vendor or manufacturer. However, some judges perceived the injustice that could arise from denying recovery in all cases where there was no direct contractual relationship between the defendant and the injured party. A party had suffered injury and could point to the person at fault, yet the injured party was without recourse. In some cases, the judges stretched the limits of the privity of contract doctrine and allowed recovery even where the injured party had no direct dealings with the defendant. The law stumbled along from case to case. For example, in a case where a woman suffered injury caused by a bottle of defective hair-wash that her husband had purchased for her, the woman could not point to a contract she had entered with the vendor-manufacturer to ground her claim. If the privity of contract doctrine were strictly applied, she had no right to recover damages for the injury she had suffered. This was plainly unjust, and the court held the vendor-manufacturer liable on the ground that he must have known that his customer had purchased the product for his wife.[10] That decision was later cited as a precedent for the proposition that recovery for losses caused by defective products did not always rest on a direct contractual relationship. Duties of care were found to arise in other situations on a case-by-case basis, despite the absence of a contract. The emerging pattern of decisions hinted that there might be a wider basis for liability, but the privity doctrine remained dominant. The gaps left by the strict rule of privity of contract were gradually filled on an *ad hoc*, case-by-case basis. These decisions created a pattern of exceptions that undermined the rule, because it was unclear whether the judge would apply the privity of contract rule or make an exception to avoid the injustice.

Ultimately, as I will explain below and in greater detail in chapter 5, in 1932, the House of Lords decided in *Donoghue v Stevenson* that the exceptions had overwhelmed the rule and announced a much broader and more general test for finding a duty of care based on the foreseeability of harm rather than privity of contract.[11]

## General Rules and Ambiguity

The problem of gaps can be alleviated by framing the law in broad terms of general standards capable of capturing a wide range of possible situations. Casting the law in terms of general standards affords greater flexibility to judges deciding concrete cases and gives them considerable scope to achieve justice and equity in particular cases. But broadly worded principles that accord a wide measure of discretion to judges permitting them to achieve what they believe is a "just" result in the individual case renders the law less certain and less predictable. So what we gain in generality of application and avoidance of gaps we pay for in terms of uncertainty and the need to rely on judicial decision-making to flesh out the details of the law. Lawyers find it difficult to predict outcomes for their clients, and judges squirm under the pressure of having to grapple with vague principles every time they decide a case. This creates pressure to move back in the direction of certainty and predictability.

For an example of a general rule that relies on judicial interpretation and case-specific adaptation, I return to the law of negligence. In *Donoghue v Stevenson*, Lord Atkin decided that the narrowly defined privity of contract rule for establishing tort liability was unduly limited and needed to be expanded. He looked to the exceptions that had arisen throughout the case law and searched for a unifying trait that could provide an explanation for them all. Lord Atkin was able to discern a general principle that could be inferred from the case law, namely, that there is a general duty to avoid harming those who, in his words, are "so closely and directly affected by my act that I ought reasonably to have them in contemplation as being so affected."[12] The new principle liberated the courts from the unacceptable constraint of the privity of contract doctrine, but it established a general principle for liability of enormous potential reach. Unless reined in, the principle raised "the spectre of indeterminate liability,"[13] and it had to be refined and limited on a case-by-case basis in a process that continues to this day.

The arguments for certainty are particularly strong in commercial law. Lord Mansfield observed that commercial dealings "ought not to depend upon subtleties and niceties; but upon rules easily learned and easily retained," and that it is "of more consequence that a rule should be certain, than whether the rule should be established one way or another."[14] Commercial actors must be able to order their affairs and plan for the future. A reliable legal regime provides the assurance that commercial actors need, namely, that their contracts will be enforced and that, in the event of a dispute, their relationships will be governed by known and established rules. The efficient functioning of the market economy requires clear legal rules that govern the conduct of market actors.

Lawyers drafting legislation and commercial agreements face the same dilemma as judges formulating common law rules. If the statute or contract is drafted too narrowly and too precisely, it may fail to provide for all contingencies. But if the instrument is drafted too broadly, it may leave too much to interpretation and result in uncertainty.

The law is constantly struggling to settle on the appropriate point in the spectrum between what a notable English judge described as the two extremes of "such certainty in the law as to obviate virtually all litigation save on disputed questions of fact" and "the goal of perfect hand-tailored justice in every case."[15] We may think of the pursuit of both legal certainty and perfect justice as a zero-sum game: as certainty increases, perfect justice diminishes, and vice versa. In the end, I suspect that we are faced with a continuous search for the right balance between the desire for clarity, certainty, and predictability on the one hand, and the wish for generality, universality of application, and individualized case-specific justice on the other.

## Law in Context

The second feature that makes law uncertain is that laws must always be applied in a factual context, and the factual context is constantly evolving and changing. The common law tradition rests on the idea that the law emerges from the pattern of decisions dealing with specific cases. Somewhat paradoxically, that same tradition stubbornly resisted the notion that the interpretation and application of legal doctrine is a contextual undertaking. The reason for this resistance is that admitting context matters appears to destabilize legal doctrine. If the answer to the question, "What does the law say about this?" is always "That depends upon the context," the law will appear to be too contingent on the circumstances and too subject to the perceptions, beliefs, biases, and prejudices of the judge deciding the case.

No one would challenge the ideal that our system of law should be as free as possible from the personal predilections of judges. Judges have sworn oaths to decide cases according to law, thereby promising not to decide cases according to their own individual opinions and preferences. One expression of this ideal is captured by the narrowly legalistic version of formalism that prevailed in Canada well into the twentieth century and that, to some extent, survives to this day. As Ernest Weinrib explains, this "justifiably maligned notion ... requires strict or mechanical adherence to the authoritatively formulated rules of positive law without reference to the rules' normative underpinning."[16]

While I accept that legal reasoning has a formal structure to which judges must adhere,[17] my daily experience of hearing and deciding cases tells me that the law does not, and cannot, operate in a vacuum. Rigid adherence to the narrowly legalistic formalist model misses, or even worse, conceals things that are very real and ever-present in my work as a judge. The legal disputes I decide arise from the realities of daily life and from a wide range of ever-changing social, economic, and political contexts. The legal texts and doctrines that I am sworn to follow and apply, whether common law or statutory in origin, are imbued with moral, philosophical, and social values. As Canadian Supreme Court Justice Gérard La Forest observed, judges have to make choices and "unavoidably adapt the law to the times." He observed that a precedent "suitable in the context of the society of the time ... may have a completely different effect in a new setting" or its "governing rationale may have been overridden by some other principle in view of changing conditions."[18] Israeli Supreme Court Justice Aharon Barak maintains that judges have an obligation to "bridge the gap between law and society," as "when social reality changes, the law must change too."[19]

To pretend that the law can be mechanically applied in a purely objective, morally neutral manner is to ignore the important question of what values actually drive and determine judicial decisions. Professor Paul Weiler wrote a stinging critique of the excessive legalism of the Supreme Court of Canada in the late 1960s. Weiler complained that the judges "wrote their opinions as if there is already an established legal rule which binds them," applying the rule "because the law requires it, not because the judges believe it is a desirable rule."[20] Legal rules are "social products with social purposes" to be interpreted through socially informed eyes" and applied in "particular social contexts."[21] Judges do not, and cannot, decide cases entirely based on neutral, objective principles. Indeed, to pretend that they do creates a serious problem. It conceals or obscures a significant component of judicial reasoning and discourages judges from reflecting upon, and, more importantly, questioning, the values they inevitably apply.

A prime example of the perils of narrow legalistic reasoning is the 1928 decision of the Supreme Court of Canada in the Persons Case.[22] The issue was whether a woman could be appointed to the Senate. The appointment provision in Canada's original constitution, the *British North America Act, 1867* (now the *Constitution Act, 1867*), section 24, provides that the Governor General shall "summon qualified Persons to the Senate."

Was a woman a "qualified Person"? The question was raised when Emily Murphy, a prominent author and activist who had been appointed as an Alberta magistrate to preside over cases involving women and children, sought a Senate seat in 1919. In response, the Department of Justice provided the government of the day with a detailed legal opinion, which concluded that women were not eligible for appointment to the Senate. The opinion was based on a line of English case law holding that women could not vote, hold public office, or gain entry into the professions or the universities. Suffragettes had argued that since legislation governing the interpretation of statutes established that "words importing the Masculine Gender shall be taken to include Females ... unless the contrary as to Gender ... is expressly provided,"[23] statutes conferring the right to vote on "every man" conferred that same right on "every woman." But judges refused to accept the argument, ruling that giving women the vote was "ridiculous."[24] This line of judicial thinking prevailed, even in the face of statutes that did use gender-neutral language. The proposition that legislation giving the vote to "all persons" who had graduated from certain universities granted the vote to female graduates was rejected out of hand as being "incomprehensible."[25] Even a statute proclaiming that "a person shall not be disqualified by sex or marriage from the exercise of any public function" or from appointment to any post[26] was not enough. When a woman inherited her father's title and sought admission to the House of Lords on the strength of that legislation, her claim was dismissed on the ground that such "vague and general" statutory language could not be interpreted as "effecting such a revolutionary change."[27]

Emily Murphy was determined to test the Department of Justice opinion in the courts, and she persuaded Prime Minister Mackenzie King to refer the question of the eligibility of women to the Supreme Court of Canada. It came as no surprise to the Canadian legal community that the Supreme Court agreed with the Department of Justice, followed the English decisions, and held that a constitutional amendment would be required to make a woman a "qualified person" for purposes of appointment to the Senate.[28] Chief Justice Frank Anglin – a judge who believed in "scientific jurisprudence," a version of legal formalism that viewed law as a set of fixed, immutable rules akin to the laws of science – was firmly wedded to the view that the values of order, predictability, and uniformity must prevail.[29] His judgment began with the proposition that the court was not "concerned with the desirability or the undesirability of the presence of women in the Senate."[30] Although the Constitution used the gender-neutral word "Persons," Chief Justice Anglin concluded that to give the word a gender-neutral meaning would amount to an unacceptable departure from past authority. He was not prepared to question the thinking of an earlier age that excluded women from public office, and he flatly rejected the argument that a woman could be appointed to the Senate.

It is entirely likely that the senior and respected judges who made these pronouncements excluding women from public office thought they were simply applying the law in a neutral fashion. Their adherence to a rigid view of legal formalism insulated them from the need to re-examine the values and assumptions animating earlier decisions in the light of modern social conditions.

But there was nothing neutral or intrinsically legal about the law's denial of equal treatment for women. It was the product of archaic social attitudes and moral values that conceived of women as inferior to men and therefore undeserving of the same opportunities or entitlements. The formalist tradition of law shielded those views from scrutiny. The judges who perceived themselves to be neutral were, in reality, actively perpetuating inequality when they interpreted "Persons," a word plainly capable of including women, as including only men.

Fortunately, in 1928, the Supreme Court of Canada did not have the last word. Emily Murphy appealed the decision to the Judicial

Committee of the Privy Council, then Canada's highest judicial authority. This august imperial institution, one of the last vestiges of Canada's colonial past, sat in London and served as the final judicial arbiter for legal disputes throughout the British Empire. It played a pivotal role in the evolution of Canada's Constitution for more than eighty years. The Privy Council proclaimed an organic and progressive theory of constitutional interpretation. The reform-minded Lord Sankey, who sat at the apex of the English judiciary as Lord Chancellor, wrote, "The exclusion of women from all public offices is a relic of days more barbarous than ours."[31]

Two themes pervade Lord Sankey's remarkable judgment. The first is the recognition that legal rules or customs are the products of a particular social and historical context. Laws may outlive the customs and traditions that gave rise to them, and courts should take this into account when interpreting the law when circumstances change. Lord Sankey carefully reviewed the legal authorities excluding women from public office. He acknowledged the centuries of legal discrimination against women but refused to view the law in static terms or be bound by the past. The word "Persons" was "ambiguous, and in its original meaning would undoubtedly embrace members of either sex." If the original meaning of the word could include women, it was social tradition and custom that excluded women, not the law itself. Lord Sankey concluded, "The appeal to history therefore in this particular matter is not conclusive."[32] In Lord Sankey's view, it was wrong "to apply rigidly to Canada of today the decisions and the reasons therefor which commended themselves, probably rightly, to those who had to apply the law in different circumstances, in different centuries to countries in different stages of development."[33] As the word "persons" could include both genders, Lord Sankey wrote, "to those who ask why the word should include females, the obvious answer is why should it not?"[34]

Lord Sankey's second theme was the difference between statutory interpretation and constitutional interpretation. He characterized the evolution of the *British North America Act, 1867* as an affirmation of Canadian unity and self-determination. Again, Lord Sankey emphasized the importance of social tradition and custom in legal development. As the final court of appeal for "the Britannic system," which includes "countries and peoples in every stage of social, political and economic development and undergoing a continuous process of evolution," the Privy Council "must take great care not to interpret legislation meant to apply to one community by a rigid adherence to the customs and traditions of another."[35] Ironically, the voice of supreme colonial power was insisting upon the very independence and legal maturity that Canada's own judges had refused to claim for themselves.

It is within this context that Lord Sankey presented what has come to be the most memorable phrase in modern Canadian constitutional law: "The *British North America Act* planted in Canada a living tree capable of growth and expansion within its natural limits."[36] The living tree metaphor described the Constitution in the organic terms of growth and evolution. It was, wrote Lord Sankey, neither the duty nor the desire of the Privy Council "to cut down the provisions of the Act by a narrow and technical construction, but rather to give it a large and liberal interpretation" to allow Canada to be "mistress in her own house."[37]

The Canadian press and popular opinion applauded the Privy Council decision[38] as reflecting widely accepted contemporary views about the role of women in society. However, the idea that the law is capable of adapting over time to meet the changing needs of Canadian society did not immediately resonate with the staid Canadian legal community. An article in the *Canadian Bar Review* defended the Supreme Court of Canada for having applied the settled rules of statutory interpretation that Lord Sankey and his colleagues had "simply ... brushed aside," ignoring points that were "obvious ... to a legal mind."[39] The author's staunch defence of Chief Justice Anglin's judgment was firmly rooted in legal formalism, which strongly opposed the contextual approach and Lord Sankey's insistence that laws be understood and interpreted in the light of the moral and political climate that produced them.

The living tree metaphor has since been accepted as a norm of constitutional interpretation. And in non-constitutional cases, the Supreme Court has accepted that "[i]t is incumbent on the judiciary to bring the law into harmony with prevailing social values."[40]

There is now a long list of cases where changing societal perceptions regarding the role of women have led courts to change the law. A 1979 ruling holding that the denial of sick-leave benefits to pregnant women did not amount to discrimination[41] was overruled ten years later because of the changed perception of gender equality and the place of women in the workforce.[42] The law relating to the evidence admissible in a case of self-defence was reformulated to ensure that juries had a full understanding of battered-wife syndrome when considering whether a woman who had killed her abusive husband was guilty of murder.[43] In a case formulating a remedy to allow a woman to secure her rightful share of matrimonial property upon marriage breakdown, the Supreme Court stated, "Many factors, legal and non-legal, have emerged to modify the position of earlier days. Among these factors are a more enlightened attitude toward the status of women, altered life-styles, dynamic socio-economic changes. Increasingly, the work of a woman in the management of the home and rearing of the children, as wife and mother, is recognized as an economic contribution to the family unit."[44]

But the "living tree" doctrine and considerations of social context still serve as a lightning rod attracting the criticism of those who reject the proposition that judges have a law-making role. How do judges decide what are prevailing social values? When do changed social values qualify as appropriate motivators for legal change? And those judges who embrace the idea that the law must move with the times are left with this question: If we abandon the idea that the law is a self-contained discipline that simply involves the objective application of morally neutral rules, are we admitting that the law is necessarily radically indeterminate? If so, what are the implications for judges? Are we free to do as we please? What are the "natural limits" on Lord Sankey's "living tree"?

## The Attack on Legal Formalism

For the past century, there have been waves of legal thinkers who have challenged the formalist ideal of law as a purely objective tool that can be mechanically applied to yield ready and clear answers. The American legal realist movement of the 1920s to the 1940s undermined confidence in formalism. Realists argued that judicial decision-making essentially turns on the facts and on the personal or political biases of judges. The realists adopted an instrumentalist view that regarded law as a tool to serve broader social purposes, perhaps reflecting American legal culture's tendency to see litigation as a means of achieving legal and social reform. The realists urged greater reliance on the use of social science insights to enhance the quality of judicial decisions and to advance social, economic, and political goals.[45] These arguments inspired the "Brandeis brief," the invention of future Justice Louis Brandeis when he was a lawyer appearing before the Supreme Court. Resisting an attack on a law limiting workday hours for women, Brandeis filed a lengthy brief that gathered empirical data on the harmful effect of long working hours. The court accepted the brief and upheld the law.[46]

In the 1950s and 1960s, the legal process school attempted to find a middle ground between the realists and the formalists.[47] These scholars rejected the formalist claim that judges do not make law but argued for limits on judicial law-making authority, insisting on the distinction between law and politics. They emphasized the need to advert to the institutional capacity of courts, legislatures, and administrative agencies. They emphasized the importance of fair process and procedure and, with respect to judicial decision-making, they stressed the importance of reasoned elaboration of principles that "in their generality and their neutrality transcend any immediate result that is involved."[48] If a judge could point to no "neutral principle," the question must be left for the legislature.

In the 1970s, 1980s, and 1990s, critical legal studies, critical race theory, and feminist legal theory took legal realism in new directions. These diverse schools of thought are premised on progressive political attitudes and claim that conventional formal legal reasoning is incoherent, indeterminate, and based upon raw political choice. The critical legal studies movement took flight in the 1970s. Critical legal studies scholars vigorously rejected the formalist vision of law and asserted that law is radically indeterminate. They argued that as rights can be manipulated, the legal process is not a neutral tool to resolve differences on a principled basis but rather a political device to ensure the protection of vested interests.[49] Critical feminist and critical race theorists borrow the rhetoric of critical legal studies to some extent but focus specifically on the evils of sexism and racism, and on the need to transform social and legal attitudes in order to achieve genuine equality.[50]

From the other end of the political spectrum emerged the law and economics movement, which shares the realist perception of law as lacking coherence or credibility as an autonomous discipline. Law and economics proponents view legal disputes as being nothing more than a point at which disparate forces and ideas compete for acceptance. Building on the utilitarian philosophy of Bentham and Mill, law and economics scholars argue that legal rules could best be explained, understood, and developed in terms of their attainment of economic efficiency.[51]

While these schools of thought have eloquent and influential adherents in the academy in Canada, they have achieved less traction
here than in the United States. They have had even less impact on
the conventional legal thought prevailing in the Canadian legal profession and the judiciary. On the other hand, I think it would be a
serious error to discount their influence. Indeed, I think that many
aspects of the once radical realist attack have been more or less absorbed into conventional legal thinking. Most Canadian lawyers and
judges today accept the notion that the law is imbued with moral,
political, and social values. We accept as well that law and legal rules
should be viewed and shaped in terms of the broader social, political, and economic context in which they operate. We no longer see
law as a self-contained end in itself but rather as a tool that can be
used to achieve social harmony, peace, and justice. We recognize that
this renders the law less than certain and that there are bound to be
challenging cases where the legal outcome is difficult to predict.

### Is the Law Indeterminate?

I accept that the open-textured nature of legal rules renders the law
uncertain in its application to specific cases and dependent to some
extent upon external moral, social, and political values. I accept as
well that law must adapt to deal with changing social reality. But
where does that leave me as a judge? Does it mean that I have to
go about my work on the basis that law is inherently indeterminate
and that I can do as I please, or am I bound to decide cases on the
premise that there is always a legally correct answer? H.L.A. Hart
aptly described these two extremes as, on the one hand, the realist
"nightmare" that judges never decide according to the law, and, on
the other, the idealist "noble dream" that judges always simply follow the law.[52]

Some judges feel liberated by the idea that the law is indeterminate. It frees them to do what they believe to be just in the cases
they decide. A prime example is Judge Richard Posner, a former law
professor, a prodigious author, and for many years a member of the
United States Court of Appeals for the Seventh Circuit. Posner argues that when legal doctrine runs out, as he believes it frequently
does, judges should approach their task as pragmatists, deciding
cases on the basis of what they believe will work best for the parties
and for society at large in both the short and the long term.[53]

But others find the idea of indeterminacy unsettling and threatening. Probably most judges, including me, fit somewhere in between these two extremes. My object in writing this book is to confront this problem as openly as I can, without hiding behind the glib assertion that I simply apply the law as it is written.

I think that most Canadian judges today reject what Justice Brian Dickson labelled "blind and empty formalism"[54] that prevailed in Canada during the early years of the twentieth century. At the same time, they realize that the abandonment of narrow legal formalism does not leave them free to decide cases on the basis of their own personal views or preferences. As Michael Kirby, formerly a member of the High Court of Australia put it, they search for a point "somewhere between the spectacle of a judge pursuing political ideas of his or her own … irrespective of the letter of the law, and the unrealistic mechanic deified by the strict formalists."[55]

It has been persuasively argued that the divide between formalists and realists has been exaggerated. "No one thinks that law is autonomous and judging is mechanical deduction, and rare is the informed jurist who thinks that judges are engaged in the single-minded pursuit of their personal preferences."[56] Putting the debate in terms of a choice between those two extremes fails to capture the basis upon which virtually all jurists proceed. The suggestion that the only choice is between the purely mechanical application of rules or deciding cases on the basis of personal preferences presents a false dichotomy. The mechanical model plainly does not reflect accepted judicial practice, but that does not leave us with the personal preferences of judges as the only other choice.

I have explained why I think there is an inherent element of uncertainty in the law that judges interpret and apply. But I do not think this makes the law indeterminate in quite the way the realists and critical legal studies scholars assert. The existence of some element of uncertainty does not mean that judges are freed from all constraints. The argument I am about to make rests on two propositions. The first is entirely practical. As a matter of fact, most of the time the law yields an answer that is reasonably clear. The second deals with the exceptional cases where the law does not yield a clear answer. These are the "hard cases" upon which skilled and reasonable lawyers and judges will disagree, the cases that go to the Supreme Court of Canada and result in a nine-judge panel splitting in a 5–4 decision. Here I admit my explanation is far more controversial. It may even amount to an article of faith rather than an argument. It is simply this. My judicial "job description" and my working hypothesis when confronted with such a case has to be that, however difficult the case may be, I am engaged in a process that aspires to find the right answer. I concede that it may be impossible for me to get my colleagues to agree that my answer is right and that I will never know for sure that I have found the right answer, but my job is to try to do so. I am bound as a judge to follow what Hart called the noble dream.

## The Practical Certainty of Law

Let me expand on the first proposition, practical certainty. It is important to put the question of judicial decision-making into proper perspective and not to exaggerate the significance of the law's uncertainty by focusing exclusively on the most difficult and contentious cases that come before appellate courts. As a practical matter, for most disputes, the law does provide a discernible rule or standard by which the parties can govern their affairs. In a very high percentage of the situations in which the law matters, there is a clear path. The law defines rights and obligations in terms sufficiently precise to provide reasonable guidance for citizens to order their behaviour and for courts and judges to decide disputes in a consistent and predicable manner.[57]

Virtually all social and economic interactions and transactions proceed without dispute about the law that the parties are able to identify, accept, and follow. When disputes arise, most settle before legal proceedings are initiated. When the parties do find themselves in litigation, most cases settle before trial. Of those that go to trial, most involve contested issues of fact, not law. Few trial decisions are appealed. So by focusing on judicial decisions, and especially appellate decisions, we are looking at the very tip of the pyramid of disputes and ignoring the vast bulk of resolved disputes that lie at the base and that are resolved without dispute about the law.

The angst produced by the abandonment of the formalist ideal is also considerably alleviated on a day-to-day basis by the experience of deciding actual cases. Judges are practical people, and, as a practical matter, the law does provide reasonably clear answers for most cases. In the relatively modest volume of disputes that end up in court, the usual task of the trial judge is to deal with the contested facts about who did what to whom. Once the factual issues are resolved, most cases lead to the relatively straightforward application of an accepted legal rule. This is why I think it is wrong to focus exclusively on the highly contentious cases where the answer is anything but clear.

It is only when we reach closer to the tip of the pyramid of disputes that we encounter the jurisprudential cases that require appellate courts to decide significant points of law. Even then, in a high percentage of those cases, judges are unanimous. At the very top of the pyramid is the Supreme Court of Canada, which hears sixty-five to eighty cases per year. The court has chosen these cases on the basis of their importance to the legal system as a whole. While we naturally focus on the contentious cases, often decided by a divided court, the statistics show that in the past decade, the Supreme Court has been unanimous in approximately 70 per cent of the cases it decides, including some of the most contentious *Charter* decisions.[58] No doubt some of those unanimous or near-unanimous decisions are not universally regarded as having been "rightly" decided. However, Supreme Court judges are strong-minded individuals who openly hold differing views and are not prone to compromise on points of principle. I suggest that the extent to which decisions attract unanimity provides some support for the proposition that the law is not radically indeterminate.

I sit in an intermediate appellate court, and a very high percentage of the 1,000 cases we decide annually – I would say that 80–85 per cent – fall into the category of "error-correction." These are cases where the issue is whether or not the trial judge erred in law or in applying a settled legal principle to the evidence. In these cases, clear law, combined with the trial judge's findings of credibility and fact, determine the result, and our decisions have little or no jurisprudential significance. They rest upon relatively well-settled legal doctrine and can be disposed of with reasons that will have little interest to anyone other than the litigants. For example, we hear many criminal appeals that turn on the credibility of the witnesses at trial. The result is obviously very important to the person convicted and to the victim. However, if the trial judge properly explained why the judge accepted the evidence of the victim and rejected that of the accused, there is nothing an appellate court can do and no reason for us to elaborate on the trial judge's reasons.

The high number of "error-correction" appeals suggests that, as a practical matter, the law usually does yield a reasonably clear answer that the judiciary, the legal community, and the public are collectively able to accept. We should not become too obsessed with hard cases, the difficult, cutting-edge cases where uncertainty reigns. As Cardozo observed, "We must not let these occasional and relatively rare instances blind our eyes to the innumerable instances where there is neither obscurity nor collision and no opportunity for diverse judgment."[59] Our encounters with trees of the tough cases may have caused us to lose sight of the forest of the law.[60]

## Hard Cases: Is There Always a Right Answer?

There are, however, cases where the correct legal result is anything but clear. These are the cases that catch the headlines and perplex legal theorists in search of a sound and coherent explanation for judicial decision-making. The prime examples arise from the interpretation of *Charter* rights and freedoms. What do we mean by equality? Liberty? Freedom of expression? The principles of fundamental justice? The precise meaning of these rights and freedoms was a matter of debate among politicians, lawyers, and moral philosophers for centuries before the *Charter*. The debate continues today. It is doubtful that we will ever arrive at a complete or settled meaning of these rights and freedoms. There are also "hard cases" involving more technical legal issues where the result is not apparent from the relevant authorities. In chapter 9, I discuss such a case that I faced dealing with the issue of privacy.

I accept that the direction the law takes in hard cases is contingent on many factors: when the case comes before the court, who argues it, who decides it,[61] and the influence of the political climate of the day. Honest and reasonable lawyers, judges, and legal scholars, doing their very best to follow the dictates of the law, will disagree about how the case should be decided.

It is here that the once-radical but now accepted critique of the formalist model – which conceives of law as a body of neutral principles that can be objectively determined and applied – comes to the fore. If the law is less than certain, imbued with moral, political, and social values, and to be shaped in terms of the broader social, political, and economic context, then what disciplines the judge's decision?

I think it is important for judges to confront this difficult issue rather than hide behind the myth of strict legalism. The role of a judge, especially a Supreme Court judge, is not, as Chief Justice John

Roberts infamously claimed, nothing more than that of the baseball umpire who simply calls balls and strikes.[62] Myths and fictions of that kind are dangerous, not only because they are wrong, but also because they discourage judges from being honest and reflective about the values they bring to judging.

If judges really believe that their personal views cannot influence their decisions, they will fail to make the necessary effort to put those personal biases and prejudices aside. The conscientious judge should not hide behind a facade of judicial neutrality but should engage in self-reflection, consciously striving to confront the influence of personal views and attitudes when making decisions.[63] The judge should not pretend to be an amoral and apolitical automaton.

H.L.A. Hart, writing from the positivist perspective, argued that in hard cases, where the law does not dictate an answer, the judge has the discretion to decide the case "according to his own beliefs and values" and "to follow standards or reasons for decision which are not dictated by the law."[64]

I accept that, where the law does not dictate a clear answer, I have a choice. But I am unable to infer from that choice that my decision-making responsibility can be accurately described as allowing me to choose from a range of equally acceptable results on the basis of my own personal views and values.[65] Indeed, Hart himself conceives of the judge's discretion as being circumscribed. He insists that the choice the judge makes must not be arbitrary, and that it should "display characteristic judicial virtues," including "a concern to deploy some acceptable general principle as a reasoned basis for decision."[66]

I recognize that any claim that a judge can confidently predict or know "the right answer" to every case that comes before the courts is doomed to fail. Such a claim would be quickly refuted by reading majority and dissenting opinions from the Supreme Court of Canada. Those judgments reveal strongly divergent judicial views with no agreement as to the "right answer." Most of these divergent views are thoughtful, forceful, well-written, and based upon accepted legal sources. Different judges see legal issues in different ways, and different judges, acting in perfect good faith and sharing an eager desire to do justice, will disagree about what is right. There is no meta-theory of justice against which we can readily measure all decisions for correctness.

On the other hand, it seems to me that when I sit down to write my reasons, my working hypothesis has to be that my job is to do my best to come up with the "right" – or at least the best possible – answer, even though I accept that I may not be able to claim with any confidence that I have found it.

I realize that many disagree with the proposition that there are "right answers." Even Ronald Dworkin, who argued that there are "right answers," was driven to rely on the Hercules construct: "a lawyer of superhuman skill, learning, patience and acumen"[67] to decide the "hard cases" that cannot be decided "under a clear rule of law, laid down by some institution in advance."[68] I am no Hercules, and my skill, learning, patience, and acumen is far from superhuman, yet I still must decide the hard cases.

I think that it is important for the judge to identify and focus on the noble dream, the ideals, and the aspirations of the law, not on our shortcomings and human failings. That I am no Hercules does not relieve me from performing my Herculean task. To carry it out in a manner acceptable in a democratic society, I must strive to identify and remain faithful to a vision of law as a coherent set of norms and standards. As a judge I work within an institutional framework and a process that aims to achieve that aspiration: a framework that guides and disciplines the process of judicial decision-making and that seeks to limit the influence of the personal views of the judge. I have to be honest and admit that sometimes the framework takes me only so far, and that I could credibly decide the case either way. I concede that the law does not dictate one right answer, but I aspire to attain a result that displays what Dworkin calls integrity: "Law as integrity asks judges to assume, so far as this is possible, that the law is structured by a coherent set of principles about justice and fairness and procedural due process, and it asks them to enforce these in the fresh cases that come before them, so that each person's situation is fair and just according to the same standard."[69]

I see the decision-maker's task as being constrained by the need to find a result that best comports with the fabric and texture of the legal rules and principles pertinent to the dispute. The integrity of the legal process compels me to define my responsibility in terms of providing a reasoned justification for my decision that aims to persuade the litigants, the legal community, and the public that I have reached the right result – the result that achieves justice under law, not justice according to my personal beliefs.

Justice John Morden of the Ontario Court of Appeal observed in one case, "In the absence of binding authority clearly on point it may reasonably be said that the law *is* what it ought to be."[70] What the law "ought to be" was not Justice Morden's personal opinion, but the product of his characteristically thorough and thoughtful review of the authorities, delving into the intricacies of the existing rules, their rationales and principles. As Benjamin Cardozo put it, "[T]he thing that counts is not what I believe to be right ... [but] what I may reasonably believe that some other man of normal intellect and conscience might reasonably look upon as right."[71]

I realize that I am only human and that my decisions may be influenced or affected by my personal views. But my oath compels me to make a conscious effort to control the direction in which my personal views take me. My personal views may well come into play in "hard cases" where precedent is not dispositive, but I have a responsibility to decide the case on a principled basis that I am prepared to live with in the future.

Lord Hoffmann, a former member of the English Court of Appeal and House of Lords, offered his perspective on Ronald Dworkin's argument that the task of the judge is to find what seems to be the "right answer." Hoffmann was under no illusion: he recognized that these cases could go either way, with neither option being conclusively "right." But when confronted with such a case and by colleagues who took a different view of how it should be decided, he thought that he was right, and they were wrong. "Our job was to find the right answer and obviously each thought we had done so." He went on to explain that while "there was no divine arbiter to say which of us was right ... the one point on which we were unanimous was that there was only one right answer."[72]

Most judges are probably less categorical. They recognize that they have a choice in hard cases, and, in the absence of a "divine arbiter" or objective test to determine who was right and who was wrong, they can go no further than saying there are better answers, or perhaps that they are in pursuit of the best[73] or optimal[74] answer. But, like Lord Hoffmann, they do their very best to persuade their colleagues and the public that they are right. Judges who say that there are no right answers are simply being honest and admitting that in hard cases the law does not dictate an outcome and that they must make choices. They recognize that a different judge might, quite legitimately, make a different choice, and, out of respect for that different choice, they refrain from claiming that they are right. But by making that concession, I do not think that they abandon the noble dream of a legal order governed by a coherent set of principles of justice, fairness, and procedural due process to govern judicial decision-making.

In chapter 9, I offer an example of a hard case I confronted. It was a case where one party's privacy had been violated by the other, and the question was whether there was any legal recourse for the party who had been wronged in this way. My instinctive response was that the party whose privacy had been invaded should be able to sue, but the existing law provided no clear answer. The protection of privacy was recognized in some legal situations, but Ontario law did not yet recognize a private right of action. There were strong arguments that it should. I canvassed the arguments and the relevant authorities and decided that recognizing a new right of action was an incremental change that was within my capacity as a common law judge to make.

Did I reach the right answer? I think so, but I cannot be sure. Could another judge have conscientiously come to a different conclusion? Almost certainly yes. Does the fact that I cannot be sure that I was right and my concession that another judge could have decided differently undermine my claim that my job was to do my best to get the right answer? I don't think so. I was not entitled to decide the case as I pleased. I thought long and hard about it. I read as much as I reasonably could about the issues it presented. I was looking for a result that seemed to best reflect the pertinent principles of justice that the law recognizes. I was looking for a result that would make the law a more coherent whole and that respected the limits of my judicial law-making authority. I fully accept that my answer was not legally inevitable, that I had a choice, and that another judge could have decided the case differently. As I see it, I was engaged in a process that has to accept the frailty of human judgment but, at the same time, must aspire to provide right answers.

## Conclusion

As a practical day-to-day matter, the law's admittedly general, open-textured norms and standards provide adequate guidance. Most of the time, the law is sufficiently clear and ascertainable to allow citizens to guide their actions and resolve their disputes without recourse to the courts. Most cases that are litigated involve factual rather than legal disputes, and relatively few cases involve questions of law that require appellate review. A significant proportion of the few cases that do go before an intermediate or final appellate court are decided unanimously.

There are, however, "hard cases" that come before the courts where the law does not yield a ready answer. These cases are relatively rare, but they raise the important, headline-grabbing issues that provide fodder for the debate about the legitimacy of the judicial role. The law imposes a significant responsibility upon judges who decide such cases. There is no clear answer, yet the judge is still duty-bound to come up with an answer that is legally acceptable. I argue that the judge's task when deciding a "hard case" is not aptly described as having the discretion to choose from a range of possible options, all of which are legally acceptable. In my view, the working hypothesis of judges deciding "hard cases" has to be that they are in search of the best answer according to law, even though they may not be able to agree on what the best answer is.

## Chapter 4

# Do Judges Make Law?

We are all familiar with the plea that the courts should just apply the law and leave it to Parliament or the legislatures to decide what the law should be. Parliament and the legislatures have the authority to decide matters of public policy and enact laws that reflect the choices of the people who elected them. The primary role of judges is to decide the cases that come before them. They have the task of applying the law to individual cases. Their role is essentially reactive, and they have little opportunity to map out or follow an agenda for change. Subject to the Constitution, "the legislature can legislate at will," but "the judge never can do so."[1] And as judges are not elected, they must accept the division of responsibility and respect the limits that our democratic order imposes upon them as lawmakers.

But the simplistic proposition that courts just apply the law fails to account for two features of our legal order.

The first relates to the law's open texture, the topic of the previous chapter. Laws enacted by Parliament and the legislatures have to be interpreted to decide specific cases. Statutes channel and define the parameters of debate, but human activity is so complex and varied that it is simply not possible to write the law in a way that anticipates every case that might arise. Many statutes explicitly acknowledge this impossibility and direct judges to decide cases based on what is "fair," "equitable," "appropriate," and "reasonable," and to avoid results that are "unconscionable." Those words are deliberately chosen to allow the judges to interpret, shape, adapt, and apply the law as is required to meet the justice of the cases they decide. Moreover, Parliament does not have the capacity constantly to revisit and revise laws to meet changing social conditions. By using broad language, legislatures leave it to the courts to update the law through judicial interpretation.

When combined with the common law doctrine of precedent, the need for judicial interpretation eats away at any attempt to maintain a strict division of responsibility between legislatures as "lawmak-ers" and courts as "law-appliers." When judges are asked to inter-pret and apply statutes, they cannot avoid making law. I explore the subject of precedent in greater detail in chapter 7. At its core, the doc-trine of precedent rests upon a simple and readily understood prin-ciple of justice: like cases should be treated alike. Central to the idea of law is the consistent application of rules and standards so that citizens can plan their affairs and so that public authorities, such as the police, can govern in an orderly manner. If a statute is interpreted in one way in a particular case, it should ordinarily be interpreted the same way in a subsequent case. A decision interpreting a statute one way constitutes a precedent that more or less fixes the meaning of the statute for the future.

A second and even more important aspect of the doctrine of prec-edent is difficult to reconcile with the view that judges simply apply the law. This aspect of the doctrine of precedent is peculiar to our common law tradition. In the common law world, a huge swathe of our law is essentially untouched by statute and is instead the prod-uct of judicial precedents. In other words, there is no written law that judges interpret and apply; rather, the law is to be found in the decisions of previous cases. Most of our laws relating to contracts, property, torts (civil liability for personal wrongs), much of family law, and administrative law, and even important parts of our crimi-nal law are judge-made laws based on the precedents established by past decisions. As the courts confront new disputes arising from constantly changing social and economic circumstances, the com-mon law is gradually shaped and moulded by the courts to suit the changing needs of our society.

When common law judges decide cases, they are engaged in a process in which they simultaneously follow and constitute the law. The judge must follow the law as it then exists, whether in the form of common law precedents or statutes enacted by Parliament or the legislature. But once the judge decides the case, the doctrine of prec-edent makes the judge's decision part of the law that subsequent judges will follow, giving it what Benjamin Cardozo called "a gen-erative power ... that begets in its own image."[2] The decision will be read by lawyers as an indication of how future cases will be decided. Clients are advised and plan their affairs in the expectation that another judge will follow the precedent in the future.

Although common law judges have always played an important role in making and reshaping the law, for a long time, lawyers, judges, and scholars were stubbornly resistant to admitting the fact. William Blackstone, an eighteenth-century professor, judge, and author of the influential *Commentaries on the Laws of England*, wrote that common law judges do not make law; they are simply "living oracles" who discover the law and declare what it always has been. Expounding the common law declaratory theory, Blackstone argued that judgments are nothing more than "the evidence of what is the common law."[3]

Most modern judges reject Blackstone's declaratory theory as a discredited fiction designed to conceal the inconvenient truth that judges *do* make law. As Lord Goff, a member of the House of Lords, stated in a precedent-setting decision, "We all know that in reality ... the law is the subject of development by the judges." We can identify "the decisions which mark the principal stages in this development, and we have no difficulty in identifying the judges who are primarily responsible." Lord Goff described the judicial development of the common law as "inevitable," since "if it had never taken place, the common law would be the same now as it was in the reign of King Henry II." He continued, "The common law is a living system of law, reacting to new events and new ideas, and so capable of providing the citizens of this country with a system of practical justice relevant to the times in which they live."[4] More than twenty-five years earlier, Lord Reid, another distinguished member of the House of Lords, described the declaratory theory as a "fairy tale."[5] Justice Oliver Wendell Holmes Jr famously wrote, "The common law is not a brooding omnipresence in the sky, but the articulate voice" of the judges.[6] In *R v Hislop*, the Supreme Court of Canada observed, "Blackstone's declaratory approach has not remained unchallenged in modern law. Commentators and courts have pointed out that judges fulfil a legitimate law-making function. Judges do not merely declare law; they also make law."[7]

The declaratory theory confronts us with a pretence that is both misleading and dangerous – misleading because it distorts a very important feature of the role of judges in our society, and dangerous because it discourages judges from openly confronting the questions of value and choice that they face.[8] On the other hand, it seems to me that the declaratory theory does contain a certain grain of truth. Judicial law-making is incidental to deciding cases.[9] When judges make law, they do so by deciding a case and by working with accepted sources and principles. They explain, extend, or restrict the reach of what was there before, but they are bound to heed the pattern of past decisions and provide an acceptable and principled justification for the change they pronounce. Lord Goff, writing extrajudicially, emphasized that judicial law-making should not be based on "purely personal judgment" but rather must be "an informed and educated judgment, formulated in public discussion" and founded upon "a shared experience of the practical administration of justice" and "an accepted basis of systematic legal principle."[10] Dean Roscoe Pound readily accepted that judges have a law-making role but argued that it was consonant with the social need for legal stability "only in case it rests upon traditional premises and is developed therefrom by the traditional technique."[11]

The issue of judicial law-making arises in a variety of ways. In chapter 3, I discussed the problem of legal gaps and ambiguities. A gap occurs when the statute or common law governing the general area of law implicated by the dispute fails to provide for the specific situation presented by the facts of the case to be decided. A claimant is injured by the negligence of the defendant. On the facts of the case, there is no previous decision establishing that the defendant owes the claimant a legal duty of care.[12] There are, however, analogous cases that rest on a general principle that could be interpreted to impose a duty of care that would favour the claimant's situation. Should judges reason by way of analogy from the existing law? If they do, they "make law" by filling in the gap. If they do not, they "make law" by closing the door to like claims in the future. Similarly, if the law is ambiguous and could be interpreted either way, once the case is decided, the precedent makes the ambiguity disappear for future cases, posing the same issue.

Filling gaps and resolving ambiguities is what legal philosopher Leslie Green describes as the judge's "law-improving" role.[13] Green argues that in addition to the obligation to apply the law and protect the law's integrity by conducting fair proceedings, judges have the obligation to "keep the law in good shape."[14] Green sees this role as being inherent in the judicial function in a society that aspires to the rule of law: "If judges find the law unclear, they have a duty to clarify it; if there are conflicts in the law, they should try to resolve them. More generally, they should improve the law's capacity to guide the conduct of its subjects."[15]

The issue of judicial law-making also arises with social change. The content of law is shaped and determined by the social context of the era in which it was written. When the social context changes, should judges reshape the law to take that change into account? If they do, they make law. If they do not, they may escape the label as a lawmaker, but their decisions may fail to meet the interests of justice and the expectations of our legal order. In chapter 3, I give the example of the Persons Case where the Supreme Court of Canada, determined to avoid "making law," was harshly criticized for excluding women from the category of "persons," while the Privy Council provided a principled justification for departing from the past practice of discrimination and exclusion.

The real question, I suggest, is how far judges should go when faced with the challenge of making or not making law. When should the courts leave it to the legislature to change a common law rule or doctrine? This is highly contentious territory both within and outside the judiciary. There is a range of opinion about the limits of the judicial law-making role, as will be apparent from the discussion that follows.

## The Experience of Judicial Law-Making

I certainly became much more aware of the problems posed by judicial law-making after I was appointed to the bench. Being the one with the responsibility to decide made me more aware of the pitfalls, and it made me more cautious about how and when to change the law. There were several reasons for this.

As a judge, one is acutely aware of certain institutional constraints that limit one's capacity to assess when and how a law should be changed. A judge gets exposed to only a part of the law, the part that is relevant to the specific dispute to be decided. Viewed through this narrow lens, a legal issue takes on a certain hue that may change when the same issue arises in the context of a different dispute. Judges respond to the arguments the litigants present. Our adversarial legal tradition discourages us from doing our own research or dealing with issues or arguments the parties have not raised and ultimately we remain prisoners operating within the walls of the specific dispute we are called to decide.

This was clearly brought home to me in a series of cases I decided that dealt with the issue of when a domestic court should assume jurisdiction over an out-of-province defendant. I was a member of the three-judge panel assigned to hear an appeal raising this issue.[16] An Ontario resident had been injured in a motor vehicle accident in Alberta. The other car was owned and operated by Alberta residents. The Alberta residents disputed the jurisdiction of the Ontario courts to hear the case. It was an important, although rather technical, legal issue. I was familiar with the issue, having taught civil procedure as a law professor and from having written a report on the subject that was subsequently published as a monograph.[17] The law on jurisdiction over an out-of-province defendant was in a state of flux and uncertainty. It was apparent that a decisive judgment from our court would establish a law-making precedent that would guide Ontario judges in the future.

We heard the case, and we came to a tentative conclusion. After the case was argued, but before we had written our decision, we discovered that there were four other cases waiting to be heard by our court that raised similar questions of jurisdiction, but on different facts. There was a risk that if five different panels of judges heard and decided five different appeals, each argued differently, and on different facts, there would be differences in the tone and emphasis of the judgments, which might leave the law in a confused state. We reviewed the matter with the Associate Chief Justice, and he agreed that it would be best to have all the cases decided by the same panel of three judges. We listed the four new cases to be heard together, and we decided to have the case we had already heard re-argued along with that group.[18] We are ordinarily reluctant to have a case re-argued because there is an additional cost imposed on the litigants. However, the issue of jurisdiction over out-of-province defendants was important, and we decided that the interest in clarity in the law should prevail.

The effect of seeing the same legal issue from the perspective of the additional cases was revealing. I did not change my mind about the ultimate outcome in the first case, but I certainly changed the way I analysed the issues and the way I wrote my reasons. This brought home to me how easy it would have been to say something in the context of one appeal that would have been awkward to deal with in the context of the others.

My decisions on the five appeals set out a framework of general principles to be used when deciding issues of jurisdiction. It served as a workable precedent for several years, and many cases were decided using the framework I had set out. It came to be known as the "*Muscutt* test" and also was the subject of a considerable volume of academic commentary.[19] The approach that I had laid down in my decisions was very flexible, and it seemed to produce sound results. It was followed in Ontario and in some other provinces, but not in others. Some provinces adopted a model uniform law, proposed by a body that aims to harmonize the laws of the provinces,[20] that arguably was clearer and more certain. While most academic commentators approved of my decision and the *Muscutt* test,[21] others expressed the concern that the test was too loose and resulted in too much costly litigation on a preliminary issue that should be dealt with swiftly and cleanly.[22]

Several years later, two contentious cases were listed for hearing that challenged the *Muscutt* test. They were not easy to decide on their facts, and they presented forceful arguments that the *Muscutt* test lacked sufficient precision to guide the lower courts. There was good reason to think it might be time to take another look at the issue of assumed jurisdiction. Since a panel of five judges is required to depart from an earlier decision of the court,[23] the Chief Justice directed that the two cases be heard together by a five-judge panel.

We now had the benefit of eight years' experience with the *Muscutt* test. There were a significant number of trial court decisions applying it. These decisions were indicative of the test's utility in a diverse array of factual circumstances. We also had the benefit of the academics who had waded in on the efficacy of the test. Because the issues were important, we also welcomed arguments from interveners who were keenly interested in the issue as it affected their interests, namely, the Ontario Trial Lawyers Association and the Tourism Industry Association of Ontario. The interveners were able to offer a wider perspective on the issues than the immediate parties. We concluded that, while the earlier decisions were essentially sound, it was time to fine-tune the test to make it simpler and easier to apply. I wrote the decision for both appeals.[24] I did my best to retain what had worked from the earlier decisions, adapting the test to take into account the need for certainty and predictability.

The Supreme Court of Canada granted leave to appeal both decisions. At the national level, the Supreme Court had the advantage of viewing the problem from a much broader perspective. The court affirmed our decisions but crafted a test intended to provide greater clarity and consistency.[25] When I wrote my reasons I had to follow the lead of the Supreme Court's earlier jurisprudence that had revolutionized this area of law.[26] Those cases rested on broad and general principles. They had insisted that the law in this area had to be flexible and that it was impossible to lay down strict rules.[27] I did my best, within that framework, to provide what I considered to be principled and practical guidance for the future. By 2012, and with the benefit of the experience reflected by hundreds of cases from the lower courts, a significant legislative initiative, and a substantial volume of academic writing, the Supreme Court decided that it was time to move from flexibility to a clearer rule-based approach.

I draw several lessons from the experience of dealing with the issue of assumed jurisdiction.

The first I have already mentioned, but it bears repetition. Courts decide specific cases on specific facts. The specific context provides a limited perspective on the general legal issue involved. Because a legal issue looks different when the specific facts change, it is only when the same legal issue is considered in the context of different facts that it can be fully and properly understood. While courts can try to overcome this limitation through procedural devices, such as grouping similar cases for common hearing or entertaining the submissions of interveners, it remains dangerous to make sweeping pronouncements about a particular legal issue based on the limited information obtained through adversarial litigation.

The narrow and fact-specific nature of the common law encourages judges to be minimalists.[28] Decide only as much as is required to deal with the case at hand and wait for another case on different facts to decide more. Minimalism does not, however, relieve the judge of the obligation to be frank and candid. Any change in the law should be identified and justified, not smuggled in or passed off as just another routine decision. On the one hand, the decision must rest upon a rule or principle of sufficient generality to avoid the appearance of being purely result-oriented, in other words, decided only with reference to what seems just in the case, without regard to workable rules or principles. On the other hand, the decision should avoid "premature and unnecessary generalization"[29] and should not be "too greedy in its occupation of space in the legal firmament."[30]

Judicial minimalism is closely linked to the idea that the common law evolves incrementally.

There are clear advantages to a minimalist and incremental approach. When a judge makes a pronouncement that will have precedential value, the judge should be cautious about trying to resolve too much all at once. In the assumed jurisdiction cases, it was very helpful to be able to revisit, reconsider, and refine the test we had laid down previously, with the experience gained from the many trial-level decisions and the insights offered by academics with special knowledge and expertise in the area.[31]

The experience of the assumed jurisdiction cases also taught me that it is a mistake to ever think that one's judgment will be the last word. This is especially true for trial judges and judges who sit on intermediate appellate courts who are subject to review by a higher court. But even Supreme Court justices must be ready for the microscopic scrutiny their pronouncements attract from the legal profession, the media, the politicians, and the academy. They too must be aware that, as time passes and new cases with new facts arise, the law will evolve.

In my view, judges making pronouncements that have precedential value should approach the task from the viewpoint of starting a conversation, an "ongoing, always provisional and never-completed dialogue between judges and lawyers, bench and bar, about what the law is and what it ought to be."[32] The judge is a participant in a complex process that will likely involve future litigation, review by higher courts, and scrutiny from external critics. It is a process that will involve many participants, probably take unforeseen twists and turns, and may take years to unfold.

## When May Judges Change the Common Law?

A leading Canadian case on the limits of judicial law-making is the Supreme Court's 1989 decision *Watkins v Olafson*.[33] *Watkins* considered the issue of how damages to compensate for future losses should be paid. Future losses might include the cost of future care, or the losses that are anticipated to arise from an impaired ability to earn income in the future. The established common law rule is that an injured party is entitled to receive a lump-sum award for future losses. The lump-sum rule has been criticized because lump-sum awards pose a serious risk of either over- or under-compensation. If injured parties live longer than expected or if there are unexpected consequences from the injury, they will be under-compensated. On the other hand, if injured parties die earlier or recover more quickly, they will be over-compensated.

In *Watkins*, an individual injured in a motor vehicle accident sued and recovered a lump-sum award that included compensation for the estimated cost of future care and future loss of income. The Manitoba Court of Appeal set aside the lump-sum award and ordered the defendant to pay monthly payments to be adjusted for inflation and subject to variation determined by the injured party's need. The Court of Appeal recognized that ordinarily the injured party is entitled to a lump-sum award but was concerned that this plaintiff might be able to secure future care assistance from the government, which would thereby make the lump-sum award an unjust windfall.

The Supreme Court of Canada accepted that "once-and-for-all" lump-sum awards were problematic. As Justice Beverley McLachlin put it, "[P]eriodic payments are more consistent than the lump-sum rule with the fundamental principles upon which the assessment of personal injury damages are founded," namely, full and fair compensation, putting the plaintiff in the position he would have been in had the injury not occurred.[34] However, as Justice McLachlin saw it, the issue for the court was not whether periodic payments would be better, but rather, whether it was appropriate for the court to change the law and take away the injured party's right to receive a lump-sum award. To that question, her answer was a firm no.

Justice McLachlin accepted that "[o]ver time, the law in any given area may change" as a result of judicial decisions, but she insisted that the judiciary is ordinarily "bound to apply the rules of law found in the legislation and in the precedents," and that the process of change through judicial decisions "is a slow and incremental one, based largely on the mechanism of extending an existing principle to new circumstances." She referred to "the long-established principle that in a constitutional democracy it is the legislature, as the elected branch of government, which should assume the major responsibility for law reform." She defended the "judicial reluctance to dramatically recast established rules of law" on the ground that the "court has before it a single case" and consequently a limited view of the perceived deficiencies in the law. As "the court may not be in a position to appreciate fully the economic and policy issues underlying the choice it is asked to make," the court could not know the consequences of changing the law. Judicial law-making is permissible "[w]here the matter is one of a small extension of existing rules to meet the exigencies of a new case and the consequences of the change are readily assessable ... [b]ut where the revision is major and its ramifications complex, the courts must proceed with great caution."[35]

Ordering periodic awards "would constitute a major revision of the long-standing principles governing the assessment of damages for personal injury." The revision would "not involve the extension of an existing rule, but the adoption of a new principle." Such a change would remove a significant common law right and would be "fraught with complex ramifications extending beyond the rights and obligations of the parties at bar." The plaintiff and the defendant would be bound to "an uneasy and unterminated relationship for as long as the plaintiff lives."[36] A review of legislation permitting periodic payments in other jurisdictions indicated that there were a variety of policy choices to be made in designing an effective scheme – choices that would require ongoing consultation with insurers and other affected interests.

Considerations of this nature are often at play in what are described as "polycentric disputes." A polycentric dispute is one that "involves a large number of interlocking and interacting interests and considerations"[37] requiring "solutions which concurrently balance benefits and costs for many different parties."[38] Polycentric issues engage the interests of parties not before the court and raise wide-ranging policy choices. Courts lack the knowledge and resources to adequately address the complex issues that arise in polycentric disputes. Courts are better suited to resolve "bipolar" disputes, where the decision and any consequent law-making effect it might have turns exclusively on the nature of the rights and the relationship of the two parties who are before the court.[39]

A little more than a year after deciding *Watkins* the Supreme Court revisited the issue of judicial law-making in *R v Salituro*.[40] The appellant had been convicted of forgery on the strength of his estranged spouse's testimony. He appealed his conviction, arguing that the trial judge should have excluded his spouse's evidence because of the long-standing common law rule that one spouse is not competent to testify against the other. The rule was based upon the assumption that allowing one spouse to testify against the other would disrupt marital harmony – an assumption that was out of keeping with

modern views on the equality of women. While Parliament had not
abolished the common law rule, it had legislated significant exceptions to it by making spouses competent and compellable witnesses
in certain cases.[41] None of those exceptions applied in *Salituro*, but
the trial judge ruled that where the spouses had separated without
any possibility for reconciliation, one spouse could testify against
the other.

The Supreme Court agreed and upheld the conviction. Justice
Frank Iacobucci ruled that an essential feature of the common law
tradition is that "while complex changes to the law with uncertain
ramifications should be left to the legislature, the courts can and
should make incremental changes to the common law to bring legal
rules into step with a changing society."[42]

The convicted man made the same argument that had succeeded
in *Watkins*: any change in the law should be left to Parliament. Parliament had, after all, changed the spousal incompetency rule for
some cases but left it intact for others. Justice Iacobucci assessed the
changes Parliament had made. They were piecemeal, and there had
been no legislative attempt at a comprehensive reconsideration of
this arcane branch of the law. He concluded that it was open to the
court to refine the law to bring it into keeping with modern values.

The extent to which Parliament had acted may have influenced the
court to take a minimalist approach. The court did not abolish the
spousal incompetency rule entirely. Instead, it crafted an exception
to it for irreconcilably separated spouses. To apply the traditional
rule in those circumstances, said the court, would be "inconsistent
with respect for the freedom of all individuals, which has become a
central tenet of the legal and moral fabric of this country particularly
since the adoption of the *Charter*."[43] Justice Iacobucci described the
new exception as "precisely the kind of incremental change which
the courts can and should make ... as the custodians of the common
law." It fulfilled the court's "duty to see that the common law reflects
the emerging needs and values of our society."[44]

*Watkins* and *Salituro*, read together, present the two ends of the
judicial law-making spectrum. *Watkins* has been criticized by many.
Professor John McCamus, an accomplished common law scholar,
sees *Watkins* as articulating "a rather cramped vision of the role to
be played by the courts in refining and reshaping common law doctrine."[45] I agree with Professor McCamus that, if read on its own,
*Watkins* gives a distorted picture of judicial law-making and depicts

an unduly restricted court. But I am not sure the Supreme Court was wrong to refrain from changing the law relating to periodic payments. *Watkins* presented an issue that posed economic and administrative questions that transcended the legal rights and duties of the litigants. Such issues are arguably beyond the capacity of the courts. The design of an effective scheme of periodic payments for injured parties could not be accomplished by looking only at the way the law defined the rights of the parties and the legal principles of fault and fair compensation. The social welfare scheme was implicated, and there were a variety of ways such a scheme could be structured. Choosing the best or most workable scheme would turn on policy choices[46] that demand an understanding of the complex and interconnected economic and administrative considerations at play. The issue presented in *Salituro,* on the other hand, was bipolar and could be resolved more or less as a matter of law and without consideration of external policy considerations. To be sure, the issue had significant moral and social implications, but the values at play had long been the subject of legal concern and debate. The question of whether one spouse should be permitted to testify against the other spouse turned upon a value-laden but essentially legal consideration of the nature of the spousal relationship. The spousal incompetency rule was the product of the mores of an earlier age when husband and wife were considered to be one person in law. That view of the spousal relationship had dramatically changed in more recent times. In virtually all other areas of family law, it had been abandoned. It was inconsistent with the prevailing legal principles on the place of women in society and with the right of every person to be treated with dignity and respect. The spousal incompetency rule did, however, reflect a rationale that is arguably still valid, namely, respecting and protecting the marital bond by not forcing one spouse to incriminate the other. However, as that rationale was not relevant where the spousal relationship had broken down, introducing an exception for separated spouses represented an incremental change that made the law more coherent as a whole. That, I suggest, is the kind of legal change that is open to judges to make.

There are many cases where, as in *Salituro,* the Supreme Court has changed the common law "to bring the law into harmony with prevailing social values."[47] As I pointed out in chapter 3, many of these cases involve significant changes to the law on account of changing societal perceptions regarding the role of women and gender equality. The courts were entitled to take those changed social perceptions into account. They were not deciding on the basis of raw public opinion. The social values upon which they relied grew out of and reflected a social understanding of fundamental legal values: the equality of all citizens and the right of every individual to be treated with dignity and respect. Changing the discrete elements of the law that did not accord with those fundamental values made the law truer to itself.

On the other hand, some changes in public opinion may have to be resisted by judges to maintain the integrity of the legal order. Judges must be steadfast and resist being swayed by populist attacks on vulnerable minorities and core values like freedom of expression and judicial independence.

Another striking modern example of judicial law-making is the transformation of the common law rules relating to the recognition and enforcement of foreign judgments. The conventional common law rules were based on English decisions from the late nineteenth century, when England was a dominant commercial and political power. Not surprisingly, the English courts adopted rules that were highly protective of English commercial interests. They prescribed a very restrictive approach to the recognition and enforcement of foreign judgments. It became apparent in the 1980s that those nineteenth-century English rules were ill-suited to meet the demands of Canada's contemporary political and commercial reality. Canada is a federation of ten provinces, and because each province had its own law relating to property and civil rights and its own judicial system, each province was considered to be a foreign jurisdiction when it came to questions of legal recognition and enforcement. Justice Gérard La Forest broke the shackles in a 1990 decision where he observed that treating each province as a foreign jurisdiction flew "in the face of the obvious intention of the Constitution to create a single country."[48] Cross-border trade between Canada, the United States, and countless other jurisdictions in the global economy had become the modern reality. "The world has changed" as have "[m]odern means of travel and communications." These changes made the nineteenth-century rules "appear parochial." Corresponding legal change to accommodate "the flow of wealth, skills and people across state lines" had, in Justice La Forest's words, "now become imperative."[49] The rigid nineteenth-century approach was abandoned in favour of principles of "order and fairness" more in keeping with modern conditions. The courts in one province should give "full faith and credit" to the judgments given by a court in another province or territory, provided that there had been "a real and substantial connection" between parties or the dispute and the deciding court to justify its exercise of jurisdiction.

### *Charter* Values

The *Charter of Rights and Freedoms* significantly enhanced judicial law-making. The capacity of the courts to strike down legislation enacted by Parliament and the legislatures has always been controversial. I will discuss that aspect of judicial law-making in chapter 11. Here, my focus will be on the influence of *Charter* values on common law adjudication.

There is now a long list of cases where the courts have applied and developed "the principles of the common law in a manner consistent with the fundamental values enshrined in the Constitution."[50] Although the *Charter* applies only to legislation and governmental action, the values of the *Charter* have strongly influenced the direction of the common law. As Justice Peter Cory explained, "Historically, the common law evolved as a result of the courts making those incremental changes ... necessary to make the law comply with current societal values." It followed that it was open to judges to make "incremental revisions to the common law" to make it "comply with the values enunciated in the *Charter*."[51]

There are many examples. Before the *Charter*, courts routinely granted publication bans on court proceedings to protect the fair trial rights of an accused. In a 1994 decision, the Supreme Court altered the common law governing publication bans to ensure that before any ban was issued, adequate consideration was given to the *Charter* values of freedom of expression and freedom of the press.[52]

Freedom of expression also led the courts to make significant changes to the common law of defamation. Traditionally, the common law strongly favoured the protection of personal reputation over freedom of expression. However, in several decisions, the courts have found that this imbalance was inconsistent with *Charter* values, and they changed the law accordingly.[53] The most notable change to the common law of defamation is the recognition of a defence that enhances the capacity of the press to report on matters of public interest. Formerly, the common law imposed a form of strict liability and required the press to prove the truth of any statement that harmed the plaintiff's reputation. In *Cusson v Quan*,[54] I wrote a judgment holding that this rule inhibited investigative journalism and open debate on matters of public interest and that the common law failed to reflect the *Charter* values of freedom of expression and freedom of the press. Provided the matter is one of public interest, the press should have a defence if it can show that it acted responsibly when investigating and verifying the story it published. The Supreme Court of Canada reversed my judgment on another ground[55] but in another case[56] agreed with the responsible journalism defence.

### Judges "Make Law," They Don't "Make Law Up"

As will be discussed in chapter 5, judicial decisions have brought about significant changes in other areas of the law. The courts have transformed law relating to the admission of hearsay evidence.[57] Claims for unjust enrichment are now accommodated under a new principled framework.[58] Good faith has emerged as an "organizing principle"[59] of contract law, and the constructive trust has become, through judicial elaboration, a new "head of obligation of great elasticity and generality."[60]

Taken as a whole, these modern Canadian examples demonstrate the significance of the judicial law-making role. I believe that role can be defended. It is a process that has always been a prominent feature of the common law. Judges certainly "make law," but they do not "make law up." Rather than ignore the past, they build upon it. In the words of Israeli Justice Aharon Barak, they give effect to the legal system's "hidden potential."[61] Their decisions are grounded in the values and principles that undergird the common law, but they are shaped to reflect the current reality. The judge, said Cardozo, is "not to innovate at pleasure," and he is not "a knight-errant roaming at will in pursuit of his own idea of beauty or goodness." Judicial law-making is "informed by tradition, methodized by analogy [and] disciplined by system."[62] To justify taking the law in a new direction, a judge must provide a reasoned decision demonstrating why a shift in direction is called for, why it can be supported by existing and recognized legal norms, and why making the change is consistent with the inherent limits of adjudication and with the role of a court in our democratic tradition.

## Leave It to the Legislature?

Every judge who is asked to make a decision that will change the law must ask if the proposed change should be left to the legislature. There is no easy or obvious answer to that question, but there are general principles to be considered. The first relates to the nature of the proposed change to the law. The second relates to its magnitude.

The first question is whether the proposed change is of a nature that falls within the capacity of the courts to decide. Judges, as I have argued, should be conscious of the inherent limits of adjudication and the fact that their view of a legal issue will necessarily be limited by the dynamics of the adversarial litigation process. That process is well-suited to deal with the issues posed by bipolar disputes and considerably less capable of dealing with polycentric issues that raise questions and pose problems that transcend the interests of the parties. Judges should hesitate to move the law in new directions when the implications of doing so are not readily captured or understood by looking at the issue through the lens of the facts of the case they are deciding. The legislative process is better suited to consider and weigh competing policy choices that are external to legal rights and duties. Elected representatives have the capacity to reflect the views of the population at large. Government departments have the resources to study and evaluate policy options. The legislative process allows all interested parties to make their views known and encourages consideration and accommodation of competing viewpoints.

The second question relates to the magnitude of the change. Common law judges constantly refer to incremental or interstitial change and characterize the development of the common law as a gradual process of evolution. Former Senior Law Lord Tom Bingham put it this way: it is very much in the common law tradition "to move the law a little further along a line on which it is already moving, or to adapt it to accord with modern views and practices." If the proposed change fits that description, there is a strong tradition to support judicial law-making. It is quite another thing, however, "to seek to recast the law in a radically innovative or adventurous way," as that makes the law "uncertain and unpredictable" and is unfair to the losing party who relied on the law as it existed before the change.[63] Developments of the latter magnitude may best be left to the legislature. But it must be said that there is no clear line here, and many of the examples I have given represent legal changes of significant magnitude.

While judges should consider the capacity of the legislature to make the proposed change, it is an important feature of our democratic tradition that legislatures avoid getting involved in the intricacies of substantive common law. The common law has always evolved as new cases present new problems, and legislatures have tacitly accepted that changing the common law is a function the courts perform. As Professor Mel Eisenberg argues, legislatures cannot satisfy the demand for "the enrichment of the supply of legal rules," and "in many areas the flexible form of a judicial rule is preferable to the canonical form of a legislative rule."[64] Legislatures tend to be preoccupied with more general issues of public policy, matters such as health, welfare, education, public safety, infrastructure, and budget. Law reform commissions with a mandate to study and make recommendations for change in specific areas of law can fill this void, but in most jurisdictions, the resources available to these bodies have been significantly curtailed. The practical reality is that legislatures rarely engage with the intricacies of the common law, so if the courts do not act, the law will remain static.

## Law-Making and the Judicial Hierarchy

The place the judge occupies in the hierarchy of courts affects the judge's law-making authority. Lower courts are bound by the pronouncements of higher courts, and there is a tendency when discussing judicial law-making to focus on appellate courts. I think this focus is misguided and underestimates the significant law-making powers of trial judges.

The first reason for this is that trial judges control the facts, and the facts are what drive change in common law. Trial judges become immersed in the facts and the details of each case they hear. They see the parties and hear the witnesses over the days, weeks, and sometimes months it takes for the trial to unfold. Their close involvement with the facts and details of the case provides the perspective needed to decide what justice requires. Trial judges are required to apply the law as laid down by appellate courts, but their authority to find the facts to which the governing legal rules and principles apply carries with it significant law-making powers. If the trial judge finds that the facts of the case are novel and do not fall within the reach of established precedent, the trial judge has the capacity to move the law in a different direction. The common law tradition depends upon this highly fact-sensitive process. The facts and circumstances of every case are closely scrutinized at the trial level and, as circumstances change and society evolves, the demands of justice influence trial judges to shape the law, slowly but surely, this way or that.[65]

The trial judge's decision will be subject to review on appeal, and that certainly operates as a constraint on the trial judge's law-making power. On the other hand, trial judges enjoy a measure of freedom not available to appellate judges. Their liberty flows not only from the authority to find the facts but also from the reality that as a trial judge's pronouncements will not bind other judges,[66] they can be less concerned about the broader consequences of their decisions. I certainly do not mean to suggest that trial judges should be cavalier or careless about their pronouncements. But they are at greater liberty than appellate judges to preoccupy themselves with the demands of justice in the particular case they are deciding. Appellate judges have additional concerns that arise from the binding nature of their decisions. All judges at the same level and below the appellate judge in the judicial hierarchy will be obligated to follow what the appellate judge has stated as the law. Appellate judges must strive to do justice in the particular case, but they have significantly more reason to worry about the consequences of the precedent they establish.

There is another marked shift as one moves from an intermediate appellate court to the Supreme Court of Canada. Intermediate appellate judges are immersed in the nitty-gritty of deciding a large volume of cases on a wide range of subjects. They have virtually no control over their docket, as most litigants enjoy a right of appeal. As mentioned in chapter 2, most of the cases heard by intermediate appellate courts fall into the "error correction" category and involve no issues of precedential value. The mindset of an intermediate appellate judge is inevitably affected by the experience of deciding many cases, most of which do not involve jurisprudentially significant issues. This encourages a cautious, minimalist, and incremental approach.

Things are quite different at the Supreme Court of Canada. That court controls its own docket. The leave to appeal process allows the Supreme Court to pick and choose the cases it hears on the basis of their national importance. The Supreme Court can defer hearing an issue until it has been dealt with by more than one provincial court of appeal. This allows the issue to ripen on the basis of a variety of facts and a variety of trial and appellate decisions. The Supreme

Court hears very few "error correction" appeals. Its task is to decide sixty-five to eighty important cases each year that raise issues of legal importance that transcend the immediate interests of the litigants. Virtually every case the Supreme Court decides has precedential value.

I suggest that a comparison of intermediate appellate judgments and the judgments of the Supreme Court of Canada reveals that the judge's approach to the challenge of judicial law-making is influenced by day-to-day routine. A judge who decides many cases, most of which are not precedent-setting, will think of judging differently from the judge who, as one of nine, deals only with cases of national importance. Intermediate appellate judgments tend to be more focused on the facts of the case, and the legal pronouncements the judges make tend to be more minimalist in nature, deciding only what is necessary to deal with the case at bar. Reading Supreme Court judgments, one regularly encounters broad general statements of principle that extend beyond the confines of the actual dispute between the parties. The temptation to settle entire areas of the law is often present and sometimes irresistible, but there are perils to be avoided. The more detached the pronouncement is from the facts of the case and the more the court deviates from established common law method, greater is the risk that the pronouncement will fail to anticipate facts or circumstances not before the court and will have unintended effects.

Now of course intermediate appellate courts do decide many precedent-setting appeals, and they do have a significant law-making role. We hear appeals raising issues of broad jurisprudential significance that require us to make pronouncements on important legal issues. Although we do not have the final word, many of our jurisprudentially significant decisions are not appealed, or leave to appeal is denied. In these cases, our role is not unlike that of the Supreme Court.

The question, then, of whether and to what extent judges make law depends on a number of factors, not the least of which is the judge's place in the court hierarchy. As one moves up the hierarchy of trial, intermediate appeal and final appeal, one moves from the specific to the general. The trial courts are the pulse of the entire system. As I have explained, trial courts are preoccupied with the facts and the justice of the specific case. Intermediate appeal courts have a more general perspective. The trial judge's case-specific findings and perceptions of what justice demands are tested at the intermediate level of appeal for legal integrity and reliability. The task of the intermediate appellate court is to ensure that trial judgments are free from legal error and that the law and the legal process are responding appropriately to the disputes that arise. The apex court has general oversight over the entire system. It is charged with settling the most contentious issues of law, and by limiting its attention to cases of that nature it is bound to have a significant law-making role.

## Conclusion

Judicial law-making is a fundamental aspect of the common law tradition. That does not mean that judges can make law as they please. Judges decide cases, and they must respect the role of the legislature as the primary source for legal change. They must also respect the limits imposed by their place in the judicial hierarchy. But judges also have a duty to maintain the integrity of the law. Their decisions should aim to enhance the law's clarity and its consistency with contemporary conditions and needs. The judicial maintenance function of "keeping the law in good shape" sometimes involves changing the law. If the judge is able to support such a change on the basis of a legally manageable and workable principle that emerges from the pattern of past decisions, legislative enactments, or *Charter* values, the judge is making law, not making up law. Changes that make the law a more complete and coherent whole fall within the judicial function.

## Chapter 5

# Rules, Principles, and Policies

When considering the judicial process, it is helpful to identify and distinguish three types of legal norms that judges work with when deciding cases: rules, principles, and policies.[1] I will describe a spectrum of norms ranging from the most specific, rules, to the most general, background principles and policies.

## Rules

At one end of the spectrum are rules, the well-established, specific, and widely accepted doctrines or categories that define legal rights and that can be readily applied to decide legal disputes. Rules are akin to what lawyers sometimes call "black letter law," a phrase derived from the practice of some publishers to highlight the most basic legal doctrines in bold letters. Rules may be written down in statutes, or they may be the product of common law precedents. Statutory speed limits and the rules of the road are obvious examples. Other examples are procedural rules that prescribe time limits to commence a proceeding, the common law rule that a contract under seal is enforceable, and the statutory requirement of two witnesses for the validity of a will.

Rules rest upon and promote background values, but they attempt to capture those values in a form that can operate independently without the decision-maker having to refer back to the value itself.[2] If the facts of the case bring it within the rule, the rule applies. If not, the rule does not decide the case. Rules tend to apply in an "all-or-nothing" fashion.[3]

The disadvantage of rules is that the justice they provide is rough and ready. Travelling at sixty kilometres per hour in a fifty-kilometre zone is an offence, even if, under the circumstances, it was perfectly safe to travel at sixty. The fifty-kilometre rule will be overly inclusive, as it will catch some safe drivers. It will be under-inclusive, as it will not catch drivers travelling at the limit when the conditions make it unsafe to do so. On the other hand, the advantage of rules is that they are relatively easy to understand and apply. The clarity of rules limits the discretion of officials and decision-makers and promotes efficient and consistent application.

It is a common misperception among lay people that the law consists entirely of readily applied rules of this nature. However, as I explained in chapter 3, the apparent simplicity of rules is misleading, and, as I will explain in this chapter, most laws have a more open texture and are expressed in terms that can be applied only through the exercise of judgment about the specific facts and circumstances of each case.

## Principles

At the next point along the spectrum are principles.[4] Principles are more general in nature than black-letter rules.[5] They cover a wider swathe than rules. Because of their generality, and because their application depends on considering the background values they promote, principles are less susceptible to mechanical application and more amenable to consideration of the particular facts and circumstances of the case. As I will explain below, principles have become a central feature of modern Canadian law.

Lawyers and judges use the term "principles" to describe a range of legal norms. Towards the rule end of the spectrum are what might be called operational principles[6] that are used to decide cases. Rather than prescribe conduct in the precise manner of a rule, operational principles require the judge to decide on the basis of more general considerations such as reasonableness and fairness. They require the judge to consider the background value the law seeks to promote and to factor that value in when making a decision on the specific facts and circumstances. To return to the speeding example: instead of specifying a particular speed, the law states that drivers shall not travel faster than a speed that is safe in all circumstances. Such a law avoids the injustice flowing from the over-inclusiveness of a rule specifying a strict limit that will catch some safe drivers or the under-inclusiveness that allows unsafe drivers travelling at the limit to escape. However, application of the "drive safely" principle requires the exercise of considerable judgment and discretion in its application, because what is "safe" largely depends on the context in which the conduct occurs. That entails a more costly and less predictable decision-making process.

An example of an operational principle used to decide cases is the norm that cases involving custody and child welfare are to be determined according to the "best interests of the child." The principle dictates that when deciding such cases, the judge must choose the option that best supports the child's development and well-being. The "best interests of the child" principle focuses and channels the debate, but it requires the judge to exercise significant discretion to reach a decision. This is because the exercise of determining what is "best" for a child is highly contextual and fact dependent. There is no specific measure that can be used to determine what is best and what is not.

The principles of procedural fairness are an example of an operational principle at the midpoint in the spectrum. In a very general way, these principles identify procedural protections that administrative agencies and other decision-makers should respect, such as the right to notice and the right to be heard. However, the precise nature of the appropriate procedures will depend upon the specific context.[7] A relatively formal oral hearing may be required, where a citizen faces a punishment such as a monetary penalty, but in other cases fairness may be satisfied by the opportunity to make written submissions.

At the far end of the spectrum, we find background principles that express basic legal values in a more explanatory and less prescriptive fashion. Background principles elucidate the basic underlying rationales and values that the rules seek to protect. They may also be used to fill in gaps when rules and operative principles run out. Courts sometimes use background principles to interpret rules or doctrines that are unclear and to deal with cases that do not seem to be covered by existing doctrine. They help to frame, guide, discipline, and serve as starting points for legal debate. In Justice Cardozo's words, they serve as "a point of departure, from which new lines will be run, from which new courses will be measured."[8]

Ronald Dworkin discusses the principle that one cannot benefit from one's own wrong.[9] This is an ancient maxim, long known to lawyers as the *ex turpi causa* principle. It applies in different ways in different contexts. Its precise meaning is sometimes highly controversial, and it does not, standing on its own, determine the result. It expresses the background legal value that the courts will protect the integrity of the legal system, and it has been recognized that, in many cases, precluding a claim on the ground that the plaintiff's conduct is tainted by wrongdoing would be unjust. So, for example, the principle will bar the claim of one who murders another to collect the proceeds of a life insurance policy, but not the claim of a party who was injured in a motor vehicle accident after allowing the defendant to drive while drunk.[10]

Other examples of background principles that embody underlying values are found in the maxims of equity: equity will not suffer a wrong without a remedy; one who seeks equity must do equity; one who comes to equity must come with clean hands; and equity will not assist a volunteer. These maxims express general ethical principles, inherent in the equitable tradition. They are distilled from the decisions of the Court of Chancery, which, until the late nineteenth century, was a separate stream of justice that ran parallel to the common law and emphasized fair dealing and good conscience. The maxims guide legal argument and explain legal doctrines, but they are very general and cannot be independently applied to decide cases. Principles in this category guide, but they do not decide. They are legal concepts or values that point in a certain direction, though their application is often uncertain.

Perhaps the most notable use of background principles in Canadian law is the 1998 decision of the Supreme Court of Canada in *Reference Re Secession of Quebec*.[11] The court was asked to decide whether Quebec had the right to secede from Canada unilaterally, a highly controversial and difficult question not covered by the text of the Constitution. The Court ruled that a constitutional amendment would be required for a province to secede but added that considerable weight would have to be given to a clear expression of the will of the people of Quebec to leave Confederation, and that the other provinces and the federal government would have to respect that democratically expressed choice and enter into negotiations with Quebec. The process would have to respect what the court called "four fundamental and organizing principles of the Constitution,"[12] namely, federalism, constitutionalism and the rule of law, respect for minorities, and democracy. These principles, said the court, are "not expressly dealt with by the text of the Constitution,"[13] but they nonetheless have normative force as operative instruments of our constitutional order. They "inform and sustain the constitutional text: they are the vital unstated assumptions upon which the text is based."[14] The four principles represent the "major elements of the architecture of the Constitution itself and are as such its lifeblood." They "infuse our Constitution and breathe life into it."[15] In a later case, *Reference Re Senate Reform*, the court insisted that "the Constitution should not be viewed as a mere collection of discrete textual provisions" and that the interpretation of the amendment provisions must take account of the Constitution's "architecture" and "basic structure."[16]

Background principles will often overlap, and, in any given case, they may conflict with one another. Likewise, operational principles may point in different directions. The principle of freedom of contract that requires courts to enforce unfair bargains conflicts with the principle of unconscionability, which precludes a party from taking undue advantage of unequal bargaining power.[17] The common law respects freedom of contract by enforcing a bargain made between two people, even where the bargain disproportionally favours one party over the other. However, where an improvident bargain was unfairly obtained, the principle of unconscionability comes into play to qualify freedom of contract and relieve against the unfairness. Claims of freedom of expression and freedom of religion often collide with the principle of equality.[18] Hate speech is a form of expression, but it also targets people on ethnic or religious grounds and thereby invades their right to be treated as equals. The right of gays and lesbians to be treated equally conflicts with some religious views and expressions of religious freedom.[19] In these cases, two established principles come into play, yet neither applies automatically. Reconciling the conflict and finding a resolution that gives proper consideration to both conflicting principles requires careful assessment and judgment.

## Policies

I distinguish principles from policies. Principles, both operational and background, arise from considerations of justice and fairness and help us define and understand legal rights. Principles are used to explain and resolve the intricacies of the relationship between the parties and the just resolution of their dispute – matters that are the very stuff of adjudication. In contrast, policies are standards that set out "a goal to be reached, generally an improvement in some economic, political or social feature of the community."[20] Policies involve matters pertaining to the common good. They are general considerations of public welfare that are to be taken into account in law-making. Policies involve values such as efficiency, community and social cohesion, deterrence of inappropriate behaviour, and the enhancement of personal and national security. Policies are instrumental in nature. When judges take policies into account, they are focusing not on justice or fairness as between the parties, but rather on the effect, impact, or implications of their decision for the community at large.

Responsibility for the definition of rules and principles is shared between courts and legislatures. Rules and principles can arise from common law adjudication, and they can be created by legislation. Given their nature, policies are matters that fall more squarely within the domain of the legislature, which has primary responsibility for the interests of society at large.

There is a lively jurisprudential debate about the use of policy-based reasoning in common law adjudication.[21] Some authors accept or even welcome consideration of policy,[22] while others argue that it should play little or no role.[23] I do not intend to enter that theoretical debate, as it seems clear to me that, rightly or wrongly, it is commonly accepted by lawyers and judges that policy-based arguments are legitimate and important tools that may be deployed when arguing and deciding cases. In my view, current practice recognizes that courts are entitled to consider policy-based arguments. This arises in at least two ways.

First, policy-based arguments play a significant role in public law cases. The proper interpretation of a statute often requires an understanding of the policy the legislature sought to advance. In a long list of decisions, the Supreme Court of Canada has accepted as "definitive" the formulation for statutory interpretation advanced by a frequently cited author: "[T]he words of an Act are to be read in their entire context and in their grammatical and ordinary sense harmoniously with the scheme of the Act, the object of the Act, and the intention of Parliament."[24] This approach recognizes that courts must be attentive to the "grammatical and ordinary" meaning of words in statutes. However, as meaning is dependent on context, courts must also be attentive to the overall object and purpose that the legislation seeks to advance.

The use of policy-based arguments is pronounced in *Charter* cases. Courts must grapple with policies when determining whether a challenged law that limits a protected right or freedom can be defended as a reasonable limit under section 1. As I will explain in chapter 11, the court must assess whether the limit imposed by the law respects the principle of proportionality. If the law is rationally connected to the legislative objective, limits the *Charter* right as little as is reasonably possible, and satisfies the overall balance or proportionality between the benefits of the limit and its deleterious effects, the law will be upheld. This is a policy-laden exercise.

Second, it seems to me that it is appropriate for courts to take into account the broader social implications of legal change when exercising their law-making role. While judges and courts are properly preoccupied with, and give primacy to, legal rights as they exist between the parties, legal rights do not exist in a vacuum. They have to be crafted and shaped in a manner that takes into account their impact on the general good of society. As Cardozo put it, "The final cause of law is the welfare of society," and when deciding whether to extend or restrict a rule or principle, the judge "must let the welfare of society fix the path, its direction and its distance."[25] In my view, it follows that while the primary consideration should be the legal principles that determine issues of interpersonal justice, there are some issues of policy that are legitimate for judges to consider when deciding cases. This has been described as the "pluralist approach."[26] As I will explain in the next part of this chapter, the development of the law of negligence provides a good illustration of how the principle is the primary tool to define legal rights and obligations and how policy considerations are a residual consideration.

I hasten to point out that the borders between rules, principles, and policies are not precise, and lawyers and judges do not always define or distinguish them in the manner I have just set out. The difference between rules and principles is very much a matter of degree. They represent points on a spectrum. At one end are very specific rules (speed limits), in the middle are operational principles (best interests of the child), and at the other end are background principles that explain the moral or ethical values that underlie legal doctrines (one cannot benefit from one's own wrong). The word "policy" is commonly used by lawyers and judges to describe general considerations of justice and fairness to be taken into account in order to reach an appropriate result.[27] While the terms are commonly intermingled, as I will explain, I believe that it is helpful to distinguish considerations of justice and fairness from considerations of general social benefit and welfare.

## The "Principled Approach"

There is a pronounced trend in modern Canadian law away from narrowly framed, specific rules and towards the flexibility of broadly worded general principles.[28]

This trend is found in both legislation and in the common law. The most striking example of a law cast in terms of general principles is the *Charter of Rights and Freedoms*. The *Charter* defines our fundamental rights and freedoms in terms of broad principles that require a massive interpretive effort when applied to specific cases. I will discuss the *Charter* in greater detail in chapter 11. It is important to point out, however, that the tendency for legislation to define rights and obligations in terms of general principles rather than specific rules is by no means restricted to the *Charter*.

Even in the area of commercial law, which puts a premium on certainty, legislation is commonly cast in vague terms of what is fair, reasonable, and conscionable. Ontario's *Unconscionable Transactions Relief Act*[29] provides for a remedy where, "in respect of money lent, the court finds that, having regard to the risk and to all the circumstances, the cost of a loan is excessive and that the transaction is harsh and unconscionable." There is no precise method of definitively determining whether something is "excessive" or "unconscionable," and the legislation leaves a large area to the discretion of the judge. The *Business Practices Act*[30] forbids anyone from engaging in an "unfair practice," which is defined to include "an unconscionable consumer representation." Both federal and provincial company law protects minority shareholder interests from "oppression,"[31] without defining what conduct is oppressive. The *Bankruptcy and Insolvency Act*[32] confers wide discretionary powers on judges, and the *Companies Creditors Arrangements Act*[33] gives the judiciary sweeping discretionary powers to supervise the restructuring of major commercial entities. Securities legislation gives the regulator the power to make orders to protect "the public interest."[34] Commercial lawyers complain of the generality and uncertainty of these measures, but legislatures insist that they are required to ensure fair dealing in the marketplace.

## The Principled Approach to Hearsay Evidence

In this part I will focus on the "principled approach" in common law decisions. I take the "principled approach" label from the modern law governing hearsay evidence. This is a difficult and complex area,[35] and I will outline the law in the most general terms simply to explore the concept of the "principled approach."

The common law rule against hearsay evidence precludes a party from introducing second-hand statements as proof of a contested fact. In other words, if a fact is contested, it cannot be proved by a witness telling the court what he heard from someone else. The rationale for the rule is that if the person who is the source of the evidence is not physically in court, the reliability of the evidence cannot be properly assessed and tested through cross-examination. But the experience of common law judges hearing and deciding cases demonstrated that such a rule could not be rigidly applied, for it tended to exclude relevant and reliable evidence. Over the years, decisions in specific cases developed an intricate and highly technical pattern of black-letter rules and exceptions allowing for the admissibility of second-hand evidence in situations where the evidence was reliable.

By the 1990s, the list of specific exceptions was long and complex, yet there were still cases that could not be decided satisfactorily either under the rule or under the exceptions. Rather than providing a reliable and predictable guide, the "black letter" approach to hearsay had disintegrated into a morass of obscure detail that had "frequently proved unduly inflexible in dealing with new situations and new needs in the law."[36] This unfortunate state was created by a legalistic and formalistic obsession with casting the law in terms of strict black-letter rules and exceptions. The underlying legal values that drove the rule in the first place were lost in all the detail.

In *R v Khan*,[37] a medical doctor was charged with sexually assaulting a three and one-half-year-old chid. The child told her mother what the doctor had done fifteen minutes after the incident. The trial judge applied the traditional hearsay rule and concluded that the mother could not testify that her daughter had reported the assault. The daughter was too young to give evidence, and the doctor was acquitted. *Khan* was the first in a series of decisions in which the Supreme Court of Canada reshaped the law of hearsay by emphasizing principles rather than rules. From the complex web of hearsay decisions, the court identified two operational principles – necessity and reliability – that explained the rationale for the hearsay rule and the detailed pattern of exceptions. While the court did not repeal the traditional rules, it enunciated what it called a "principled approach," which allows a judge to accept second-hand evidence provided it meets the broad criteria of necessity and reliability.[38] The court concluded that a new trial was required to determine whether the child's statement to her mother satisfied these criteria.

The principled approach affords trial judges considerable flexibility when deciding on the admissibility of hearsay evidence. The flexibility inherent in the principled approach may appear to render the law uncertain. However, the black-letter rule and the long list of exceptions were anything but certain. The Supreme Court concluded that the flexibility derived from clearly articulated principles better equips the judge to achieve justice in the individual case. And as judges work with and apply the principled approach, patterns of decision may be traced, and a new body of doctrine directly and explicitly related to the underlying values will emerge.

## The Modern Law of Unjust Enrichment

Another example of the principled approach is found in the law of unjust enrichment.[39] The background principle that a person who has been enriched unjustifiably at another's expense should not be entitled to retain the benefit has emerged as a significant source of obligation in private law. The principle of unjust enrichment is derived from specifically recognized claims, some of which had exotic sounding names: money had and received, *quantum meruit*, constructive trust, tracing, subrogation, waiver of tort, and breach of fiduciary duty. Each of these claims had developed along its own separate path. Each one had its own specific rules and application, creating what lawyers sometimes call a "pigeonhole" pattern. If a claim fit into one of the pigeonholes, the claimant would succeed; if the claim did not fit, the claimant would fail. Justice was achieved in cases that fit one of the pigeonholes but not in cases falling outside. The legal rules were narrowly framed without explicit reference to the underlying principles, leaving significant gaps in the law.

The pigeonholes often failed to respond to the interests of justice in contemporary society. The case of *Pettkus v Becker*[40] provides a good example. Rosa Becker lived with Lucas Pettkus for almost twenty years. They never married, but they worked together to build a successful beekeeping business. When their relationship broke down, Pettkus, the legal title holder, sold the property and kept the proceeds. The law seemed to give Rosa Becker no recourse. She was not a spouse, nor was she an owner, and although she worked to build the business, there was no established legal category that allowed her to advance a claim. When her case was decided by the Supreme Court, modern Canadian law took a turn. The majority judgment of Justice Brian Dickson identified the unifying background principle of unjust enrichment that would allow Rosa Becker to recover.

The principle of unjust enrichment explains the justice achieved by the complex and seemingly disparate historic pigeonhole doctrines. The traditional categories remain, but the principle of unjust enrichment equips the courts to develop the law to meet new situations consistent with the traditional categories. Where there has been the conferral of a benefit upon the recipient, a corresponding deprivation to the claimant, and the absence of any juristic reason that entitles the recipient to retain the benefit, there is a legally enforceable claim. Unjust enrichment, said the Supreme Court, is a "third head of obligation, quite distinct from contract and tort ... an obligation of great elasticity and generality."[41] The Supreme Court has described these as a "malleable" principle to be "shaped" by the judiciary "so as to accommodate the changing needs and mores of society, in order to achieve justice."[42]

As in the law of hearsay, a broad, overarching principle of unjust enrichment has emerged from the pattern of traditional narrow, technical, and specific rules. The generality and flexibility of the principle of unjust enrichment reveals a tolerance for a considerable degree of uncertainty in order to equip judges to achieve a just result.

### Good Faith in Contract Law

The Supreme Court of Canada's identification of good faith as a general "organizing principle" in contract law in the case of *Bhasin v Hrynew*[43] is another prime example of the principled approach. Common law lawyers were reluctant to admit that contractual rights should be qualified by the concept of good faith. If the parties have made a bargain, they should stick to it. If things turned out badly for one side, the courts had no business rewriting the deal. On the other hand, it had to be acknowledged that there were situations where the common law would prevent one party from taking unfair advantage of the other. There was, however, no unifying principle that captured when those situations would arise.

Bhasin and Hrynew both sold registered educational savings plans for the same company. The company appointed Hrynew as a compliance officer and misled Bhasin about why it had done so and about the access Hrynew would have to Bhasin's customer information. Hrynew, who had long coveted Bhasin's business, used his position and the information to secure it for himself. The Supreme Court of Canada found that the company should pay Bhasin damages for breach of what it called the duty of honest performance of the contract. The court decided that it was consistent with its duty to develop the common law in an incremental fashion to keep it in step with the "dynamic and evolving fabric of our society"[44] to recognize a background principle of good faith in order to "bring a measure of coherence and predictability to the law" and "bring the law closer to what reasonable commercial parties would expect it to be."[45] The principle found support in scholarly writing.[46] It is a feature of Quebec's civil law and has gained some acceptance in other common law jurisdictions. It was an explicit feature of some lines of common law authority such as unconscionability and implicitly recognized in others, including the law relating to implied terms and the rules of contract interpretation. However, as Justice Thomas Cromwell put it, "Canadian common law in relation to good faith performance of contracts is piecemeal, unsettled and unclear."[47] He concluded that "enunciating a general organizing principle of good faith and recognizing a duty to perform contracts honestly will help bring certainty and coherence to this area of the law in a way that is consistent with reasonable commercial expectations."[48]

The court made it clear that the principle of good faith draws upon and does not obliterate the existing common law categories where good faith had operated in the past. Justice Cromwell also cautioned that "[g]enerally, claims of good faith will not succeed if they do not fall within these existing doctrines." The existing list is not closed, and the organizing or background principle of good faith may be developed incrementally "where the existing law is found to be wanting" and where the change would be "consistent with the structure of the common law of contract" and "the importance of private ordering and certainty in commercial affairs."[49]

The recognition of a general principle of good faith was explicitly modelled on the court's approach to unjust enrichment where it identified a principle that had "grown out of the traditional categories of recovery." Those categories continue to operate as specific instances of the organizing principle, but they do not limit its development, "allowing the law to develop in a flexible way as required to meet changing perceptions of justice."[50]

Justice Cromwell cautioned against using the organizing principle as "a form of *ad hoc* judicial moralism," or "'palm tree' justice," or "as a pretext for scrutinizing the motives of contracting parties." Due weight must be given to the traditional common law value respecting "the freedom of contracting parties to pursue their individual self-interest," and the principle should not be allowed "to undermine certainty in commercial contracts."[51]

On the facts of the case before it, the court took the limited step of enunciating "a general duty of honesty in contractual performance." In other words, "parties must not lie or otherwise knowingly mislead each other about matters directly linked to the performance of the contract,"[52] allowing "the implications of the broader, organizing principle of good faith ... to evolve according to the ... incremental judicial approach."[53]

## The Law of Negligence

As the examples of hearsay, unjust enrichment, and good faith show, courts often rely on broad statements of principle as a first step in making a fundamental change in the law. The general principle explains or rationalizes the body of strict rules that have become unworkable, outmoded, or incoherent. When a unifying principle first emerges, it will often be possible only to sketch it out in a broad outline. Over time, as cases are decided and a body of doctrine develops, flesh is put on the bones of the broad principle.[54] But the principle remains as a background value that can be deployed to meet new situations.

The classic common law example is Lord Atkin's use of the good neighbour principle as the basis for a duty of care in his 1932 decision, *Donoghue v Stevenson*.[55] On 26 August 1928, May Donoghue went with a friend to a Glasgow cafe. Her companion ordered and paid for Donoghue's drink, a ginger beer that came in a dark bottle that concealed its contents. Donoghue drank some of the ginger beer. When her friend poured the rest into a glass, the remains of a partly decomposed snail dropped from the bottle. Donoghue later complained of stomach pain and was diagnosed with having gastroenteritis and being in a state of severe shock. The cafe had purchased the ginger beer from a distributor who had purchased it from the manufacturer, the defendant Stevenson. If anyone was at fault, it was the manufacturer, Stevenson, but Donoghue had no contract upon which she could base her claim.

Was the manufacturer of a product under a legal duty to a consumer to take reasonable care to ensure that the product is free from defect likely to cause injury to health? As I explained in chapter 4, the answer to that question at the time was by no means clear. The common law courts, as Lord Atkin put it, had been "concerned with the particular relations which come before them in actual litigation" and "had been engaged upon an elaborate classification of duties."[56] This produced a classic example of a set of detailed rules that left gaps. In the case of negligently manufactured products, the consumer had no privity of contract with the negligent manufacturer to support a legal claim. Contract law demanded privity, and tort law had not yet identified a duty of care to support a claim for negligence. The facts of the case did not fit "some particular species which has been examined and classified,"[57] and the common law's preoccupation with the details of each individual instance had failed to identify the "common element" or principle "common to the cases where [a duty] is found to exist" and upon which liability "must logically be based."[58]

To derive the common element or principle necessary to solve the problem, Lord Atkin turned to public morality and the precept or background principle that "you are to love your neighbour." Liability in negligence, he wrote, "is no doubt based upon a general public sentiment of moral wrongdoing for which the offender must pay."[59] But he recognized that the sentiment found in public morality was too general to provide a legal answer. Liability for injuries had to be tempered and limited in keeping with what he described as the needs of the "practical world" as revealed and understood by the experience of the common law. The background moral value is reformulated and made operational for legal purposes in two ways. First, the rule "that you are to love your neighbour becomes in law, you must not injure your neighbour." Second comes what Lord Atkin describes as the "lawyer's question": Who is my neighbour?[60] That question "receives a restricted reply": "Who, then, in law is my neighbour? The answer seems to be – persons who are so closely and directly affected by my act that I ought reasonably to have them in contemplation as being so affected when I am directing my mind to the acts or omissions which are called in question."[61]

In this passage, Lord Atkin planted the seeds from which modern negligence law would grow: foreseeability and proximity. The background good neighbour principle is operationalized by reference to foreseeability of harm, where the relationship is sufficiently close and direct, or proximate, to justify imposing liability.

I suggest that this very wise judgment and its Canadian progeny reveal a great deal about how legal rules and principles emerge from moral and ethical values, and how courts use rules, principles, and policies to form and shape the law in a creative but disciplined manner.

At the core of the hodgepodge of the common law precedents that emerged from fact-specific judgments, Lord Atkin found implicit the good neighbour principle. While that broad principle captured what the law should achieve, by itself it lacked the precision required to achieve justice in the real world. It had to be refined and narrowed to be useful as an operative principle of law. The lawyer's skill is to craft, interpret, and apply rules and principles so as to arrive at a workable and coherent scheme of justice. The lawyer takes the ethical or moral value and asks questions that explore and elucidate the issues of practicality and implementation in the social and economic context within which it must operate.

The full implications of Lord Atkin's operational principles of reasonable foreseeability and proximity are still being worked out by the courts. In 2001, and with the benefit of seventy years of jurisprudence, the Supreme Court of Canada reformulated the inquiry in a case called *Cooper v Hobart*.[62] I suggest that the evolution from *Dongohue v Stevenson* in 1932 to *Cooper v Hobart* in 2001 serves as a useful model to explore the relationship between rules, principles, and policies and the way in which the common law evolves through judicial decision-making.

In *Cooper v Hobart*, several mortgage investors alleged that the Registrar of Mortgage Brokers had failed to take adequate steps to deal with their mortgage broker who had used the funds for unauthorized purposes. The investors claimed damages from the Registrar to compensate them for the losses they had suffered. The issue was whether the defendant Registrar owed the plaintiffs a legal duty of care.

The decided cases following *Donoghue v Stevenson* had dealt with specific fact situations and determined that certain relationships give rise to a legal duty of care. Those decisions established what the Supreme Court called "categories,"[63] which correspond to what I am calling "rules." If the facts of a case fall within a pre-established category or rule, a duty of care exists, and, provided the other elements of the tort of negligence are established, liability may be imposed. As the Supreme Court put it, the use of categories "provides certainty to the law of negligence." The Supreme Court concluded that no precedent had established a duty of care that covered the situation of the investors and the Registrar.

But just as Lord Atkin had found in 1932, the Supreme Court held that the body of common law rules or categories established by the precedents was not exhaustive. The rules emerging from the precedents were incomplete. The gaps left by the categories could be filled by reference to the broader principles of reasonable foreseeability and proximity. Judges can resort to these general principles to consider novel situations not previously considered so that the law can "evolve to meet the needs of new circumstances."[64] The court refused "to be confined by arbitrary forms and rules where justice indicates otherwise" and referred to the proximity principle as "not so much a test in itself, but as a broad concept which is capable of subsuming different categories of cases involving different factors."[65]

The inquiry involves two stages. At the first stage there are two questions. Question one is essentially Lord Atkin's reasonable foreseeability test: "Was the harm that occurred the reasonably foreseeable consequence of the defendant's act?" Question two relates to Lord Atkin's warning that the relationship between the claimant and the injured party must be sufficiently close and direct. Foreseeability of harm is a necessary but not sufficient condition for the imposition of a duty of care. Question two is: "Are there reasons, notwithstanding the proximity between the parties established in the first part of this test, that tort liability should not be recognized here?"

The second stage of the inquiry turns to "whether there are residual policy considerations outside the relationship of the parties that may negative the imposition of a duty of care."[66]

The focus at the first stage is "on factors arising from the relationship between the plaintiff and the defendant." I understand this first stage to be a reiteration of what Lord Atkin described as the "lawyer's questions" on the details of the case and the practicality of imposing a legal duty of care – questions of principle that probe and explore the nature of the parties' relationship and the justice and fairness of making someone legally liable for the injury suffered by another. The established categories, while not closed, provide guidance on "the type of relationship in which a duty of care may arise"[67] that may be used by way of analogy.

While the court added that the proximity inquiry involves questions of policy "in the broadest sense of that word," it seems to me that the court must be using "policy" at the first stage to refer to the assessment of the justice and fairness of imposing liability as between the parties. This might be described as "legal policy," as distinct from pure public policy.[68] The court spoke of the "distinctive policy considerations which impact each stage" of the analysis[69] and stated that the proximity analysis at the first stage "focuses on factors arising from the *relationship* between the plaintiff and the defendant."[70] Was the defendant in a sufficiently close and direct relationship with the plaintiff that it is just to impose a duty of care?

In *Cooper v Hobart*, the legal policy component at the first stage involved consideration of the source and general nature of the Registrar's statutory powers and duties. The court found those duties to be wholly public and, according to the court, the Registrar owed a duty "to the public as a whole." In the court's view, the Registrar's public duties required him to "balance a myriad of competing interests" to ensure the efficient operation of and public confidence in the operation of the mortgage market. To impose a private law duty to individual investors would impair "other important interests," including "efficiency" and "public confidence in the system as a whole."[71]

While that was enough to decide the case, the court also dealt with the second stage of the proximity inquiry and the "residual policy considerations" that might nullify a duty of care. These residual policy considerations, said the court, "are not concerned with the relationship between the parties" but rather "with the effect of recognizing a duty of care on other legal obligations, the legal system and society more generally" – in other words, pure public policy.

In *Cooper*, the court referred to the immunity extended to government policy decisions (as distinct from operational decisions) where the imposition of liability would constitute an undesirable intrusion into government policymaking. Governments have to make choices when allocating limited resources. The government might know that if it spends money on education or hospitals rather than road improvement, there will be more road accidents. But that sort of trade-off is exactly what government is all about, and courts will not interfere by imposing civil liability for the consequences of the choices governments make, even where the harm suffered is foreseeable. The court reiterated the concern, often expressed when an extension of tort liability is in play, of "the spectre of indeterminate liability."[72] The court also concluded that to impose a duty of care would "effectively create an insurance scheme for investors at great cost to the taxpaying public."[73]

These considerations take into account the broader societal consequences that could arise from the imposition of a new legal duty of care. When crafting rules and principles for liability, the court must achieve an appropriate reconciliation of individual rights with the general social good. But as the court made clear in *Cooper*, policy considerations of this nature are clearly "residual," and liability should "be primarily determined by reference to established and analogous categories of recovery."[74] In other words, the second stage policy consideration should rarely be determinative, and virtually all cases deciding whether to recognize a new duty of care will turn on the proximity analysis at the first stage.

## The Principled Approach: An Assessment

I suggest that the principled approach to hearsay, the law of unjust enrichment, the principle of good faith in contract law, and the law of negligence reveal a similar pattern of judicial analysis. The judge starts with the established categories or rules. The judge realizes, however, that it may not be possible or advisable to apply the categories and rules mechanically. Behind the rules are principles that identify the underlying considerations of justice and fairness that motivate the rules. Those principles are set out in a deliberately broad-brush fashion. They may be used to interpret the existing rules and they may accommodate cases not caught by the existing rules. New categories or rules can emerge, subject to residual considerations of policy or general social welfare that might require some limitation of application.

To conceive of the law as a body of both rules and broad overarching principles affords the judge the flexibility to achieve justice in each case, but also disciplines the judge to reach decisions that respect the coherence and integrity of the law. Past cases and existing rules provide stability and may be applied by analogy to new circumstances. Because of their breadth, principles give coherence to the law by identifying the moral and ethical content of the considerations of justice and fairness that the law seeks to protect. Identifying and focusing on the motivating principles ensures that the law will be interpreted and developed in a coherent manner. Justice E.W. Thomas, a New Zealand judge who advocates the principled approach as an antidote to what he perceives to be an excessively rigid adherence to rules and precedents, argues that "principles deserve primacy in the adjudicative process," given their "unique capacity to provide the judicial process with coherence and continuity." Principles also "make the law more sensitive to the achievement of justice in the individual case and to securing a law which is in harmony with the times."[75] Principles help us decide the "hard cases" where the law appears to offer no clear answer. When the law seems to have run out, we turn to principles to fill in the gaps.

Policy considerations are to be distinguished from concerns of justice and fairness as between the parties. Defined as considerations of the general good of society, policy considerations are properly considered, but they are residual rather than primary. The focus of adjudication should be on rights, and on the parties and the nature of their relationship or interaction. However, legal rules and legal rights have to be formulated, interpreted, and enforced in the real world. It is appropriate for judges to consider the wider societal ramifications of creating a rule or legal right.

The principled approach also reflects a resurgence of the same spirit that motivated the ancient tradition of equity. Until the fusion of law and equity in the late nineteenth century, there were two broad streams in English and Canadian law. The first stream, the common law, reflected the need for certainty. The common law provided a body of highly specific rules that emerged inductively from the precedents established by judicial decisions rather than deductively from general principles. The second stream, equity, consisted of a body of general principles that could be applied deductively to fill in the gaps and relieve against the strictures and harshness of the common law. To take a familiar example, one party holds the legal title to property in which another party has a legitimate interest. The common law insisted that the legal title holder's rights were exclusive.

Equity did not deny the legal title but imposed on the title-holder a duty of trust to reflect the legitimate interest of the other party.

We no longer think in terms of a bifurcated legal system consisting of law on the one hand and equity on the other. However, the modern principled approach to law accomplishes many of the same objectives of good conscience and fair dealing as the ancient court of equity. By stating the law in terms of overarching principles, considerable flexibility is left to judges when deciding specific cases. Principles fill gaps and accord flexibility in decision-making similar to the discretion afforded by equitable doctrines. In a 1992 decision rejecting a claim for unjust enrichment, Justice Beverley McLachlin described the need to strike "an appropriate balance between predictability in the law and justice in the individual case" by choosing "a middle course between the extremes of inflexible rules and case by case 'palm tree' justice." She described the "middle course" as "adhering to legal principles, but recognizing that those principles must be sufficiently flexible to permit recovery where justice so requires having regard to the reasonable expectations of the parties in all the circumstances of the case as well as to public policy."[76]

### But Is It Law?

Some may ask whether the law should rely so heavily on general overarching principles. Do they supply sufficient precision to allow citizens to plan and regulate their affairs with a reasonable degree of certainty about the consequences of their conduct? Are they sufficiently precise to provide a sound and reliable basis for judicial decision-making?

These are very basic questions about the nature and character of law. There is an ongoing debate over the relative advantages and disadvantages of relying on rules or principles.[77] The English and Australian courts have been considerably less enthusiastic than Canadian courts about the principled approach, precisely because they believe it to be too uncertain. In a 1990 decision, the House of Lords recognized "the importance of the underlying general principles common to the whole field of negligence" but favoured "attaching greater significance to the more traditional categorisation of distinct and recognisable situations as guides to the existence, the scope and the limits of the varied duties of care which the law imposes."[78] A year later, the House of Lords overruled *Anns*, the foundation of the Supreme Court of Canada's principled approach for negligence, describing it as a "remarkable example of judicial legislation."[79] Instead, they agreed with a judgment of the Australian High Court that insisted "that the law should develop novel categories of negligence incrementally and by analogy to defined categories."[80] The Australian courts have also been unreceptive to the principled approach to unjust enrichment, describing it as a form of impermissible "top down reasoning."[81] The House of Lords rejected a unifying principle or theory for economic torts on the ground that its very generality sowed seeds of confusion by obscuring required elements of distinct torts.[82] Lord Hoffmann wrote, "The example of what Lord Atkin achieved for negligence in *Donoghue v Stevenson* always beckons. But this too is a form of seduction which may lure writers onto the rocks."[83] This echoed another English jurist, Lord Goff, who warned against "the temptation of elegance" rather than accepting that "the law has to reflect life in all its untidy complexity."[84] In England, the law of hearsay was reformed by legislation, not by judicial decision, in terms more specific, precise, and rule-bound than the principled approach enunciated by the Supreme Court of Canada.[85]

The concern expressed by English and Australian jurists is the risk that general principles may obscure the details and nuances that have been built out of the experience of deciding cases in the common law tradition. To decide cases in an orderly and consistent manner, we also need the accumulated wisdom that is reflected in a body of common law doctrine. The experience of deciding cases teaches that the devil is very often in the details and that we cannot escape those details by reverting to overly simplistic formulae. In the search for principle we risk losing or obscuring the nuance and subtlety revealed by the pattern of past decisions. General principles are very useful to enhance understanding of the basic values that drive our legal regime, but we also need to hold on to the categories established by past decisions to guide, structure, and discipline judicial decision-making.

I suspect that there are two reasons why Canadian law has tended to favour the principled approach. The first is the influence of the civilian tradition. As Stephen Waddams points out, since the eighteenth century, common law scholars "seeking order, simplicity, logic and elegance in English law look, somewhat enviously, towards civil law systems."[86] The Supreme Court of Canada regularly hears appeals from Quebec, where private law is governed by the

*Civil Code*. One of the chief characteristics of the civilian tradition is that the law is codified in terms of provisions that cover large areas and that define rights and duties in terms as general as the principles developed by the Supreme Court for negligence and unjust enrichment.[87] Familiarity with the civilian approach may well have influenced the court to conceive of the common law in terms of broad principles. The principled approach may well reflect something of a convergence between the two streams of Canadian jurisprudence: the common law and the civil law.[88]

The other influence is the *Charter of Rights and Freedoms*. Although the *Charter* does not directly apply to the common law, the experience of dealing with its very general provisions has likely had an effect in making the court more receptive to articulating the law in terms of general principles, even when it comes to common law adjudication.

While the principled approach seems ascendant, it has not gone unchallenged. The Supreme Court regularly debates the relative advantages and disadvantages of rules and principles when developing the law. As the following two examples will show, sometimes the court finds that clear-cut rules are required, and other times it opts for broad principles.

*R v Jordan*[89] involved the contentious *Charter* right of an accused person "to be tried within a reasonable time."[90] Barrett Richard Jordan was arrested in December 2008 and charged together with several other individuals with various drug offences. He remained in custody for two months before securing bail on strict conditions. In May 2011, two and one-half years after his arrest, he was committed for trial after a nine-day preliminary hearing. His trial commenced in September 2012 but was adjourned, and he was eventually convicted in February 2013, forty-nine and one-half months after his arrest.

Jordan's motion to have the charges stayed on account of delay was dismissed by the British Columbia courts. They applied a very flexible and contextual test laid down in *R v Morin*,[91] a prior Supreme Court decision. *Morin* required the court to balance a list of factors, namely, the length of the delay, the conduct of the defence and the Crown, the reasons for the delay, including institutional constraints, and the prejudice to the accused's interest in liberty, security of the person, and a fair trial.

The five-judge majority judgment in the Supreme Court, jointly authored by Justices Moldaver, Karakatsanis, and Brown, decided that it was time to overrule the flexible and contextual *Morin* test and replace it with a clearer standard. Emphasizing the importance of timely justice, the majority found that "a culture of complacency towards delay has emerged in the criminal justice system."[92] The flexible and contextual approach had failed. It was unpredictable, confusing, and too complex. The emphasis on prejudice to the accused ignored the public interest in timely justice. The flexible case-by-case retrospective analysis rationalized delay and failed to provide the clear standard that was required to motivate all actors in the justice system to achieve timely justice.

The majority laid down a presumptive ceiling, with deduction for any delays caused by the defence, of eighteen months for provincial court trials and thirty months for superior court trials. In cases exceeding those limits the Crown must establish exceptional circumstances to rebut the presumption of unreasonable delay and avoid a stay dismissing the charges. If the case is tried within those limits, it is for the defence to rebut the presumption to show that the delay was unreasonable. The presumptive ceiling, said the majority, was required "to give meaningful direction to the state" and to "court administration, Crown prosecutors, accused persons and their counsel and judges" to ensure the constitutional obligation to provide timely justice was satisfied.[93]

Justice Cromwell, writing for the four dissenting judges, insisted that a reasonable time for trial cannot and should not be reduced to simple numerical ceilings and that the right is "multi-factored, fact-sensitive, case-specific," and "unavoidably complex."[94] "Reasonableness is an inherently contextual concept"[95] that cannot be judicially determined with precision or "captured by a number."[96] The minority advocated readjusting rather than rejecting the *Morin* framework and viewed the majority judgment as an unacceptable form of judicial law-making that was likely to cause chaos in the justice system.

The difference between the majority and minority judgments is striking. The majority is focused on the need to instruct and discipline the actors in the justice system. The system is too slow, and that needs to be corrected. The correction can be achieved only by the creation of a clear and firm standard. That clear standard will exact a price, as guilty parties will go free. But that is a price that must be paid for the system to become more efficient and just overall. The minority is focused on reaching just results in specific cases. A clear rule lacks the subtlety required properly to determine the contours of an important constitutional right. There is no escape from a careful, contextual, case-by-case analysis to achieve justice in each case.

We see a similar debate with a different outcome in the Supreme Court's decision in *R v NS*.[97] The issue was whether a Muslim woman should be allowed to testify in court in a sexual assault trial while wearing a niqab covering her face. The court had to reconcile the fair trial rights of the accused, who asserted that they could not properly cross-examine the complainant if her face was covered, with the claim of religious freedom asserted by the complainant, who had a sincere religious belief that she ought to wear the niqab when in public. The court sharply divided on whether to adopt a clear rule or to opt for a more general principle.

I sat on the case when it was at the Court of Appeal for Ontario.[98] We decided that it was not possible to devise a clear-cut rule that would satisfactorily reconcile the competing claims of religious freedom and fair trial rights.

Writing for the four-judge majority, Chief Justice McLachlin essentially agreed with our approach and held that a rule-based approach that would either always require the complainant to remove the niqab or always allow her to wear it was untenable. She favoured what I would describe as a flexible principle-based approach that identified several factors to be weighed on a case-by-case basis in order to strike "a just and proportionate balance"[99] between freedom of religion and trial fairness, based on the particular facts of the case before the court. Justices Lebel and Rothstein, dissenting, favoured "a clear rule"[100] that would always require witnesses to have their faces uncovered to respect the fair trial rights of the accused. A clear rule avoided adding "a new layer of complexity to the trial process"[101] and upheld both the fair trial rights of the accused and the values of openness and religious neutrality in the justice system. Justice Abella, highly doubtful of the impact of wearing a niqab on the fair trial rights of the accused, favoured a clear rule in the other direction – one that would allow the witness to wear the niqab except in cases where her identity was in issue.

The members of the Supreme Court in *Jordan* and in the niqab case were debating substantive constitutional law, but they were also debating legal method. I am a strong believer in the benefits of identifying principles and deploying them as a core component of legal analysis. I also think that there are cases, like the niqab case, that do not lend themselves to resolution on the basis of a clear "black-and-white" rule. However, cases like *Jordan* point out that an unyielding emphasis on general and flexible principles may be problematic in terms of maintaining a clear and disciplined approach in certain areas.

General principles require the exercise of a considerable degree of individual judgment in their application. That makes cases more difficult to argue, decision-making less predictable, and the entire process more costly. In a justice system already plagued by delay and excessive cost, the principle-based approach does exact a price. And in some situations it may be better to forgo the aim of perfect justice in all cases. As Professor Frederick Schauer puts it, "[T]he best legal rule may at times be one that will produce an unjust result in the present case but which will produce better results in a larger number of cases, the result in the present case notwithstanding."[102] In my view, this argument is particularly pertinent to questions of procedure and evidence where we need quick and predicable answers to ensure accessible justice. It also carries weight in areas such as commercial law, where business people require the assurance of a stable and certain body of law to govern their affairs. Even in areas like family law, where the desire to do justice in the individual case is very strong, the parties often lack the resources for drawn-out litigation, and there are advantages to rough-and-ready rules that produce predictable outcomes, discourage litigation, and provide a clear framework for consensual resolution.

There is an interesting parallel to be drawn between the level of generality of the kind of principles I have been discussing and what the Supreme Court of Canada has said counts as a "law" under the *Charter of Rights and Freedoms*. The issue arises under two sections of the *Charter*. Section 1 provides that the rights and freedoms guaranteed are "subject only to such reasonable limits *prescribed by law* as can be demonstrably justified in a free and democratic society."[103] When is a limit on a *Charter* right sufficiently precise to qualify as a limit "prescribed by law"? Section 7 of the Charter provides, "Everyone has the right to life, liberty and security of the person and the right not to be deprived thereof except in accordance with the principles of fundamental justice." In some cases, it has been argued that a law that limits life, liberty, or security of the person lacks the precision necessary to provide citizens with the guidance required by the rule of law and the guarantee of fundamental justice.

On both questions, the Supreme Court has consistently resisted the argument that to qualify as a law, a legal norm or standard must provide crystal clear and immediate answers. On the other hand, the court has insisted that there must be an intelligible standard, capable of providing "an adequate basis for legal debate … as to its meaning by reasoned analysis applying legal criteria."[104]

In *Irwin Toy*,[105] a 1989 decision challenging a restraint on advertising as an infringement of freedom of expression, the majority wrote that "absolute precision in the law exists rarely, if at all" and that the real question is "whether the legislature has provided an intelligible standard according to which the judiciary must do its work." Because a legal standard cannot "specify all the instances in which it applies," decision-making necessarily calls for the exercise of judgment or discretion in particular cases. But there is a baseline of precision below which a standard ceases to have the legitimacy of law. "Where there is no intelligible standard" and where the decision-maker has been "given a plenary discretion to do whatever seems best in a wide set of circumstances," the essential minimum requirements of the rule of law are not met.[106]

The notion of "an intelligible standard" was echoed in the judgment of Justice Antonio Lamer in the *Prostitution Reference*, where he spoke of "an ascertainable standard of conduct, a standard that has been given sensible meaning by courts."[107] The theme was taken up again in *R v Nova Scotia Pharmaceutical Society*.[108] There the court had to contend with the offence of conspiracy to "lessen competition unduly" under the *Competition Act*. Justice Charles Gonthier explained the relationship between a general legal rule and a specific judicial decision in the following terms: "Legal rules only provide a framework, a guide as to how one may behave, but certainty is only reached in instant cases, where law is actualized by a competent authority."[109]

The legal rules define "the boundaries of permissible and nonpermissible conduct" and thereby provide substantive norms that permit and structure debate, limit the risk of abusive or undisciplined exercise of discretion, and "sufficiently delineate an area of risk to allow for substantive notice to citizens." The suggestion that laws "can and must provide enough guidance to predict the legal consequences of any given course of conduct in advance" reflects an unrealistic perception of the precision that language can achieve.[110]

These statements reflect a judicial recognition that the problem of uncertainty of result in any given case is pervasive and inherent in any standard phrased broadly enough to provide us with guidance in more than one fact situation. The objective of law is not and cannot be complete predictability of results – a workable legal standard must leave some room for judgment in deciding specific cases.

We should keep in mind, however, that the *Charter*'s constitutional standard sets out the minimum that is required to comply with the rule of law, not the ideal level of clarity and precision. Citizens require adequate guidance provided by law to govern their conduct and to order their affairs. Lawyers need to know the boundaries of acceptable legal argument. Judges require adequate standards to guide and discipline their decisions.

We encounter here the basic conundrum that pervades the legal system: how to strike the right balance between, on the one hand, certainty and predictability, and on the other, ensuring just results in all cases.

## Chapter 6

# Disciplined Judicial Decision-Making

I have argued in earlier chapters that there are cases where the law is less than certain and that judges sometimes make law when they decide cases. To some, this may sound surprising – even alarming – but in my view, these are inevitable features of our common law tradition.

In this chapter, I will discuss the factors that discipline the decision-making powers conferred upon judges. Judges work within the confines of our legal order. Judges must do their work with scrupulous care and attention to the constraints under which they function.

The first constraint is that the judge's task is to decide according to law. Judicial decision-making is not an open-ended pursuit of the judge's personal views of right and wrong. A judge must accept that the law will not always lead to the result the judge thinks is right. The legal system as a whole aspires to reach just results in all cases, but judges have to live and work in the real world. No legal system is perfect. The inherent flexibility of the law leaves judges with considerable room to manoeuvre, but that is not a licence to ignore the law. The role of the judge is to find the result that best fits with the relevant legal rules and principles, not to find the result that comports with the judge's personal view of right and wrong.

The second and related constraint is that judges are required to provide a reasoned explanation for the decisions they make. This means that judges must expose their thinking to the litigants and to the public and demonstrate that they have been faithful to the obligation to decide the case according to the law. If a judge fails to do so, the decision may be reversed on appeal, it may be subjected to professional and public scrutiny and criticism, and it may shake public confidence in the justice system.

## Follow the Law or Make the "Right" Decision?

When they take their oath of office, all judges make a solemn commitment to decide cases according to the law. This commitment is the most fundamental and obvious constraint that judges must accept.

Legal reasoning of the kind employed by lawyers to argue cases, and accepted by judges to decide cases, has much in common with forms of argument used outside the law.[1] Lawyers and judges use the methods of philosophy, reasoning by analogy and logical progression from moral and ethical principles. To discern the meaning of legal doctrines, they look to history and the way the law has evolved. And like the social sciences, they examine legal doctrine from the perspective of social values, mores, and welfare.

But while lawyers and judges draw on other disciplines to do their work, there are distinctive features that are peculiar to legal reasoning.[2]

Philosophy and the social sciences have much to teach about general principles of justice. But lawyers and judges have the special skills required to craft workable legal standards by which specific disputes may be decided in a fair and just manner. The distinctive task of the law is to move from the general to the particular and to deal with the crucially important details about the fair resolution of disputes, the precise contours of legal rights, and their enforcement at the level of particular cases.[3] Law "is ethics subjected to the discipline of practical application in decisions which have to be made, day after day, in the full light of publicity and under the pressure of the elementary requirement of justice that like cases be treated alike."[4] So, for example, the law's commitment to the overarching principle that promises should be kept derives from both moral philosophy and social sciences such as economics. However, the important details of contract law are derived from the practical experience of lawyers and judges resolving issues on a case-by-case basis.

A critical feature of legal reasoning is that issues about rights and their enforcement must be resolved within a defined framework that requires arguments to have a certain pedigree to qualify them as legitimate.[5] This limits the bite of arguments that lack that pedigree and that are based on factors external to it. Fundamental to the very idea of law and to the nature of legal argument is the idea that the choice a judge exercises when deciding a case must be constrained. Simply put, a judge is not free to decide cases on the basis of what seems to the judge, all things considered, to be the best possible outcome. The judge is not allowed to consider all things. The judge is to consider only those things that have a sufficient legal pedigree, even if the result the law yields is not the result that the judge thinks is best. As Frederick Schauer argues, perhaps with some exaggeration, "[E]very one of the dominant characteristics of legal argument and legal reasoning can be seen as a route towards reaching a decision *other than* the best all-things-considered decision for the matter at hand."[6]

We prefer the discipline of law to the whim of individual judgment. As Aristotle observed, "It is better for the law to rule than one of the citizens," and "so even the guardians of the laws are obeying the laws."[7] Lawyers and judges are expected to work within the bounds of the law and to decide cases according to the appropriate legal standard, whether they agree with that standard or not. The law is wary of placing undue reliance on individual judgment in individual cases lest the standard of the law disintegrate into a mess of shifting and unpredictable caprice.

I would be very concerned about a judge who has never felt compelled to decide a case in a way that goes against the judge's personal views. That is simply an unpleasant but familiar part of the job. We are prepared to put our personal views to one side because that is what we have promised and because, at the end of the day, we must accept that it is necessary to tolerate occasional outcomes that we personally regard as wrong or unjust in order to preserve the overarching ideal of a legal order that exists separately and independently from the personal views of judges.

## Formalism

While the label has become unpopular, I think judges have to accept that there is a necessary element of formalism in the law.[8] Legal doctrine does matter, and the law limits our choices. We have to apply constitutionally valid statutes as they are written, and we have to follow binding precedents that pertain to the dispute before us, even if we do not like the result the authorities prescribe.

Accepting the limits on our choice that are imposed by legal authority distinguishes legal reasoning from other modes of analysis. Scientists, philosophers, and social scientists are engaged in a search for the truth unconstrained by authority. Sir Edward Coke, the great legal scholar and judge who fought to establish the fundamental principles of the English constitutional order in the early seventeenth century, spoke of the "artificial reason" of the law, which he distinguished from "natural reason." Coke argued that even if the King was endowed with "excellent science," the rights of the King's subjects were not to be decided by the King using natural reason but by the judges using the "artificial reason and judgment of law."[9]

The "artificial reason of the law" does not put judges and lawyers in an impossible straitjacket of strict legalism. As discussed in chapter 3, legal standards are, by nature, general and often open-ended. They afford judges considerable latitude to reach just results in individual cases, and there is certainly scope for judges to develop the law to make it more just. Legal standards are also shaped and influenced by a broader background of moral, social, and economic considerations. The wise judge will certainly take account of the moral, historical, and philosophical roots of the legal standards the judge is interpreting and applying. The wise judge will also probe and prod to see if there are not holes to be poked in a legal argument that leads to an unjust result. Former Israeli Supreme Court Justice Aharon Barak insists that "judges must not impose their own personal, subjective perceptions"[10] but adds that "judges ... must aspire to reach just solutions," and if the law seems to point to a result that contradicts the judge's sense of justice, "the judge must retrace his footsteps" to see "whether he has strayed from the path, for law's aspiration is to be just, and the judge's aspiration is to do justice."[11]

But wise judges also must recognize that the discipline of law imposes limits on their capacity to make the world a better place and that they must abide by certain constraints, even if at times those constraints lead to a result with which they do not personally agree. The "pervasive formality of law" and the "tendency to take its rules and their words seriously even though in some cases they might work an injustice – is what distinguishes law from many other decision-making contexts."[12]

For example, there is a common law rule requiring "consideration," a term indicating the exchange of something of value, to support the enforcement of a contract. Suppose that I think the need for consideration is outmoded and that all promises should be enforced. I hear a case where enforcement of a promise is resisted on the ground that there was no consideration for the promise. If I cannot fit the facts of the case into a recognized exception to the traditional consideration rule, I have no choice. Much as it may pain me to render what I consider to be an unjust result, I cannot enforce the promise.[13]

The discipline of law forces us to accept that perfect justice in every single case is humanly impossible. Legal standards apply across the board. They are not framed to decide specific cases but to provide a workable framework that fosters results that are, on the whole, right and just. Given the unpredictability of events and the uncertainty of human affairs, it is impossible to come up with legal standards that will yield justice in every single instance. It is inevitable that even the best legal standard we can hope to devise, one that produces just results almost always, will occasionally yield a result that seems unjust. If we are to maintain the general standard, there is an unfortunate price to be paid. We must remain faithful to the generally just standard, even when it yields a result that we do not like, for if we were free to depart from the standard when we do not like the result it produces, the standard would cease to have any meaning.

## Precedent

The discipline of maintaining a legal standard that produces awkward results is an explicit feature of adherence to the precedents laid down by past decisions, a topic I will discuss in greater detail in chapter 7. Like cases should be decided in a like fashion. I may disagree with the way my colleagues decided a case last week, but if I have to decide a case this week that raises the same issue, I have no choice: I must follow the precedent my colleagues laid down. As the great American judge Louis Brandeis stated, "[I]n most matters it is more important that the applicable rule of law be settled than that it be settled right."[14] When common law judges follow a past decision, they do so not because they agree with it but because it is there. They recognize that the interests of justice in general are served by following the precedent and that maintaining the stability of legal doctrine will often transcend the interest of reaching a just result in a particular case. Certainty and predictability are legitimate and necessary values to any system of law. The rule will survive only if we are willing to follow it even when we do not like the result it produces.

Even when deciding a "hard case" for which the precedents provide no clear answer, the doctrine of precedent constrains me as a member of an intermediate appellate court. My decision in the "hard case" will stand as a precedent that I, and all the other judges at or below my level in the judicial hierarchy, must follow in the future. As I will explain in chapter 7, the decision of one three-judge panel is considered binding on a subsequent panel. That means that all of my colleagues will be stuck with what I say, even though they do not participate in my decision. That gives me enormous power that I am bound to exercise in a responsible and restrained manner. Knowing that my decision will bind my colleagues and other judges constrains any wish I might have to decide the case on the basis of my own personal views. It reinforces my obligation to decide cases in a principled legal fashion, one that best fits with the established law and the prevailing norms and standards of our legal system.

The situation is different at the Supreme Court of Canada (and most other, but not all,[15] apex courts), where, if possible, all members of the court sit on significant cases. In a Supreme Court case where five judges decide one way and the other four dissent, the decision of the majority is binding on the four dissenting judges unless and until it is overruled. Nevertheless, the four dissenters cannot complain, for they were participants in the precedent-setting decision, and they had the opportunity to persuade their colleagues to decide the case the other way.

As an intermediate appellate court, the Ontario Court of Appeal will depart from a prior decision only if a five-judge panel determines that the rather stringent conditions for overruling it have been met. And even then, most members of the court are not involved in the decision.[16] We do not have *en banc* sittings, a practice of some American appellate courts,[17] where all members of the court sit to resolve important issues. Nor do we follow the practice of some provincial courts of appeal of circulating significant draft judgments to all members of the court for comment or reaction.[18]

The fact that my pronouncement will bind my absent colleagues and the lower courts makes me cautious. I have only one case, one set of facts and arguments, and whatever I say will bind me and my colleagues in the future. I cannot shirk or avoid the responsibility of deciding the case that is presented, however significant its consequences. But I have to be very careful about unanticipated consequences. As a general rule, I will avoid saying more than is necessary to decide the case at hand. My role as a judge on an intermediate court of appeal points to a minimalist approach – say and decide no more than is necessary to decide the case.

## *Legislation*

Legislation lays down standards that, however sound in general, require judges to impose harsh or undesirable results in some cases. Take, for example, statutory limitation periods that require a plaintiff to commence an action within a prescribed period of time. The rationale for limitation periods is based on both justice and efficiency. Stale claims are difficult to decide fairly, as memories fade and evidence is lost as time passes. At some point, potential defendants are entitled to be left at peace. On the other hand, the application of a specified time limit is bound to seem arbitrary and to operate unfairly in some cases. Even if the claim could be tried fairly in a particular case and even if it seems just that the defendant should still have to face it, if the prescribed period has passed, the claim must be dismissed. If we refuse to enforce the specified limit, we lose the undoubted benefits of the rule. While modern limitation statutes go a long way to alleviate unfairness through the doctrine of discoverability (a concept first elaborated by the courts[19]), which fixes the time to sue from the point at which the plaintiff knew or should have known of the claim, there will still be cases where the sympathy factor will be high and where judges have to bite the bullet and dismiss meritorious time-barred claims.

Even where judges do not agree with the underlying rationale for a law, they are still required to respect the law-making authority of our democratically elected Parliament, provincial legislatures, and municipalities. Provided that those institutions act within the limits imposed by the Constitution, judges must accept the laws enacted, even when the judges do not like or agree with them. For example, most judges disagree with mandatory minimum sentences, which limit their capacity to impose a sentence that best fits the crime and the offender. This causes anguish to the judge who is required to sentence an offender for whom, all other things considered, the mandatory minimum seems to be too severe. But if the legislation imposing the mandatory minimum passes constitutional muster,[20] the sentencing judge has no choice. However much the judge may disagree with the result it produces, the judge has to accept the authority of Parliament to pass the law and follow its dictates.

## *Collegial Decision-Making*

Another constraint is that, as a judge of an appellate court, virtually every decision I make is reached through a collegial process.[21] Collegial decision-making is a strong counterweight to any tendency to be influenced by values extraneous to the law. The collegial process accomplishes this in two ways. First, it requires me to engage not only with the arguments presented by the litigants and the lawyers, but also with any opposing views from my colleagues when we debate the case in the conference room and as we prepare our reasons for judgment. That obligation represents a significant discipline on how I decide. I have to take my colleagues' views into account and, if I disagree with what they say, be prepared to have our disagreement publicly displayed through dissenting reasons. Second, the collegial process ensures that the personal extraneous views of the judge are diluted – in my court, by two and sometimes four other judges. At the Supreme Court, one judge's decision is diluted by eight other judges. Related to this is a kind of "team spirit" that prevails in most collegial courts. A decision of one panel reflects upon all of us. We share a common interest in maintaining and enhancing the reputation of our institution as stable, reliable, independent, and committed to the legal integrity of its work.

## *Respecting the Boundaries of Decision-Making Authority*

Judges operate within a legal and constitutional order that defines the decision-making powers of various actors.

In chapter 10, I discuss obligations imposed upon judges to respect the decision-making authority conferred on other adjudicators. Administrative agencies and tribunals are empowered to decide myriad issues and disputes. Provided that those agencies and tribunals are acting reasonably and within the limits of the powers they enjoy, judges must accept their decisions, even in cases where the reviewing judge would have decided otherwise.

In chapter 10, I also explain the division of decision-making authority within the judiciary. Trial judges have primary responsibility to find the facts, and, unless the finding was unreasonable, appellate judges must respect that authority. Many decisions by first-instance decision-makers are discretionary. A judge who sits higher in the legal hierarchy may disagree with the first-instance adjudicator's exercise of discretion, but if the decision was reasonable and provided it falls within the margin of appreciation allowed by the law, the reviewing judge must swallow any personal misgivings and uphold the decision. The obligation imposed on appellate courts to defer to the factual findings and discretionary decisions of trial judges represents a very significant discipline on appellate decision-making.

## The Evidence, the Record, and the Parameters of the Dispute

Another constraint and discipline judges must respect is that they are confined by the way the parties have defined the dispute and by the evidence the parties have led. Party definition of the issues and presentation of the facts are fundamental features of the adversarial system. Judges do not define or shape the scope of the dispute they are to decide. That is left to the parties who have the right to plead their case as they see fit. The parties also control the evidence that is put before the court. It is only in rare and exceptional cases that a trial judge is permitted to insist that a witness be called. If a litigant decides not to advance an issue or an argument, judges almost always respect the litigant's choice, even if the judge would have presented the case differently. While modern procedural rules involve more and more judicial case-management, the parties retain control over the definition of the issues and decide what evidence and arguments to present.

If a trial decision is appealed, the trial record is all-important, and its limits effectively bind the appellate court. Appeal judges are quite properly very reluctant to consider arguments or facts that were not placed before the trial court. Allowing a losing litigant to shift ground and advance a new argument on appeal would be unfair to the opposing party, particularly in cases where the opposing party could have introduced evidence to rebut the argument at trial. It would also undermine the integrity of the trial process if a party were free to ignore the trial and retry the case on a different theory or on different facts on appeal. Nor will an appellate court ordinarily deal with an issue or argument that the parties have not advanced. It is very dangerous for a court to base its decision on a point not raised by the parties. Often there was a good reason why the point was not raised or, if given a chance, the party affected would have a good answer. If the court thinks that the case cannot properly be decided without reference to an issue or argument not advanced by the parties, it will notify the parties to invite their submissions on the point. Sometimes this will happen before the hearing of the appeal, but more often it occurs after the judges have fully engaged with the case, following oral argument.[22]

## The Discipline of Reasons

There are certainly legal scholars and many lawyers and judges who doubt the integrity of the constraints I am describing. Political scientists tend to be particularly sceptical of claims the law controls judicial decision-making and argue that what I call constraints "serve only to rationalize ... decisions and to cloak the reality"[23] that judges decide on the basis of their personal ideologies. Those critics acknowledge that the *form* of legal argument and judicial reasoning reflects those constraints, but, in their view, form is little more than a convenient mask for what really drives judicial decision-making – namely, the judge's personal, moral, and political views.

This brings me to what I will describe as the discipline of reasons. The discipline of reasons requires the judge to expose to the litigants, and to the public, the path the judge has taken to arrive at a decision. Requiring reasons is the way our legal system enforces the obligation of judges to follow the law and not their personal opinions. If the judge cannot provide a reasoned justification, the decision may be set aside on appeal and subjected to professional and public scrutiny and criticism. The obligation to give reasons is much more than a legal formality.

Popular opinion is increasingly sceptical of those who have and exercise authority. The modern culture of transparency demands justification from all who wield power in contemporary democratic societies. The judiciary cannot escape the kind of scrutiny to which other public officials are exposed. The public wants to know what values, opinions, and attitudes judges bring to bear on the task of deciding cases.

Related to this is the parallel phenomenon of an erosion of confidence in the objectivity of law. One does not have to be a legal realist or an adherent of the critical legal studies movement to be sceptical of Chief Justice Roberts's claim that he just "calls balls and strikes" like an umpire in baseball.[24] Because of our scepticism, we do not allow the Chief Justice to simply say "strike." We require a reasoned opinion based upon recognized and accepted legal sources to explain why.

The demand for transparency and accountability, familiar to all public officials, poses particular problems for judges. Judges wield public power, but they operate in the cloistered world of the courts, and judges speak to the litigants and to the public only through their judgments. If a judgment is criticized, the judge cannot respond. The judgment must stand on its own. Out-of-court explanations from judges, explaining why they decided as they did or rebutting criticism of their judgments, are seen as unprofessional. Such pronouncements would cloud the authority of the judgment and require lawyers and litigants to track down and digest extrajudicial statements from the judge that might qualify or explain the judgment itself.

This limit places enormous weight upon reasons for judgment, since reasons are the one and only way judges can communicate with the public. Absent misconduct in office, it is exclusively through reasons that judges are accountable to the lawyers and litigants who appear before them, to appellate courts, to the legal community, and to the public at large. The legitimacy of judicial authority ultimately rests on the integrity of reasons for judgment.

## Who Is the Audience?

Judges frequently ask themselves: For whom am I writing this judgment? There are, I suggest, three audiences that correspond to the three purposes of reasons that I elaborate in greater detail below.

The first and, for most judges, probably the most important audience is the parties to the case, and in particular, the losing party. The second audience is the Court of Appeal or the Supreme Court of Canada, depending where the judge sits in the judicial hierarchy. The third audience is the public, not just the wider legal community, but also the public at large.

### THE PARTIES AND THE RIGHT TO REASONS

The parties have a right to reasons, and when writing reasons the judge is speaking directly to them. Judges try to demonstrate, as best they can, that they have heard and understood the evidence, the arguments, and the relevant law presented by the parties. They aim to explain their reasoning in a way that explains and justifies why one party lost and the other party won.

Litigants are entitled to reasons as a simple matter of justice and fairness. The right to a reasoned decision may be seen as an aspect of the right to be heard. As an English judge observed in this regard, the most important person in the courtroom "is the litigant who is going to lose."[25] Without a reasoned decision to explain why they lost the case, litigants can have no confidence that the judge actually understood and grappled with their position. As the English Court of Appeal stated, "[J]ustice will not be done if it is not apparent to the parties why one has won and the other has lost."[26] Lord Denning explained that reasons give "proof" that the judge "has heard and considered the evidence and arguments" and that the judge "has not taken extraneous considerations into account."[27]

The Supreme Court of Canada has described this as "the dignity interest ... an interest at the heart of post–World War II jurisprudence."[28] An academic commentator puts it this way: "[R]easons may be regarded as an integral part of treating a disappointed litigant with the respect which his dignity as a citizen demands."[29] In a like vein, another author states that reasons have a "humanizing" effect, demonstrating the judge's respect for the losing party.[30] And as Sir Robert Megarry put it years earlier, "[T]o be condemned without being understood is as bad as to be condemned unheard."[31] We will never make losing parties happy, but reasoned decisions are more acceptable, because they demonstrate to the losing parties that they were heard and that their arguments were understood and grappled with.

### THE APPELLATE COURT AND THE FACILITATION
### OF APPELLATE REVIEW

For all but the judges of apex courts, the second audience when writing reasons is the Court of Appeal or the Supreme Court. Judges know that their reasons are subject to scrutiny by a higher court, and that their decision may be reversed if it reveals legal error. Judges must do their best to explain their decisions in a way that shows the higher court precisely why they decided as they did, so that the higher court can exercise its oversight role and ensure that the decision comports with the law.

The requirement for reasons is formally cast by appeal courts as a means to facilitate appellate review.[32] From that perspective, reasons have an informational effect. They let the parties know why the decision was made so that they can decide whether to take the next step and appeal to a higher court. Reasons also provide appellate courts with the tools they need to review trial decisions. An appellate court needs to be able to see the basis for the trial judge's factual findings and the train of legal reasoning that led to the decision. As the Supreme Court of Canada has explained, adequate reasons are essential to maintaining the boundary between the trial and appellate functions: "A clear articulation of the factual findings facilitates the correction of errors and enables appeal courts to discern the inferences drawn, while at the same time inhibiting appeal courts from making factual determinations 'from the lifeless transcript of evidence, with the increased risk of factual error.'"[33]

### THE PUBLIC AND THE INTEGRITY OF THE LEGAL PROCESS

The third audience is the public, not just the wider legal community but also the public at large. Judges have to realize that their decision-making authority is an exercise of public power and that the integrity and authority of the court on which they sit will suffer if their decisions are not based on legally accepted standards.

Reasons make judges publicly accountable for the power they exercise and may be seen as an element of the open court principle, the idea that the public has a right to attend court to see justice openly administered. Justice must not only be done, but also seen to be done.[34] Members of the public, as well as the litigants, are entitled to an explanation. As Professor Hamish Stewart observed, "[R]easons provide a basis for ... public and political debate about the justice of the particular decision and of the underlying law that authorized it."[35]

The obligation to provide reasons fosters public confidence in the judicial process by forcing judges to be transparent. The "legal culture of justification"[36] comports with the more general culture of justification that pervades modern democratic life.[37] Reasons shed light on why a decision was made, and that, in turn, assures the public that the decision was not arbitrary. The Supreme Court of Canada sees the need to provide reasoned judgments as "central to the legitimacy of judicial institutions in the eyes of the public."[38] Reasons for judicial decisions are necessary to bridge the gap between judicial power and democratic legitimacy: reasons allow unelected judges to demonstrate to the public that the judicial process is legitimate and based on sound principle and rationality. By providing reasons, judges expose to public view the basis for their decisions and provide the means for public scrutiny, accountability, and, where appropriate, criticism.

I believe that the obligation to expose one's reasons to the legal community and the public at large represents a significant constraint on the exercise of judicial power. Judges are members of the legal community and the legal culture that publicly proclaims its integrity, propriety, and commitment to the rule of law. Reasons cement the judge's adherence to those values and the obligation to abide by the limits they impose. By providing reasoned decisions, judges demonstrate that they are not, as the realists and judicial cynics claim, simply deciding on the basis of their own personal views but rather are operating within the limits imposed by the legal regime and the judicial function. American Judge Patricia Wald explains that any temptation to reason backwards from desired result to rationale is inhibited on an appellate court: "[T]here are judges of other persuasions to brake the momentum; there are precedents galore that must be acknowledged and accommodated; there is always the judge's own sense of integrity toward the development of coherent law."[39] And as New Zealand's Justice E.W. Thomas puts it, judges "are constrained by their adherence to the rule of law ... [and] they will consciously strive to reach a decision which is acceptable within the bounds of that concept rather than self-indulgently impose their own will or ideal."[40]

Reasons are intimately linked to the concept of "public reason" and public justification that lies at the heart of the modern liberal democratic state.[41] Reasons reflect our obligation to expose our thinking to the parties, the appeal process, the academics, the media, the public, and the politicians. If our reasons are not based upon sources and arguments accepted by the legal community and fail to abide by the relevant accepted legal norms, they will not survive scrutiny, whether in the court of appeal or in the court of public opinion. Reasons thereby constrain judicial power and simultaneously limit and legitimate judicial creativity by demonstrating that we are not simply deciding the case on the basis of our own personal views or predilections, but rather operating within the circumscribed boundaries implicit in the judicial function and imposed by the law.

Ronald Dworkin links the obligation to provide reasons with the virtue of integrity that requires all who exercise power "to act in a principled and coherent manner toward all citizens."[42] Reasons encourage judges "to conceive of the body of law they administer as a whole rather than as a set of discrete decisions that they are free to make or amend one by one."[43] Reasons ensure that judges avoid arbitrary distinctions between similar cases and that they base their decisions on principles that together form part of "a single, coherent scheme of justice and fairness."[44]

## Legal Sceptics and the "Judicial Hunch"

Jerome Frank, an American realist judge, insisted that decisions "are not and cannot be described in terms of legal rules and principles."[45] The legal realists and their modern critical legal studies disciples argue that there is always more than one correct answer available, and the one that the judge chooses will depend upon a variety of factors, including the current temper of the court and the "sense of the situation as seen by the court."[46]

The realists extolled "judicial intuition" and the "judicial hunch" as a way of describing how judicial decisions are made. A respected American judge writing in the realist tradition described how he decided cases: "[A]fter canvassing all the available material at my command, and duly cogitating upon it, [I] give my imagination play, and brooding over the cause, wait for the feeling, the hunch – that intuitive flash of understanding which makes the jump spark connection between question and decision, and ... where the path is darkest ... sheds his light along the way."[47]

That view, expressed over eighty years ago, is still heard today. When discussing how to construct a winning argument, lawyers and judges frequently minimize the importance of legal doctrine. Seasoned advocates frequently say, "Only the facts count. Let me put the facts of the case forward in a sympathetic way from my client's perspective and then we'll find some law that will allow the judge to do what seems to be right." I often hear judicial colleagues say, "I want to know the facts and where the equities lie. I am not looking for some formal technical jurisprudentially correct solution. I just want a practical solution that works for these people."

Writing in the modern era, Albie Sachs, formerly a judge from the South African Constitutional Court, provides a compelling account of judicial decision-making. Sachs once stated, "Every judgment I write is a lie."[48] Why is it a lie? Because, according to Sachs, contrary to their appearance, "[l]egal judgments ... [do] not emerge from the dispassionate placing of logical propositions in rationally ordained

sequence" but rather from "an inchoate – even chaotic – mental firmament" with "an enormous amount of random intuitive searching
and a surging element of unruly, free-flowing sensibility."[49] The final
form of the judgment fails to reveal the complex mental process that
the judge follows to come to a decision.

If Sachs had stopped there and we were to accept the "judicial
hunch," "only the facts matter," "every judgment is a lie" school of
thought as the whole story, judicial decision-making would be reduced to nothing more than a shallow charade and subterfuge for
judges to decide cases on the basis of their own private and personal
predilections.

But Sachs goes on to provide a valuable insight that significantly
qualifies his claim that every judgment is a lie. Sachs identifies two
phases of the judicial decision-making process. The first phase he
calls the "logic of discovery." This corresponds with the "judicial
hunch"/"only the facts matter" account of decision-making. The
logic of discovery refers to the mental process of sifting through the
evidence and the legal arguments to come to an initial tentative conclusion. The second phase Sachs calls the "logic of justification." The
product of the initial journey through the logic of discovery will not
suffice unless it can be justified: "[A] discovery that cannot be justified simply cannot stand."[50]

The sound and conscientious judge will not decide a case solely
on the basis of an initial hunch about what seems to be the right
result. The sound and conscientious judge must justify the result on
the basis of what Sachs describes as "accepted principles, rules, and
standards to arrive at a conclusion that is consistent with those rules,
principles and standards."[51]

Every judge has had an "it just won't write" moment. After hearing the argument, at the "discovery" stage, the decision seems clear.
But after sitting down and trying to write reasons for a decision, it
becomes clear that the discovery cannot be justified. A discovery
that "won't write" cannot survive as a judgment. There are many
documented cases of Supreme Court of Canada judges changing
their minds after expressing their views at the post-hearing conference.[52] The judicial reasoning that starts with intuition and flashes of
inspiration must end with a reasoned judgment capable of justify-
ing the result, even if that means, in Sachs's words, "causing [the
judge] to abandon even the strongest initial intuitions."[53] Justice
Ruth Bader Ginsburg of the United States Supreme Court makes a

similar observation: "A court charged with defining the law may not rely on unarticulated intuition ... the court is obliged conscientiously to reason why."[54] Even Jerome Frank, who adhered to the "hunch" school of jurisprudence, accepted that the discipline of reasons had to prevail: "Often a strong impression that, on the basis of the evidence, the facts are thus-and-so gives way when it comes to expressing that impression on paper."[55]

I believe that Albie Sachs's account of the "logic of discovery" and the "logic of justification" provides a useful framework for thinking about how judges decide cases. It suggests that the judicial hunch theory accurately captures one aspect of judicial reasoning but that the initial hunch needs to be managed and controlled.

We know from the work of psychologists that "hunches," first impressions, and intuitive thinking are important elements in the way the human mind processes information and formulates decisions. Cognitive psychology teaches that we should be aware of the way the intuitive process works and recognize when hunches and intuitions can lead us astray.

The hunch, in Sachs's terms, the discovery, yields an almost automatic response and corresponds to what has been called "system 1" thinking. It is quick, effortless, and simple. The final judgment, or the justification, corresponds to what has been called "system 2" thinking. It is slow, reflective, deliberate, and complex.[56]

It seems to me that as "system 1" thinking is a prominent feature of human cognition, what lawyers and judges call "hunches" are bound to play some role in judicial decision-making. A judge hearing a case is confronted with a mountain of information about the parties and their dispute. That information does not always come neatly packaged in the appropriate legal categories. To address this flood of information, the judge will develop what Justice John Morden described as "a necessary initial organizing technique."[57] The judge needs to quickly develop a framework to be able to integrate the evidence and the arguments into orderly and manageable categories or packages. The cardinal rule of legal advocacy is to present – at the earliest possible opportunity – a simple, clear, and compelling overview that presents the client's case in the most attractive light. The effective advocate will whet the appetite by planting the "hunch" or "instinctive flash" in the judge's mind to frame a favourable hypothesis into which the judge can readily assimilate the evidence and the arguments.

It is, however, dangerous for the judge to rely too heavily on an initial impression of the case. To leap from an initial hunch to the final decision without reflection is to risk producing aberrant and undesirable results. The conscientious judge must be prepared to jettison the tentative conclusion if the result cannot be justified on the basis of legally accepted sources and argument. Roger Traynor, an American appellate judge, observed that the obligation to provide reasons that "analyze issues that have been disputed every inch of the way" serves "to guard against premature judgment."[58] The hunch or instinctive flash should be allowed to survive only if the judge can marshal arguments with an accepted legal pedigree to justify the result.

Lurking behind the judge's immediate intuitive response to the case may well lie unexamined but deeply ingrained discriminatory and prejudicial ways of thinking. An apparently benign desire to "do justice" and not get too caught up in the technicalities may allow unthinking, stereotypical thinking or irrelevant and extraneous factors to supplant reason and sound judgment.

Another reason why judges need to be cautious about their hunches is that undue reliance on a hunch can lead to what is sometimes described as "result-oriented" reasoning, or what psychologists call "confirmation bias."[59] The judge makes a quick, intuitive decision about the case, then closes his or her mind to the possibility that the intuition might be wrong. The judge proceeds to look only for ways to support the desired result without engaging in the critical and probing thought that is needed to satisfy the logic of justification. This type of reasoning is a familiar feature of wrongful conviction cases where police adopt a "tunnel vision" approach to the investigation of a crime.[60] To counter the dangers of confirmation bias, the judge must approach the task of making a final decision with an open and questioning mind. The judge must recognize that the hunch is only a first impression and that it needs to be re-examined in the cold light of day. Can the result that I *think* looks right be justified on the basis of the record before me and on the basis of the applicable legal authorities?

Psychologists identify several other pitfalls in intuitive, system 1–type thinking, some of which are particularly pertinent to judging.[61] "Anchoring" is the tendency to rely on the first value given when making numerical estimates.[62] The initial value "anchors" the subsequent estimation process and may lead to a higher or lower final number than is actually appropriate. The risk of "anchoring" pertains to decisions on matters such as damage assessment or sentencing. The starting point of one party for an appropriate damages award or sentence, often nothing more than a tactical ploy, may exert an undue influence on the outcome.

"Hindsight bias" is the tendency to overestimate the predictability of past events. The bias "arises from an intuitive sense that the outcome that actually happened must have been inevitable."[63] "Hindsight bias" may affect a judge's assessment of what was foreseeable or reasonable. Knowledge that a certain event did happen can distort the judge's appraisal of the predictability of that event before it took place.

These cognitive tendencies indicate that there are clear dangers in judges relying too heavily on their hunches and intuitions. We need to understand, however, what experienced lawyers and judges are describing when they talk of "following intuition," "deciding on the equities," "using common sense," and "finding practical solutions." I would argue that, perhaps without consciously intending to do so, they are actually referring to something that is highly sophisticated and laudable. The initial perceptions of judges and lawyers who have spent their entire professional lives resolving legal problems are the tentative judgments of educated legal minds.

Judicial decision-making is a much more complex task than the mechanical application of black-letter rules. I argue in chapter 5 that in difficult cases, judges necessarily look beyond the black letter to the broad legal principles and values that structure our legal order. Lawyers and judges who have struggled to work their way through intricate legal problems throughout their legal careers are imbued with the law's fundamental principles and values. Their instincts do not spring from a vacuum, and their common sense is not based on "blind, untutored," or "highly subjective predilections"[64] but on "trained intuition" that can often lead the judge to the right result.[65] As Professor Rachlinski, a leading scholar on the lessons of cognitive psychology for law, puts it, "The conversion of deliberative judgment into intuitive judgment might be the hallmark of experience."[66]

Viewed in that light, the "judicial hunch" school of jurisprudence reflects something that is entirely healthy and to be encouraged in judicial decision-making. The judicial hunch approach reflects an unwillingness to make decisions based on an automatic or purely technical application of the formal rules. The judicial hunch school of thought reflects a willingness to view the case from 10,000 feet where the entire field of relevant rules, principles, and legal values can be surveyed. The judicial hunch, when combined with the need to justify the result, reflects a willingness to decide cases in a manner that coheres with the grand panorama of the basic rules, principles, and values that undergird our system of justice.

### Political Preferences

There is a significant volume of empirical attitudinal studies examining the effect of the political preferences of judges on judicial decision-making. Most of this work has been done in the United States,[67] where the selection of judges, whether by appointment or election, is more highly politicized than in Canada. There is, however, an emerging literature in Canada as well.[68] To the extent these studies show that judicial choices are based on politics and personal preferences rather than law, they challenge my view of judicial decision-making. On the other hand, we have to be wary of falling into the trap of thinking that because *some* judges are *sometimes* influenced by their political views in deciding *some* cases, we have uncovered the phenomenon that explains judicial decision-making.[69] Empirical studies have been shown to have low predictive value. They are purely quantitative studies based on voting records and take no account of qualitative factors – in particular, the reasons judges give for their decisions.[70] In other words, they deliberately ignore the very feature that judges claim is the driver of decision-making. The Canadian studies also suggest that the link between outcomes and the political party that appointed the judge is weaker in Canada than in the United States.[71]

As a lawyer and judge, I approach the issue from a normative rather than an empirical perspective. I accept that judges are influenced by their personal and political views, and I am interested to learn how often that occurs. However, I argue that the legal system in which judges work discourages and inhibits decisions based on such views. I am interested in learning that judges do not always follow the norms, but that fact does nothing to dispel the propriety of the norms and should only strengthen our resolve to insist that the norms be respected and followed. And we need to be wary of the danger that "judges, told often enough that their decision-making is crucially informed by their politics, will begin to believe what they hear and to respond accordingly."[72]

## Conclusion

At the end of the day, after I have rendered my judgment and I ask myself, "Did I reach the right answer?" I may be unsure. But I must feel certain of a number of things: that my reasons demonstrate to the litigants that they were fairly heard; that I grappled with the arguments that they made; that I assessed and analysed those arguments in a manner that comports with accepted legal principles and norms of our legal culture; and that I have clearly explained why I decided the case as I did. I also want to be sure that if another litigant comes before me tomorrow and cites my decision, I will be prepared to adhere to what I have written.

## Chapter 7

# Working with Precedent

The proposition that judges should follow prior decisions is hardly surprising. At its core, the doctrine of precedent rests on the idea that, as a simple matter of justice, like cases should be decided in a like manner. Long used by common law judges to capture the idea of precedent, the Latin phrase *stare decisis* means "we stand by the things that have been decided."

Implicit in the doctrine of precedent is the idea that consistency with past decisions and certainty for the future prevail over ensuring the best possible result in every case. Parties need to be able to plan their affairs and to rely on the courts to provide consistent and predictable justice. If one judge or one panel of judges were free to disregard past decisions, the law would become unpredictable, haphazard, and unacceptably dependent upon the personal views of the judge or judges assigned to hear the case. This would erode legal certainty and threaten the public's confidence in the legitimacy of the judicial process.

If it is just for Jane to succeed in her suit against Pablo, then it seems only right that when Kyra brings the same claim against George, she too should win her case. Once decided, Jane's case becomes a reason for Kyra to win her case, even if, when looking back, the judges hearing Kyra's case have misgivings about the reasoning that allowed Jane to win hers.

Once Jane's case has been decided, the precedent it sets allows Kyra to plan her affairs accordingly. Kyra should be able to assume that if she does so, her expectations will not be upset on the whim of another judge who disagrees with the result in Jane's case. The legal system and society at large benefit from the stability provided by precedent and from the efficiency gained by avoiding the cost of re-litigating settled points.

But like so many other fundamental legal concepts, the doctrine of precedent is far too subtle and nuanced to be reduced to a simple mechanical formula. There is no easy answer that tells us when to follow a precedent and when not to. There is a decided modern trend towards relaxing the weight attached to precedent. As the Supreme Court of Canada observed in its 2015 decision on assisted suicide: "The doctrine that lower courts must follow the decisions of higher courts is fundamental to our legal system. It provides certainty while permitting the orderly development of the law in incremental steps. However, *stare decisis* is not a straitjacket that condemns the law to stasis."[1]

So a trial judgment in Jane's case will not strictly bind the trial judge hearing Kyra's, nor will a judgment from the court of another province. Even if Jane's case was upheld on appeal, George might be able to persuade the judge hearing Kyra's claim that there are factual differences sufficiently significant to warrant "distinguishing" and not following Jane's decision. Nor will every word in Jane's decision bind the court that hears Kyra's case. George can argue that the judicial comment upon which Kyra relies was not an essential part of the reasoning in Jane's case and is therefore not binding.

And it has been increasingly accepted that precedent would be an impossible trap if there were no room at all left to correct mistakes. At some point, the values of certainty and predictability must yield and allow the law to purge itself of past errors and decisions that no longer serve the interests of justice. So even if Kyra can bring her claim squarely within the decision favouring Jane, and even if Jane's decision was upheld on appeal, it is possible, although exceptional, for an appellate court to take a fresh look at the matter and overrule one of its own decisions.

In chapter 5, I suggested that Canadian law has moved away from an emphasis on certainty and, increasingly, in the direction of more flexible general principles that aim to ensure justice in individual cases. I suggest that the same pattern can be seen in the way we deal with precedent. While following precedent is still the general rule, modern Canadian courts – in particular the Supreme Court of Canada – have relaxed their insistence on adhering to precedent and have moved steadily towards the "get it right" end of the spectrum.

## What Does a Case Decide?

I will begin with the traditional techniques lawyers and judges have used for generations when working with precedents.

When asked to follow a precedent, the first question a judge must ask is, "What did that case decide?" We cannot read prior decisions as if they were statutes where every word counts as binding legal authority. The reasons for judgment in the prior case almost inevitably say more than was strictly necessary to decide the case and, in the often-quoted words from an early twentieth-century House of Lords judgment, "[A] case is only an authority for what it actually decides."[2] What a case "actually decides" is determined by looking at its facts: "[T]he generality of the expressions" used to decide a case, the House of Lords went on to say, "are not intended to be expositions of the whole law," and the precedential weight to be attached to the words of the prior judgment is "governed and qualified by the particular facts of the case in which such expressions are to be found."[3]

First-year law students quickly learn that, when working with precedent, the fact-sensitive nature of common law decision-making is very important. They learn how to read a case and how to identify the essential facts. Their professors bombard them with seemingly endless factual hypotheticals designed to test the precedential value of the prior decision. What is the *ratio decidendi*, commonly referred to as the *"ratio,"* the essential core of the reasons for a decision to which the authority of precedent is attached? If the facts of the case to be decided are significantly or materially different, we can say that the prior decision can be distinguished and that its *ratio* therefore does not apply.

For example, in its 2014 decision in *Sattva Capital Corp v Creston Moly Corp*,[4] the Supreme Court of Canada held that the interpretation of contracts was essentially a factual question that affected only the immediate parties to the contract and that an appellate court must defer to a trial judge's decision unless the interpretation was unreasonable.[5] Two years later in *Ledcor Construction Ltd v Northbridge Indemnity Insurance Co*,[6] the court distinguished *Sattva* when interpreting a standard-form contract. Standard-form contacts are non-negotiable, pre-printed agreements prepared for general, across-the-board use in certain industries or activities. Their interpretation is not affected by the facts of the dealings between the parties, and an interpretation in one case would have precedential value in another involving the same standard-form agreement.

When the judge says more than is necessary to decide the case, a subsequent court need not follow the parts of the judgment that were unnecessary to the core of the prior decision. Those parts of the prior judgment that fall outside the *ratio* of the case are labelled *obiter dicta*, things said by the way or in passing, and therefore not necessary for the decision. An *obiter* statement may have persuasive value in subsequent cases, but it does not have the same binding force as the *ratio*.

Discerning the *ratio* of a case, and thereby determining its jurisprudential reach, is very much a matter of argument and judgment. There is no mechanical rule or test that can be uniformly applied.[7] There are several reasons why efforts to come up with a fail-safe method for determining the *ratio* of a case have proved futile.

Often it will be apparent that even the court that decided the case was not certain about the *ratio*. A judge may offer more than one line of reasoning for the result. There may be more than one set of reasons. One judge will offer this reason and another judge that reason. The very existence of concurring reasons for judgment demonstrates the inability of the court to agree on the precise reason for deciding the case.

Even if the judge who wrote the decision tries to state the *ratio*, that judge cannot control the way in which the decision will read in the future. If the judge were able to do so, the judge would become a mini-legislature with virtually unconstrained power to make law. The judge is simply deciding one case, and it will be for later courts to interpret the decision and determine the *ratio* and evaluate the extent of its worth as a precedent.

The most important reason why it is difficult to fix on the precedential value of a decision takes us back to the facts. The common law process is one in which general propositions are constantly tested by factual variations. Sometimes the factual variations are hypotheticals imagined by law professors, lawyers, and judges designed to probe the limits of the reasoning. Sometimes the factual variations arise in actual litigation. Rarely, if ever, will precisely the same facts arise. Subsequent courts will have to determine which facts were central to the prior determination and whether the facts of the case now being decided are materially different.

The distinction between the *ratio* of a case, which is binding, and *obiter dicta*, which are not binding, is notoriously difficult to draw, but it represents a vitally important aspect of the common law tradition of precedent. It is a distinction that allows the law to achieve an appropriate balance between certainty, on the one hand, and growth and creativity, on the other. The authority of precedent provides the legal system with stability and predictability, while the ability to probe and test the limits of the reasoning of prior decisions allows the law to respond to changing mores and conditions and to purge itself of past missteps. As Justice Brian Dickson explained in a 1980 lecture, "By the genius of distinguishing facts the courts escaped the folly of perpetuating to eternity, principles unsuited to modern circumstances."[8] The flexibility at play in the analysis of prior judgments is one of the ways the common law develops. Judges should, and generally do, refuse to stifle the process of development by placing undue weight on every word and phrase uttered in the prior decision.

What was necessary for the prior decision and what was not? The judge writing the decision would not have included the passage if he or she did not think it important, but the subsequent court may not agree with that assessment. Judges try to make their judgments readable, understandable, and persuasive. When deciding a specific point, it will often serve the explanatory effort to stray from what is strictly necessary and use hypothetical examples and even the odd rhetorical flourish. Some of these examples and flourishes will survive as valuable insights worthy of repetition, but inevitably others will flounder.

Some *obiter* statements prove to be persuasive and workable in practice. They are followed in later decisions and become the law. *Obiter* statements become the law not because other judges are bound to follow them but because experience demonstrates their wisdom and soundness. As an English legal scholar observed, "*[D]icta* are of varying degrees of persuasiveness."[9] At one end of the scale are the *obiter* statements that reflect the considered opinion of all nine members of the Supreme Court of Canada who have heard a case upon which leave to appeal was granted because it raises a point of public importance. At the other end of the scale are statements that are made in passing by one judge sitting alone or with two others and without the reflection and consideration that is to be expected when a binding pronouncement is intended. In the words of an early

English case dismissing the authority of an *obiter* statement, "It was not only an *obiter dictum*, but a very divaricating *dictum*."[10]

In this constant process of testing the appropriateness of applying prior judicial statements to new situations, some decisions emerge as resting upon or establishing a rule or principle that proves to be sound and reliable. Those are the decisions that fit comfortably with generally prevailing legal norms and that consistently yield just results. They grow in precedential stature over time, and their *ratios* are read generously.

The classic example is the 1932 decision of the House of Lords in *Donoghue v Stevenson*,[11] discussed in chapters 3 and 5. When deciding that a ginger beer manufacturer could be liable to a consumer who suffered injury because the product was defective, Lord Atkin enunciated the "good neighbour" principle for establishing a duty of care in tort law. The case went on appeal to the House of Lords on a preliminary ruling on a point of Scottish law, and thus all that Lord Atkin decided was that it was *possible* that the claim would succeed at trial. When the decision was first released, it was far from certain that the good neighbour principle would gain traction as the dominant idea in the common law of negligence. It was for subsequent courts to determine how broadly or how narrowly that principle should apply. Did it apply only to defective food products? Did it extend to all manufactured goods? Should it govern other forms of negligent conduct outside the realm of product liability? Subsequent courts tested and applied the good neighbour principle to these and many other cases. As they adopted and reshaped the principle to meet unforeseen facts, it proved to be a powerful and enduring tool that has shaped a huge part of modern tort law.

Other decisions fare less well. When tested with new fact situations, they prove less resilient. The reasoning may prove lacking in congruence with related legal principles and doctrines. When their application fails to satisfy the demands of justice, their *ratio* is read narrowly, and even some decisions of the highest appellate courts wither and end up standing as authority for little more than the law on the exact facts of the case they decided.[12] They are, in Lord Denning's colourful words, dismissively marked "not to be looked at again."[13]

Most decisions probably fall somewhere in between. When the House of Lords decided in *Rylands v Fletcher*[14] that a non-negligent landowner was strictly liable for damage caused by water that escaped from a reservoir he built on his land, the decision did not lead to a significant expansion of strict liability. It was extended to apply to any dangerous substance that is accumulated on land and escapes, but it has been restricted to neighbouring occupiers, and the strict liability it imposes remains an exception to the dominant theme in modern tort law of fault-based liability.

So the answer to the question "What does a case decide?" is usually "Only time will tell." We will probe and test the reasoning as new facts emerge. It is through the crucible of the common law fact-specific method that we determine the precedential value of a prior decision.

## "Get It Right" or Follow the Precedent?

If a prior decision cannot be distinguished, and if the prior judicial statement relied on by a litigant cannot be characterized as *obiter dicta*, the judge who is persuaded that the precedent yields the wrong answer is left with a stark choice. The judge must follow the decision and accept what seems to be an unjust result or overrule the decision and undermine the certainty of the law. The conventional view is that the judges must follow the decision, however much they may disagree with it. As Lord Reid stated when reluctantly following a criminal law decision from which he had dissented, "I still think the decision was wrong ... But I think that however wrong or anomalous the decision may be it must stand ... unless and until it is altered by Parliament."[15] Some American judges "repeat" their dissents each time the issue arises.[16] In my view, it is preferable for judges to follow Lord Reid's example and, unless they can justify overruling the precedent, concede that they are bound to follow it, although they continue to believe that the precedent is wrong.[17]

When can the court overrule or refuse to follow a precedent? Obviously, much will depend upon the provenance of the prior decision and the place in the judicial hierarchy occupied by the judge who has to decide. A judge of a lower court is obliged to follow the prior decisions of a higher court. However, if the decision cited as a precedent emanates from the same court on which the judge sits, as I will explain, the law accepts that under certain circumstances the prior decision can be overruled.

## *Vertical Precedent*

Past decisions may be divided into two categories.[18] First are decisions of courts that occupy a higher position in the judicial hierarchy and that attract the weight of vertical precedent. Under the category of vertical precedent, courts lower in the judicial hierarchy are required to follow the decisions of higher courts. Vertical precedent is implicit in the hierarchical nature of our court system and the division of labour between the various levels. It is an element of an orderly and efficient scheme of justice. As a judge of the Court of Appeal for Ontario, I am required to follow the decisions of the Supreme Court of Canada. Trial judges are required to follow the decisions of both the Court of Appeal and the Supreme Court of Canada.

Is a judge lower in the judicial hierarchy bound to follow statements by higher courts that were not necessary for the decision and are therefore *obiter* in nature? At one time, it was thought that lower courts were bound to follow everything said by the Supreme Court of Canada, however tangential the statement may have been to the dispositive facts and law at issue. The high-water mark for the authority of *obiter* statements was set in a 1980 judgment by Justice Julien Chouinard. In a much-criticized passage, he stated that even where "it was not absolutely necessary" to rule on the point "in order to dispose of the appeal," the *obiter* statement from the Supreme Court "must prevail."[19] The Supreme Court has since rejected that proposition. In the words of Justice Ian Binnie, "The notion that each phrase in a judgment of this Court should be treated as if enacted in a statute is not supported by the cases and is inconsistent with the basic fundamental principle that the common law develops by experience."[20]

On the other hand, it is often difficult to discern exactly where the *ratio* of a decision ends and where the *obiter* begins. Again to quote Justice Binnie, the jurisprudential "weight decreases as one moves from the dispositive *ratio decidendi* to a wider circle of analysis."[21] Where the wider circle of analysis reflects the appellate court's considered view of an area of law and is clearly intended to provide guidance for the future, a judge lower in the hierarchy will naturally be very hesitant to depart from the statement, even though it may technically qualify as *obiter* but may do so where statement appears to conflict with other decisions.[22]

*Obiter* statements of an intermediate appellate court, it seems to me, fall into a different category. The law-making role of an intermediate appellate court is necessarily more constrained than that of the Supreme Court of Canada. Intermediate appellate courts are more focused on the specifics of the cases they hear. They hear a large number of cases and, unlike the Supreme Court, do not sit *en banc* to allow all members of the court to express their views on all the important legal issues. The nature and volume of cases intermediate courts decide and the fact that they ordinarily sit in panels of only three judges are factors to be taken into account when considering the weight to be attached to *obiter* statements made by one judge in one case. However, there are carefully considered *obiter* statements from intermediate appellate courts that should and will be ordinarily respected, especially where it is clear that the court has deliberately taken on the task of surveying a subject or area of law with a view to clarifying the law for the future.

## Horizontal Precedent

When it comes to decisions of courts at the same level, referred to as horizontal precedent, the situation becomes more complicated. With horizontal precedent, in most jurisdictions, distinctions are drawn between trial and appellate courts and between intermediate appellate courts and supreme or apex courts that occupy the highest level of judicial authority in the country.

### TRIAL COURTS

A trial judge is not strictly bound to follow the decisions of another trial judge of the same court. However, trial judges will ordinarily follow decisions of their colleagues absent strong reasons to the contrary. The reasons to the contrary include: the authority of the prior decision has been undermined by subsequent decisions; the decision was reached without consideration of a relevant statute or binding authority; or the decision was not fully considered but given "where the exigencies of the trial require an immediate decision without opportunity to fully consult authority."[23] The obligation to follow another trial decision is sometimes expressed as a matter of "comity" (courtesy and respect), but the better reason is that not to do so "will unsettle the law" and confront the "unhappy litigant ... with conflicting opinions emanating from the same court and therefore of the same legal weight."[24]

Much will depend upon the nature of the trial decision relied upon as a precedent. If it is a fully and carefully considered decision based upon full argument and obviously intended to provide guidance for the future, certainty and predictability favour standing by that decision.

There are, however, good reasons why the doctrine of precedent does and should allow room for one trial judge to depart from a colleague's decision. The job of a trial judge is to find the facts and focus on the demands of justice in each particular case. Trial judges know that their decisions will be cited as authority in subsequent cases, but their essential and primary task is to focus on the details of the case they have to decide rather than to settle the law. In most instances, they decide the case and write their reasons accordingly. While the interests of certainty and predictability militate in favour of adhering to decisions of coordinate authority, imposing a strict requirement on trial judges to follow decisions of their colleagues would, I think, introduce a level of undue rigidity. As I argue in chapter 4, trial courts and their focus on the facts and details of individual cases are the lifeblood of the common law tradition. New cases bring new twists on seemingly familiar problems, and it is the collective wisdom that can be gleaned from the judgments of different judges confronting new facts that keeps the common law vital. That vitality could be stymied if every trial judge strictly had to follow every decision of every other trial judge.

### APPELLATE COURTS

Different considerations apply at the appellate level. Appellate courts treat their past decisions as binding and will ordinarily not depart from one of their own prior decisions. This flows from the function performed by appellate courts. Appellate courts are constrained by the standard of review, a topic discussed in chapter 10. They do not retry cases as if at first instance but exercise a supervisory legal function. They are charged with the duty to oversee the work of the trial courts and to correct legal errors. For the vast majority of cases, they are the court of last resort, as very few cases are granted leave to appeal to the Supreme Court. While appellate courts are very much concerned about the rights and wrongs of particular cases, their capacity to "get it right" is necessarily tempered by their duty to provide general guidance on the law. If "getting it right" means unduly sacrificing the clarity and coherence of the applicable law, the latter must prevail. The appellate judge is necessarily preoccupied with the overall integrity of the legal system. So when an appellate judge says something in Jane's case, that judge knows and intends that a future court will do the same in Kyra's case.

However, the duty to adhere to past decisions is not absolute, and appellate courts now accept that there are times when a prior decision can be overruled. It is here that we confront the fundamental tension between the need for certainty and predictability and the desirability of reaching a just result in the specific case to be decided. When we reach the point at which the injustice produced by adhering to a precedent exceeds the justice to be gained from stability and certainty, appellate courts may overrule their own prior decisions.

In a 1944 decision,[25] the English Court of Appeal announced the traditional and relatively strict rule for intermediate level courts. The rule admitted only three narrow exceptions, and the list certainly did not include a situation where the decision is deemed to be wrong. First, if the court is confronted with conflicting decisions – something that could happen only through inadvertence – it can decide which one to follow. Second, the court is not bound to follow one of its prior decisions that "cannot, in its opinion, stand with a decision of the House of Lords."[26] Third is the rather slippery *per incuriam* category: the court is not bound to follow a decision of its own if it is satisfied that an earlier decision was given in ignorance of the terms of a statute, rule, or an earlier binding decision. I say "slippery" because it is almost always possible to cite authority and frame an argument in a different light. The doctrine of precedent would be rendered utterly unstable if the binding effect of a decision were dependent upon "whether, in the opinion of succeeding courts on an examination of the available record, the case was properly argued or not."[27]

As intermediate appellate courts have become more willing to reconsider their past decisions, resort to the *per incuriam* principle has become less necessary and less frequent. In its place we find identified a more flexible and fully articulated factor that focuses on an assessment of the nature of the decision. As the Manitoba Court of Appeal put it, a court will be more prepared to overrule a purely conclusory decision than one that was fully reasoned: "The court's freedom to depart from a prior, incorrect decision should logically increase in direct proportion to the extent to which that prior decision lacks a fully reasoned, analytically sound foundation."[28]

It has also been held that an appellate court is not bound to follow a prior decision that was based on a "manifest slip or error."[29] This category has been applied to allow a court to correct "an error so obvious and clear that, as soon as pointed out, it is beyond any argument."[30] Whether it is because such obvious errors are rarely encountered or because it is often recognized that the clarity of an error is merely in the eye of the beholder, this escape from precedent is not commonly used.

The practice of the Ontario Court of Appeal and several other Canadian intermediate courts of appeal[31] is that a three-judge panel will not overrule one of our own previous decisions. Only a panel of five judges can do so. In Ontario, if a party intends to ask us to overrule a decision, an application is made to the Chief Justice asking the court to strike a five-judge panel. Sometimes the Chief Justice will strike a five-judge panel on his or her own initiative, or at the suggestion of a judge or panel of judges. This occurs particularly where there appear to be conflicting decisions.[32] In other provinces, the decision to strike a five-judge court is made by a panel of three judges.[33]

I think there are valid reasons for an intermediate court to take a stricter view of precedent than the more relaxed approach that prevails at apex courts. An obvious difference is that, if a decision of an intermediate appellate court needs to be overruled, the problem can be fixed by the highest court in the land. Apex courts also have the advantage of a different perspective. A central purpose of having an apex court is that it can focus on the most difficult and contentious legal issues and provide general guidance to the country as a whole. The Supreme Court decides relatively few cases, and the cases it does hear are specifically selected for their public importance. This both allows and encourages the Supreme Court to adopt an expansive role in its decision-making authority.

When the House of Lords announced that it would no longer be strictly bound by its prior decisions, it made it clear that the change it announced was "not intended to affect the use of precedent elsewhere,"[34] and it subsequently affirmed that the English Court of Appeal remained obliged to follow its own decisions.[35] Similarly, the Supreme Court of Canada is now prepared to depart from its prior decisions but has said nothing to alter the proposition that an intermediate court of appeal should exercise considerable caution and restraint before departing from one of its own decisions. However, just as the Supreme Court has become more willing to reconsider its past decisions, so too have the intermediate appellate courts.

In *Polowin*,[36] a 2005 judgment written by Justice John Laskin, our court explained its approach to precedent and overruling prior decisions. Justice Laskin considered the five factors identified by the Supreme Court of Canada in the late 1980s and 1990s that I will discuss below. He described the list as a "useful, though not exhaustive, checklist for provincial appellate courts."[37] The court must "weigh the advantages and disadvantages of correcting the error," focusing on its nature and "the effect and future impact of either correcting it or maintaining it," taking into account "the effect and impact on the parties and future litigants" and "on the integrity and administration of our justice system."[38]

At first blush, the case for overruling the prior decision in *Polowin* did not seem to be very strong. The point at issue was the interpretation of a term in a standard motor-vehicle insurance policy. The Supreme Court of Canada had refused leave to appeal our earlier decision, and the contested wording of the standard insurance policy had already been changed by legislation. None of the five factors identified by the Supreme Court of Canada's list to justify a departure from the precedent were present. However, Justice Laskin gave persuasive reasons why the earlier decision should be overruled. The wording of the contested provision was used across Canada, and the courts of two provinces had questioned our court's previous decision and come to the opposite conclusion. The result was that the same provision meant different things in different provinces. There is a strong case to be made for consistency across the country. Although the actual result had been reversed by legislation, there was a broader issue of the interpretation of standard terms that needed to be clarified. The value of certainty was not undermined, as the prior ruling was not one that anyone would have relied on to plan their affairs.

While being wrong may not be enough, the error of the earlier decision weighed heavily in the balance. The earlier panel had been presented with an incomplete account of the legislative history, and the fuller record now available presented a very different picture of the purpose and meaning of the contested policy term.[39] The prior decision was of recent vintage, had not been reaffirmed, and, as Justice Laskin put it, "Better then to correct an error early than to let it settle in."[40] A related point is that in a system where leave to appeal to the Supreme Court is granted only on questions of national importance, an intermediate court cannot always rely on the apex court to correct its errors. It was far from clear that the Supreme Court would grant leave to appeal if the Court of Appeal refused to reconsider the prior decision. "For the people of Ontario, the Court of Appeal for Ontario is the final court in the vast majority of cases."[41] This means that, when it comes to precedent, there are times when an intermediate court must assume the mantle of an apex court.

### APEX COURTS[42]

While common law judges have always been guided by the experience of the past, it was not until the late nineteenth century that *stare decisis* crystallized as a firm rule. Apex courts became wedded to the proposition that certainty and predictability should prevail at all costs and that if the law laid down in a prior ruling was to change, it would require an act of Parliament to bring about that change. In 1898, the Earl of Halsbury, Lord Chancellor, proclaimed, "[O]nce given upon a point of law," a decision of the House of Lords "is conclusive upon this House afterwards, and that it is impossible to raise that question again." This meant that a decided point of law could never be argued afresh and that the earlier decision could never be reversed.[43] The Supreme Court of Canada took a similar approach.[44]

Such an unbending adherence to precedent proved to be unworkable. There are several reasons for this.

First, as I argued in chapter 3, the law necessarily evolves with changing social and economic conditions. It would surely be odd if common law judges had no ability whatsoever to change the law they themselves had made. Parliament and the legislatures are routinely preoccupied with larger issues of politics and policy, and the intricacies of the common law regularly escape their attention.[45] As a practical matter, there is often no other place to go for reform and change, apart from the courts. As the common law emanates from the courts in the first place, it seems inevitable that the courts should retain some capacity to develop the law as circumstances change, even if that means reversing a prior decision. As the Supreme Court of the United Kingdom put it in a 2016 decision,[46] *R v Jogee*,[47] "[I]f a wrong turn has been taken, it should be corrected," and, since the court had created the problem, it was for the court to set the matter right rather than leave it to Parliament.[47]

Another problem is the recognition that the commitment to prec-edent will not always prevent lawyers and judges from finding creative ways to avoid or evade troublesome precedents. Forced to meet the current demands of justice, courts craft complex exceptions or intricate distinctions to reach just results. Sometimes we reach the point at which clarity and certainty, the very goals precedent is meant to serve, will be undermined if we continue to pretend that a hoary old precedent actually reflects the current state of the law.

By the mid-twentieth century, it was accepted that adherence to precedent had to soften. Strict and unquestioning adherence to precedent put the law into a straitjacket. It was inconsistent with the suppler notion of precedent that prevailed in earlier times that had given the courts more freedom to reshape the law as circumstances required. Both the House of Lords and the Supreme Court of Canada announced that while they would ordinarily follow their past deci-sions, they would no longer be strictly bound by them.

At first, the change was explained only in the most general way. In 1966, the House of Lords issued its famous *Practice Statement (Ju-dicial Precedent)*[48] announcing that it now recognized that "too rigid adherence to precedent may lead to injustice in a particular case and also unduly restrict the proper development of the law." The Lord Chancellor, Lord Gardiner, cautioned that the use of precedent re-mained "an indispensable foundation upon which to decide what is the law and its application to individual cases," as "[i]t provides at least some degree of certainty upon which individuals can rely in the conduct of their affairs, as well as a basis for orderly development of legal rules." However, while the House would continue to treat its decisions as "normally binding," it would feel free to "depart from a previous decision when it appears right to do so." The only guidance as to when it would appear "right to do so" was the observation that the House would "bear in mind the danger of disturbing retrospec-tively the basis on which contracts, settlements of property and fiscal arrangements have been entered into," as well as "the especial need for certainty as to the criminal law."

The Supreme Court of Canada accepted the possibility of overrul-ing one of its prior decisions in the late 1950s[49] but initially gave little guidance as to when this would be appropriate. The court has con-sistently maintained that it will do so only where there are "compel-ling reasons,"[50] but it has overruled past decisions with increasing frequency, particularly in *Charter* litigation.

I suggest that we can divide this development into three stages during which the Supreme Court has moved gradually but steadily away from strict adherence to precedent and towards a much greater willingness to reshape the law.

In the first phase, from the late 1950s to the 1980s, the court acknowledged that it could overrule a prior decision, but it rarely acted on that power, and even when it did, it offered little or no explanation for why it saw fit to do so.[51]

The second phase was reached in the late 1990s, when the court looked back on the experience reflected by the cases and adopted a non-exhaustive list of factors identifying when it would be appropriate to overturn a precedent. The list was first articulated by Dickson CJ in a 1988 dissenting judgment,[52] but later adopted by the court.[53] Each of these factors takes into account the values that underlie the doctrine of precedent itself. The factors reflect what a more recent case describes as a "balancing exercise between the two important values of correctness and certainty."[54]

First, the Court will reconsider decisions that are inconsistent with or fail to reflect the values of the *Charter of Rights and Freedoms*. This reflects the view that the *Charter* brought about a fundamental change to our legal system and, that given the supremacy of the Constitution, *Charter* rights and values must prevail. The doctrine of precedent is not so strict as to countenance giving priority to a judicial pronouncement over the supreme law of the land. As the court stated in its 2013 decision striking down provisions of the *Criminal Code* dealing with prostitution laws that it had upheld[55] just over twenty years earlier, "[T]he common law principle of *stare decisis* is subordinate to the Constitution and cannot require a court to uphold a law which is unconstitutional."[56]

Second, where a decision has been "attenuated" by subsequent decisions, it may be appropriate to overrule that earlier decision. Some decisions simply do not withstand the test of time. They are qualified and distinguished to the point that they no longer accurately reflect the state of the law. The interests of certainty and predictability are better served by simply abandoning the prior ruling and admitting that it should no longer be followed.[57]

The third factor is where the social, political, or economic assumptions underlying a previous decision are no longer valid in contemporary society. As I will explain below, this has become a very significant factor in *Charter* ligation where parties are able to present a comprehensive factual record to demonstrate that the actual operation and effect of a law is other than what was found or assumed by the court when it made a prior determination of constitutional validity. But even in non-*Charter* cases, changed circumstances may justify departing from a prior ruling. In a 1978 decision, the Supreme Court recognized a wife's entitlement to a share in property held in her husband's name on the basis that failure to recognize her indirect contribution would unjustly enrich her spouse.[58] The court adopted the dissenting opinion in a recent decision to the contrary[59] on the basis that the majority opinion in the former case failed to reflect modern social reality. The court noted that we now have a "more enlightened attitude toward the status of women" and a growing recognition of "the work of a woman in the management of the home and the rearing of children ... as an economic contribution to the family unit."[60]

The fourth factor is similar to the second. Some decisions fail to articulate a workable rule or standard having content sufficient to guide behaviour. Adhering to the decision produces uncertainty, and it is better, in the name of predictability, simply to overrule it. For example, in a 1982 decision the Court concluded that the category of *persona designata* to identify certain decisions from which there could be no appeal "was a source of more confusion than enlightenment" and that the very values underlying precedent – certainty and predictability – favoured overruling a previous decision in order to get rid of the troublesome doctrine.[61]

The fifth factor identified in the 1980s involved considerations peculiar to individual rights and the criminal law. The court said it would not ordinarily overrule a prior decision where the effect would be to expand the reach of criminal liability or restrict the liberty of the subject. As Dickson CJ put it, "It is not for the courts to create new offences, or to broaden the net of liability, particularly as changes in the law through judicial decision operate retrospectively."[62] In subsequent cases, the Supreme Court reiterated the principle that it should hesitate to change the law where doing so would expand the scope of criminal liability.[63] The court has also stated that it "should be particularly careful before reversing a precedent where the effect is to diminish *Charter* protection."[64] Conversely, the court will feel less constrained when convinced that a prior decision restricting the liberty of the subject was wrongly decided.[65] However, the courts have not always adhered to the idea that they should not overrule a precedent where the effect would be to expand criminal liability. For example, in 1992, the House of Lords overruled the common law rule that a husband cannot be found guilty of raping his own wife,[66] and the Supreme Court of Canada has reversed *Charter* decisions and common law rules favourable to the accused on more than one occasion,[67] although when doing so in one case, the Court stated that it "should be particularly careful before reversing a precedent where the effect is to diminish *Charter* protection."[68]

Notably absent from this list of reasons to depart from precedent is the suggestion that a decision can be overruled simply because a subsequent court thinks it was wrongly decided. While only prior decisions that the court now thinks are wrong are candidates for reversal, the doctrine of precedent would disappear if wrongness alone were sufficient grounds for overruling, for it would mean that the Court could always ignore decisions with which it did not agree.

The pattern of recent decisions suggests that we may have entered a third phase reflecting a growing willingness of the court to depart from past rulings with which the judges no longer agree, particularly in *Charter* cases. The court has insisted that it "does not and should not lightly overrule its prior decisions, particularly when they have been elaborated consistently over a number of years and when they represent the considered view of firm majorities."[69] However, there is now a long and growing list of cases where the Supreme Court has overruled its own prior *Charter* decisions.[70] The willingness of today's Supreme Court of Canada to review its prior decisions is striking, particularly when compared to the rigid view the same institution took fifty or sixty years earlier. This may be explained, at least in part, by the changed role played by the court in the modern era. Again, we can identify three stages of development.

First, Parliament gave the court control over its own docket in 1975 when as-of-right appeals were largely abolished and the leave to appeal requirement was introduced. Before 1975, virtually any judgment could be appealed to the Supreme Court, and it heard a significant number of cases that did not raise issues of public importance. The court no longer exercises an error-correction function, and it now hears only about eighty cases per year. In most of these cases,[71] litigants must now apply to the court for leave to appeal, and the court grants leave only in cases that raise issues of national importance. By reshaping the jurisdiction and function of the court through the leave to appeal process, Parliament implicitly invited

the court to focus its attention on cases raising contentious legal issues where the law is unsettled. When the leave to appeal process
was introduced, Chief Justice Bora Laskin wrote in the *Canadian Bar
Review* that this change meant that the court's "main function is to
oversee the development of the law" and "to give guidance in articulate reasons ... on issues of national concern."[72]

Second, the introduction of the *Charter of Rights and Freedoms* in
1982 represented a major change to the fabric of Canadian law. As I
will explain in chapter 11, the *Charter* changed the role of the courts
in Canada's modern democratic society, and with that change came
a significant law-making function for the Supreme Court. This function necessarily involves reconsideration of some of the court's past
decisions.

Now, more than thirty years after the *Charter*'s introduction, we
seem to have reached a third stage of development. Initially, the
*Charter* provided the justification for reconsidering pre-*Charter* decisions. But now the court is reconsidering and reversing its own post-
*Charter* decisions with some frequency. When the Supreme Court
refuses to overrule, it regularly does so on the basis that there is no
reason to think that the prior decision was wrongly decided.[73] The
court has never said that it can overrule any decision it thinks was
wrong. However, implicit in the court's current approach to precedent, at least in relation to *Charter* rights, is that "getting it right"
is the dominant concern and that certainty and predictability, the
considerations that dominated in an earlier era, have faded into the
background.

As I have already noted, the court has stated that "*stare decisis* is
subordinate to the Constitution and cannot require a court to uphold
a law which is unconstitutional."[74] I am not sure how much this tells
us as the determination of whether or not a law is unconstitutional
must turn largely upon the relevant precedents. Other cases suggest
restraint. In *Henry*, a *Charter* decision overruling an earlier case, Binnie J provided a list of factors that suggest that "getting it right" is
not the only consideration:

1. The prior decision departed from the purpose of a *Charter* provision as articulated in an earlier precedent.
2. Experience shows that the prior decision is unworkable, as its
   application is unnecessarily complex and technical.

3. The prior decision is contrary to sound principle.
4. The prior decision results in unfairness.[75]

There are sound reasons to justify overruling a constitutional decision that, with the benefit of hindsight and experience, a later court
can say was wrongly decided. The Constitution is the fundamental
law of the land. Missteps in other areas can be fixed by the legislature, but those on constitutional issues are more difficult to repair,
requiring either a constitutional amendment or, in the case of most
*Charter* decisions, resort to the notwithstanding clause.[76] We can tolerate compromises in other areas of the law where the interests of
certainty and predictability may trump correctness. But if precedent
has proved to be unworkable or problematic in realizing the purpose
of a *Charter* guarantee, better to overrule it than to allow it to frus-
trate our basic law and our fundamental rights and freedoms. This is
especially so where the precedent denies or narrows a *Charter* right,
whereas if overruling would cut back on a *Charter* right previously
recognized, the Supreme Court is reluctant to do so.[77]

On the other hand, considerations of institutional integrity suggest that courts should be cautious about too readily overruling
*Charter* decisions. Judicial review under the *Charter* is contentious
and often controversial.[78] *Charter* rights and freedoms are rooted in
the fundamental values of our political and legal tradition. One can
expect and accept a process of evolution and change to meet new
circumstances, but to make frequent departures from past decisions
would be inconsistent with the image of a permanence implicit in
a constitution. The public, the politicians, and the legal community
are entitled to expect a body of stable and predictable doctrine upon
which they can rely. If the courts routinely overrule past decisions,
the judicial process takes on the appearance of a political game in
which the personal views of the judges are all that counts.

In *Canada (Attorney General) v Bedford,*[79] a *Charter* challenge to laws
related to prostitution, and in *Carter v Canada (Attorney General),*[80]
which dealt with the prohibition of assisted suicide, the applicants
faced prior rulings of the Supreme Court upholding the very laws
they contested.[81] In both cases, the applicants mounted a substantial
factual record that painted a different picture of the contested laws'
impact on *Charter* rights, raising legal arguments that had not been
advanced in the earlier cases. In both cases, the Supreme Court held

that it was open to the trial judge to consider the new evidence, and, if persuaded that it made out a *Charter* breach, to strike down the legislation despite the earlier ruling. While insisting that precedent is "the foundational principle upon which the common law relies" and that "[c]ertainty in the law requires that courts follow and apply authoritative precedents,"[82] the court held that a trial judge "can consider and decide arguments based on *Charter* provisions that were not raised in the earlier case" as well as "new legal issues ... raised as a consequence of significant developments in the law" or a change "in the circumstances or evidence that fundamentally shifts the parameters of debate."[83]

The same proposition was applied in *Saskatchewan Federation of Labour*,[84] a case that did not involve a fresh factual record. In the face of Supreme Court of Canada authority that the *Charter* right to freedom of association did not protect the right to strike,[85] a trial judge struck down legislation banning strikes by public sector unions. The Supreme Court agreed with his right to do so: "Given the fundamental shift in the scope of s. 2(d) ... the trial judge was entitled to depart from precedent and consider the issue in accordance with this Court's revitalized interpretation of [freedom of association]."[86]

In *Bedford*, the court reversed its prior ruling upholding *Criminal Code* provisions dealing with prostitution on the ground that the factual record was different. To justify that result, the court also overruled another prior ruling,[87] now declaring that a trial judge's factual findings relating to the impact and effect of legislation, known to lawyers as "social and legislative" facts, attract a very high level of deference on appeal.

This significantly attenuates the doctrine of precedent. It means that a trial judge can now depart from an earlier ruling of the Supreme Court by accepting a new factual argument that the impact of the legislation brings it into conflict with the *Charter*. Social and legislative facts are essentially matters of opinion that are proved by tendering expert social science evidence. On issues of this kind, the line between legal argument and fact is difficult to draw. However, if the Supreme Court sticks to what it said, the trial judge's findings are entitled to deference on appeal. This means that neither the court of appeal nor the Supreme Court of Canada can interfere with the trial judge's decision striking down a law in the face of a prior Supreme Court ruling on the grounds that the facts have changed, unless the trial decision reveals "palpable and overriding error."[88] This weakens the force of precedent and significantly diminishes the capacity of appellate courts, including the Supreme Court of Canada, to have the final word on the constitutionality of legislation.

I find the proposition that trial judges effectively have the last say on the constitutionality of legislation troubling and problematic. We could well have different trial judges in different provinces coming to opposite conclusions on the constitutionality of legislation based upon expert opinion evidence. It is quite conceivable that both findings could be reasonable and effectively immune to appellate review. How would the Supreme Court deal with conflicting but reasonable findings by different trial judges in different provinces on the constitutionality of the same legislation?[89]

### ARE DECISIONS THE SUPREME COURT IS LIKELY TO OVERRULE BINDING ON LOWER COURTS?

If the Supreme Court is increasingly prepared to depart from its own prior decisions, what does a trial judge or intermediate appellate court do when faced with a Supreme Court decision that it thinks the Supreme Court itself is likely to overrule? Do the lower courts have to obey the prior ruling of the Supreme Court and leave it to the litigants to take the case higher, or is it permissible for the lower court to predict the outcome at the Supreme Court and rule accordingly?

In 2011, the Federal Court of Appeal was confronted with a much criticized 1978 decision of the Supreme Court interpreting a provision of the *Income Tax Act*. Another panel of the Federal Court of Appeal had carefully considered the 1978 Supreme Court decision in 2006, and, in light of the criticism the 1978 decision had attracted as well as the practical difficulties it had caused, the 2006 panel declined to follow it.[90] The 2011 panel decided that it was bound to follow its own decision and not that of the Supreme Court. The Supreme Court of Canada held that the Federal Court was wrong, both in 2006 and in 2011, not to follow the problematic 1978 Supreme Court decision.[91] Writing for the Supreme Court, Rothstein J said that the Federal Court of Appeal should have followed the 1978 decision, providing reasons explaining why the 1978 decision was problematic. It was for the Supreme Court to overrule itself, and that is what the court proceeded to do.

However, as noted above, the decisions in *Bedford*, *Carter*, and *Saskatchewan Federation of Labour* indicate a very different approach in *Charter* cases. The Supreme Court appears to have opened the door to permit trial judges to refuse to follow earlier Supreme Court *Charter* decisions where there have been significant changes in fact or law. Not only is the Supreme Court prepared to overrule its own rulings, the court places such a high premium on "getting it right" in *Charter* cases that it is prepared to allow, if not encourage, lower courts to depart from the court's earlier *Charter* pronouncements if either or both the factual and legal landscape have changed. The Supreme Court retains the last word, but even that has been attenuated by the holding in *Bedford* and *Carter* that findings on social and legislative facts are entitled to deference on appeal.

## Conclusion

Precedent is a foundational principle of the common law. But the weight attached to precedent cannot be reduced to a set of mechanical rules. It is the starting point to legal analysis. For most disputes, precedent will be decisive. But the capacity of the common law to evolve is inconsistent with rigid, unbending adherence to past decisions. We must keep in mind that the ultimate purpose of precedent is to foster certainty, predictability, and coherence in the law. Blind adherence to *stare decisis* may not only perpetuate an unjust rule but may also conflict with the very purpose of the doctrine itself.

The doctrine of precedent is a prime example of the kind of disciplined decision-making I discussed in chapter 6. It is easy to follow precedents with which we agree. The hard part of precedent kicks in when we disagree with the prior ruling or with the result it produces in the case at hand, but we know that we must allow the values of certainty and predictability to prevail.

However, the doctrine of precedent is also a prime example of the principled approach to legal reasoning that I discussed in chapter 5. Those principles recognize that certainty and predictability exact the price of injustice when circumstances unforeseen by past decisions arise. This creates a tension between, on the one hand, the certainty and predictability we need to satisfy the rule of law and achieve systemic justice, and, on the other hand, our perfectly proper concern over achieving justice in the individual cases we decide. And, in the words of Lord Denning, a great English judge notable for his impatience with what he regarded as the dead hand of the past, "The doctrine of precedent does not compel your Lordships to follow the wrong path until you fall over the edge of the cliff."[92]

As we edge towards that cliff, we have various tools at our disposal. We may be able to distinguish the precedent, read it narrowly, or find exceptions or qualifications to restrict its reach. Over time, this may so undermine the precedent that it becomes unstable, and it is better, in the name of certainty and predictability – the very goals precedent is meant to serve – that it be jettisoned. Sometimes we realize that the precedent was simply wrongly decided or that it was the product of another era when very different conditions prevailed. But when we are tempted to jettison a precedent to avoid the injustice side of the cliff, we must remain mindful to avoid falling off the other side into uncertainty and *ad hoc* decision-making.

Neil Duxbury, an English legal scholar argues, "The common law requires not an unassailable but a strong rebuttable presumption that earlier decisions be followed."[93] I suggest that the "strong rebuttable presumption" approach to precedent accurately reflects the way intermediate appellate courts in Canada use precedent. When it comes to apex courts, some scholars argue that the presumption should shift. Decisions now thought to be wrong should be overruled, "unless their retention can be justified in the circumstances by overriding *stare decisis* values."[94] That shift in presumption has not been formally accepted by our Supreme Court, nor, so far as I am aware, by any other common law apex court. However, as the number of instances in which the Supreme Court reverses itself rises, it may be that the shift in presumption accurately reflects the direction that precedent has taken in the modern era.

## Chapter 8

# Authority: What Counts?

I argued in chapter 6 that judges have a legal and professional obligation to provide reasons for their decisions based upon legally accepted sources. But what is a legally accepted source? It may come as a surprise that this question is not readily answered and that the acceptability and weight attached to legal sources shifts over time.

In this chapter, I will discuss the sources judges look to when deciding cases that are not readily determined by the governing statutes and case law. I will focus, in particular, on two areas where we have seen significant changes in our legal culture over the past fifty years. First, the influence of English judicial decisions in Canadian courts. Second, the use of scholarly articles. I will discuss the waning influence of the former and the rising prominence of the latter. I will argue that these marked shifts in judicial practice stem largely from the demise of the narrowly legalistic version of legal formalism that prevailed in Canada until the 1970s and 1980s.

## Binding and Persuasive Authority

There is a basic distinction to be drawn between what is regarded as binding authority and what is considered to be an acceptable source that does not bind the court but that may carry persuasive weight. Binding authority includes any relevant provision of the Constitution, relevant statutes, and governing precedential judicial rulings. It is universally accepted that the Constitution and the statutes enacted by Parliament or the provincial legislature and regulations enacted pursuant to statutory authority (including municipal by-laws) must be considered and applied when a court has to decide an issue controlled by those authorities. Likewise, as discussed in chapter 7, judicial precedents must be considered and followed if applicable.

Of course, even with these sources, the question of whether a particular authority is binding in any particular case is far from automatic. The Constitution or the statute must be interpreted, and the judge must decide whether or not the provisions cited are relevant to the dispute before the court. Similarly, as I discuss in chapter 7, precedents have to be read and dissected. They cannot be applied mechanically. They should be followed if the facts are similar and the reasoning remains pertinent and apt. But they can be distinguished if the facts are materially different, or read narrowly if the strength of the reasoning in the prior decision seems outmoded or inappropriate. Precedents can also be overruled. But subject to that kind of judgment call, if the binding authority does apply, the judge has no choice but to apply it. Failure to do so will amount to a legal error that renders the decision vulnerable to appeal.

The other category of authority is a much larger and more fluid one. It consists of those sources that have a sufficient legal pedigree to be acceptable for citation and reliance but are regarded only as persuasive. It is legitimate and even expected that the judge will cite and consider such sources when deciding a difficult case. But the weight these sources carry depends upon the persuasiveness of their reasoning. By "persuasiveness" I mean that the legal analysis and reasoning is convincing and consistent with the relevant legal rules and principles. The judge does not have to follow persuasive authority, but it makes sense to do so where the authority points to an answer that is sound in law as well as just and appropriate in the circumstances of the case.

I suggest that the distinction between binding and persuasive authority is important, as it puts in proper perspective the wide range of sources that judges can cite in their judgments. The binding authorities define the parameters of the debate. It is only where the case cannot readily be decided on the basis of binding authority that non-binding sources will have a material effect on the decision. But even when the binding authorities fail to provide enough guidance to actually decide the case, the judge must work within the framework, however incomplete, defined by the binding authorities. The judge will look to non-binding but persuasive authorities and accept or reject them on the basis of how well they fit within that framework. In other words, the judge should strive to maintain the coherence and integrity of the law as defined by the binding authorities, using persuasive authority to elaborate and flesh out its basic structure.[1]

## What Is a Persuasive Authority?

We have no clear rule of recognition to define precisely what counts as a legitimate source of persuasive authority. It is simply a matter of practice and usage. We find that, in a manner entirely characteristic of the common law, what counts as persuasive authority and the weight attached to various kinds of persuasive authority shifts and evolves with changing patterns of judicial usage. From this perspective, the use of persuasive authority may seem arbitrary, as the judge has a certain freedom to choose from an ill-defined range of non-binding sources. But as Patrick Glenn argued, "[O]nce it is perceived that each decision by a legal official involves personal choice and can never be purely mechanical in character," by providing a bridge between "mechanical jurisprudence on the one hand and arbitrary personal choice on the other," resort to non-binding persuasive authority makes judicial decision-making more principled.[2]

## Decisions of Extra-Provincial Courts

In chapter 7, I discuss how courts use prior decisions as precedents. I explain how Canadian judges use decisions from courts higher and lower in the judicial hierarchy to decide questions of law. Courts of one province can also make use of decisions of courts of other provinces. In this chapter, I consider the use of non-Canadian judicial decisions as authorities.

## *English Decisions*[3]

Until the 1970s, Canadian common law remained very much a product of English common law. Canadian courts routinely followed English decisions as if they were binding authority. Until 1949, the Judicial Committee of the Privy Council was Canada's court of last resort in civil cases, and this inevitably led the Canadian courts to adhere to the law as laid down by the House of Lords. The judicial members of the House of Lords were the dominant force on the Privy Council,[4] and the Law Lords could be expected to speak with the same voice, whether sitting in the Lords at Westminster or in the Privy Council in Downing Street.

The imposition of the House of Lords, the Privy Council, and the English courts as the infallible oracle for the entire empire was readily accepted in Canada. As future Chief Justice Bora Laskin put it, English decisions "were accepted and applied without any consciousness of obligation but because they reflected agreeable propositions of law."[5]

Several factors contributed to this obedient attitude. Canadian judges revered their English brethren, especially those who had reached the pinnacle of the House of Lords. This reverence was partially a product of colonialism, but it also flowed from a genuine admiration of the strength of the English bench and bar and a respect for the high quality of English decisions.

The reverence for the work of the English courts blended with the Canadian profession's acceptance of Blackstone's theory of a universal and immutable body of common law, untouchable except by Parliament.[6] On this theory, the common law was conceived as an integral existing body of rules, there to be discovered, not made, moulded, or changed by judges, who simply applied it. The Canadian legal profession had no doubt that English judges were the most reliable and authoritative judges to ascertain and reveal the common law for the entire empire. The remarkably strong Canadian adherence to a rigid version of legal formalism lasted well into the 1960s and 1970s. The common law was seen as a body of rules that could be objectively and mechanically deduced from prior decisions without reference to social, political, or economic contexts. The formalist vision of the law and legal reasoning was unreceptive to arguments that Canadian judges should shape the common law to reflect Canadian experiences and conditions. The judicial role was limited to applying the common law as laid down by the highest authority. Legal order, predictability, uniformity, and stability required an ultimate authoritative source for common law doctrine, and that was the House of Lords.

This powerful colonial-formalist legal tradition led Canadian judges to place the House of Lords on a pedestal. The Supreme Court of Canada meekly accepted its subservience and conceded that "[a] decision of the House of Lords should ... be respected and followed though inconsistent with a previous judgment of this court."[7] Justice Frank Anglin wrote in 1923, a year before he was named Chief

Justice of Canada, that the House of Lords "carries authority almost equal to that of an Act of Parliament."[8] Canadian courts readily acquiesced to the Privy Council's 1927 pronouncement that the House of Lords was "the supreme tribunal to settle English law" and that a "Colonial Court, which is bound by English law, is bound to follow" the pronouncements of the House of Lords.[9]

From the time of its creation in 1875 until the early 1960s, the Supreme Court of Canada tended to await "the last word from the English courts"[10] before daring to change the law, even in emerging areas. As the author of a leading study of the Supreme Court of Canada observes, the Court's "subservience to English cases was very much a Canadian creation."[11] It was, wrote Bora Laskin in 1951, "difficult to ascribe any body of doctrine to [the court] which is distinctively its own, save, perhaps, in the field of criminal law."[12] In 1959, another prominent Canadian scholar protested that Canadian judicial decisions read as if they were written by "English judges applying English law in Canada, rather than those of Canadian judges developing Canadian law to meet Canadian needs with guidance of English precedent."[13] It was not until the 1960s that the Supreme Court of Canada cited more Canadian cases than English ones.[14]

The first cracks in Canada's colonial-formalist legal foundation appeared in relation to our constitutional law and the Privy Council's interpretation of the provisions of the *British North America Act, 1867* allocating legislative powers as between the federal and provincial governments. In a series of post–First World War decisions, the Privy Council restrictively interpreted two key federal powers, "trade and commerce," and the residual "peace, order and good government" clause. The Privy Council refused to read the federal power in relation to "trade and commerce" as conferring broad authority to regulate the national economy.[15] Similarly, the residual "peace, order and good government" power, thought by many Canadian scholars to reflect the intention of the Fathers of Confederation to confer a general power to deal with matters of national concern, was reduced to little more than a power to respond to national emergencies.[16] These decisions were widely criticized as "the precise opposite of that which our fathers hoped and endeavoured to attain"[17] and as seriously at odds with the needs of a modern federation.[18]

Particularly galling was the Privy Council's 1926 decision in *Nadan v R*,[19] striking down a section of Canada's *Criminal Code* that barred appeals to the Privy Council in criminal cases. Prominent constitutional litigator and future Chief Justice of Ontario Newton Rowell described the Privy Council's decision as "startling and re-actionary."[20] The suggestion that Canada could never have its own court of last resort provoked Chief Justice Frank Anglin – a judge who strongly supported the supremacy of the House of Lords on matters of common law – to take the unusual step of protesting to Prime Minister Mackenzie King, "My Canadianism leads me to the opinion that we should finally settle our litigation in this country."[21]

But for almost twenty more years, the Canadian attachment to the ideal of a uniform body of common law enunciated by the courts of England remained more powerful than any concerns over the Privy Council's constitutional doctrines. The desire to keep Canadian "jurisprudence in harmony with that of Great Britain and the Empire" and to maintain the Privy Council's "steadying influence on our jurisprudence," as well as the need to resist the strong pull of the United States, were cited as reasons to forgo Canadian judicial autonomy.[22] It was not until 1949 that appeals to the Privy Council were finally abolished in civil cases.

The attraction of the colonial-formalist tradition was bound to fade once appeals to the Privy Council were abolished. The idea of a uniform body of common law that could apply throughout the empire was an impossible dream. The law inevitably adapts to distinctive local conditions, cultures, and mores. By the 1960s and 1970s, Canadian lawyers and judges began to recognize the House of Lords for what it was: an English court comprising English judges deciding English cases in light of English values. The House of Lords could certainly be relied upon as a source of English law. However, English judges could not be expected to understand, let alone consider, Canadian values when deciding English cases. There was bound to be a tension between our reverence for the English legal tradition and the authoritative pronouncements of England's highest court, and the inevitable failure of that court to understand or reflect our unique experience when crafting its decisions. This was not a criticism of the House of Lords – the problem rested in Canada, where judicial adherence to a form of narrowly legalistic formalism more or less immunized the authority of English decisions from being adapted to meet the exigencies of the Canadian experience.

After 1949, relieved of the influence of the Privy Council as the court of last resort, Canadian judges gradually began to develop what Chief Justice Brian Dickson would later describe as "a distinctively

Canadian jurisprudence."[23] Canadian courts continued to look to the English courts for authoritative statements of common law principle, but English jurisprudence was no longer accorded automatic precedence, and its acceptance rested entirely upon its persuasiveness.

The House of Lords, now the Supreme Court of the United Kingdom, continues to play an important role in the evolution of Canadian law, but this role is based upon persuasion rather than obedience. The Supreme Court of Canada recognizes that "the English legal background necessarily sets the stage for our own experience,"[24] and when it is necessary to go to "first principles,"[25] the court frequently looks to the English courts for non-binding but helpful guidance.

So, for example, in the area of negligence, discussed in greater detail in chapters 3 and 5, the decision of the House of Lords in *Donoghue v Stevenson*[26] remains the core source and inspiration for the Canadian law of negligence, as do the landmark House of Lords decisions that followed in the 1960s and 1970s: *Hedley Byrne & Co Ltd v Heller & Partners Ltd*,[27] *Home Office v Dorset Yacht Co Ltd*,[28] and *Anns v Merton London Borough Council*.[29] But when the House of Lords subsequently overruled *Anns* in *Murphy v Brentwood District Council* on the grounds that "it did not proceed on any basis of principle at all, but constituted a remarkable example of judicial legislation," and it "introduced a new species of liability governed by a principle indeterminate in character,"[30] Canadian and English tort law parted company. The Supreme Court of Canada continues to rely on the *Anns* test, insisting that *Anns*, not *Murphy*, harmonizes better with the traditional law of negligence that flows from *Donoghue v Stevenson*.[31] The Supreme Court of Canada rejected "the insistence on logical precision of *Murphy*," preferring an approach "more consistent with the incremental character of the common law [that] ... permits relief to be granted in new situations where it is merited."[32] This open acceptance of law-making and the willingness to pick and choose from various strands of authority on the basis of what best meets Canadian needs stands in stark contrast to the court's earlier colonial-formalist tradition.[33]

## Decisions from Other Common Law Jurisdictions

Canadian courts routinely cite American, Australian, and New Zealand decisions as authorities, although less frequently than English decisions. We share the common law tradition with these jurisdictions, and, like us, they draw upon the basic principles of English common law. Their style of analysis and reasoning is similar and readily understood and, if appropriate, may be adopted by a Canadian judge to decide a point of Canadian law.

In the nineteenth century, Canadian courts regularly cited American authority. American reports and texts provided readily available sources and decisions tended to track English common law with variances appropriate to North American experience.[34] However, as Canadian law developed its own distinctive qualities and as American law diverged from the English common law, Canadian judges became more guarded in their use of American law. This is perhaps, in part, a product of the general Canadian wariness of being too closely drawn-in by our very close, large, and powerful neighbour, and our determination to maintain our own distinctive legal and political culture. In the early years of the *Charter*, the Supreme Court resisted what might have been a natural inclination to look to the vast body of American Bill of Rights decisions, given the similarities of the two instruments, and insisted instead upon the development of a "distinctively Canadian jurisprudence."[35]

But there are also some practical reasons why citing American decisions remains the exception rather than the rule in Canada. One is that there are differences in our legal culture: we do not have elected judges, we use juries much less frequently, and we probably have a less litigious population. Another factor is the multiplicity of jurisdictions. American law is diverse and far from uniform across the fifty states. Often American decisions reflect a wide range of legal opinion on any particular point.

At the same time, it would be a mistake to minimize the influence of American law in Canada. American jurisprudence, especially decisions of the United States Supreme Court, have been influential in some areas. Leading texts and scholarly articles that distil the essence of American decisions are frequently cited by Canadian judges as authoritative sources on contested points of law. A prime example is the American Law Institute's Restatement of the Law series. With extensive input from legal academics, judges, and practitioners, the Restatements reflect the consensus of the American legal community on the current state of the law and offer suggestions for improvement and future development.[36] Another factor favouring the influence of American law is that most Canadian legal academics have done graduate studies in the United States. Their teaching and their scholarly writing is influenced by American legal thinking, and, as I will argue later in this chapter, the courts increasingly look to the academic writing as a source of persuasive authority.

## Non–Common Law Jurisdictions and International Law

Until recently, one would rarely encounter a reference by a Canadian judge to the decisions of a non–common law court (other than in Quebec, with its civilian tradition) or to international law. This has changed. The Supreme Court has stated courts should interpret legislation "in a way that reflects the values and principles of customary and conventional international law" and that "legislation is presumed to comply with Canada's international obligations."[37]

The influence of international law has been significant with respect to fundamental human rights in the era of the *Charter* for two reasons. First, *Charter* rights and freedoms are emanations of the same principles that underlie instruments such as the *European Convention for the Protection of Human Rights and Fundamental Freedoms* and the *Universal Declaration of Human Rights*.[38] Those same rights and freedoms are also found in the constitutions of other countries. As there is a universal quality to basic human rights, it is to be expected that we would pay heed to how other jurisdictions have interpreted and applied those rights. Decisions of the European Court of Human Rights have been frequently cited. One also finds occasional references to the decisions of the German and South African Constitutional Courts, as well as the Israeli Supreme Court.[39] The resistance to citing foreign authorities led by Justice Scalia in the United States[40] has no parallel in Canada.

The second reason is that many *Charter* rights reflect international commitments assumed by Canada as a signatory to the *International Covenant on Civil and Political Rights*,[41] the *International Covenant on Economic, Social and Cultural Rights*,[42] and other covenants. Canada adheres to the "dualist" tradition, according to which international commitments are not directly enforceable in domestic courts unless specifically incorporated into domestic law by Parliament. However, the Supreme Court has held that, where possible, *Charter* rights and freedoms should be interpreted in a manner consistent with Canada's international obligations.[43] Although international law is not "controlling in itself," the Court looks to it "as evidence of" the fundamental principles that underlie and motivate protected rights and freedoms.[44] The court has described "Canada's current international law commitments and the current state of international thought on human rights" as a "persuasive source for interpreting the scope of the *Charter*."[45] The court has stated that "the *Charter* should be presumed to provide at least as great a level of protection as found in the international human rights documents that Canada has ratified."[46]

## Academic Writing

In recent years, academic writing has played an increasingly central role in judicial decision-making.[47] It was not always so. In 1950, the Chief Justice of Canada refused to allow counsel to cite an article published in the *Canadian Bar Review* during oral submissions on the ground that scholarly writing was "not an authority in this Court."[48] This thinking, lamented at the time by scholars as unduly constraining,[49] was ostensibly based on the fear of relying on the works of living authors who might later rescind or disavow their published statements. But more fundamentally, the refusal to look beyond case law and statutes was a product of a highly formalist and anti-intellectual judicial culture that prevailed in Canada, the United Kingdom, and the Commonwealth until well into the mid-twentieth century.[50] Counsel who found academic writing helpful were forced into the regrettable practice of adopting, but not citing, scholarly positions as part of their own argument.[51] The best outcome legal scholars could hope for was to have their views smuggled into the process by counsel and unwittingly plagiarized by the judges.

In the 1970s and 1980s, two chief justices, Bora Laskin (a former academic) and Brian Dickson, helped remove the shackles of this unnecessarily restrictive position and encouraged the shift towards intellectualizing the Supreme Court.[52]

By 1985, recognition of the enhanced status of legal scholarship was unofficially formalized with the addition of the "authors cited" rubric in the *Supreme Court Reports*, the official reporter of all Supreme Court decisions. At the start of each published judgment, one finds a list of the scholarly writings cited immediately following the traditional lists of cases and statutes cited.[53] Only thirty-five years after scholarly citation was forbidden, reliance on academic writing had been consecrated as "a significant component of the decision writing style" at the Supreme Court.[54] The use of academic writing is now firmly entrenched in judicial decision-making at all levels.[55] One even finds reference to the writings of philosophers, particularly in *Charter* cases where the courts strive to get to the root of fundamental concepts such as freedom of expression and liberty.[56]

It should be noted that the former aversion to scholarly writing was a distinctly Anglo-Canadian common law phenomenon. American common law judges were much more receptive to scholarly writing. In an introduction to a text written in 1931, Supreme Court Justice Benjamin Cardozo praised the use of legal scholarship as advancing the intellectual discourse surrounding the legal discipline and in addressing the demands of immediate and routine day-to-day decision-making. Cardozo observed that "leadership in the march of legal thought has been passing in our day from the benches of the courts to the chairs of universities" and that this trend had "stimulated a willingness to cite the law review essays in briefs and in opinions in order to buttress a conclusion."[57]

In the civilian tradition, "doctrine" as espoused by legal scholars has long been a revered source of legal authority. Indeed, the civil and common law traditions were at polar opposites as, until recently, civilians tended to prefer scholarly writing as a source of authority over past judicial decisions.[58] As Professor Roderick Macdonald observed, in the civilian tradition, scholarly opinion "is not simply writing about law; it is, in some measure, thought to be constitutive of law."[59]

## When Do Judges Cite Academic Writing?

### READY AND RELIABLE

Judges invoke scholarly works for a variety of reasons. The first is pragmatic. The adversarial system of justice, combined with the demands of workload and timely decision-making, compels judges to rely upon the efforts of others – counsel and legal scholars, sometimes supplemented by law clerks – for their legal research. As Brian Dickson explained, "The volume of litigation facing the courts today puts increasing pressure on judges, robbing them of time for thorough research and meditation. It forces them to be more dependent on the research of others."[60] Scholarly writing often serves as a convenient and reliable source for a legal proposition, especially where the commentator has carefully sifted through the authorities and coalesced them around clear and readily understood overarching principles.

Even in the dark days when most judges refused to admit that they relied on scholarly writing, some members of the English judiciary acknowledged the intellectual value associated with the product of leading text writers. These works were described as "repositories of principles," written by scholars "who have studied the law as a science with more detachment than is possible to men engaged in busy practice."[61]

I share the concern expressed by many judges over "academic writing becoming esoteric,"[62] written for a narrow, specialized audience and not easily accessible to practising lawyers and judges. However, there remains a considerable volume of scholarship that is helpful. Appellate courts routinely substantiate points of law or other legal propositions with citations to scholarship that have already performed the legwork and conveniently assembled relevant sources and precedents for ease of reference. Courts tend to favour certain "go-to" scholarly sources.[63] In the realm of constitutional law, appellate courts routinely cite Peter Hogg's scholarship as an authoritative source.[64] Few statutory interpretation cases fail to refer to either Sullivan and Driedger[65] or Côté.[66] Sopinka, Lederman, and Bryant[67] feature in most evidence decisions. The works of Waddams, McCamus, and Swan on contracts[68] have attracted considerable judicial respect, while torts decisions routinely cite Linden and Feldthusen.[69] Authors of this stature who are leading exponents of particular areas of law provide readily available sources that lend legitimacy to the resolution of difficult points of law.

Moreover, it would be wrong to minimize the influence of more esoteric forms of legal scholarship. Judges discuss the decisions they have to make with their law clerks, and the annual infusion of bright law clerks, fresh from the academy, ensures that new ways of thinking about law filter into the decision-making process.

### SETTLING UNSETTLED AREAS

Where a court is called upon to revisit an unsettled area or to change the law, sound academic writing that considers the possible legal responses and their implications can be very useful. Courts frequently look to the academy to ensure that their treatment of an unsettled point corresponds with emerging or evolving legal trends.[70] Academic writing helps to situate the specific issue in the broader context of the subject as a whole by providing the overarching theoretical and doctrinal structure into which the court must fit its decision. As Justice Michel Bastarache explained, "The work of academics serves to provide a contextual social background for legal disputes, helps to make judges aware of the underlying reasons for the decision that they make and offers useful suggestions for reform. No principled approach to decision-making can ignore the contribution of academics."[71]

Taking stock of the literature gives judges the benefit of in-depth, thorough research and analysis not always available from the partisan arguments of counsel. Lord Goff, a scholar and a judge, observed that in the courtroom "single points of law are placed under the microscope," a process that may obscure the broader picture of principle that can be painted by legal scholars.[72] Well-argued and well-researched scholarly works that go beyond merely surveying past cases is very helpful to appellate courts when there is a precedential void or when an issue on appeal arises in an unsettled legal field. By turning to legal scholarship, judges are exposed to theoretical considerations that structure the law but are not readily apparent from reading nothing but the cases. This was described by a Supreme Court judge as promoting "stability and coherent changeability by affecting the substantive content of rights and by providing a rational basis for judicial decision-making."[73]

Scholarly writing may also assist judicial decision-making in ways that go unacknowledged. Appellate judges will frequently take account of academic writing to vet the implications of a particular decision without providing citations to those works in their reasons for judgment. While unfortunate for the uncited authors, their work will still have played a crucial role in the judgment-writing process.[74] Scholarly writing may also assist judicial decision-making by laying out a proposition or a theory that the appellate court decides to reject. An appellate court may benefit from a scholar's assessment of potential avenues for change or reform but decline to heed the author's recommendation in its decision.[75] Although the academic work does not attain its objective, it nonetheless plays an important role in the decision-making process by stimulating dialogue and promoting critical self-reflection by the judiciary.

## DIALOGUE BETWEEN THE JUDICIARY AND THE ACADEMY

Judges often accuse academics of lying in the weeds, waiting to pounce after the court pronounces upon a contentious point. The court's judgment appears to be little more than fodder for the academic mill. But this judicial perception is neither accurate nor fair. Academics *should* criticize judges. No public institution with the power to make important decisions affecting the lives of citizens should be immune to scrutiny – appellate courts are no exception. Recognizing that the academy serves an important watchdog role, Justice Dickson urged his judicial colleagues not to "resent criticism by the legal community," as "[i]t is the function of the scholar to point out to the judiciary the error of their ways."[76]

A healthier and more apt approach is to see the relationship between judges and scholars as symbiotic and dialogic. Academics may not always comment on specific cases as those disputes wend their way up the judicial hierarchy but, as Professor Vaughn Black and Nicholas Richter observe, "a certain portion of academic writing – in particular, a preponderance of law review articles – is written as more or less a direct exhortation to judges about how to decide cases expected to come before them."[77] Appellate courts draw on academic writing to decide cases, and reasons for judgment provoke further academic comment. This, in turn, causes judges to react and respond in subsequent decisions to academic criticism, either heeding or rejecting critiques or proposals advanced by scholars.

The Supreme Court's jurisprudence offers many examples where the court has paid attention to the critical assessments of scholars. When the court found that there was a "general organizing principle" of good faith in contract law, it placed considerable reliance on academic writing.[78] In *General Motors of Canada Ltd v City National Leasing*,[79] Chief Justice Dickson drew approvingly from scholarly writing that criticized the court's prior decisions as "abstractly legal, divorced from commercial effect."[80] In upholding a *Competition Act* provision enabling a private right of action, the court concluded that the earlier case law failed to "correctly [assess] the balance to be struck between s. 91(2) and s. 92(13)."[81] Similarly, when the Supreme Court's family law *Pelech* trilogy[82] established a "causal connection" test for individuals attempting to have support agreements reconsidered, an instantaneous academic backlash was provoked, and Justice L'Heureux-Dubé responded in subsequent decisions.[83]

The Ontario Court of Appeal's jurisprudence on assumed juris-diction over foreign defendants provides a good example of the possibility for fruitful dialogue and interplay between the bench and the academy. As I mentioned in chapter 4, in *Van Breda*,[84] I sat on a five-judge panel that revisited the eight-part test for assumed jurisdiction that I had developed in an earlier judgment.[85] The ear-lier decision made extensive reference to academic writing and, in turn, had provoked an extensive body of case law and scholarly commentary. In the subsequent five-judge decision, I observed that "the *Muscutt* test has been critically assessed by a number of legal scholars in academic articles,"[86] some favourable and some highly critical. We specifically acknowledged that this corpus of academic commentary played a significant role in our reconsideration and adjustment of the *Muscutt* test: "This extensive body of writing pro-vides us with a wide range of assessments of the *Muscutt* test from experts in this field that we can and should take into account along with the experience reflected by the case law. Many scholars who have written on the subject have expressed disagreement with the *Muscutt* test. These criticisms of *Muscutt* arise from what many legal scholars perceive to be undue complexity and lack of predictability in the eight-factor test."[87]

I suggest that the interplay between our use of scholarly writing in *Muscutt*, the ensuing scholarly critique of that decision, and our subsequent use of that criticism to reformulate the test in *Van Breda* illustrates how there can be a productive symbiotic partnership be-tween the bench and the academy.

### SOCIAL CONTEXT

Academic work can fill gaps in judicial expertise when courts are faced with issues that involve broad social implications that require consideration of other disciplines. There seems to be a proportional nexus between the social implications of a given appeal and the ex-tent to which judges rely on scholarly works in deciding that appeal. Most judges feel ill-equipped to tackle the social or interdisciplinary aspects of a case. In a number of cases, scholarly writing, particularly in the realm of social sciences, has assisted the judiciary. Scholar-ship that elucidates the social context within which legal issues arise can be valuable, especially when a given case has significant public policy implications.

In the post-*Charter* era, judges have increasingly turned to academic writing to come to grips with underlying assumptions and to frame legal issues within a broader socio-political context.[88] An openness to consider insights from interdisciplinary scholarship prompted Chief Justice Dickson to draw on critical race theory when upholding hate propaganda legislation in the *Keegstra* decision.[89] Similarly, Justice La Forest's 1992 judgment in *M(K) v M(H)* is replete with references to Canadian and American law review articles and other relevant literature on "accommodation syndrome" or "post-incest syndrome."[90]

The influence of social sciences scholarship has been particularly significant in the family law context. As Justice Claire L'Heureux-Dubé stated, the court "recognized the usefulness of social science research and judicial notice of social context in debunking myths and exposing stereotypes and assumptions which desensitize the law to the realities of those affected."[91] The Supreme Court relied on social science writing when it recognized the battered woman syndrome in *R v Lavallee*.[92] The court held that expert evidence was admissible, because without it a juror would have difficulty comprehending the situation of a battered woman. There was a common misconception that a woman would not remain in a relationship with a man who abused her, and therefore women alleging abuse who remained in the relationship could not have been as badly beaten as they claimed. A related misconception was that battered women had masochistic tendencies. These stereotypes adversely affected the perceived credibility of a battered woman's claim of self-defence. Social science evidence permitted the court to dispel such harmful myths.

The Ontario Court of Appeal's decision in *Peart v Peel Regional Police Services Board*[93] illustrates the use of social context scholarship in appellate adjudication. Mr Peart claimed that his arrest and apprehension had been the product of racial bias, and he sought damages against the police officers under section 24(1) of the *Charter*.[94] Justice David Doherty cited scholarly articles by Richard Devlin,[95] Kent Roach,[96] and David Tanovich[97] on the practice of racial profiling. Justice Doherty acknowledged the role of academic writing in this difficult and contentious area: "Racial profiling can seldom be proved by direct evidence. Rather, it must be inferred from the circumstances surrounding the police action that is said to be the product of racial profiling. The courts, assisted by various studies, academic writings, and expert evidence have come to recognize a variety of factual indicators that can support the inference that the police conduct was racially motivated, despite the existence of an apparent justification for that conduct."[98]

There is, however, a limit on the use of social science writings cited as authorities. The Supreme Court has warned against bootlegging "evidence in the guise of authorities."[99] A line has to be drawn between the use of social science literature to bolster a legal argument and the use of social science to establish a "legislative" or "social" fact. "Legislative" or "social" facts relate to the causes and effects of social, cultural, and economic issues that the legislation addresses. Social science evidence of this nature has become a prevalent feature of constitutional litigation. *Charter* challenges involving major social issues such as prostitution and assisted suicide now rest on sworn expert evidence.[100] When legislative or social facts are contested, they must be proved by evidence. Rather than simply cite an article or a book, the party seeking to establish the fact must lead sworn opinion evidence from an expert witness.

## Conclusion

The treatment of English case law, international law, and academic and scholarly writing demonstrates how judicial attitudes and practices regarding non-binding authority change. English cases, at one time considered to be more or less binding, are now treated as persuasive at best. International law, formerly thought to be irrelevant to domestic decision-making, is now accepted in the area of fundamental rights and freedoms. Academic writing, at one time banned from consideration, has become a routinely accepted source. The same applies to the writings of philosophers and social scientists that occasionally appear in *Charter* decisions.

These changes have occurred in typical common law fashion. They have been gradual and piecemeal. There is no discernible rule or standard to tell us what sources have a legal pedigree and what sources do not. We simply have to look to see what pattern can be traced from judicial practice. I suggest that if there is an explanation, it is probably this: with the retreat from the narrow vision of legalist formalism that prevailed in the early part of the twentieth century, we see an increasing tendency to search for broad principles of justice to structure and guide judicial decision-making.[101] That approach is bound to be more receptive to academic writing and to decisions from other jurisdictions.

## Chapter 9

# Judicial Decision-Making: A Case Study

In this chapter I present a case study on judicial law-making in the common law tradition. My aim is to provide a concrete illustration of many of the points I have discussed in earlier chapters of this book.

*Jones v Tsige*,[1] a case that came before our court in 2012, posed an issue with which common law courts had been wrestling for over 100 years: Is there a common law right to personal privacy that can be remedied by an award of damages?

The facts were simple, straightforward, and not in dispute.[2] Sandra Jones and Winnie Tsige worked at the same bank, but they were not personally acquainted. Tsige had developed a romantic relationship with Jones's ex-husband. Tsige had used her workplace computer to snoop into Jones's bank records at least 174 times. The information displayed included details of Jones's financial transactions as well as personal information such as date of birth, marital status, and current address. Tsige was contrite and admitted that she had acted inappropriately and contrary to the bank's policy. Her motivation was unclear. Jones did not accept Tsige's explanation that the reason for her snooping was that she was in a financial dispute with Jones's ex-husband and wanted to see whether he was paying Jones child support as he claimed.

Jones claimed damages for the invasion of her privacy. She faced a significant problem. She did not have what lawyers call a "cause of action" giving her the right to sue. After hearing the argument, and after considerable reflection, my colleagues and I decided that the time had come to change the law and allow Jones's claim. In this chapter I will attempt to explain why and how we reached that conclusion.

I realize that many, perhaps even most, judges would not think it appropriate to say anything more about one of their decisions than what they said in their reasons. The prevailing view is that a decision should speak for itself and that it is dangerous for the judge to say more. Extra-curial comments risk clouding the authority of the written decision. Lawyers and litigants should not have to look beyond the decision itself to know what it stands for.

It is evident from the very fact that I have written this book that I take a different view, perhaps because of my academic background. Against the risks posed by extra-curial statements must be weighed the benefits. In my view the benefits include providing a window into the judicial decision-making process with a view to enhancing public understanding of how that process works and what it entails. That is the purpose of this book, and I believe it justifies the following discussion.

*Jones v Tsige* attracted considerable attention in the profession and in the academy. I have frequently been asked to speak to law students, judges, and lawyers about the case. In this chapter I will follow the pattern I have adopted when I have spoken about the decision to legal audiences. I will review my reasons as they were written, and I will not add to or embellish what I wrote. I will, however, attempt to explain the process that my colleagues and I followed in coming to the conclusion that we should take the step of recognizing a new common law cause of action.

Successful arguments in cutting-edge cases such as *Jones v Tsige* tend to involve four interrelated components: facts, rules, principles, and policies. Let me explain what I mean by each of these components and how they relate to one another.

### Facts

The facts come first. Common law lawyers and judges are trained to focus on the facts. Our method is inductive rather than deductive. We infer general principles from the pattern of specific decisions. It is only after we have absorbed the factual details of the case that we begin to work towards the applicable or governing legal norm or standard. Skilled advocates will often say that the facts are more important than the law. That is because great advocates are almost always masterful storytellers. They have a knack for distilling the details of the case and painting a picture that casts their client and their case in the best possible light. The advocate's aim is to tell an attractive story that reflects well on their client and that will make the judge want to decide the case in the client's favour.

But a winning argument cannot be spun out of facts alone. The fact-finding process necessarily evolves in the shadow of the law. The judge will be able to base the decision only on facts that are relevant to the governing legal norm. Facts irrelevant to the law must be disregarded. This means that the fact-finding process is selective. The skilled advocate knows that the conscientious judge will have to justify the decision as being consistent with the law. To win the case, the advocate will select and emphasize facts that bring the case within the legal norm upon which the advocate relies.

The instinctive response or reaction of most common law lawyers and judges to the facts of *Jones v Tsige* was that Jones ought to have a remedy. I have argued in chapter 6 that the "judicial hunch" is very much a feature of judicial decision-making. If properly managed, I think judicial hunches can play a positive role in judicial reasoning, as they reflect a willingness to avoid a mechanical and unduly formalistic approach. But judges must be careful not to put undue reliance on their hunches. They must consciously examine hunches to ensure they are not the product of ingrained or unconscious bias or prejudice. The judge must also be prepared to subject the hunch to the test of justification. If the judge cannot present a reasoned explanation based upon arguments and sources that have the acceptable legal pedigree, the judge must be prepared to jettison the hunch and decide the case differently.

I sat on *Jones v Tsige* with two very experienced judges, Chief Justice Warren Winkler and Associate Chief Justice Douglas Cunningham of the Superior Court, sitting as an *ad hoc* judge[3] of our court. When the three of us retired for our post-hearing conference, we all leaned in favour of recognizing the claim Jones asserted. When I tried to explain the significance of our instinctive reaction to an audience of eager young law students after our decision had been released, I was somewhat alarmed to realize that between the three judges who sat on the case, we collectively had over 100 years of experience in the law. I like to think that our instinct or hunch was not a raw gut reaction but rather the product of three educated and experienced legal minds.

As we discussed the case, we all recognized that our instinct was not enough. Accepting Jones's claim would involve taking a significant step in the law. This was not a case where we could return to court in a few minutes and deliver an oral judgment. This was a case we could decide only after considerable reading, study, and reflection. We knew that we had to subject our hunch to the rigours of legal analysis and that if our tentative decision "would not write," we would have to decide the case the other way.

## Rules

Legal norms or standards, as I have argued in chapter 5, come in three categories: rules, principles, and policies. By rules I mean the relatively clear, hard-edged legal doctrines that lend themselves to immediate application. The plaintiff, Jones, could point to no established rule that supported her claim, but she urged us to establish one. The defendant Tsige argued that, as there was no rule in Jones's favour, we should simply dismiss the case for lack of requisite authority. To win her case, Jones had to convince us to accept that she presented a valid legal claim that should be recognized in Ontario law.

Jones could point to no definitive statement from an Ontario or Canadian judge identifying a "black-letter" rule to support her claim. The recognition of the distinct right of action for breach of privacy remained uncertain. But the case law was not silent on the point, and after doing a considerable amount of reading, I discerned a gradually evolving acceptance of claims for breach of privacy.

Tsige, and the judge who had granted summary judgment dismissing Jones's claim, relied on one of our court's recent decisions. The case involved a claim for damages for negligence, assault, civil conspiracy, and breach of certain *Charter* rights, all while in police custody.[4] Our court observed that "[the plaintiff] properly conceded in oral argument before this court that there is no 'free-standing' right to dignity or privacy under the *Charter* or at common law."[5]

The judge who decided *Jones v Tsige* at first instance thought that this was a precedent he was bound to follow and that it was fatal to Jones's claim. I considered the earlier case and concluded that the statement could not have been intended to express any definitive opinion on the existence of a tort claim for breach of a privacy interest. The plaintiff in that case had not advanced such a claim, and the point at issue in *Jones v Tsige* had not been argued. The statement could be distinguished as what lawyers call an *obiter dictum*, that is, a judicial statement that did not resolve a contentious point at issue and therefore has no binding effect as a precedent.

There were a few trial judgments where judges had been prepared to award damages for claims similar to that advanced by Jones using traditional causes of action. None of these labelled the claim as invasion of privacy. I thought that these cases were significant. In the great tradition of the common law, they reflected the wisdom of trial judges. Being fully immersed in the facts of the cases they heard, they knew that some remedy was called for. The awards in these cases were small, the judgments had not been taken to appeal, and the reasoning was less than crystal clear. While far from decisive, I saw these decisions as having planted seeds for the recognition of Jones's claim.

There were also cases, including a decision of our court, accepting claims for appropriation of personality where the defendant had used the plaintiff's name or likeness for its own advantage.[6] This was not enough to cover Jones's claim, but it did show that our law was receptive to some claims that, broadly speaking, could be described as breaches of privacy.[7]

Yet another line of cases involved pretrial motions by defendants asking a judge to strike out claims similar to the one advanced by Jones on the ground that they had no hope of success. While some had been struck on the ground that the law had not recognized a claim for breach of privacy, several judges had refused to strike out such claims as hopeless.

There is a strict test for establishing whether a judge should dismiss a claim as hopeless before trial where the facts can be fully explored. The claim will not be struck merely because it is novel. The allegations of fact pleaded in the claim must be accepted as if they have been proven, and the defendant must show that it is "plain and obvious" – or beyond doubt – that the plaintiff could not succeed if the matter were to proceed to trial.[8] This strict test is a product of our strongly fact-oriented common law tradition. The reluctance to strike claims without a trial reflects the recognition that the common law is a living organism capable of growth and development. Even if the claim is novel, it should be allowed to proceed to trial, where the facts can be fully developed so that the judge can fairly assess the justice of the case.

Given the strictness of that test, judgments refusing to strike claims fell well short of establishing the legitimacy of Jones's claim.

However, these decisions gave some support for recognizing the claim advanced by Jones. As one judge stated in his decision refusing to strike, "[T]he time has come to recognize invasion of privacy as a tort in its own right."[9]

As discussed in chapter 8, when facing a difficult decision on a point not expressly covered by our own case law, we often look to the decisions of other common law courts. While those decisions are not binding on us, they can be persuasive on a contentious point if their reasoning is sound and if they are consistent with a pattern or trend in a certain direction. A review of the case law from other jurisdictions supported recognizing Jones's claim. While no Canadian court had expressly approved a comparable right of action, two provincial appellate courts had indicated an openness to doing so.[10] There was also a long line of American case law accepting claims for breach of privacy.[11] English law had steadfastly rejected the proposition that there was a common law right of action for invasion of privacy,[12] but at the same time, English judges had reshaped the claim of breach of confidence and allowed what amounted to privacy claims to be advanced under that rubric.[13] The courts of Australia[14] and New Zealand[15] had indicated a clear willingness to entertain claims for breach of privacy.

When I stood back and considered the impact of this entire body of case law defining the applicable black-letter rules, I concluded that while it was certainly far from conclusive, the trend was in the direction of recognizing Jones's claim.

## Principles

As I had concluded that the precedents and established legal rules neither accepted nor precluded Jones's claim, I turned to what seemed to be the applicable legal principles to see if they supported what I had discerned to be the drift or tendency of the case law. In taking this step, I engaged the legal tools I discuss in chapter 5 of this book. Principles are the values and organizing ideas that underlie the law. Principles provide the legal regime's architecture. They are legal in nature, as they must be drawn from accepted sources – cases, statutes, the Constitution, and scholarly writing. They are not, however, cast in the form of a specific rule that can be applied immediately to decide a case. Principles guide, but they do not decide. Principles are important tools that judges use to assess legal issues where the rules are less than clear, or where there appears to be no established rule capable of answering the case.

Principles are often deployed when a rule is challenged as having outlived its usefulness or where the law needs to evolve to accommodate social or technological change. As I argued in chapter 4, the common law has long recognized that judges can and should take into account changed social conditions, and they should reshape the law to meet those changed conditions. We were faced with that situation on *Jones v Tsige*. For over 100 years, technological change has motivated the legal protection of the individual's right to privacy, starting with the advent of photography.[16] Legal scholars have warned that the exponential acceleration of technological change poses a threat to personal privacy and that the law has to respond.[17] The facts of *Jones v Tsige* demonstrated that ready access to the huge volume of sensitive personal information routinely stored in electronic databases poses a serious new threat to personal privacy. Digital technology has changed the way we communicate and our capacity to capture, store, and retrieve information. Technological change makes sensitive personal information readily available: details about our finances, health, the books we borrow or buy, the movies we rent or download, where we shop, where we travel, whom we talk to, and what we say. I concluded that it was within the capacity of the common law to evolve and to respond to "the problem posed by the routine collection and aggregation of highly personal information that is readily accessible in electronic form."[18]

I was persuaded that the individual's privacy interest was a fundamental value underlying several traditional and existing claims or causes of action. As scholars had been pointing out for over a century, claims for breach of confidence, defamation, breach of copyright, nuisance, and breach of certain other property rights all rest to some extent on the principle that individuals have a fundamental interest in protecting and assuring their privacy.[19] As one Ontario judge had perceptively observed after a detailed consideration of the case law, "[I]nvasion of privacy in Canadian common law continues to be an inceptive, if not ephemeral, legal concept, primarily operating to extend the margins of existing tort doctrine."[20] While no Ontario court had taken the next step to find explicitly that a breach of privacy constituted a legitimate legal claim, accepting Jones's claim would be entirely consistent with an accepted value in our legal system.

The argument from principle was considerably bolstered by *Charter* jurisprudence. The way *Charter* jurisprudence applied in this case nicely illustrates the difference between two of the concepts I discuss in chapter 5: rules, which apply directly, and principles, which are background legal values that may be used to explain rules or fill in gaps.

The *Charter* did not apply in a rule-like fashion to Jones's claim because the *Charter* applies directly only to the actions of government.[21] Jones did not challenge any statute, regulation, or action by an arm of the government. Her claim was that of one individual citizen against another, and it rested entirely on the common law. However, when the Supreme Court determined that the *Charter* applied only to government, the court made an important qualification. Even where the *Charter* does not apply directly in a rule-like fashion, the court held that the courts should develop the common law in a manner "consistent with the fundamental values enshrined in the Constitution."[22] The values of the *Charter* are fundamental principles of our legal order. Judges may use them to understand, interpret, and develop the law, even where the *Charter* itself has no direct application to the case.

The text of the *Charter* does not specifically contain or define a right of privacy. However, in one of its early *Charter* decisions, the Supreme Court held that the right to be free from unreasonable search and seizure, conferred by section 8, could be understood only in terms of the fundamental value it protected, namely, every individual's reasonable expectation of privacy.[23] This led the court to hold that privacy is an important value "worthy of constitutional protection."[24] In a later *Charter* case, the court identified three distinct privacy interests: personal privacy, grounded in the right to bodily integrity; territorial privacy, protecting the home and other spaces where the individual enjoys a reasonable expectation of privacy; and informational privacy: "[T]he claim of individuals ... to determine for themselves when, how, and to what extent information about them is communicated to others."[25] While not dispositive, the explicit recognition of privacy as an important value attracting constitutional protection supported the recognition of the civil right of action that Jones asserted. The common law was already tending towards recognition of a right of privacy, and the *Charter* value served as a fundamental legal principle that could be used to fill the gap in the current state of the law.

In our search for the governing legal principles, we also turned to the very considerable body of academic writing on privacy where legal scholars had explored the need for, and the implications of, affording legal protection to privacy. As Brian Dickson observed, "[T]he quality of the law achieved by the courts bears a direct relationship to the quantity and quality of analysis offered by the academic community."[26] As I pointed out in chapter 8, when faced with a difficult issue such as whether to recognize a novel claim, academic writing that considers possible legal responses and their implications can be immensely useful to an appellate judge.

A significant volume of writing by legal scholars from Canada and elsewhere argued that it was time for Canadian courts to recognize a common law right of action for invasion of privacy. Two seminal American articles were particularly persuasive. The first,[27] co-authored in 1890 by Louis Brandeis, a future justice of the Supreme Court of the United States, argued that recognizing a right of action for invasion of privacy was needed to deal with the issues posed by technological and social change that saw "instantaneous photographs" and "newspaper enterprise" invade "the sacred precincts of private life."[28] The article pointed out that privacy was a fundamental value underlying various existing causes of action and that it was time to openly recognize it as the basis for an independent tort. The allusion to technological change was striking: the accumulation and ready access to digitized personal data of the twenty-first century struck me as a threat to privacy that easily matched the threat to privacy posed by photography in the nineteenth.

The second seminal article[29] was written in 1960 by William Prosser, an eminent scholar of tort law. Prosser picked up the threads of the American jurisprudence that had developed in the seventy years following the first article. He argued that from the hundreds of decisions on privacy, what emerged was not one, but four torts. Although the four torts were tied together by a common theme and name, they comprised different elements and protected different interests. He summarized the four torts as follows:

1. Intrusion upon the plaintiff's seclusion or solitude, or into his private affairs;
2. Public disclosure of embarrassing private facts about the plaintiff;

3. Publicity that places the plaintiff in a false light in the public eye;
4. Appropriation, for the defendant's advantage, of the plaintiff's name or likeness.[30]

That classification had been adopted by the American Law Institute's influential *Restatement (Second) of Torts (2010)*. The first tort, "intrusion upon seclusion," the one that corresponded to Jones's claim, is described as follows: "One who intentionally intrudes, physically or otherwise, upon the seclusion of another or his private affairs or concerns, is subject to liability to the other for invasion of his privacy, if the invasion would be highly offensive to a reasonable person."[31]

I found this four-part classification, and the specific category of "intrusion upon seclusion," to be very important. It emerged from the case-law of our close common law neighbour and its acceptance in the *Restatement* gave it a legitimate juridical pedigree. It was strongly rooted in principle, and it put into sharp focus the specific issue we had to decide.

The four-part classification also allowed us to focus on the precise type of privacy claim Jones was making. As I suggested in chapter 3, judges must always remain conscious of their institutional limitations when it comes to making law. We had only one case and one set of facts before us, and we were naturally reluctant about deciding more than was necessary. I feared that if we accepted the invitation to recognize a general right to sue for invasion of privacy, we might be biting off more than we could chew and creating an "unmanageable legal proposition" that could "breed confusion and uncertainty."[32] By situating Jones's claim within one of the four categories, we were able to decide her case and leave the very different issues raised by the other three categories to be decided if and when an appropriate case was argued. To accept intrusion upon seclusion as a tort was already a significant step, and when a court changes the law, it is almost always best to proceed one step at a time.

### Policy

If principles are used to develop the law along a new path, policies come into play. Judges must ask, Is taking that new path consistent with sound policy? What are the broader social implications of going down that path? Is the proposed legal development consistent with the common good? Are the considerations of justice and fairness that support the new legal development outweighed by any adverse social or economic impact that the new development might cause?

Every time a common law judge decides a case involving a potential change in the law, the judge must consider the respective roles of the courts and the legislature or Parliament. Courts are best suited to deciding specific disputes, while questions of general policy should ordinarily be left to Parliament or the legislature. In *Jones v Tsige*, we had two distinct arguments to consider.

The first was that the legislature and Parliament had already spoken by enacting a rather complex framework of privacy legislation.[33] Counsel for Tsige argued that expanding the reach of the common law would only interfere with the policy choices that had been made through the democratic process.

The second argument was that proclaiming a right to privacy would usurp the legislative role, as it involved a sensitive policy choice in a difficult area, affecting a wide variety of interests and institutions.

We rejected both arguments. With respect to the first, while the legislative regime that had been created was indeed complex, it was directed to the issue of privacy at an institutional level and did not speak to the issue we had to decide, namely whether there should be a right of action between two private parties. The statute most clearly in play, a federal statute that governed banks,[34] contained a complaint mechanism but one that provided no effective remedy for the individual whose rights had been infringed. Through this mechanism Jones could only complain about the Bank's conduct, not that of Tsige. She had no statutory right to recompense for any wrong she had suffered. The bank felt it had satisfied its duty under the Act by punishing Tsige for her transgression with a one-week suspension without pay and the denial of a bonus.

Simply put, it did not appear to us that Parliament had turned its mind to the issue we had to decide, and we could not see how giving an individual a common law right of action would disrupt or interfere with anything Parliament had done. We decided that "it would take a strained interpretation to infer … a legislative intent to supplant or halt the development of the common law in this area."[35]

Nor were we persuaded by the second argument that the issues of policy involved were so complex that they could be dealt with only by the legislature. I agree that issues raising difficult and contentious policy choices are ordinarily left to the legislative process. When it comes to law-making, judges operate at a disadvantage. As I tried to explain in chapter 3, the perspective of a court is confined by the need to decide a specific case arising from a relatively narrow set of facts. But on the other hand, judges are very skilled at dealing with claims to legal rights. The definition, refinement, and application of rights as between individuals all fall squarely within the judicial role. It is very much in the common law tradition to find a legal remedy to respond to a compelling individual claim.

I found instructive the legislation of other provinces that had created a private right of action to sue for invasion of privacy.[36] The legislation enacted by four common law provinces and by the legislature of civilian Quebec revealed a pattern. The legislation was uniformly general and lacking in specificity. None of the provincial laws went beyond a general proclamation of right by providing that "[i]t is a tort, actionable without proof of damage, for a person, wilfully and without a claim of right, to violate the privacy of another."[37] There was no precise definition of what constitutes an invasion of privacy, and the legislatures had simply left it to the courts of their province to define the contours of the general right that had been proclaimed. This pattern confirmed my impression that we were dealing with an issue legitimately within the judicial function, namely, defining the precise contours of a legal right. There was a strong basis in the common law to recognize the right, and legislation suggested that defining the details of that right was within our judicial competence.

Having decided that it was open to the court to recognize the new right, the next question was how to define that right. Here again, we were mindful of the need to proceed with caution and to avoid taking on more than was prudent on the basis of the limited factual record before us. Defining the right was largely a matter of principle. In other words, defining the right was a legal question that turned on the details of the relationship between the parties. But as we were expanding the range of tort liability, we also had to consider questions of policy. We had to think about the social and economic consequences of recognizing a new legal right. This meant defining the elements of intrusion upon seclusion with sufficient precision to avoid opening what legal discourse describes as the "floodgates" to claims of dubious merit.

As I have already mentioned, one feature I liked about the approach taken in the *Restatement of Torts* was the four-part classification that carved privacy into manageable chunks. Jones's claim fell within the first category of intrusion upon seclusion, and we could decide the case without going beyond that category. To ground a successful claim in this category, the plaintiff would have to show that:

1. the defendant acted intentionally or recklessly;
2. the defendant invaded, without lawful justification, the plaintiff's private affairs or concerns; and
3. the invasion was one that a reasonable person would regard as highly offensive, causing distress, humiliation, or anguish.

We cautioned that the claim we recognized was not absolute and that it would have to be reconciled with, and perhaps even yield to, the competing claims of freedom of expression and freedom of the press.

Finally, and perhaps more controversially, came the issue of damages. We accepted that proof of actual out-of-pocket loss should not be required, but we held that absent provable pecuniary damage, recovery should be modest to avoid windfall claims but sufficient to mark the wrong. After reviewing the awards made for similar wrongs by the Ontario courts and the courts of other provinces under protection of privacy legislation, we fixed the range for damages for non-pecuniary loss at up to $20,000.[38]

I concluded that by limiting our decision to intrusion upon seclusion, avoiding a more general proclamation of a right to privacy and limiting the amount of damages available, the move we were making was "an incremental step that is consistent with the role of this court to develop the common law in a manner consistent with the changing needs of society."[39]

## Making Law, Not Making Up Law

I suggest that one way of looking at the kind of judicial law-making involved in a case like *Jones v Tsige* is this: judges are entitled to make law when they decide cases, but they are not entitled to make law up. As I argued in chapter 4, judicial law-making is an essential part of our common law tradition. But judges are not entitled to make up law or create it out of thin air. They must provide reasoned decisions, based upon existing and recognized legal norms and arguments acceptable to the community and consistent with the limits inherent in our democratic tradition.

I certainly do not adhere to Blackstone's declaratory theory that common law judges do not make law but rather simply discover the law and declare what it always has been.[40] Yet it seems to me that at some level Blackstone's theory contains the grain of an important insight. I knew that we were making law in *Jones v Tsige*. Before we decided the case, the tort of intrusion upon seclusion did not exist in Ontario. But *something* did exist within the law before my decision. I was not just making the whole thing up on my own. The tort of intrusion upon seclusion did not come out of thin air. It was based on pre-existing, recognized legal principles and persuasive authorities. It took our decision in *Jones v Tsige* to show that the time had come for those principles to crystallize and establish the new tort. In my reasons for judgment, I did my best to explain to Tsige, the losing party, as well as to the legal community and the public at large, that the new tort was far from an invention out of whole cloth.

## Conclusion

At the end of my judgment in *Jones v Tsige*, I summarized the factors that I thought justified recognizing a right of action to cover Jones's claim.

First, the case law, while far from conclusive, was steadily drifting in Jones's direction. Second, there was a principled basis for the claim flowing from the values underlying several recognized claims. This was significantly bolstered by the recognition of privacy as a *Charter* value. Third, a very considerable body of legal scholarship supported the development. Fourth, there had been technological change. If the advent of photography was enough to prompt a future judge of the Supreme Court of the United States to advocate a change to the common law in the nineteenth century, then surely the problems posed by modern digital technology supported a similar change in the twenty-first century. Finally, we had before us facts that seemed to me to cry out for a remedy. Tsige's conduct was deliberate. Anyone in Jones's position would be profoundly upset, and, in my view, "the law of this province would be sadly deficient if we were required to send Jones away without a legal remedy."[41]

As the decision in *Jones v Tsige* was not appealed to the Supreme Court of Canada, it stands for now as the law of Ontario. While it has been generally well received,[42] the decision has not achieved universal acceptance,[43] and it certainly will not be the last word. In the tradition of the common law, this area will continue to evolve as new fact patterns emerge for judicial consideration and as technology and social conditions continue to change.

## Chapter 10

# Standard of Review and Discretion

## Standard of Review

Legal adjudicators – administrative tribunals, trial and appellate courts – have distinctive roles in our legal system. When a first-level adjudicator's decision is challenged in a court by way of judicial review or appeal, those distinctive roles are reflected in formal legal terms by what lawyers and judges call "the standard of review." The standard of review defines what an appellate or reviewing court can and cannot do in relation to a first-instance decision.

In some cases, the appellate or reviewing court is entitled to scrutinize the first-instance decision on a "correctness" standard: Was the decision right or was it wrong? The appellate or reviewing court will affirm the challenged decision if it thinks it is right and reverse it if it thinks it is wrong. However, in a long and growing list of situations, the appellate or reviewing court is required to defer to the first-instance decision. Even if the appellate or reviewing court disagrees with the decision under review, it cannot interfere unless the decision is unreasonable or rests upon a certain type of readily identifiable legal error.

An unfortunately complex body of law has developed in this area. Justice Rosalie Abella described the standard of review in administrative law as the Supreme Court's "prodigal child."[1] Justice David Stratas, a member of the Federal Court of Appeal, has lamented the fact that "[d]octrinal incoherence and inconsistency plague the Canadian law of judicial review."[2] It is not my intention in this chapter to deal with all of the intricacies in this difficult area. However, the concept is vital to a proper understanding of the judicial role. In virtually every case I decide as an appellate judge, the first question I have to ask is, What is the applicable standard of review? Very often the answer to that question determines the outcome of the case. Accordingly, I will endeavour to explain in simple terms the broad outlines of the law relating to the standard of review.

## Deference and Legality

At the core of the debate over the appropriate standard of review are the competing principles of deference and legality.

Deference defines the measure of respect the reviewing or appellate court must accord the decision under review. Deference reminds the reviewing or appellate court that first-instance decision-makers have certain institutional advantages in dealing with questions of fact, policy, and certain questions of law that are central to their mandate. Deference instructs reviewing or appellate courts to refrain from approaching the case as if they were the first-instance decision-maker. First-instance decision-makers are given a margin of appreciation, protecting their decisions from unduly strict scrutiny. This means that even if the reviewing or appellate court would lean towards deciding the case differently, ordinarily, it may not interfere with the decision unless it can say that the decision was "unreasonable" (a concept I explain below) or infected by certain kinds of legal error.

Deference also reflects legislative supremacy and the right of Parliament and the legislatures to assign decision-making powers to administrative agencies – for example, human rights commissions, labour boards, and immigration and refugee tribunals. Provided the legislation that assigns decision-making authority does not infringe upon the constitutionally protected authority of the courts,[3] the legislator's choice must be respected.

But deference has its limits and at a certain point confronts the competing principle of legality and the ideal of a uniform standard of justice. A reviewing or appellate court must reconcile the need to defer to first-instance decisions with the duty to ensure the overall legal integrity of the decision-making process. Reviewing and appellate courts are instructed by the principle of deference to refrain from unduly meddling with specific decisions but, at the same time, are encouraged by the principle of legality to intervene when first-instance decisions do not respect the law's general standards.

As we shall see, knowing where to draw the line between the principles of deference and legality has proven to be a notoriously difficult task. While this may sound like a purely technical question, it is probably the question that gnaws at my judicial conscience more than any other. The reason is very simple. As a judge, I am committed to the idea that every case should be decided justly. Yet the standard of review and the principle of deference instruct me daily to keep my appellate judicial hands off decisions that I would have made differently – decisions that I think are wrong but not so wrong that I can call them unreasonable.

## Administrative Law

Deference has been a particularly significant theme in the law that governs the activities of governmental administrative agencies. A detailed consideration of administrative law is beyond the scope of this book, but some discussion is appropriate, as it was in the administrative law context where the theme of deference emerged in modern Canadian law.

The courts have always played a role in the supervision of the administrative apparatus of the state. A complex body of law determines when a citizen can challenge an administrative decision before the courts. Historically, judicial review of administrative decisions was justified on the basis that the courts were duty-bound to ensure that government officials and administrative agencies established by statute did not exceed the limits of their jurisdiction. If a statute provided that an administrative tribunal could make an order if both conditions A and B were satisfied and the administrative tribunal made an order on the basis of conditions A and C, the reviewing court could nullify the order on the ground that the tribunal had exceeded its jurisdiction. Jurisdictional review was seen to be an essential aspect of the rule of law. Government officials and administrative tribunals had to respect the statutory and legal limits on their powers, and if they failed to do so, a court could intervene.

An important feature of jurisdictional review was the distinction between correctness and legality. The court could not quash a decision simply because it thought the decision was wrong. It could do so only on the ground that the administrative decision-maker had exceeded the legal limits of its powers – in other words, had gone beyond where its enabling statute permitted it to go. This restriction on judicial review was meant to preclude judges from quashing administrative decisions simply because they disagreed with what had been decided.

However, courts were wary of the growth of the modern administrative state[4] and did not hesitate to subject administrative decisions to close scrutiny. There was a pronounced tendency for courts to characterize issues as jurisdictional and thereby expose them to correction by the courts. Many techniques were deployed to justify judicial intervention, and even some factual findings were characterized as being jurisdictional.

This interventionist stance was replaced by a prevailing and dominant norm of deference. The watershed moment in Canada arrived with Justice Brian Dickson's 1979 decision in a labour relations case, *CUPE v New Brunswick Liquor Corporation*.[5] Dispute resolution in labour relations is highly complex and specialized. Courts had proven themselves inept at resolving such disputes, and legislatures responded by establishing specialized tribunals that had the requisite expertise. The courts, ever protective of their powers, retaliated with aggressive judicial review of labour board decisions.

In *CUPE*, Justice Dickson tried to put an end to what he and many others saw as excessive judicial intervention. He insisted that courts must refrain from labelling doubtful legal issues as jurisdictional to justify judicial intervention. He drew a firm line of deference to protect the decisions of administrative tribunals from being second-guessed by judges. A labour board, he wrote, was "not required to be 'correct.'"[6]

Whether rightly or wrongly decided in the eyes of the court, a labour board's decision had to be respected because the board had specialized expertise and experience in labour-management relations. Labour boards, not courts, have the required knowledge or background to cope with the "delicate balance between the need to maintain public services and the need to maintain collective bargaining."[7] The courts were entitled to intervene, he wrote, only if "the Board's interpretation was so patently unreasonable that its construction cannot be rationally supported by the relevant legislation."[8] A leading scholar of administrative law described this decision as a "refreshing change" and "a significant advance," because it recognized the "autonomy and prerogatives of expert statutory authorities."[9] Justice Dickson cared deeply about getting to the right decision. But he also understood that judges do not always have a premium on right answers. He realized that sometimes the interests of justice and the objective of getting to the right answer were best served by respecting the decision-making capacities of others.[10]

The phrase "patent unreasonableness" defined the standard of review for many years. While it has now evolved into "reasonableness," the high level of deference to be accorded to administrative tribunals is firmly entrenched in Canadian law. *Dunsmuir v New Brunswick*[11] states: "Reasonableness" is "a deferential standard animated by the principle that ... certain questions that come before administrative tribunals do not lend themselves to one specific, particular result," and that tribunals are to be accorded "a margin of appreciation within the range of acceptable and rational solutions."[12] The task of a judge reviewing an administrative decision for reasonableness is restricted to ensuring that the decision reveals "justification, transparency and intelligibility within the decision-making process," and that "the decision falls within a range of possible, acceptable outcomes which are defensible in respect of the facts and law."[13] The Supreme Court agreed with a leading administrative law scholar who described "deference as respect" that requires of the courts "not submission but a respectful attention to the reasons offered or which could be offered in support of a decision."[14] Judicial distrust has given way to a recognition that administrative tribunals and agencies have both specialized expertise and the capacity to resolve certain disputes in a timely and efficient manner, one that enhances access to justice.

At the same time, however, the principle of legality must be respected. The courts have a constitutionally protected role to maintain the rule of law and ensure the integrity of decisions that affect legal rights. The first-level decision-maker is expected to provide a reasoned justification for the decision.[15] If the reasons fail to demonstrate a reasonable result or if the decision was reached in violation of procedural fairness, the decision will not be tolerated and will be vulnerable to judicial review.

There are certain legal issues that are reviewed on a correctness standard and upon which the courts have the final say. On those issues, deference does not apply, and the court is entitled to set the decision aside if it concludes that the decision-maker's decision was wrong in law. Identifying legal issues that are reviewed on a standard of correctness has been difficult and controversial. Courts are discouraged from characterizing issues that involve a mix of fact and law or policy as questions of law or jurisdiction to be reviewed on a correctness standard. The norm of deference may be reinforced where the statute creating the administrative agency explicitly states that decisions of the administrative agency are final and conclusive and not subject to appeal or judicial review.[16] Even where there is a statutory right of appeal, the reasonableness standard applies.[17] Another important limitation on judicial review is that courts are required to defer to decisions involving the interpretation of an agency's "own statute or statutes closely connected to its function, with which it will have particular familiarity."[18] Deference is also appropriate for related general legal issues where the agency has developed a particular expertise.[19] On the other hand, legal issues that are of "central importance to the legal system ... and outside the ... specialized area of expertise" of the administrative decision-maker will attract a correctness standard.[20]

The prevailing norm of deference significantly limits my right as a judge to interfere with an administrative decision simply because I think the decision was wrong in law. But the competing norm of legality remains as a central feature of modern administrative law. Despite being significantly controlled and constrained, the courts still play a role in ensuring the integrity of the decision-making process. We are left with what appears to be a perpetual search for the right balance between deference and legality.

## Trials and Appeals

Deference is also a dominant theme in defining the respective roles of trial and appellate courts.[21] Essentially, the division is between questions of law, on which appellate courts are supreme, and questions of fact, on which trial courts usually have the final say.

My primary role as an appellate judge is to define, explain, and elucidate the law, and to ensure its uniform application. When filtered through the screen of deference, this means that as an appellate judge, I apply a standard of correctness to a trial judge's conclusions in law. If I identify a legal error in the trial judge's decision, I can correct it.

On the other hand, I must accept and respect the trial judge's primary role of deciding specific disputes on their facts. I must defer to a trial judge's findings of fact, and I may reverse only factual findings that exhibit a demonstrable error at the heart of the case, or to use the technical label, a "palpable and overriding error."[22] A palpable error is one that is obvious. For example, if there is no evidence to support a factual finding, it is obviously wrong. If one finding conflicts with another finding, there is an obvious error. Speculative findings and findings based on a misapprehension of the evidence are further examples of obvious or palpable errors.[23] An "overriding" error is one that is of sufficient gravity to "vitiate the challenged finding of fact" – in other words, an error that "goes to the root of the challenged finding of fact such that the fact cannot safely stand in the face of that error."[24] Errors of this nature implicate the integrity of the legal process and accordingly are not protected from appellate review. So if the finding is "contrary, not merely to what the appellate court would have done, but contrary to what any trier of fact could reasonably have done,"[25] the appellate court must intervene.

*Cottrelle v Gerrard*[26] illustrates when an appellate court will intervene. This was a difficult case involving a diabetic woman who had to have her leg amputated. She maintained that her physician fell below the standard of care in her treatment. The real issue was causation: Did the physician's alleged failure to render proper treatment cause the woman to lose her leg? The law sets a clear standard: the patient had to show on a balance of probabilities – that is, more than a 50 per cent probability – that but for the negligent treatment, she would not have lost her leg. The plaintiff will not succeed where the probability is less than 50 per cent, as the law does not allow partial compensation for the "loss of a chance" of a better outcome. Regrettably, in this case, the evidence of causation to meet the legal standard simply was not there. The expert witnesses agreed that while proper treatment *might* have saved her leg, because of her severe pre-existing atherosclerosis, it was more likely than not that she would have lost her leg even with proper treatment. We concluded that the trial judge, understandably sympathetic to the plight of the patient, had either misapplied the law on causation or misunderstood the evidence. We had no choice but to set aside the trial judge's judgment in favour of the woman.

There are good reasons for the division of labour between trial and appellate courts. Let me first consider questions of law. It is basic to a sound system of justice that the law be applied uniformly to all. This is sometimes referred to as "the principle of universality" that ensures "that the same legal rules are applied in similar situations."[27] Appellate courts have the duty to monitor and supervise the legal integrity of decision-making. They have an overview of the legal system and are ordinarily better placed to decide points of law than a single trial judge, who is necessarily immersed in the facts and details of the specific case. Appellate decisions have precedential effect and will be binding in the future. This means that appellate judges have to focus not only on the specifics of the case but on the broader implications of the decision. This gives rise to a certain expertise in assessing how a specific ruling in one case may affect other cases in the future. Appellate courts also sit in panels of three or more judges. This ensures that points of law are decided on a collegial basis and insulates decisions from the personal or idiosyncratic views of one judge.

When we turn to questions of fact, it is widely accepted that trial judges have the advantage. Trial judges are "in the trenches" and on the front lines of justice. They see and hear the parties and the witnesses. They watch the narrative of the case unfold, and they guide the case from its start to its completion. The trial judge lives with the case for the duration of the trial, often days or weeks. This puts the trial judge in "a privileged position"[28] to deal with issues of fact. By dealing with the dispute hands-on, trial judges gain an intimate understanding of the case. This first-hand perspective is impossible to replicate on appeal. In the words of an author cited with approval by the Supreme Court of Canada, the trial judge is "exposed to the entire case" and gains a "total familiarity with the evidence," which facilitates a "far deeper" insight than is possible on appeal.[29] An appellate judge can only read the paper record. Oral argument on appeal will be time-limited. The view of the case is "telescopic"[30] or "myopic"[31] rather than at large.

Appeal courts are required to defer to the trial judge's findings of fact for three reasons.[32]

First, it is unlikely that the quality of decisions on questions of fact would be improved by allowing open-ended appellate review. There is a significant risk that without the first-hand familiarity with the case that can be gained only by hearing and seeing the witnesses, appellate decisions on factual questions will be of a lower quality than those made by trial judges. So, however paradoxical it might seem, the curtailment of appeal rights and the restraint imposed on appellate judges from interfering with factual findings is motivated by a desire to get to the right result.

Second is the interest in efficiency and minimizing the cost of litigation. As there is nothing to be gained in quality, the interests of efficiency strongly favour limiting appeals on questions of fact. It would be costly and time-consuming to give appellate judges the time and resources they would require to be in the position where they could safely second-guess trial judges on questions of fact. And even then, it is unlikely that a full-blown appeal on factual issues would yield better or even equally sound results. Saddling the parties, especially litigants with limited resources, with the cost of such an appeal would be both inefficient and unfair.

I am generally wary of allowing systemic efficiency to trump individual justice. However, I accept that if the justice system is too costly, access to justice is lost, and with lost access goes the protection of individual rights. Appeals are expensive and can be used by wealthy litigants to wear down their opponents. Modern civil procedure emphasizes the principle of proportionality, the idea that the nature and cost of the process should be proportionate to the value, complexity, and importance of the case so that civil justice is more timely, efficient, and affordable. This curtails the unbridled pursuit of "justice at all costs" that can put justice out of reach. Open-ended appeals could undermine the principle of proportionality and the encouragement of cost-effective justice.

The third reason for limiting appeals on questions of fact is promoting the integrity of the trial process. Allowing appeal courts to review all trial decisions on a correctness standard could undermine public confidence in the trial process. Trials would become nothing more than the first crack, and if one party did not like the result they could have a second crack at the court of appeal. As the Supreme Court of Canada put it, an appeal should be "the exception rather than the rule."[33]

While there is general agreement that appeal courts should defer to trial judges on questions of fact, like many judges and lawyers, I have reservations about how far deference should go.

Appeal courts are required to defer to findings of fact, even when the case did not involve oral evidence and was based on a purely written record.[34] The advantage possessed by the trial judge in such a case is considerably less apparent than where the findings were made after a full-blown trial involving oral evidence. Requiring deference in cases decided on a written record essentially rests on the ground that appeals should be limited for reasons of efficiency.

Techniques like summary judgment allow judges to decide cases on a paper record to avoid lengthy and costly trials, where the judge decides that the case for allowing or dismissing the claim is clear.[35] Those gains in efficiency would be impaired if we allowed for open-ended rights to costly and time-consuming appeals.

Another and more significant extension of deference turns on the elusive question of whether an issue is one of law or of fact. There is no clear test that draws a precise line between questions of law and questions of fact. All trial decisions necessarily involve issues of both law and fact, and it is not always easy to say whether an issue that has been appealed involves a question of law or a question of fact.

A trial judge must do three things in order to decide a case: first, determine what actually took place between the parties on the basis of the evidence led in the case; second, determine the applicable legal standard that applies; and third, apply the legal standard to the facts as found.

The first step obviously involves a question of fact to which deference is owed. A finding of fact may be infected by a legal error if, for example, the trial judge made a legal error on the admissibility of evidence. However, there is a growing tendency to treat many rulings on evidence as being discretionary, and discretionary decisions also attract appellate deference. So if a trial decision is appealed on a factual issue, deference will almost always apply to limit the scope of the appeal.

The second step involves a question of law. If the trial judge misstates the law or selects the wrong legal test, the court of appeal is entitled to correct the legal error. The correctness standard applies, and the court will reverse the decision.

The most contentious issue arises at the third step, applying the legal test to the facts or determining whether the facts satisfy the legal test. This third step is commonly referred to as "a question of mixed fact and law." Whether this step is reviewable on a standard of correctness or a standard of deference varies, but in modern Canadian law, the general tendency is to accord trial judges applying the law to the facts the same deference they are accorded to findings of pure fact.

In *Housen v Nikolaisen*, the leading Canadian case on the standard of review,[36] the issue was whether a municipality had been negligent in maintaining a road. The trial judge made factual findings on what the municipality had or had not done. He concluded that there were shortcomings in road maintenance and that the municipality had fallen below the required standard of care. The result was that the municipality was negligent and liable to the person injured because of the poor road maintenance.

That decision involved an element of legal judgment. Deciding that the municipality acted unreasonably required a legal evaluation of the municipality's conduct, not just a factual finding about what the municipality had or had not done. However, the Supreme Court insisted that the decision was essentially factual and could be reversed on appeal only if it revealed "palpable and overriding" error.

The court held that questions of mixed fact and law lie along a spectrum. A correctness standard should apply only if the trial judge made what it described as an "extricable" or clearly identifiable error in legal principle. This would arise, for example, if the trial judge misstated the legal test or without explicitly stating the legal test, implicitly applied one that is wrong.[37] Or, having stated the test correctly as involving a consideration of factors A, B, C, and D, the trial judge proceeded only to consider factors A, B, and C.[38] However, most trial judgments correctly recite the law, and the devil lies in the details of its application to the facts. This means that the palpable and overriding error standard effectively immunizes most trial decisions applying the law to the facts from review.

There is a marked trend to accord substantial deference to decisions on questions of mixed fact and law. In its 2014 decision in *Sattva Capital Corp v Creston Moly Corp,* the Supreme Court acknowledged, "Historically, determining the legal rights and obligations for the parties under a written contract was regarded as a question of law" but announced that the old approach should be abandoned.[39] Contrary to the traditional approach, where contractual interpretation focused strictly on the legal document, courts increasingly look to the circumstances surrounding the formation of a contract to decipher its intended meaning. As that is essentially a factual inquiry, contractual interpretation has become a question of mixed fact and law. Absent an extricable error of law such as "the application of an incorrect principle, the failure to consider a required element of a legal test, or the failure to consider a relevant factor,"[40] the standard of deference applies, and an appellate court cannot interfere with the trial judge's decision.

Within two years, faced with several decisions from provincial appellate courts pointing out problems caused by *Sattva,*[41] the Supreme Court pulled back and held in *Ledcor Construction Ltd v*

*Northbridge Indemnity Insurance Co*[42] that where a court is interpreting a standard-form contract, the standard of review is correctness.
Standard-form contracts, sometimes called "contracts of adhesion,"
are non-negotiable, pre-printed agreements prepared for general,
across-the-board use in certain industries or activities. They are described by a leading contract law scholar as "a pervasive and indispensable feature of modern commercial life."[43] The court found that
the rationale for the *Sattva* reasonableness standard did not apply for
most standard-form contracts, as there were no circumstances surrounding the formation of the contract to consider, and the decision
in one case would have precedential value in another case involving
the same standard-form agreement.

While *Ledcor* qualifies *Sattva,* it does not question the general policy
objective of limiting intervention from appellate courts. The role of
an appellate court is to ensure consistency in the law, not to provide
a "new forum for parties to continue their private litigation."[44] This
means that appellate courts should intervene only where the answer
to the question of law posed is likely to have an impact beyond the
confines of the particular case. As it was put in an earlier decision,
the question is "whether the dispute is over a general proposition
that might qualify as a principle of law" and is therefore reviewable,
or whether it is "over a very particular set of circumstances that is
not apt to be of much interest to judges and lawyers in the future,"
in which case it is not.[45]

Another striking extension of the deference principle is found in
the realm of constitutional law. The Supreme Court of Canada has
held that even on highly contested issues of great public importance, deference may prevail. *Bedford,* the decision striking down
criminal prohibitions against certain activities associated with prostitution, turned on the claim that the existing laws infringed upon
the constitutionally protected right to security of the person in a
manner that did not accord with the principles of fundamental justice.[46] Prostitution is not, in itself, an illegal activity, and one of the
purposes of the impugned laws was to protect vulnerable sex-trade
workers. Those challenging the laws presented a substantial volume of expert social science evidence showing how the laws actually operated. The evidence demonstrated to the satisfaction of the
trial judge that rather than protect vulnerable sex-trade workers,
the impugned laws had the effect of putting them at greater risk.

The laws were accordingly found to be inconsistent with the principles of fundamental justice. They were arbitrary, as there was a lack of connection between the effect and the object of the law; they were overbroad, as the laws went too far and interfered with some conduct that bore no connection to the objectives; and the harmful effect of the law was found to be grossly disproportionate to the state's objective. Despite an earlier Supreme Court of Canada decision upholding the constitutionality of the same laws,[47] the trial judge struck them down as an infringement of the sex-trade workers' section 7 *Charter* rights.

The "legislative" or "social fact" evidence used in *Bedford* is different from more routine evidence about "who did what and when" that had been considered in the cases establishing the deferential "palpable and overriding" error standard. Legislative or social fact evidence relates to the actual impact and effect of legislation. This is a matter of opinion ordinarily proven by experts trained in the social sciences. As opinion of this kind involves judgment about the operation and effect of the law, it seem to lie more towards the legal end of the law-fact spectrum. Until *Bedford*, findings based on legislative or social fact evidence had not been accorded deference on appeal but were reviewed more or less on the same basis as were questions of law.[48]

This approach was reversed in *Bedford*. The Supreme Court held that a trial judge's findings on legislative or social fact evidence must be treated as factual and be reversed only if infected by palpable and overriding error. In coming to that conclusion, the court was daunted by the prospect of appellate courts "duplicating the sometimes time-consuming and tedious work"[49] of the trial judge and the consequent cost and delay that such an exercise would entail. Again, the policies of efficiency and protecting the integrity of the trial process pushed the court to a deferential standard.

The implications of *Bedford* are significant and demonstrate how far we have gone with deference. A trial judge now has the power to strike down a law previously found valid by the Supreme Court on the basis of new facts about the law's operation. Neither an intermediate appellate court nor the Supreme Court of Canada can review that decision unless it can be said that the trial judge's findings reveal palpable and overriding error. This represents a significant shift of decision-making authority away from the appellate courts, including the Supreme Court of Canada, in favour of trial judges.

## Deference: Conclusion

The expanding reach of the deference doctrine imposes a significant qualification on the capacity of appellate judges to right perceived wrongs. And as Professor Jutras noted, "[E]xplaining to ordinary litigants that the Court of Appeal must on occasion uphold a 'mistaken' decision is not an easy thing to do."[50] But without deference, we would risk "effectively compressing the system into a single rank of court."[51] We limit the capacity of appellate courts to correct errors of fact, and we trust trial courts to administer fair justice when resolving specific disputes that have little or no impact beyond the immediate parties. This respects the integrity of the trial process and encourages appellate courts to devote their efforts to the jurisprudential task of ensuring that a sound body of law is applied evenly and consistently.

But there is always the question of where to draw the line between deference and legality. That line has steadily been pushed very far in the direction of deference by the Supreme Court. Decisions like *Bedford* seem to me to go too far, and the instability of the Supreme Court's administrative law jurisprudence suggests that the time for readjustment may not be far away.

## Discretion

Discretion is an important and frequently discussed feature of judicial decision-making.[52] It is closely related to the standard of review. Many decisions that attract a deferential standard of review are discretionary.

The central idea behind discretion is that it is not possible to know or to predict every situation that might arise. We must rely on the capacity of decision-makers to reach appropriate outcomes. Rather than dictate outcomes, the law lays down general standards and principles and trusts decision-makers to reach fair and appropriate results by considering the particular circumstances of each case.

The concept of discretion has been described by Aharon Barak as "central to an understanding of the judicial process."[53] Yet despite its significance, the meaning of discretion is variable and uncertain. It has been described as a "chameleon concept,"[54] one that is not "simple or single."[55] I will argue that the purpose, meaning, and proper use of discretion depends very much upon the context in which the term is used.[56]

## Discretion: Good Judgment or Uncontrolled Power?

What do we mean by "discretion"? The *Shorter Oxford English Dictionary* definition of "discretion" includes two quite different meanings:

1. The action of discerning or judging; judgment; discrimination.
2. Liberty or power of deciding, or acting according to one's own judgment; uncontrolled power of disposal.

There is an obvious tension between these two meanings. The first suggests good judgment, consistent with the idea of disciplined decision-making based upon recognized and accepted legal standards. The second connotes the opposite: the autonomy to decide according to personal views, irrelevant and extraneous to the law.

The tension between these two definitions is reflected in judicial decisions discussing discretion. Lord Mansfield adhered to the first meaning: "Discretion when applied to a court of justice means sound discretion guided by law. It must be governed by rule not by humour; it must not be arbitrary, vague and fanciful; but legal and regular."[57]

This meaning recognizes the need to give judges a margin of discretion to allow them to decide cases fairly and justly by taking into account specific or distinctive features of the case that cannot be captured by the generality of the pertinent legal rules. But it also circumscribes discretion by requiring it to be "sound," "guided by law," "governed by rule," and "legal and regular." It is what Professor Kent Roach has described as "principled discretion" that lies at a midpoint between strictly rule-bound decision-making and unconstrained choice.[58]

Another eighteenth-century judge, Lord Camden, perhaps more cynical than Lord Mansfield, saw discretion more in terms of the second definition: "The discretion of a judge is the law of tyrants. It is always unknown. It is different in different men. It is casual, and depends upon constitution, temper, passion. In the best it is of-tentimes caprice. In the worst it is every vice, folly, and passion, to which human nature is liable."[59]

This description paints discretion as a dangerously ill-defined and undisciplined doctrine capable of opening the floodgates to rule by "vice, folly and passion."

In chapter 6, I presented the arguments for what I call disciplined decision-making. Is reliance on a healthy measure of discretion con-sistent with disciplined decision-making? How do we ensure that judges have the discretion required to decide cases justly and fairly but at the same time ensure that judges do not decide cases on whim or caprice?

The first and most fundamental answer is that the law has insisted that Lord Mansfield's definition of discretion prevails over that of Lord Camden. In the legendary Supreme Court of Canada decision *Roncarelli v Duplessis*,[60] Justice Ivan Rand recognized that, if accepted, Lord Camden's idea of discretion would undermine the very idea of justice under law. The issue was whether Maurice Duplessis, the Pre-mier of Quebec, had acted unlawfully when he ordered that a Mon-treal restaurant owner's liquor licence be terminated. Duplessis's motivation was his ill-will towards the restaurant owner for having bailed out of custody several devout and proselytizing Jehovah's Witnesses who had been arrested for distributing their literature in violation of a municipal by-law. The liquor licensing regime gave broad discretion, but Justice Rand held that "there is no such thing as absolute and untrammelled 'discretion.'"[61] A decision-maker must act for a reason that comports within the letter and purpose of the law that confers the discretion. The religiously motivated activities of the restaurant owner had nothing to do with the purpose and ob-ject of the liquor licensing regime, and therefore it was an abuse of power to revoke the liquor licence on those grounds.

The meaning attributed to discretion by Lord Mansfield and Jus-tice Rand answers Lord Camden's worst fears about the arbitrary nature of discretion. The legal system must rely on the discretion of decision-makers to deal efficiently, effectively, and fairly with the day-to-day administration of justice. But the legal system must also insist that the discretion be channelled and controlled.

Decision-makers who make discretionary decisions must remain within the parameters that the law defines, and if they exercise an adjudicative function, they must provide a reasoned justification for the decision. As I will explain, it is open to an appellate court to reverse a discretionary decision where the trial judge mistook the applicable legal test or principle defining the limits of the discretion or reached a decision that was unreasonable. The decision is not subject to review simply because the appellate court thinks it was wrong. However, the decision will be subject to review if the appellate court finds that the decision failed to comply with governing legal norms, including the duty to provide a reasoned justification.

## Discretion in Context

In legal discourse, we frequently describe discretion as "the power to choose between two or more courses of action, each of which is thought of as permissible."[62] To understand the implications of this view of discretion and to determine its consistency with the principle of disciplined decision-making, it is helpful to consider discretion in three different contexts.

The first context relates to the generality of legal standards. Laws set general standards and leave it to judges to decide specific cases. The room left to decide is commonly referred to as discretion.

The second context relates to institutional advantage. As I have attempted to explain in the first part of this chapter, the law recognizes that certain decisions are best left to first-instance decision-makers. The law limits the capacity of appellate or reviewing courts to interfere with those decisions. We tend to label those decisions as discretionary. There may be an appeal, but the appellate court will recognize that the decision falls within the field where the first-level decision-maker is better situated to make the call, and, as with questions of fact, the appellate court will defer to that call, even where it might have decided differently.

The third context relates to the need for finality. Like the second context, this relates to the distinctive roles of first-level decision-makers and reviewing or appellate courts. There are situations where it is in the interest of efficient justice to insist that the parties accept a decision, right or wrong, rather than to permit an appeal. Decisions with limited rights of appeal, again, tend to be labelled as discretionary.

Attention to these three contexts facilitates our understanding of discretion. It also mitigates against the mistaken impression that a judge who exercises discretion and thereby receives relative immunity from appellate review is somehow relieved of the over-riding responsibility to make the right – or at least the best pos-sible – decision.

My basic argument is that it is essential to keep in mind that dis-cretion has two aspects. The first, what I will call discretion as defer-ence, relates to the power to choose from a range of possible courses of action. Discretion as deference pertains when we are considering the reviewability of decisions. The reviewing court must respect and defer to the first-instance decision, subject only to legal error or un-reasonableness. The second aspect is what I will call discretion as good judgment. That aspect of discretion is appropriate to describe the task of the first-instance decision-maker who is assigned the re-sponsibility of deciding issues labelled discretionary.

## Discretion and the Generality of Legal Standards

In chapter 3, I argue that the need for generality of legal standards makes the law to some extent inherently uncertain. Laws cannot be framed in a way that provides an automatic answer for every case. The law's general standards define the parameters of legal debate but, at the same time, leave room for judgment in application to specific cases. The room or space left by the broadly framed legal standard gives the judge a margin of appreciation to decide the case justly and fairly by applying the general legal standard but also to take into account the particular or peculiar features of the case at hand. This well-recognized and desirable feature of judicial deci-sion-making falls into the category of discretion. As Aharon Barak puts it, the law defines "a zone of lawful possibilities"[63] and gives the decision-maker the power "to choose between two or more alter-natives, when each of the alternatives is lawful."[64] Discretion in this sense is the oil that makes the machinery of justice run smoothly. It recognizes that the law cannot contemplate in advance all possible situations and that the general standards it lays down require indi-vidualized judgment when implemented.

The "power to choose" concept explains both discretion as defer-ence and discretion as good judgment. Discretion as deference relates to the task of appellate or reviewing courts. They must accept that, very often, individualized judgment is best exercised by the first-instance decision-maker who is immersed in the details of the case.

Discretion as good judgment defines the task of the first-instance decision-maker. There is a choice to be made, but the law does define a "zone" and the factors the judge is required to consider. The law contemplates "sound discretion guided by law." Decisions based upon a judge's "constitution, temper, passion" are excluded.

There are many situations where the law insists upon judgment and discernment according to a defined legal standard but falls short of providing a formula capable of deciding all cases. Take the rules determining the availability of equitable remedies.[65] The common law tradition favours damages as a remedy for civil wrongs. In some situations, however, where damages are "inadequate" to compensate for the wrong, it is appropriate for the court to order an injunction requiring that a party do, or refrain from doing, the particular activity at issue. In most cases, a party who breaches a contract will be required to pay damages but where damages are "inadequate," the court may make an order of specific performance requiring the defaulting party to perform the contract as promised. The test to determine the adequacy of damages is very general, and while there is an extensive body of case law dealing with the concept, it is not possible to define the standard in a way that allows for automatic application. The standard can be applied only after careful consideration of the facts and the relationship between the parties, a determination that necessarily involves the exercise of judicial discretion. For that reason, the remedies of injunction and specific performance are said to be discretionary.

As Professor Kent Roach has shown, remedies under the *Charter of Rights and Freedoms* have a similar quality.[66] Decisions regarding matters such as the exclusion of evidence obtained in violation of a *Charter* right involve a variety of factors that cannot be reduced to a simple set of rules. Yet *Charter* rights are meaningless without effective remedies, and it is essential that remedial decisions be made in a principled fashion. Remedial discretion must be "conceptualized in a manner that makes it part of the *Charter*" and is consistent with the emphasis on "rational explanation and principled reasoning"[67] that should permeate the interpretation and application of our most fundamental rights and freedoms.

A judge who must decide a case under broad and general principles has a difficult task. The result is not neatly supplied by mechanical operation of a fixed rule. But from the perspective of the judge who has to decide the case, is the concept of discretion not best captured by the idea of good judgment? The judge faced with a discretionary decision certainly cannot say, "I have discretion and that means I can do what I please." Nor can the judge credibly say to the loser, "The law provided me with no more guidance than this: among the legally acceptable outcomes, there were several. I could have decided the case either for or against you. I have chosen to decide it against you." As in any other case, the judge must carefully consider and weigh the facts and delve deeply into the applicable legal rules and principles. The judge must strive to come up with a result that can be defended as the correct or, at the very least, the best possible result. As Professor Denis Galligan has argued, "Discretionary power is often characterized in terms of the authority to choose amongst alternative courses of action." However, the obligation to provide a reasoned decision means that "discretion consists not in the authority to choose amongst different actions, but to choose amongst different courses of action for good reasons."[68]

So even if, from the perspective of discretion as deference, an appellate court must defer because the lower-level decision was discretionary, the unlikelihood that the decision will be reversed does not detract from deference as good judgment and the duty of every judge *always* to come to a decision that best coheres with the governing legal principles and the pattern defined by past decisions. As Professor Stephen Waddams observes, "[I]t cannot be credibly maintained, simply because the judge has what is called 'discretion,' that one decision is as good as another."[69]

Judges making discretionary decisions know that their reasons for decision will be closely studied by the parties and by the legal community of which they are a part. The reasons must stand up to legal scrutiny. The decision may be appealed, and even if it was discretionary, it is not immune to review. The judge will also be aware that the decision may have an impact on how similar cases are decided in the future. The standards of the legal community and the private and public expectations of our legal system compel judges to do their very best to decide cases in accordance with the appropriate legal rules and principles. These expectations and aspirations explain deference as good judgment and constrain and control the exercise of discretion by first-instance decision-makers.

## Institutional Advantage

There are many situations where first-instance decision-makers have an advantage over appellate courts and where the law accordingly insists that the appellate court accord deference to the first-level decision. In these situations, it is commonly said that the first-level decision-maker has a discretion that the appellate court must respect.

In some cases, the institutional advantage is expertise. This, as I explained earlier in this chapter, is a prominent feature of modern administrative law where the legislature has assigned decision-making responsibility to a specialized tribunal. Legislatures confer powers on officials and create specialized agencies and tribunals to deal with particular matters. Courts have the inherent right to supervise the exercise of discretionary powers, but it is recognized that a complex modern society could not function without the exercise of discretion by public officials and administrative agencies. Modern administrative law doctrine is characterized by judicial restraint and deference. Subject to review for jurisdictional excess (now strongly discouraged and accordingly rare) and "unreasonableness,"[70] those who have been given discretionary powers have the right to decide and, so far as the reviewing court is concerned, the right to be "wrong" if the decision is not what the reviewing court would have chosen.

Conceptualizing discretion as a process more or less immune to review is also used with respect to judicial decisions. There are many decisions made by trial judges that the court of appeal will not review on a correctness standard because they are said to fall within the discretion of the trial judge. Many of the decisions that fall into this category are procedural – decisions on pretrial matters, many evidential rulings, and routine decisions made during the course of the trial process.

Decisions of that nature often require an intimate familiarity with the flow of the litigation that is readily available to trial judges and elusive to appellate courts.

In some areas, appellate courts accept that specialized trial judges have an expertise that calls for deference, namely in the areas of insolvency, commercial law, and class actions. These are areas where appellate courts recognize the advantage possessed by trial judges who may be assigned to sit for extended periods on particular kinds of cases because of their familiarity with a difficult and often technical area.

Another category of decisions deemed discretionary are those that are fact-sensitive and require a hands-on understanding of the intricacies of the case. Trial judges are clearly in the best position, for example, to assess the credibility of witnesses, to make findings of fact, and to assess the costs of an action. So too are trial judges best placed to make the difficult and sensitive assessments required to decide custody cases and issues of spousal support in the event of family breakdown. There is a clear advantage available to trial judges when making such decisions: the trial judges see and interact first-hand with the parties and witnesses over an extended period.

Many of the criminal appeals I decide fall into this category. They involve the sentence imposed by the trial judge. The law sets out in very general terms the principles of sentencing[71] but leaves it largely to the discretion of the judge who has tried the case to determine a fit sentence. Trial judges have the pulse of the communities in which they sit. They also have the opportunity to observe and assess the accused, the victim, and the witnesses, and that is a distinct advantage in determining a fit sentence.[72] This limits my role as an appeal judge. I must respect the primary role of the trial judge, and I can interfere with a sentence only if I conclude that the trial judge erred in principle or imposed a sentence that is manifestly unfit.

Where one of these institutional advantages exists, an appellate court is not as well placed as the trial judge to make the decision. So from the perspective of enhancing the quality of decisions, it is best for the appellate court to accord deference to the first-level decision-maker. Even if the appellate court is just as likely to reach the best decision, the time and cost involved in an appeal may not be warranted.

Some appellate judges say that they would not have come to the same decision, but they cannot say it was so wrong as to be unreasonable. They might even say that another judge might have come to a different decision. I find such statements unsettling. I have to admit that they are technically correct in law, but I do not like telling litigants, in effect, that the result reached in their case turned on the luck of what judge they happened to draw. On their face, these statements seem to refute the idea that the legal system aspires to get to the right or even the best possible answer. How can there be a right answer if the legal system gives the decision-maker a choice among more than one outcome and tolerates different answers from different judges?

I suggest that it is important to put these statements in their proper context. In my view, they refer only to discretion as deference, the power of the trial judge to choose, and the limitations that imposes on the role of the court of appeal. They do not refer to discretion as good judgment and the obligation that imposes on trial and sentencing judges to make the correct or the best possible decision. These statements also obscure, if not ignore, the reason for giving the first-level decision-maker the discretion to decide the case. We restrict intervention on judicial review or appeal precisely because we want to enhance the quality of decisions. The hypothesis upon which discretion as deference rests is that the first-level decision-maker is more likely to come up with the right or the best possible decision than an appellate or reviewing court. The relative immunity to review implicit in discretion as deference does not relieve the first-instance decision-maker of the obligation to provide the best possible answer, and it does not diminish the overarching goal of the legal system to provide the best possible answer. It simply prevents the court of appeal from getting in the way. Simply put, in these cases, appellate judges must accept that their perception of the right or the best answer may not be as reliable as that of the trial or sentencing judge.

So I reiterate the point I made in relation to the discretion that flows from the generality of legal standards. I do not think it is accurate to say that a decision-maker who is accorded discretion because of institutional advantage is freed from the duty to make the right decision according to the evidence and the law. Trial judges do not think that because the law gives them discretion to decide credibility, find the facts, determine the custody of an infant, or impose a fit sentence, they need not strive to make the right decision about who is telling the truth, who is best-suited to have custody of a child, or what is a just sentence. Discretion as deference is the flip side of discretion as good judgment. Relative immunity to appellate review does not amount to a licence to decide as one pleases.

## Finality

The third context to which the label "discretionary" pertains is that of pretrial procedural decisions from which there are narrow or restricted rights of appeal. Decisions involving preliminary procedural matters of this nature will rarely end the case. For example, does the written statement of claim filed to launch an action or the statement of defence comply with the rules of pleading? Such decisions are merely steps taken along the way to trial, and most jurisdictions impose limits on appeal rights. There are many other decisions of this kind, including decisions on rights of discovery, interlocutory injunctions, and security for costs. Such decisions may have a significant practical impact upon the litigation but, as they do not end it legally, appeal rights are limited for reasons of efficiency.[73] Allowing an automatic right of appeal on such matters would allow one litigant to bury the other with procedural appeals on peripheral and non-decisive issues. Some jurisdictions require leave to appeal and, even in jurisdictions where there is an appeal as of right, the trial level decision will be accorded significant deference. Appeal rights are also often restricted for "real-time" litigation such as decisions in insolvency and restructuring litigation, where immediate decisions are required to allow the process to unfold in an orderly and commercially appropriate manner. Appeal rights may also be restricted for small claims, as permitting appeals would defeat the objective of providing proportionally cost-effective justice.

Many decisions that fall into this category are labelled "discretionary." In my view, this simply means that whether right or wrong in the eyes of the appellate or reviewing court, the decision will not be reversed. As Roger Kerans, a retired member of the Alberta Court of Appeal, observed, calling the decision discretionary "does not adequately serve as a guide for a standard of review."[74] Professor Stephen Waddams explains the same point: "In these cases, it is more accurate to say that there is discretion because appeals are restricted, than to say that appeals are restricted because there is discretion."[75] The law imposes a restricted right of appeal in the interest of finality, fairness, and efficiency. We need a decision so that the parties can get on to trial or to an efficient resolution of their dispute. From the perspective of discretion as deference, the appellate court cannot intervene, but from the perspective of discretion as good judgment, deference on appeal does not detract from the duty of the first-instance judge to decide the case correctly.

An analogy on this point is commonly drawn to referees or umpires. There is no review of a called third strike in baseball, and yet there is no doubt about the obligation of the umpire to be right when making the call. The absence of the right to appeal the called third strike does not mean that the umpire has an unconstrained choice to decide what is a ball and what is a strike.[76] There is a need for an immediate and final decision so that the game can proceed. But that certainly does not mean that the umpire need not care about making the right call. A similar concern motivates the restriction on rights of appeal on interlocutory procedural matters or rulings made during the course of trial. The judicial system would become paralysed if parties could appeal every decision along the way. A stronger, richer party could beat an opponent into submission with a never-ending series of appeals on inconsequential matters. The demands of finality and efficiency prevail, and therefore sole responsibility to decide certain issues resides with the trial judge.

So again, in this third context, calling a decision discretionary does not tell the judge, "You should approach your task as picking among a range of acceptable choices." Rather, the judge should strive to make the right decision. Discretion invests the decision-maker with a measure of both freedom and power. But the freedom is constrained, and the power must be exercised responsibly. The decision-maker must strive to find a just outcome. That is very different from the freedom to do whatever the decision-maker wants. The absence of an automatic or full right of appeal should not divert judges from the duty to decide cases as best they can and according to the law.

## Chapter 11

# Role of the Judge in a Constitutional Democracy

In this chapter I consider the role judges play as interpreters of the *Canadian Charter of Rights and Freedoms*.[1] The *Charter* constitutionally protects fundamental rights and freedoms. The *Charter* creates an awesome constitutional duty: judges are required to declare to be of no force or effect those laws enacted by Parliament or a legislature that are inconsistent with protected rights and freedoms.

The courts – in particular, the Supreme Court of Canada – have fully accepted and embraced the *Charter*'s mandate. They have generously interpreted the rights and freedoms protected by the *Charter* and have not hesitated to strike down or rewrite laws that infringe upon *Charter* guarantees. Judges now confront some of the most controversial issues in Canadian society, and their decisions have had a significant impact on public life generally. The power of judges to review legislation for compliance with the Constitution shapes public debate on many significant issues – abortion,[2] religion in schools,[3] assisted suicide and euthanasia,[4] gay marriage and discrimination on grounds of sexual orientation,[5] the limits of police investigative powers,[6] the design of our public health-care system,[7] and national security in the age of international terrorism.[8]

The generous judicial interpretation of the *Charter* has provoked a lively and ongoing debate about the legitimacy of judicial review. I will consider that debate in this chapter, but it is important to keep judicial review under the *Charter* in proper perspective. *Charter* cases involving challenges to the validity of legislation are high-profile headline-grabbers. They are not, however, the daily fare of trial or appellate judges. *Charter* cases do not reflect the reality of the vast bulk of the work of the courts, and they should not be allowed to define and thereby distort the nature of the judicial role. Even at the Supreme Court of Canada, in 2017, only 26 per cent (11 per cent criminal and 15 per cent non-criminal)[9] of the cases heard involved the *Charter*. At an intermediate appellate court, the proportion is even lower. Most *Charter* issues arise in criminal cases, where the concern usually relates to the legality of police conduct and not the constitutionality of legislation. In my twenty-three years on the bench, I have faced relatively few cases where I have been asked to strike down a law enacted by Parliament or the legislature as inconsistent with the rights and freedoms guaranteed by the *Charter*. I have decided only two cases where that argument succeeded.[10]

I accept, however, that in view of the importance of the *Charter* and the power it confers on judges, no study of judicial decision-making in Canada would be complete without some consideration of the legitimacy of judges interfering with the laws enacted by Parliament and the legislatures.

What principle or philosophy of the *Charter* should guide judges in this difficult area? I do not pretend to have a definitive answer. This is a controversial topic, and there is a range of different and conflicting views that vie for acceptance by judges and, more importantly, by the broad Canadian polity. I will consider five different schools of thought. I conclude that no single approach has all the answers but that each school of thought offers important insights into how judges should discharge their duties under the *Charter*. Drawing on the metaphor I described in chapter 1, based upon Monet's series of impressionist paintings of Notre Dame Cathedral at Rouen, I see these schools of thought as five different "views of the cathedral."

I will begin with what I will call majoritarianism – the argument that the only legitimate way to decide controversial issues of fundamental rights is by a majority vote in Parliament. Majoritarians argue that because judicial review involves unelected judges overriding the decisions of democratically elected legislators, it is essentially undemocratic and therefore should be sharply curtailed, if not eliminated. Second, I will consider the converse of majoritarianism, the democratic process model. Adherents to this view see judicial review as the friend, not the enemy, of democracy, because by protecting fundamental rights and freedoms, judicial review enhances the preconditions for democratic life. Third, I will consider "originalism," the argument that judicial review is legitimate, but only if the courts stick to the literal meaning of the Constitution as intended by the framers. Fourth, I will explore the "fundamental rights" or "rights as trumps" school of thought, which posits fundamental rights as beyond the reach of politics and democratic choice and views judicial review as the means to ensure that fundamental rights prevail. Fifth and finally, I will discuss "dialogue theory," which situates judicial review in the context of an ongoing dialogue between the courts and legislatures in which neither the legislature nor the courts are supreme.

## Majoritarianism

Some critics argue that judicial review under the *Charter* is inherently anti-democratic as it allows non-elected and unaccountable judges to interfere with the will of Parliament and the provincial legislatures.[11] These critics accuse the courts, especially the Supreme Court of Canada, of "judicial activism," a phrase that suggests the courts have exceeded the acceptable limits of judicial authority and usurped the role of the democratically elected legislatures. Critics of "judicial activism" view the Supreme Court's approach to *Charter* interpretation as an undisciplined, unprincipled, and unwarranted assertion of judicial power. The charge of "judicial activism" alleges that the courts have been too willing to "make law" under the *Charter*, usually by striking down the laws enacted by legislators,[12] and occasionally by rewriting the law to make it comply with the *Charter*.[13] According to these critics, the courts have been too generous in their interpretation of the fundamental rights and freedoms guaranteed by the *Charter*, and, contrary to our democratic tradition, matters that should be resolved by elected representatives are now being decided by judges.

It is interesting to note that the criticism of the Supreme Court has come from both ends of the political spectrum. The first wave of assault on judicial activism under the *Charter* came from the political left.[14] These critics were wary of what they saw as the constitutionalization of individualistic, liberal values. They distrusted the judiciary as an essentially conservative institution and feared that the *Charter* would do little more than allow those who already enjoyed wealth and power to attack legislation designed to improve the interests of the weak and vulnerable.

More recently, the focus of the criticism of judicial activism has come from the political right.[15] The expansion of rights for those accused of crime and the generous interpretation accorded to minority rights, especially rights for gays, lesbians, and Indigenous peoples, have been attacked by these critics. They urge a program of judicial restraint and long for the era of parliamentary supremacy when the democratically elected legislatures could rule without interference from the courts. These critics suggest that *Charter* litigation is little more than a subterfuge that enables liberal academics and left-leaning special interest groups, labelled the "court party," to implement views that would not otherwise attract majority support from the populace at large.[16]

Although their politics differ, critics of judicial power share some common concerns.[17] They both contend that judges have too much discretion to read their own personal preferences into the vague words of the *Charter*. They argue that the *Charter* gives some groups too much power. The left is troubled by corporations and other advantaged interests using the *Charter* to strike down progressive laws curtailing their power and wealth. The right says that minorities and special interest groups use the *Charter* to gain advantages they could not achieve through democratic politics. And in the political middle there is a respectable philosophical argument that judicial review sits uneasily with democracy.[18]

I will make two observations about majoritarianism. First, judicial review has a legitimate democratic pedigree. Second, however, I think that it would be wrong for judges to ignore the fact that when deciding *Charter* cases, they are sitting in judgment of laws that have been enacted by democratic legislators. Judges must be mindful of the inherent limits of adjudication and the limits of their judicial authority when they approach that awesome task.

## The Need for Judicial Interpretation

In chapter 3, I rejected the claim that only Parliament or the legislature can make law and that judges can only apply it. The regulation of human affairs by law is simply too complex to allow for a strict division of responsibility: legislatures as "lawmakers" and courts as "law-appliers." Such a strict division of authority ignores our common law tradition and the fact that the essential and residual source for the definition of rights and obligations is the body of precedents made by judicial decisions.

When we come to the Constitution, it seems to me inevitable that the courts will have a significant interpretive and law-making role. Constitutions are intended to be permanent and, as we Canadians know from the bitter experience of the failure of the Meech Lake and Charlottetown Accords in the late 1980s and early 1990s, constitutions cannot be amended easily. Constitutions are necessarily written in terms of general principles intended to cover a vast array of subjects. The constitution is written in the language of one era, but it is intended to be a lasting instrument that will served the changing needs of succeeding eras. It does not and cannot provide obvious answers to every issue that might arise. As the great American jurist John Marshall put it, "We must never forget that it is a constitution we are expounding."[19]

Canadian courts were already charged with the responsibility of constitutional interpretation long before the *Charter of Rights*. Canada is a federal country with a Constitution that divides legislative authority between the federal and provincial levels of government, and it falls to the courts to resolve disputes about the limits of federal and provincial legislative power. This means that judicial review of legislation has always been a fact of Canadian legal and political life. In a case argued in the early years of Confederation, Edward Blake, a lawyer-politician who argued many constitutional cases, submitted that, given the "magnitude of the subjects with which it purports to deal in a very few words," the Constitution has to be "interpreted in a large, liberal and comprehensive spirit."[20] We could not have survived as a nation under the text of our original 1867 Constitution without a healthy dose of creative judicial interpretation. The drafters of the *Constitution Act, 1867* could not have anticipated the issues and problems of today, so the language they used has to be interpreted in a manner that is appropriate to account for current needs and circumstances. A constitution is meant to be a permanent, enduring statement of the fundamental values of the nation. It will serve its purpose only as long as it is capable of meeting present demands. As United States Supreme Court Justice Benjamin Cardozo put it, "The great generalities of the constitution have a content and a significance that vary from age to age."[21] He also noted that a "constitution states ... not rules for the passing hour, but principles for an expanding future."[22] In my view, the inherent need for the interpretation of the law and the Constitution means that the courts must have a law-making role. I suggest that the failure of majoritarians to take this into account undermines the force of their arguments.[23]

## History and Evolution of the Charter

When we look at the circumstances surrounding the *Charter*'s creation, it seems to me very difficult to sustain the majoritarian position that *Charter* review is nothing more than a judicial power-grab. It was politicians, not judges, who enacted the *Charter*.[24] Judges played no role in the creation of the *Charter* in 1982. Indeed, most judges were sceptical about the *Charter* when it was enacted. Even Justice Brian Dickson, arguably the greatest judicial exponent of the *Charter*, once said that the judges of Canada "did not ask for the enactment of the *Charter*. It was thrust upon us."[25] That sentiment was repeated by Justice Bertha Wilson, who argued that the judiciary "didn't volunteer" for judicial review; the duty was deliberately conferred by those democratically elected.[26]

The *Charter* was adopted in the shadow of the Supreme Court's decisions under the 1960 *Canadian Bill of Rights*,[27] a non-entrenched, statutory declaration of rights and freedoms that required all federal legislation to be "construed and applied as not to abrogate, abridge or infringe"[28] the enumerated rights and freedoms. With one or two notable exceptions,[29] the Supreme Court of Canada was very cautious in its interpretation of the *Bill of Rights*. By the mid-1970s, the court had more or less succumbed to the majoritarian argument that the courts lacked a mandate to give priority to the individual rights the Bill protected over laws enacted by Parliament. The rights and freedoms protected by the *Bill of Rights* were almost invariably interpreted in a formal and narrow fashion.

In *Canada (Attorney General) v Lavell*,[30] an Indigenous woman challenged the loss of her *Indian Act* status when she married a non-Indigenous man on the ground that a man with *Indian Act* status did not lose status when he married a non-status woman. The court dismissed what seemed to be an obvious form of sex discrimination, adopting a purely formal definition of equality, asserting that the law was applied equally to all women in Lavell's situation. In another notorious decision, *Bliss*, the court held that the refusal of unemployment insurance benefits to pregnant women did not amount to sex discrimination, even though the same benefits were available to other workers on medical leave.[31] The court's reluctance to give the right any meaningful content was attributed largely to the uncertain constitutional status of the *Bill of Rights* as an ordinary Act of Parliament.

These decisions were strongly criticized. When the *Charter of Rights* was proposed in the early 1980s, civil liberties associations and women's groups mobilized to secure meaningful constitutional protection for fundamental rights and freedoms. Witnesses testified before a joint parliamentary committee, and the draft *Charter* was significantly strengthened to avoid what was widely regarded as the debacle of the *Bill of Rights* experience. The entrenchment of the *Charter*, with its strongly worded equality rights provision and explicit supremacy and remedies clauses, reflected a conscious and deliberate choice by the political actors for a stronger judicial role. By enacting the *Charter* the elected representatives of the people were sending the courts a message: stop interpreting fundamental rights and freedoms narrowly and stop being afraid to assert the judicial authority to strike down laws that violate those fundamental rights.

I suggest that the history of the adoption of the *Charter* supports the argument that the Supreme Court's generous and liberal interpretation is not an unwarranted assertion of judicial power. Rather, it indicates the acceptance of the invitation the court received when Parliament adopted the *Charter* so that the judiciary could meet the expectations of justice, deeply felt by the Canadian public. As Justice Frank Iacobucci explained in a case dealing with discrimination against gays and lesbians, it is "misleading and erroneous" to suggest that a *Charter* challenge "represents a contest between the power of the democratically elected legislatures to pass the laws they see fit, and the power of the courts to disallow those laws." The Constitution, not the courts, limits the legislatures, and "[c]itizens must have the right to challenge laws which they consider to be beyond the powers of the legislatures."[32]

## International Human Rights

The enactment of the *Charter* and its authorization of judicial review also fulfilled Canada's international responsibilities as a signatory to several human rights conventions.[33] The decision to adopt a constitutional *Charter of Rights* brought Canada into line with the international community. Most countries that aspire to the principles of liberal democracy have a judicially enforced bill of rights. The prevalence in other democratic countries of constitutional human rights protections, and of judicial review as the means to ensure that those rights are respected, indicates that by the standards of the international community, there is nothing anti-democratic about the *Charter*.[34]

## Majoritarianism and Judicial Deference

Although majoritarianism on its own does not provide an acceptable guide to the scope of judicial review under the *Charter*, I suggest that we would be wrong to disregard the position entirely. Majoritarianism, after all, has a very respectable constitutional pedigree. Under the tradition of parliamentary supremacy that prevailed until the advent of the *Charter*, subject to judicial review on grounds of federalism, the courts had no right to strike down the laws that Parliament enacted. Canada followed the British tradition that saw Parliament as the best place to define an appropriate balance between individual rights and the broader public interest. Professor Jeremy Waldron, a judicial review sceptic, argues that in a functioning democracy that generally respects fundamental rights and freedoms, it is preferable and more legitimate to allow the political process to work out the details of what those rights and freedoms entail.[35] There is a danger that judicial review will, in Professor Peter Russell's words, "judicialize politics and politicize the judiciary"[36] by unduly shifting debate on questions of social, economic, and political justice from the legislatures to the courts. Litigation in the courts replaces open public debate on important issues of public policy, to the detriment of both the judicial and legislative process.

I suggest that judges should be mindful of the inherent limits of adjudication as a way of deciding complex issues of social, economic, and political policy and accord appropriate deference to the choices made by the elected representatives of the people. As I suggested in chapter 3, there are institutional constraints inherent in the judicial process that limit the capacity of judges as lawmakers. Judges view legal issues through the lens of the particular dispute and specific facts of the case they are deciding. The colour of the legal issue may change when the same issue arises in the context of a different dispute. Judges are also required to respond to the arguments the litigants present, and they are discouraged from exploring the full

ramifications of issues outside the limits of the adversarial presentation. While these limits can be alleviated to some degree by allowing
for interventions from interest groups, judges remain, to a significant
degree, prisoners confined by the walls of the specific dispute they
are called to decide. They seldom have the vantage point or the resources fully to understand or assess the broader social and political
ramifications of changing the law.

So while I believe that judges would be wrong to accept the majoritarian argument and abdicate responsibility for applying the *Charter*
in a generous spirit, I think that they should carry out that task with
a judicious sense of restraint and deference to legislative choices.

### The Democratic Process Model

The next school of thought I examine turns the argument that judicial review is "anti-democratic" on its head. Proponents of the democratic process model argue that *Charter* critics who equate democracy
with majority rule have an impoverished vision of democracy. These
scholars argue that there is much more to democracy than raw majority rule. Real democracy involves a legal framework that protects
the rights of individuals, guards against discrimination and margin-
alization of minorities, and encourages the full participation of all
citizens.[37] Proponents of the democratic process model believe that
the *Charter* advances democracy because judicial protection of fundamental rights and freedoms safeguards and enhances the preconditions for democratic life. This makes judicial review the friend, not
the enemy, of democracy.[38]

The most obvious precondition to democracy is the right to vote – a
right that "underpins the legitimacy of Canadian democracy and Parliament's claim to power." Judges, who are "unaffected by the shifting winds of public opinion and electoral interests,"[39] should robustly
defend this right against legislative curtailment. These statements
were made by the Supreme Court in the context of a decision striking
down a law that denied penitentiary inmates the right to vote.

A healthy democracy can exist only within a legal and political
framework that allows for free and open debate and protects the
values of individual dignity, autonomy, and freedom of choice. A
legal framework that insulates from majoritarian attack freedom
of thought, religion, the right to equality and the protection of life,

liberty, and security of the person, is a necessary condition for democracy. As Chief Justice Dickson stated, "The ability of each citizen to make free and informed decisions is the absolute prerequisite for the legitimacy, acceptability, and efficacy of our system of self-government."[40] A later Supreme Court decision refers to this as the "democratic imperative" that everyone be encouraged to participate fully in public life.[41]

Unfortunately, majorities of the day are often hostile to minorities and are prone to use, or abuse, their power to suppress opinions that threaten the status quo. Baroness Brenda Hale, sitting in the UK Supreme Court – a court that is cautious when asked to review legislation for violation of human rights – explained, "Democracy values everyone equally even if the majority does not."[42] Although he was not writing from the democratic process perspective, Professor Jacob Weinrib aptly described this as the problem of accountability.[43] The majority is entitled to govern, but it must respect the rights of the governed to be treated justly and to have their inherent dignity respected: "The right of each person to bring a constitutional complaint before a politically independent judicial body, empowered and obligated to effectuate constitutional norms, reflects the most basic commitment to the modern constitutional paradigm: that each person subject to public authority must enjoy the legal capacity to respond to a public wrong by standing on his right to just governance."[44]

Judicial enforcement of minority rights protects those whose voices are too few or too unpopular to be adequately heard in political debate. The Supreme Court's focus on the disadvantaged and on historic patterns of discrimination in its interpretation of the *Charter*'s equality guarantee[45] was based explicitly on the need to protect vulnerable groups who lack an effective voice in majoritarian politics. In 1998, when the Supreme Court held that the failure of Alberta's human rights legislation to protect gays and lesbians from discrimination violated the guarantee of equality, it based its decision on the basic democratic idea that every citizen is entitled to the protection of the law, and that the Constitution simply does not allow the majority to deny such protection to vulnerable minorities. As Justice Iacobucci stated, "[J]udges are not acting undemocratically by intervening when there are indications that a legislative or executive decision was not reached in accordance with the democratic principles mandated by the *Charter*."[46]

   Proponents of this democracy-driven justification for judicial review see judicial review under the *Charter* as counteracting and correcting malfunctions in the operation of the democratic process. The underlying assumption is that Parliament and the legislatures should be left with considerable scope to make determinations about the shape of public policy, but the *Charter* ensures the health of rights essential to the democratic process.[47]

   The strength of the democratic process model is that it endeavours to reconcile judicial review with the values of democracy. Its weakness is that, in the end, it is very difficult to explain all aspects of judicial review in terms of what is required to make the democratic process work. Some *Charter* rights, such as the protections accorded to persons accused of crime, are more tenuously connected to what is needed for a functioning democracy than, for example, equality, the right to vote, and freedom of expression. The democratic process model also fails to account for the fact that our constitutional order protects rights because of their intrinsic worth, not just because they promote some other value such as democratic governance.

### Originalism or Framers' Intent

Proponents of originalism argue that judges should constrain democratically elected legislatures only if they have a clear mandate to do so in the actual text of the Constitution. They argue that the intent of those who framed the Constitution, and not evolving judicial interpretation, is the only reliable and legitimate way to determine the meaning of the text. In the words of Justice Antonin Scalia, "[T]he provisions of the Constitution have a fixed meaning, which does not change: they mean today what they meant when they were adopted, nothing more and nothing less."[48] On this view, judges should not interpret *Charter* rights to mean anything other than what was explicitly guaranteed or contemplated at the time the *Charter* was adopted.

   A leading proponent of this theory, Robert Bork, a former judge of the United States Court of Appeals for the District of Columbia Circuit, was highly critical of the Canadian decision striking down the *Criminal Code* prohibition of abortion.[49] The Supreme Court of Canada ruled that, because of its uneven and unfair application, the law that regulated medically approved abortions failed to comply with the section 7 right not to be deprived of life, liberty, and security of the person except in accordance with the principles of fundamental justice. Bork argued that because the *Charter* is "silent" on the specific issue of abortion, the Supreme Court should have dismissed the case, stating that because the text of the *Charter* "avoided the issue" it was one that "must remain with the legislature."[50]

The argument that courts act legitimately only to the extent that they implement the intent of the framers of the Constitution has had significant influence in the United States[51] but very little influence in Canada.[52] There are many problems with the framers' intent approach that have led the Canadian courts to reject it.

Who were the framers, and how do we know what they intended? In an early *Charter* case,[53] the Supreme Court ruled that a mandatory term of imprisonment for an individual who did not know that his driver's licence had been suspended violated the section 7 right to "life, liberty and the security of the person and the right not to be deprived thereof except in accordance with the principles of fundamental justice." The court flatly rejected the argument that it was bound to interpret section 7 as a purely procedural guarantee because that was the apparent intention of the senior civil servants who helped to draft the *Charter*. The adoption of the *Charter* followed a complex political process of federal-provincial conferences, backroom drafting, scrutiny before a parliamentary committee, and general public debate. "The intention of the legislative bodies which adopted the *Charter*," said the court, is a "fact which is nearly impossible of proof."[54] The intent of the senior public servants who drafted the *Charter* did not preclude the court from holding that the "principles of fundamental justice" had substantive content and that mandatory imprisonment of the morally innocent violated those principles.

If the *Charter* is to remain relevant to the needs of a rapidly evolving society, it must be interpreted in a manner that allows for growth over the years. The Supreme Court has held that basing its interpretation of the *Charter* on the drafters' expectations would put the *Charter* at risk of becoming "frozen in time to the moment of adoption with little or no possibility of growth, development and adjustment to changing societal needs ... If the newly planted 'living tree' which is the *Charter* is to have the possibility of growth and adjustment over time, care must be taken to ensure that historical materials ... do not stunt its growth."[55]

The "living tree" metaphor and the adaptive nature of Canadian constitutional interpretation have their roots in the famous Persons Case,[56] which was decided in 1929, more than fifty years before the

enactment of the *Charter*. The courts had to decide whether the constitutional provision that provided for the appointment of "qualified
persons" to the Senate allowed for the appointment of women as well
as men.[57] The drafters of the *Constitution Act, 1867* certainly did not
consider women to be "qualified persons" for Senate appointment,
since in 1867 women could not hold public office or vote. However,
in one of its most celebrated constitutional decisions, the Judicial
Committee of the Privy Council, then Canada's highest court, described the exclusion of women from public office as a "relic of days
more barbarous than ours"[58] and refused to interpret "qualified persons" as the phrase was understood in 1867. Lord Sankey described
the Constitution as a "living tree capable of growth and expansion
within its natural limits."[59] It is a document that is in "a continuous
process of evolution."[60] The Constitution should not be cut down by
"a narrow and technical construction" but instead should be given
a "large and liberal interpretation."[61] Recognizing that the role of
women in the life of the nation had radically changed since 1867, the
Privy Council interpreted the words of the Constitution in a manner
that took into account that fundamental social change.

The *Charter*, like other bills of rights, is generally framed in terms
that are "vague and open" and whose meaning "cannot be determined by recourse to a dictionary, nor for that matter, by reference
to the rules of statutory construction."[62] It is very unlikely that the
framers had precise definitions of the various rights and freedoms
in mind when the *Charter* was adopted. It is more plausible to think
that they intended merely to identify a general principle, knowing
that it would be fleshed out by the courts on a case-by-case basis
over the years to come.

*Charter* rights and freedoms are, to an even greater extent than
qualifications for appointment to the Senate, defined in general and
abstract language. The *Charter of Rights and Freedoms* requires the
courts to interpret broadly worded rights such as "freedom of expression," "life, liberty and security of the person," as well as equality
"before and under the law" and "equal protection and equal benefit
of the law." Adopting the "living tree" metaphor, the Supreme Court
has said that the *Charter* must "be capable of growth and development over time to meet new social, political, and historical realities
often unimagined by its framers."[63] *Charter* guarantees are interpreted with reference to "the character and the larger objects of the
*Charter* ... the historical origins" of the rights it protects and, where

relevant, "to the meaning and purpose of ... other specific rights and freedoms." The Supreme Court has insisted that the "interpretation should be ... a generous rather than a legalistic one, aimed at fulfilling the purpose of the guarantee and securing for individuals the full benefit of the *Charter*'s protection."[64]

But even if we reject originalism or framers' intent as the best way to define and shape judicial review, as I think we must, we should remain mindful of the need for judicial discipline and restraint. The Supreme Court has rightly insisted upon "the primacy of our written constitution,"[65] and when rejecting proposals for Senate reform, the court placed considerable weight on the intention of the framers to create an appointed upper house with no fixed-term membership.[66] *Charter* interpretation must be grounded in the words of the Constitution. As one commentator puts it, "A constitution that can mean anything is one that means nothing,"[67] and "[t]he further the Court strays from the text, the more its legitimacy ... is jeopardized."[68]

The court has not ignored certain understandings and intentions that prevailed in 1982 and that helped shape the *Charter*. Despite their importance in our legal and political tradition, rights of property, contract, and social welfare were excluded from the *Charter*. The Supreme Court has remained faithful to this original constitutional vision when interpreting the *Charter*. The court has, so far at least, consistently refused to interpret the open-ended language of section 7 and the right to "liberty" as including the right to property[69] when asked to review laws regulating business and commerce.[70] Nor has the right to "security of the person" yet been interpreted as protecting social welfare rights.[71]

While the image of the Constitution as a living tree leaves considerable scope for interpretation, the flexibility it implies does not mean that judges have the freedom to make the Constitution say whatever they want it to say. Although cast in terms of generalities rather than specifics, the text of the Constitution does define the parameters of judicial interpretation. The "living tree" is capable of growth and expansion, but only "within its natural limits." Those natural limits are to be found in Canada's fundamental legal values and principles. Those legal values and principles lie at the heart of our legal culture and democratic tradition. They are found in the text of the Constitution, in the statutes enacted by Parliament, in previously decided cases, in the writings of legal scholars, and in the internationally accepted legal norms of civilized society.

Judicial interpretation is a rational, objective process, and this too constrains what judges can do. As discussed in chapter 6, the judge is required to give a reasoned opinion, and that reasoned opinion must be based on recognized principles, not upon the judge's personal views. Judicial interpretation must be rooted in, and consonant with, the basic principles and values of our legal system. These constraints – the text of the Constitution and the need for a reasoned opinion based upon accepted legal principles – impose "natural limits" on the growth of the living tree.

## "Rights as Trumps"

Another school of thought emphasizes individual autonomy as having central importance in our conception of rights and freedoms. *Charter* rights are seen as inherent rights of personhood that define the relationship between the citizen and the state. The courts are charged with the responsibility of enforcing the rights of the individual against the state. As with the democratic process model, this approach is based on the perception that majoritarian politics have deficiencies that require correction through judicial review. However, "rights as trumps" proponents support a more robust role for the courts. *Charter* rights do not exist only by virtue of their instrumental capacity to strengthen democracy – they are valued for their own intrinsic worth as the inherent attributes of citizenship and personhood.

This justification for judicial review is captured by the idea of "rights as trumps" over the policy preferences of governments.[72] As Lorraine Weinrib, a proponent of this model of judicial review, summarizes it, "Underlying this model is respect for the dignity, equality and autonomy of each member of the community. The individual must be able to espouse, and follow, and modify his or her own conception of the good. Whatever the sources and trajectories of these commitments, the aim of collective political life is to create and preserve a structure in which each of us, to an equal extent, may pursue and act upon these commitments, either alone or in a given or chosen community."[73]

It seems to me that the "rights as trumps" metaphor captures a central feature of the *Charter*. The *Charter* identifies and protects those rights and freedoms that are essential to individual autonomy and dignity and creates a relationship between the individual citizen and the state that ensures that those rights will be respected.

On the other hand, when we come to the role of the courts in interpreting those rights, it seems to me that the idealism or perfectionism[74] implicitly embodied in the "rights as trumps" metaphor does not entirely correspond with important structural features of the *Charter*.

*Charter* rights are not as absolute as the "rights as trumps" theory might suggest. They are, by virtue of section 1, subject to "such reasonable limits ... as can be demonstrably justified in a free and democratic society." Parliament can limit *Charter* rights, provided it has a good reason for doing so. The objective of the measure must be important enough to warrant overriding a *Charter* right, but it is very rare for the courts to rule that the legislative objective does not meet this test. Provided the limit imposed by the law respects the principle of proportionality by being rationally connected to the legislative objective, limiting the *Charter* right as little as is reasonably possible and satisfying the overall balance or proportionality between the benefits of the limit and its deleterious effects, the law will be upheld. When it comes to the crucial section 1 stage of *Charter* analysis, it seems to me the "rights as trumps" metaphor has considerably less explanatory force.

First, the courts have interpreted the section 1 "reasonable limits" clause in a way that gives Parliament considerable latitude. In most cases, the courts find that even though the impugned law infringes upon a right, it should be upheld under section 1. Furthermore, as discussed below, even in those cases where a law is struck down for having a disproportionate effect on a *Charter* right, it is almost always possible for Parliament to come back with another law that accomplishes the same objective, but in a way that has less impact on the right or freedom at issue.

Second, although the courts are charged with the responsibility of interpreting *Charter* rights, the courts do not have the final say, since judicial interpretations of most *Charter* rights are subject to the "notwithstanding clause." This clause – section 33 of the *Charter* – allows Parliament or a provincial legislature to declare that a law shall operate "notwithstanding a provision included in section 2 or sections 7 to 15" of the *Charter*. A law containing this simple declaration will be protected from judicial review and will be legally valid even though it violates a *Charter* guaranteed right or freedom listed in the enumerated sections. The notwithstanding clause applies to the fundamental freedoms (expression, religion, association, and assembly), the right to life, liberty, and security of the person, legal rights in the criminal process, and the right to equality.[75] The reach of the legislative notwithstanding clause does not extend to democratic rights (the section 3 right to vote, the section 4 and 5 requirements of regular elections and sessions of Parliament and the legislatures), mobility rights (the section 6 right of citizens to enter, leave, and move about the country), or language rights (sections 16–23).

Sections 1 and 33 are structural features of the *Charter* that expressly qualify both the extent to which rights are protected and the exclusive role of the courts in interpreting rights. These features of the *Charter* seem to me to fit awkwardly with the idea of "rights as trumps." Rights do not always trump other interests.[76] This leads me to conclude that while the idea of "rights as trumps" sheds considerable light on the judicial task, standing alone, it fails to provide a completely adequate explanation for judicial review under the Canadian *Charter*.

### The Dialogue Theory of Judicial Review

I come finally to the school of thought that perceives judicial review as part of an ongoing dialogue between courts and legislatures in which neither has the last word.[77] As I have mentioned, the section 1 reasonable limits clause almost always gives legislatures some room to manoeuvre. This means that judicial decisions invalidating laws are usually not the final word. Very often, legislatures can find a way to achieve the legislative objective by reformulating the impugned law to make it less intrusive on the protected right or freedom. The law can then be defended under section 1 as a "reasonable limit."

Although largely overlooked or discounted by judicial activism critics, the possibility of a legislative response to an adverse court decision has proved to be a very important feature of judicial review. Decisions striking down laws are frequently followed by the enactment of improved laws that better respect the right or freedom in question.[78] Usually the legislative response is to enact a more carefully tailored law that has a less drastic effect on the protected right or freedom. For example, the Supreme Court's decision[79] striking down a law banning tobacco advertising was answered with a more narrowly framed law that restricted the most objectionable forms of tobacco advertising. That law survived *Charter* challenge.[80]

Judges responding to a *Charter* challenge often recognize that they do not have the capacity to provide a complete answer. *Charter* cases frequently involve multidimensional problems that cannot be entirely resolved by a judicial pronouncement of rights. The court can confidently say that a *Charter* right has been invaded, but the judges are not the ones to decide what other law Parliament might wish to enact to accomplish its legislative objective. The effect of striking down a law may be to invite further legislative consideration. Some of the Supreme Court's most controversial rulings – those striking down the laws relating to abortion,[81] assisted suicide,[82] and prostitution[83] – expressly leave open the option of new legislation to accomplish the legislative objective in a manner less intrusive on the protected right or freedom. Very often, courts temporarily suspend a declaration of invalidity explicitly acknowledging that new legislation to deal with the same issue is expected. This allows the legislator to reassess the problem, this time taking into account the right the court has declared.

Peter Hogg points out that a judicial decision striking down a law provokes a "public debate in which *Charter* values play a more prominent role" than they would without the decision. It is left to the legislature "to devise a response that is properly respectful of the *Charter* values that have been identified by the Court, but which accomplish the social or economic objectives that the judicial decision has impeded."[84] So judicial decisions striking down laws under the *Charter* rarely end the debate. More often than not, Parliament or the legislature is free to enact another law that has the same objective but that pays proper heed to the fundamental right or freedom at issue.

Less common are "in your face" legislative responses,[85] essentially replicating the law that was struck down and requiring the court to take a second look at the issue. The most notable example concerned the law relating to the disclosure of treatment records of alleged victims of sexual assault. A 5–4 Supreme Court decision held that those accused of sexual assault could compel disclosure of such records.[86] That decision was met with a new law that essentially adopted the position of the four dissenting judges and imposed significant restrictions on disclosure. A challenge to that law was rejected in a subsequent case where the court stated that it did "not hold a monopoly on the protection and promotion of rights" and that "Parliament also plays a role ... and is often able to act as a significant ally for vulnerable groups."[87] Some have suggested that the court should defer to Parliament's judgment in "second-look" cases, thereby making *Charter* interpretation a truly cooperative exercise.[88] However, the Supreme Court rejected that proposition in the prisoners' voting cases. After striking down an absolute ban on voting by persons in prison under sentence after conviction for a criminal offence,[89] the Supreme Court was faced with a law that denied the vote for all serving sentences of more than two years in federal penitentiaries. The majority struck the new law down for failure to identify a valid legislative objective, Chief Justice McLachlin observing, "The healthy and important promotion of a dialogue between the legislature and the courts should not be debased to a rule of 'if at first you don't succeed, try, try again.'"[90] This reiterated the view expressed in the tobacco advertising litigation that "the mere fact that the legislation represents Parliament's response to a decision of this Court does not militate for or against deference."[91]

The second structural feature of the *Charter* that relates to the dialogue theory is the notwithstanding clause. As I have already explained, section 33 of the *Charter* permits Parliament or a legislature to immunize a law against *Charter* scrutiny by declaring that a law or provision of a law shall operate notwithstanding section 2 or sections 7 to 15. Section 33 has a "sunset" provision. A declaration that a law shall operate notwithstanding the violation of a protected right or freedom remains in effect for a maximum period of five years, which is roughly tied to the length of a parliamentary term.

Shortly after the *Charter* was enacted, Quebec adopted a general notwithstanding clause that exempted every Quebec statute from the *Charter*. The measure was taken in protest by the separatist Parti Québécois government, which had opposed the 1982 amendments to the Constitution and the enactment of the *Charter*. The Quebec Court of Appeal held that such a sweeping and general declaration of override was invalid,[92] but the Supreme Court of Canada disagreed and held that the courts could not second-guess even this extreme use of the notwithstanding clause.[93] This avoided what would have been an explosive confrontation with Quebec nationalist sentiment and left control of the notwithstanding clause in the hands of the politicians.[94] The control on the use of the notwithstanding clause has been public opinion, which, at least at the national level, has been solidly against its use.

Parliament has never invoked the override, but several provincial and territorial governments have.[95] Quebec invoked section 33 to override the Supreme Court of Canada's decision that a law requiring all commercial signs to be in French was contrary to freedom of expression.[96] The court had recognized Quebec's right to act to preserve and enhance the French language but held that it had failed to justify the virtual total prohibition of the use of English and other languages on such signs. Quebec did not renew the override when it expired in 1993, and the language law now generally allows the use of languages other than French in commercial signs so long as French remains the predominant language. In 2000 a private member's bill invoking the override to prevent *Charter* challenges to restrictions on marriage to opposite-sex couples was passed by the Alberta legislature. That law lapsed after five years. There have been many other uses of the override by provincial and territorial government that surprisingly have escaped media and public attention.[97]

The very existence of the notwithstanding clause is an important structural feature of our Canadian Constitution. The notwithstanding clause recognizes that elected legislators have a constitutional role in defining an appropriate balance between the rights of the individuals and the interests of society at large. With the notwithstanding clause, the *Charter* constrains the power of both legislatures and the courts. On the one hand, the *Charter* significantly curtails legislative power by conferring a broad mandate upon the judiciary to protect fundamental rights and freedoms. On the other hand, the court's power is also restricted through the inclusion of the notwithstanding clause. The *Charter* framework, including section 33, ensures that no one has the last word. Even if the notwithstanding clause is invoked to overcome judicial review, the five-year sunset provision ensures that the issue will have to be revisited by a differently constituted Parliament or legislature after an election has taken place and the people have had the opportunity to hold their representatives accountable. The net effect of the *Charter* is to achieve a subtle and effective check on both legislative and judicial power.

I agree with dialogue critics that, to the extent the word "dialogue" conveys the idea of an open-ended two-way conversation, the metaphor is inapt. Judges do not sit down with legislators to discuss the meaning of the *Charter*. When it comes to the meaning of *Charter* rights, the judges do "most of the talking" while the legislatures do "most of the listening."[98] Courts consider their decisions to be final and authoritative pronouncements on rights, not mere suggestions inviting a discussion. Nor do legislatures enact laws in order to invite a conversation with the courts about their constitutionality. What the dialogue metaphor describes is "less like a conversation and more like a complex division of labour where each branch has its own distinct, though complementary, role to play in a joint enterprise."[99] I suggest that the dialogue is the sort of conversation one can imagine between an architect and an engineer on the design and construction of a building. They both have their own distinctive role and expertise, but they must work together, and the building will not be built without a dialogue between the two of them.

When understood in this light, it seems to me that the dialogue metaphor does account for the structural features of the *Charter* that allow legislatures to limit or even override rights as they are interpreted by the courts. The possibility and the propriety of legislative response significantly qualifies the counter-majoritarian aspect of judicial review. The courts do not have the last word and, while it is crucial that they exercise independent legal judgment, they do not operate in isolation. The problems posed in *Charter* litigation are often complex and multidimensional, and judicial pronouncements on rights must be understood as part of a larger process in which the legislative and executive branches are also involved.

### Conclusion: Views of the Cathedral

So my conclusion is that none of the five theories is entirely satisfactory, but that each one has something to offer. Majoritarianism teaches us that judicial review should be deployed in a manner that respects the legislative process and pays heed to the inherent limitations of judicial law-making. The democratic process model suggests that judicial review can and should be deployed to enhance and reinforce, rather than undermine, our democratic tradition. Originalism reminds us that the "living tree" does have its "natural limits" and that our elaboration of *Charter* rights must be rigorous, disciplined, and reasoned. The "rights as trumps" metaphor teaches us that *Charter* rights are ideals to be accorded respect as the fundamental attributes of individual citizenship and personhood. Finally, the dialogue metaphor instructs us that judges do not always have the last say and that Parliament and the legislatures have a significant role to play in the realization and protection of *Charter* rights in the legislative process.

## Chapter 12

# A Judicial State of Mind

Integrity, independence, impartiality, and compassion are qualities judges should exhibit in their work to meet the legitimate expectations of the public and to satisfy the ideal of doing justice in a diverse society.

## Integrity

Integrity is plainly central to the judicial role. To sit in judgment on one's fellow citizens is a weighty responsibility. To carry it out, the judge must be worthy of public respect and confidence and be trusted by the bar and by the litigants.

The good judge is scrupulously honest and above suspicion in personal and professional conduct. As Justice Charles Gonthier stated in a decision dealing with the removal of a judge who had failed to disclose a criminal conviction before his appointment, "The public will ... demand virtually irreproachable conduct from anyone performing a judicial function."[1] Judges suspected of dishonesty in their personal or professional affairs are plainly unfit to sit in judgment on others. Such an individual, however skilled in the law, would lack the moral authority necessary to carry out the duties of judicial office.

But there is much more to the integrity required of a judge than personal honesty. The good judge is one who comes to the case with an open mind, determined to decide the case without fear or favour, on the basis of the evidence and the arguments presented in open court. The good judge owes nothing to powerful interests, be they public or private. There can be no suspicion that the judge decided a case in the hope or expectation of some future reward or benefit, including an appointment to higher judicial office. The good judge is certainly aware of the prevailing public mood but cannot be swayed or influenced by fear of making a decision that is unpopular or controversial.

An essential element of integrity is faithfulness to the law. Judges have a duty to decide cases according to the law – not in accordance with their personal views about what is right and wrong. The good judge accepts the discipline of the law when striving to achieve justice and understands that the law imposes very real constraints on the exercise of judicial power. The good judge certainly brings a strong sense of the community's moral and ethical values to the bench, but the desire to do what is right and just must never cause the judge to stray beyond the discipline of the law. To demonstrate integrity and faithfulness to the law, the good judge renders reasoned decisions, candidly and carefully explaining the grounds for the conclusion. Integrity in judicial office depends upon the transparent exercise of judicial power based upon the evidence and accepted legal sources. The litigants, especially the losing parties, are entitled to a clear explanation of the decision, an explanation that demonstrates the judge's dedication and faithfulness to the law.

## Independence

Judicial independence secures the institutional arrangements necessary to ensure that the judiciary can be impartial and free from interference from the executive branch of government, the legislature, or the litigants. Judicial independence is guaranteed by the *Constitution Act, 1867*,[2] by the *Charter of Rights and Freedoms*,[3] and by international norms and standards.[4] The central tenets of judicial independence are threefold.[5] First, judges enjoy tenure of office and are removable only for a cause related to their capacity to perform the judicial function. Second, judges enjoy financial security so that they need not fear diminution in remuneration because of judgments that are unpopular or unfavourable to the government. Financial security also ensures that judges are paid sufficiently to avoid any dependence on or pressure from outside forces, whether actual or perceived. Third, institutional independence ensures judicial control over court administration, including the assignment of judges to particular cases.

These principles of judicial independence posit judges as impartial, independent actors, not beholden to any group or interest. Judges are accorded the status and protection necessary to enable them to stand above the political fray, immune to the pushes, pulls, and swings of popular opinion. They must stand free from all forms of external pressure, whether from litigants, fellow judges, or court officials. As stated in a leading study of judicial independence and accountability in Canada, judges necessarily occupy a "place apart."[6] The Constitution guarantees judicial independence precisely because it is a necessary condition for the fundamental goal of impartiality: "[J]udicial independence is but a 'means' to this 'end' ... Independence is the cornerstone, a necessary prerequisite, for judicial impartiality."[7] Chief Justice Brian Dickson aptly described judicial independence as "the lifeblood of constitutionalism in democratic societies,"[8] and Justice Aharon Barak observed that "[w]ithout judicial independence, there is no preservation of democracy and its values."[9]

## Impartiality

Impartiality, in broad terms, refers to a "determination to deal equally with both or all parties to a dispute and not to favour any."[10] Impartiality has been defined judicially as "a state of mind or attitude of the tribunal in relation to the issues and the parties in a particular case ... it connotes absence of bias, actual or perceived"[11] and as "a state of mind in which the adjudicator is disinterested in the outcome, and is open to persuasion by the evidence and submissions."[12] This may be contrasted with the partial judge, "who has certain preconceived biases, and who will allow those biases to affect his or her verdict despite the trial safeguards designed to prevent reliance on those biases."[13]

Impartiality is difficult to achieve in a modern multicultural society. Canada has always had a diverse society, one increasingly varied through significant demographic change. Our unique historical mix of Indigenous, French, and English is enriched by the significant influx of immigrants from all corners of the globe in the twentieth and twenty-first centuries. In my city of Toronto, and in many other cities across Canada, the demographic changes resulting from immigration are obvious and striking. The diversity of our population has a direct bearing on our justice system and our commitment to impartiality and equality. We have attempted, sometimes successfully and sometimes not, to accommodate and to reconcile the racial, cultural, and linguistic differences of our peoples, and sadly our legal history is far from free from discrimination and oppression.

Impartiality, dignity, and respect are fundamental to our justice system. Litigants routinely present issues arising from differences in gender, sexuality, age, language, culture, race, poverty, and ability. Judges regularly confront the intersection of any permutation of these issues. Despite the personal differences of the litigants, the judge must apply the law equally and impartially.

Trial judges are required to assess the credibility of witnesses, many of whom come from diverse social and cultural backgrounds. A judge "sizes up" a witness to determine credibility. Can the judge safely assume that the witness's habits and demeanour are similar to those of the judge? Must the judge make allowances for possible differences in the witness's social and cultural background? Sexual assault trials, unfortunately a staple item of our criminal courts, confront us with issues of gender equality. In family law disputes, judges deal with differing views on the situation of women in a modern society. Differences in religion and culture influence views on the upbringing of children and on the spousal relationship. Do we act with an even hand as we assess the personal injury claims of the upper-middle-class homemaker, the man of Italian origin, a woman of East Indian birth, or an unemployed construction worker? Issues of race and cultural difference are very often at the forefront in criminal trials – now explicitly so when juries are selected.[14]

## Categories of Bias

The common law traditionally divided bias into two categories, actual or presumed bias and apparent bias.

Actual bias refers to situations where a judge has a direct interest in the outcome of the litigation. Actual bias rests on the proposition "that no man is to be a judge in his own cause." This principle extends beyond the judge's "own cause" and includes cases where a judge "has an interest."[15] Usually the interest is financial, but the principle also applies to preclude a judge from sitting in a case where the judge has supported the cause of one of the parties. This arose in rather dramatic fashion from a decision by the House of Lords setting aside its earlier 3–2 decision rejecting former Chilean President Pinochet's claim that state immunity precluded his extradition on changes of crimes against humanity including torture. One member of the three-judge majority, Lord Hoffmann, served as director of a registered charity affiliated with and controlled by Amnesty International (AI), a human rights public interest group, to support AI's educational work and research. AI had been granted standing as an intervener in the appeal. Pinochet asked that the decision be set aside, arguing that Lord Hoffmann's involvement with the charity, closely associated with AI, made him a person with an interest in the outcome and therefore disqualified him from sitting. That request was granted on the basis that no one can be a judge in their own cause.[16] The appeal was re-argued before a panel of seven Law Lords that ordered extradition, but on narrower grounds.[17]

The second category, apparent bias, rests on the proposition that "[j]ustice should not only be done, but should manifestly and undoubtedly be seen to be done."[18] The test laid down by the Supreme Court of Canada is "what would an informed person, viewing the matter realistically and practically – and having thought the matter through – conclude? Would she think that it is more likely than not that [the decision-maker], whether consciously or unconsciously, would not decide fairly?"[19] The reasonable observer is not a person with a "very sensitive or scrupulous conscience"[20] but rather the "sort of person who always reserves judgment on every point until she has seen and fully understood both sides of the argument" and "who takes the trouble to read the text of an article as well as the headlines."[21]

In application, there is really no difference between "actual" and "apparent" bias, as both rest on an objective assessment of reasonable apprehension of bias.[22] In the leading case on "actual bias," the House of Lords distanced itself from any suggestion that the judge could have been "in the remotest degree, influenced by the interest that he had in this concern." It insisted that judges must "take care not only that … they are not influenced by their personal interest, but to avoid the appearance of labouring under such an influence."[23] Despite the different labels, it all comes down to appearances. The dividing line is more apparent than real, and the Supreme Court of Canada has held that there is no need to maintain the separate category of "presumed" bias.[24]

## Recusal and Disqualification

Bias and impartiality are the subject of a set of formal legal rules to determine when a judge should not sit on a case.[25] These rules, I will argue, only scratch the surface of impartiality. For good reason, the law limits the chance a litigant has to challenge the judge or judges assigned to hear the case. Allegations of bias cause delay, undermine public confidence in the justice system, and may be abused as a form of "judge-shopping." On the other hand, impartial justice is fundamental to the integrity of the administration of justice, and we must ensure that judges deliver unbiased justice. I will argue that satisfying the minimal standard set by the formal rules falls well short of what is needed to satisfy the judge's professional duty to be impartial. We cannot realistically expect more from the formal rules, but we must expect much more from individual judges, and it would be a grave error to assume that satisfying the formal rules ensures impartiality. It is only by insisting that judges engage in careful and scrupulous introspection that we can hope to attain the goal of providing impartial justice.

A party challenging a judge on grounds of partiality faces an uphill fight. Judges are presumed to be impartial. As Blackstone explained, "[T]he law will not suppose a possibility of bias or favour in a judge, who is already sworn to administer impartial justice, and whose authority greatly depends upon that presumption and idea."[26] Significant weight is placed on the oath of office and on professional integrity, pride, and training. The litigant cannot question or cross-examine the judge on any statement the judge makes about the allegation of bias, because "the law does not countenance the questioning of a judge about extraneous influences."[27]

The limited scope of the inquiry is justified on several grounds. The law generally discourages challenges on preliminary issues and favours getting to the merits of a case as quickly as possible on grounds of both efficiency and fairness. Any benefit to be gained from an open-ended inquiry into the partiality of the judge is unlikely to outweigh the costs. The judiciary may not be perfect, but the risk that the orderly hearing of cases could be disrupted by "judge-shopping," or tactical manoeuvring to avoid a judge, cannot be ignored.[28]

Another legal rule that limits challenges for bias is the doctrine of waiver. If aware of some fact that would disqualify the judge from sitting on the case, a party must make a timely objection. If there is no objection and the case proceeds, the party will be taken to have waived the objection, and it will be too late to raise the point on appeal. The rationale for the waiver rule is fairness and efficiency. Failure to make a timely objection implies that before the result was known, the party did not reasonably apprehend bias. A party should not be permitted to "lie in the weeds," saving the objection to be used only in the event that the party loses the case. Allowing that tactic to succeed would be unfair to the opponent who fought the case all the way to judgment, and it would be costly in terms of wasted litigation expenses and judicial resources.[29]

Practical and tactical considerations may also limit the capacity of a party to challenge a judge for bias. A challenge for bias must be made to the very judge assigned to hear the case. Even in the case of collegial courts, the challenge is decided by the judge whose recusal is sought.[30] While judges should treat challenges for bias in a professional manner, most lawyers will naturally be cautious about advancing a bias challenge at the start of the case that could antagonize the judge who might dismiss the complaint and end up deciding the case. For this reason, it has been suggested that it would be fairer to provide for another judge to hear the challenge,[31] in the case of a collegial court, the full panel.[32]

On the other hand, judges are encouraged to take a proactive approach if aware of a potential bias issue. Judges will ordinarily discuss with their colleagues or with the Chief Justice any matter that might seem to give rise to a conflict of interest to gauge the likely reaction of the parties. The English Court of Appeal has stated that if there is any real ground for doubt, the prudent course is to step aside, especially if the recusal can occur in time to find another judge to sit on the case.[33] In my experience, that reflects the practice in Canada as well. A study of judicial practice in this area suggests that judges readily recuse themselves if there is any suggestion of bias.[34] On the other hand, I think judges have to beware of being unduly fearful of potential bias challenges. This pertains in particular to appellate courts, where there are fewer judges to step in and where decisions are collegial. As Justice Anthony Mason of the High Court of Australia observed, judges have a duty to sit, and "acceding too readily to suggestions of appearance of bias" may encourage parties to seek disqualification in the hope "they will have their case tried by someone thought to be more likely to decide the case in their favour."[35]

Allegations of bias pose special problems for apex courts which sit
*en banc* and are therefore not in a position to find another judge. In
a case dealing with a challenge to the legality of a decision taken by
President Mandela, the South African Constitutional Court provided
a thorough discussion of the appearance of bias test.[36] The applicant
challenged several members of the court because of their prior membership in the African National Congress and their close association with the President. In rejecting that challenge, the court defined
the test as "whether a reasonable, objective and informed person,"
knowing the facts, would reasonably apprehend that the judge will
"bring an impartial mind to bear on the adjudication of the case, that
is, a mind open to persuasion by the evidence and the submissions
of counsel."[37] The test is objective, and the onus rests upon the applicant. The reasonableness of the apprehension, said the court, must
be assessed in light of three factors. First, "the oath of office taken
by the judges to administer justice without fear or favour"; second,
"their ability to carry out that oath by reason of their training and
experience"; and third, their "duty to sit in any case in which they
are not obliged to recuse themselves." The Court added, however,
"[I]t must never be forgotten that an impartial judge is a fundamental prerequisite for a fair trial and a judicial officer should not hesitate to recuse herself or himself if there are reasonable grounds on
the part of a litigant for apprehending that the judicial officer, for
whatever reasons, was not or will not be impartial."[38]

## The Need for Judicial Introspection

I suggest that the achievement of true impartiality depends more
upon the professional integrity and ethical standards of the bench
than upon the formal legal test for bias. To reject the challenge of partiality in the case just mentioned, the South African Constitutional
Court had to rely on judges being mindful of the oath of office, faithful to professional training and experience, and consciously committed to bringing an open mind to bear upon the case, whatever their
background or personal opinions.

This point becomes even more obvious when one considers the test
laid down for apparent bias in the leading English case. The Court
of Appeal divided potential grounds for bias into three categories.[39]
First were attributes that could not conceivably ground a challenge
for bias: "the religion, ethnic or national origin, gender, age, class,

means or sexual orientation of the judge." Second were matters that would ordinarily be insufficient: the judge's social, educational, or previous political associations; judicial decisions, extra-curricular writing; or prior legal representation and associations. Third were matters that gave rise to a "real danger of bias": personal friendship or animosity between the judge and any member of the public involved in the case; prior credibility rulings in outspoken terms; or the expression of extreme or unbalanced views.

What distinguishes the third category from the first two is that it describes specific relationships or involvements between the judge and the parties or issues in the case. These are case-specific facts that zero in on the associations that give rise to concern. The first two categories, on the other hand, involve general personal traits or attributes that we all have. Every judge has views on religion, just as every judge has a gender identity, ethnicity, sexual orientation, age, and education. A legal test that allowed detailed scrutiny of these qualities in the absence of something more to show that the judge had a closed mind would be highly problematic.

First, it would open the door to costly and time-consuming inquiries in a large number of cases. Second, it is difficult to see how such inquiries would yield a material benefit. For example, a judge's views on religion certainly could come into play when deciding a case involving abortion, gay rights, school prayer, funding for religious schools, or resuscitation of a terminal patient.[40] But where would disqualification on such grounds end? If we were to exclude the Catholic judge from hearing a case involving school prayer, would we not also have to exclude the atheist judge? Because the grounds describe traits all judges have, albeit leading in different directions, allowing challenges on such grounds would open the floodgates to judge-shopping and tactical manoeuvring. It seems to me perfectly understandable why the law should more or less foreclose challenging the partiality of the judge on such grounds absent some clear evidence to demonstrate that the judge's views were so fixed that the judge would be incapable of bringing an open mind to the case.

However, it would be a serious mistake to deny that the traits listed in the first two categories could have a significant effect on the thinking of the judge. It is at this point that we encounter the limits of the formal legal test and the need to insist upon more. As a leading scholar observed, "The 'appearance of justice' standard can best be understood as an unsatisfactory attempt to mediate between introspection and objectivity." It "invites judges to rest on appearances, instead of looking deeper."[41] I suggest that it would be a serious error for judges to take the formal legal test literally.

Surely, no judge believes that one's personal views on religion, age, gender, sexual orientation, education, and social background could not affect one's decision. To achieve true impartiality, to remain faithful to the judicial oath, and to maintain the professional standards of the judiciary, judges must adopt a consciously self-reflective approach. If their personal religious or moral views on a matter are so strong that they would effectively trump the law, judges should recuse themselves. But even judges who feel confident that they can decide the case fairly on the law should still recognize the influence of their personal beliefs and attributes, and instruct themselves to check that influence when making judicial decisions.

The classical image depicts justice with a blindfold. At one level, this image is a powerful metaphor, graphically depicting the ideal of impartial justice. If taken literally, I suggest, this stylized ideal conveys an artificial and misleading image that has little to do with reality. If the classical image holds that judges are, or should be, divested of all preconceptions and identifications, I would categorically reject it as both unrealistic and undesirable. The human condition is such that the blindfolded judicial paragon does not exist. If there were such an individual, I suggest that he or she would make a terrible judge. Justice in the courtroom is not a mere abstraction, but a value realized in the cut and thrust of the very human process of trial and argument. The facts do not come neatly packaged in legal categories, but have to be sifted, sorted, and understood. The events under scrutiny are intensely human in nature, often sinking to the depths of our experience. The law, in all its majesty, represents the ultimate standard against which human conduct is judged in the courtroom. But judges necessarily draw upon their own non-legal experience in assessing what passes before them in the courtroom. They do not "function as neutral cyphers."[42] The blindfold has to be removed to let in the light of experience. The realities of life must filter through and temper our understanding of the law. Using "blind justice" as the ideal may discourage self-reflection and, at the same time, ignore the usefulness that experience can bring to the judicial process.

The blindfold, however, does represent an important point. There are certain things that should be excluded from consideration if the goal of impartial justice is to be achieved: "Justice is portrayed as

blind not because she ignores the facts and circumstances of individual cases but because she shuts her eyes to all considerations extraneous to the particular case."[43]

The judge needs to be shielded from what is unworthy, irrelevant,
or inappropriate for consideration in the case at hand. The values
of impartiality and equality are so strongly ingrained in our legal
system that overt prejudice or deliberate discrimination is rarely the
concern. The real danger is unintended, unthinking, or unconscious
bias that flows from internalized ways of thinking that we simply
take for granted. It is crucially important for judges to recognize that
it is only human to have this tendency. Rather than deny it, we need
to confront it.

It is important to recognize two basic points. First, the judge must
necessarily draw upon personal experience and should not resist
doing so. Second, however, the judge must rely upon these experiences judiciously and with circumspection. The judge who aspires to
render impartial justice must be aware that it is not enough to be free
of conscious bias or overt prejudice. Judges must also be prepared
to re-examine and reconsider some of the lessons their experience
seems to teach.

The challenge is to know when to let our experience lead us towards humane and compassionate decision-making, and when to
guard against it diverting us from the goal of impartiality. Some
judges may feel threatened by the suggestion that from time to time
they may exhibit unworthy thoughts, tendencies, or biases. They
may resist the plea for introspection as nothing more than an appeal to "political correctness." I take a more benign view. Conscious
attention to social context issues should be seen as an aid to better judging and as a way to come to grips with a problem even our
greatest judges have recognized: that acknowledging and confronting our biases and prejudices is a necessary first step to the realization of the ideal of impartial judging.

We must not confuse the ideal of impartial justice with the reality
of what and who we are. The experience we bring to bear on our
work contains many worthy attributes. At the same time, our experience inevitably includes biases and prejudices that we need actively
to guard against.

As the great American judge Oliver Wendell Holmes said,
"[A]ny man who says he is impartial about any subject on which
he speaks is either ignorant or a liar, and that the honest man is one

who, aware of his partiality, guards against its abuse."[44] The same point was made by Chief Justice Brian Dickson in his 1979 Goodman Lectures on the art of judging: "Judges are human. They have been molded by all they have experienced prior to elevation to the bench. They may hold strong views on many issues; yet when presiding at a trial, those views must be set aside."[45] Lord Justice Scrutton, an English judge, notable for his commercial law work, recognized the same problem: "I am not speaking of conscious impartiality; but the habits you are trained in, the people with whom you mix, lead to your having a certain class of ideas of such a nature that, when you have to deal with other ideas, you do not give as sound and accurate judgments as you would wish."[46]

In his classic book, *The Nature of the Judicial Process*, the great American jurist Benjamin Cardozo struck a similar theme: "There is in each of us a stream of tendency, whether you choose to call it philosophy or not, which gives coherence and direction to thought and action. Judges cannot escape that current any more than other mortals."[47]

Humane and compassionate judges, like Holmes, Dickson, Scrutton, and Cardozo, were not blindfolded automatons or legal technocrats. As great judges, they quite properly drew on their life experiences and upon their knowledge of what makes people and the world tick. But they did so with a sense of caution and introspection, and they were open to change. They were careful with their experience and warned of the need constantly to examine and re-examine the assumptions and the values that inform our experience. They exhibited what Justice Rosalie Abella described as the "crucial difference between an open mind and an empty one"[48] and the distinction drawn by Justice Edwin Cameron of the Constitutional Court of South Africa between "colourless neutrality" and "judicial impartiality."[49]

All judges need to consider and question the assumptions they bring to bear on their judicial work. We need to re-examine and reconsider our assumptions and our own notions of "common sense" to make sure they accord with the facts, with social reality, and that they are consistent with our ideals of impartiality and equality. We are the product of our backgrounds and of what we have imbibed at our parents' knees. We need to remind ourselves constantly that we are members of a financially and socially privileged elite. If we are to realize the ideal of impartiality in our work, we must confront the limitations that are imposed upon us by our own limited experience. We need to make sure that we are not guilty of attributing to the individuals who come before us characteristics or traits on the basis of their association or membership in a particular group. We need to guard against stereotyping, where we assume a trait, attribute it to an entire group, and judge members of that group accordingly, without regard to the facts pertaining to the individual before us. In particular, we need to guard against making decisions based on assumed characteristics such as age, gender, religion, race, class, or other personal traits, whatever we think our experience or our common sense tells us. Assumptions of that kind are ill-founded. They violate the goal of impartially judging the individual who stands before us. They reflect a "pigeonhole" style of reasoning that only obscures the truth and gets in the way of our ideal of justice for every individual based on that individual's worth, thoughts, and actions. The point is well made in the Canadian Judicial Council's 1991 *Commentaries on Judicial Conduct*: "[T]he wisdom required of a judge is to recognize, consciously allow for, and perhaps to question, all the baggage of past attitudes and sympathies that fellow citizens are free to carry, untested, to the grave. True impartiality does not require that the judge have no sympathies or opinions; it requires that the judge nevertheless be free to entertain and act upon different points of view with an open mind. To keep that mind truly open, the judge, more than most, must respond to the challenge of self-examination."[50]

Judicial education has an important role to play. All courts have judicial education programs. Some politicians have proposed making judicial education on difficult and controversial subjects such as the law's treatment of sexual assault mandatory. While I am entirely in favour of judicial education, I am highly dubious about the need for or workability of these proposals. As matters now stand, it would be very difficult for any Canadian judge to avoid education on these topics. The National Judicial Institute, Canada's national body that coordinates and provides education to judges at all levels, has made a concerted effort to provide social context education for judges. The social context approach asks judges to view legal issues from a perspective other than their familiar world of statutes and case law. Judges are encouraged to consider factors and forces external to the formal legal rules that nevertheless have a direct bearing on the operation and application of the law. How do the traditional legal rules operate if the social facts and the social context are not what we have assumed them to be? How do these rules operate for those members of our society from backgrounds different from our own? Social context education encourages self-reflection and asks judges to examine and question the underlying assumptions and attitudes they bring to their work. The National Judicial Council's program has been very well received by Canadian judges, and I doubt that forcing judges to attend programs would be as effective.

The difficulty in knowing when it is appropriate to rely on one's experience is illustrated by the Supreme Court of Canada's decision in *R v S (RD)*.[51] The case involved a black youth charged with assaulting a white police officer and resisting arrest in Nova Scotia. The youth and the officer, the only witnesses, gave very different versions of what had occurred. The judge, a black woman, acquitted the youth. In her reasons, she observed that "police officers do overreact, particularly when they are dealing with non-white groups" and went on to state that she has a "suspicion that this police officer may have lied and overreacted in dealing with this non-white accused."[52] The Crown appealed, arguing that the trial judge's comments gave rise to a reasonable apprehension of bias, as they indicated she had found, without evidence, that the police officer had been motivated by racism.

The judges of the Supreme Court of Canada divided sharply on the propriety of the trial judge's comments. Four members of the court[53] held that it was appropriate to assess the claim of reasonable apprehension of bias by taking a "contextualized understanding of the issues in the case." The reasonable person "understands the impossibility of judicial neutrality, but demands judicial impartiality" and "is cognizant of the racial dynamics in the local community."[54] The trial judge had reviewed the evidence and explained why she had a reasonable doubt, and she was entitled "to take into account the well-known presence of racism in [her] community and to evaluate the evidence as to what occurred against that background."[55]

Three members of the court[56] saw the case quite differently and dissented. They allowed that "[t]he life experience" of the trial judge "is an important ingredient in the ability to understand human behaviour, to weigh the evidence, and to determine credibility" but that "life experience" is of "no value ... in reaching conclusions for which there [was] no evidence."[57] In the view of the dissenting judges, there was no evidence of racism, and they interpreted the trial judge's comments as indicating that she had "stereotyped" the police officer.

The remaining two judges found that the trial judge's impugned comments were "worrisome and come very close to the line."[58] However, as she had given other adequate reasons explaining why she had reasonable doubt, the verdict could not be set aside on grounds of reasonable apprehension of bias.

I do not share the concerns of the judges who were critical of the trial judge. She did not make a finding of racism against the police officer; she simply found that the prosecution had not proved the case beyond a reasonable doubt. I think she was entitled to draw upon her experience living as a black woman in her community and on her experience as a judge trying cases involving violent interactions between black youths and the police. I agree with the four members of the court who saw her behaviour as informed and impartial judging.

## Behavioural Bias

To this point, I have been discussing attitudinal bias and the problem of dealing with ingrained attitudes or beliefs that may stand in the way of impartial judging. Most bias cases that are litigated arise from things done or said during the course of a trial or other proceeding indicating that the judge has predetermined the result and closed his or her mind to being persuaded by the evidence and argument. These scenarios may be described as instances of behavioural bias.

The decision of the Supreme Court of Canada in a case involving minority language rights illustrates the difference.[59] The trial judge found that the Yukon government had failed to comply with its constitutional obligation[60] to provide minority language education to francophones. His decision was challenged on grounds of bias.

The appellant argued that there was a reasonable apprehension of attitudinal bias because of the judge's past membership in a philanthropic organization in Alberta dedicated to the advancement of francophone rights. There was, however, no evidence that the objectives of that organization aligned with the position taken by the minority rights claimant. The court stated that it expected "a degree of mature judgment on the part of an informed public" recognizing that "not everything a judge does or joins predetermines how he or she will decide a case." The court added that Canada had endeavoured to create a more diverse judiciary and "that very diversity should not operate as a presumption that a judge's identity closes the judicial mind."[61]

However, the Supreme Court found that the judge's conduct during the trial exhibited behavioural bias. When counsel for the board cross-examined a witness based on confidential information in a student's file, the other side objected. The trial judge invited submissions on the point but then ruled against the board before it had the opportunity to make its argument. When counsel for the board objected, he accused counsel of playing games. The trial judge also criticized the board's counsel for the way he dealt with a request to file affidavit evidence from a witness who had suffered a stroke. On several other occasions, the trial judge disparaged and criticized counsel without valid reason. When it came to costs, the trial judge refused to allow the defendant to file reply submissions to a request for solicitor-client costs. Ruling on crucial points without allowing a party to make submissions and unfairly berating counsel are indicative of a closed judicial mind and inimical to impartiality.

## Compassion

Our most respected judges are often described as compassionate. But what exactly does it mean to judge with compassion? The law is the law. It must be applied with an even and consistent hand. It cannot be bent to meet every individual circumstance, nor can it be modified on grounds of sympathy or emotion.[62] Is judging with compassion compatible with the ideal that the law is to be applied in an even-handed, rational and objective manner?

Judging is not an abstract or mechanical process. A retired member of my court, highly respected for his meticulous intellectual rigour, insisted that judging calls for qualities of both "head" and "heart." He described the "good judge" as "a person who has a passion to do justice combined with the knowledge and skills necessary to give effect to this passion."[63]

Judging is an intensely human process. The judge is engaged in unravelling and resolving disputes that often have had a profound impact on the lives of the litigants. To render justice, it is essential that the judge understand the litigants and all the implications of their dispute, both present and future.

Compassion is related to impartiality or not being "partial." Just as a judge must not bring a biased view to bear, nor should the judge take a partial or incomplete view of the case. As Chief Justice Beverley McLachlin explained, for judges "to see all sides of the problem is to have a better chance of making a decision that is both fair and just and seen as fair and just."[64] Justice Claire L'Heureux Dubé expressed a similar view, urging judges to develop "a willingness and a sense of responsibility to understand perspectives which differ from our own and to reflect these in the law."[65]

I suggest that the capacity to see all sides of the problem and to understand the perspectives of the litigants helps us understand the quality of compassion the judge should exhibit. Chief Justice Brian Dickson saw compassion as "a feeling of empathy, or sympathy for the hardships experienced by others – a feeling, which extends to a sense of responsibility and concern to alleviate hardship at least in some measure." He thought compassion to be an essential element of justice: "For a judge to reach decisions which comport with justice and fairness, he or she must be guided by an ever-present awareness and concern for the plight of others and the human condition ... Compassion is not some extra-legal factor magnanimously acknowledged by a benevolent legal decision-maker. Rather, compassion is part and parcel of the nature and content of that which we call 'law.'"[66]

Compassion, then, is the capacity to understand fully and empathize with the situation of the litigants.[67] The compassionate judge is one who has the capacity to understand and empathize with the litigants at a very human level. Professor Jennifer Nedelsky persuasively argues that judges must avoid a formal vision of impartiality that assumes a core identity shared by all.[68] "Universal rules only make sense if there is something universally identical about the ruled."[69] Judges need to engage in an "enlargement of mind" and "taking different perspectives into account ... is the path out of the blindness of our subjective private conditions" and the way to make "autonomous, impartial judgment possible."[70]

Compassion, in this sense, does not permit the judge to make one-off decisions on the basis of sympathy or emotion that cannot be justified under the governing legal standard. The judge must be able to offer a coherent explanation for the result based upon a principle that the judge is prepared to apply to the next case. The compassionate judge remains faithful to the law and to the integrity of its steady and even application,[71] but the compassionate judge also demonstrates the ability and the determination to grapple with and accommodate the entire picture of the human drama that unfolds in the courtroom. Compassionate judges have the ability to put themselves in the shoes of the litigants and to mete out measured justice.

Compassion overlaps with wisdom and the capacity to marry faithfulness to the law with a rich understanding of the human complexities the case presents. Wisdom involves a combination of knowledge, intelligence, and practical common sense. Judges are expected to know the law and to have the intelligence required to understand, analyse, and explain the issues they decide. But the good judge brings much more to bear on decision-making than raw knowledge and intelligence. Good judges must also have some "street smarts." They have to understand how the world works and to have the capacity to grasp the practical consequences of a decision. The law is not an abstraction that can operate satisfactorily by rigorously logical application of black-letter rules. The good judge will be faithful to the law but will understand that the law is not an end in itself. The law operates in the practical world, and judges should resist "theoretically correct but practically unworkable rules."[72] The law is a tool, and its application must be balanced and nuanced if it is to achieve the goal of social peace and justice.

The compassionate judge recognizes that in some cases it is appropriate to take differences into account. Again, we encounter the classical ideal that holds that we must judge everyone the same, regardless of race, gender, religion, or other prescribed grounds of discrimination. Does this mean that we must proceed on the assumption that everyone is exactly the same? The answer seems to me to be, quite obviously, no. Sometimes differences, especially those arising from race or other suspect grounds, are very much a part of the picture we need to see and consider. If we fail to pay heed to those differences we risk violating the second meaning of impartiality, that of judging on only a partial or incomplete view of the relevant facts. Again, to quote the Canadian Judicial Council's *Commentaries on Judicial Conduct*, "Impartiality is one thing, indifference is another. A judge may show alertness to problems of our days without putting his impartiality into jeopardy."[73]

When does taking difference into account amount to invidious bias, and when is it necessary to take difference into account to avoid partiality or incompleteness? Judges need to guard against stereotyping or assuming that generalizations apply to individuals without looking at the facts. But to achieve true equality, we also need to take the social context into account. We need to try, as best we can, fully to understand the individuals we judge and the context in which they act. In so doing, we should be conscious of the fact that their experience may be different from our own, and the difference may have a bearing upon the issue we are asked to judge. Chief Justice McLachlin urges judges to engage in what she calls "the practice of conscious objectivity." The judge should "consciously put oneself in the shoes of first one party, and then the other. How would I feel if I were in this person's position? the judge should ask. In an act of imagination, the judge should attempt to see life through each litigant's eyes, much as an actor attempts to see a situation through the eyes of the character being portrayed. If the character is unsympathetic, the effort may be difficult, even distasteful. Yet it is important. For it is in this way that the judge sees the larger picture; it is in this way that the judge moves from partiality to impartiality."[74]

Professor Richard Devlin has persuasively argued that it may never be possible for us to achieve completely impartial justice. He observed that we will never be able to truly put ourselves in the shoes of the litigants, never wholly understand everything that passes before us, and never be able to entirely eradicate all of our biases and prejudices.[75] He suggests a more modest objective, namely minimizing the risk of partiality by adopting a "situationalist" posture, frankly recognizing the unavoidable limits on our ability to be completely impartial but promoting a sensitivity to these barriers: "[E]veryone who is involved in the legal process – both those who judge and those who are judged – are deeply affected by their experiential contexts …. [C]ultural forces are always crucial variables and that judging can only aspire to impartiality if it is sensitive to social phenomena such as racialization."[76]

There are many examples to illustrate the point that we will fail to deliver impartial justice if we fail to take difference into account. Cultural differences may affect assessment or credibility. In many Indigenous communities, looking someone in the eye is considered rude because it signals that the person being looked at is inferior.[77] Many Indigenous children are taught from an early age not to interfere with the choices of another and not to criticize another's actions in that person's presence.[78] This may explain a great deal about the discomfort of an Indigenous child called as a witness in a criminal trial. These habits come from a world view quite different from that of the non-Indigenous majority, including most judges. To judge this behaviour without making appropriate allowance or taking into account all the social facts could lead to an unjust and partial decision.[79]

A woman's plea of self-defence to a charge of murdering her husband by shooting him in the back may not satisfy the standard applicable to two men in a barroom brawl. It may, however, be quite compelling if the facts reveal her to be the victim of a history of spousal abuse.[80] Rather than being simply a woman who shot her husband in the back, the full factual context of her situation may reveal her to be a woman who was certain that if she did not shoot at that moment, then the man would certainly kill her later and that she actually *does* satisfy the criteria for a plea of self-defence.

Stereotypical thinking has also plagued our treatment of sexual assault cases. Our Supreme Court has held unequivocally that silence, passivity, or ambiguous conduct does not amount to consent[81] and that "complainants should be able to rely on a system free from myths and stereotypes, and on a judiciary whose impartiality is not compromised by these biased assumptions."[82] By the standards of the middle-aged male judge, an allegation of sexual abuse made long after the fact may well sound highly suspect. But should it when due consideration is given to all aspects of the complainant's experience, including the fear and shame felt at the time the abuse occurred?

The *Criminal Code* directive to give special consideration to alternative measures for Indigenous offenders[83] illustrates the point. From the perspective of a purely formal view of equality, it may appear to be nothing more than a race-based preference. With a fuller picture of all the facts, including the grossly disproportionate representation of Indigenous inmates in our prison population, the directive seems a legitimate attempt to deal with a "sad and pressing social problem."[84]

## Conclusion

As the Constitution of the State of Massachusetts provides, "It is the right of every citizen to be tried by judges as free, impartial and independent as the lot of humanity will admit."[85] Judges are human, and they are the products of a lifetime of experience. They cannot avoid the impact of that experience upon their thinking. Indeed, they necessarily rely upon their life experience when weighing the decisions they make. Formal legal rules disqualify judges in clear cases of bias, but that does not go far enough. Achieving our aspiration for impartial justice depends upon the professional training and integrity of judges to engage in careful and solemn introspection about the values and attitudes they bring to bear to their work on the bench. Compassion is an aspect of impartiality. The compassionate judge is one who understands the litigants and their circumstances and, by taking their circumstances into account, ensures that they are judged with an even hand.

# Conclusion

This book represents one judge's view of the art of judicial decision-making in the common law tradition.[1] The life of law, said Holmes, is not logic but experience,[2] and my views on judging have certainly been shaped by my experience. I have practised and taught law, and I have been a trial and appellate judge for over twenty years. My account is no doubt influenced by my academic background, but it is written primarily from the perspective of a sitting judge, and it attempts to explain the task of judging as simply and as honestly as possible.

I believe that my discussion of the judicial role pertains to the work of all judges, be they trial judges, appellate judges, or judges of an apex court. My emphasis, however, is on the work of an intermediate appellate court. Sitting between the trial court and the Supreme Court, we play a crucial and distinctive role.

Trial judges are the engine of the judicial process. All cases begin and most cases end in the trial court. Trial judges become intimately familiar with the litigants, and they become immersed in the facts of the dispute. Trial judges find facts, and they strive to reach just decisions based on the law as they understand it. The primary task of trial judges is the just resolution of the particular cases they hear.

The Supreme Court determines the major jurisprudential issues of the day. The Supreme Court deals with a very small number of important cases having national importance. The Supreme Court controls its docket by determining which cases should be given leave to appeal. The Supreme Court almost always has the advantage of having both a trial and an appellate decision exploring the issue it has to decide, and, in many cases, it will have the views of the courts of other provinces on the same or similar points. The importance of the Supreme Court is particularly marked in constitutional cases where the court shapes the structure of our democracy and determines the nature and meaning of our fundamental rights and freedoms. The primary task of the Supreme Court is to provide general guidance and direction on the law.

Intermediate courts have a distinctive jurisprudential role. Our role is to maintain the overall integrity of the judicial process by monitoring the work of the trial courts on a regular basis and by ensuring that judicial decisions respect the law. We decide a high volume of cases, and we have a significant influence on the direction of the law. However, we have virtually no control over our docket. Unlike the Supreme Court, we cannot restrict our attention or our resources to a small number of cases of national importance. Nor are we preoccupied with constitutional decision-making. Our jurisprudential role is grounded in the duty to hear and decide a large number of cases raising issues from all areas of the law. And for almost all litigants, we are the court of last resort. That places upon us a heavy burden to make decisions that respect the integrity of the law. These factors combine to make intermediate appellate courts the jurisprudential workhorse of the system.

The central theme or focus of the book is an attempt to explain and reconcile two fundamental features of judging at all levels of the judicial hierarchy: judicial choice and judicial discipline.

I think it is quite wrong for judges to pretend that they are nothing more than neutral umpires who simply apply clear rules that always dictate predictable results. I reject the view that judges can or should decide cases in mechanical fashion, strictly applying the applicable rules of law without regard to their normative underpinnings and with no account of social or political context. Judges must look beneath the surface of the rules and identify the underlying general legal principles that structure the legal regime as a whole and do their best to ensure that their decisions comport with the overall integrity of the legal order.

The law does not always provide clear answers to the cases that come before the courts, and judges are left with difficult choices to make. I have argued that the law leaves judges room for choice in its application in particular cases for two reasons. Legal rules and doctrines are necessarily general in nature. That is what gives rules the universal character that qualifies them as law. Legal rules also have to be interpreted and applied to different facts and to changing contexts. The generality and contextual nature of law confers significant power on judges. It affords them room to reach just results in specific cases, and, when combined with the idea of precedent, it gives judges the power to make law.

The choices judges make are vitally important. We live in a society that aspires to live by the rule of law. The just determination under the law of the legal rights and responsibilities of all citizens is crucial to the realization of that ideal. And because of our belief that like cases should be decided alike and our adherence to precedent, the decision a judge makes in one case has implications for future cases. When a common law appellate judge decides a case, the judge simultaneously follows and constitutes the law. Judicial law-making is an inherent, inevitable, and desirable part of our common law tradition. It allows the law to evolve to meet changing circumstances, and it reflects the important judicial role in keeping the law current.

On the other hand, I insist that the power of judicial choice is disciplined and constrained. Legal uncertainty means that judges often have to make difficult choices, but it does not leave them free to decide cases according to their own personal sense of justice. Judges are judges, not legislators, and they must act accordingly. Judges are duty bound to decide cases in a principled fashion and in a way that respects the inherent limits of the litigation process and the judicial role.

The obligation to decide cases according to law is not, as some argue, a mere pretence. When a judge finds that the law is uncertain or contested, the judge must still strive to reach a result that respects the coherence and integrity of the law. The judge must work within the law's existing framework and parameters and work towards a resolution that coheres with what is already there and makes the law a more complete whole. By seeing law as both rules and overarching principles, the judge finds the flexibility to achieve justice in each case, but also the discipline to ensure that decisions respect the coherence and integrity of the law. Rules provide stability, while principles give the law coherence by explaining the moral and ethical values the rules advance, and by identifying the considerations of justice and fairness the law seeks to protect. Principles help us apply rules justly, and when the rules run out and leave us in doubt, principles help us to fill in the gaps.

Judges are obliged to use the law's distinctive form of reasoning. Ours is a form of practical reason, wedded to the highest ideals of justice, but aimed at reaching results that are workable in the real world. We must base our decisions on certain sources that have a particular legal pedigree. We must respect institutional boundaries. We must justify the results we reach with reasons that will stand up to legal and public scrutiny. The obligation to give reasons imposes a significant discipline on judicial decision-making. It makes judging transparent and renders judges publicly accountable for the decisions they make.

Judging is also a very human process. The problems posed by the cases we decide display the best and the worst of human behaviour. They are the product of love, passion, greed, and wickedness, and the duty to decide them justly imposes a heavy burden. Judges, like the cases they decide, reflect the human condition. We are appointed because we are "learned in the law." But we also have a life story that has shaped our thinking and that can influence the way we decide cases. Judges, I have argued, should think about the experiences and values they bring to bear upon the work of deciding cases. We need to be aware that in addition to our legal skill and knowledge, our decisions may be affected by our background and experience. We necessarily use that experience to understand the cases we hear, but we must be careful about relying too heavily on our "common sense" or intuitive notion of right and wrong. Our experience can help us reach wise and compassionate decisions, but we are judges sworn to uphold the law, and that duty must remain paramount.

The subtle play of forces that empower judges to make law and that constrain judges in the choices they make is not well understood by the lay public, by politicians, or by scholars of other disciplines. Judges are at least in part responsible for that lack of understanding. When challenged, judges often hide behind the facade of an exaggerated form of judicial neutrality, proclaiming that they are no more than umpires applying the rules of the game. That protestation is unpersuasive and dangerous. It is unpersuasive as it fails to take account of an important part of the judicial function. It is dangerous, for if the judge actually believes it, there is a worrying risk that the judge has failed adequately to reflect on the ideas and values the judge has brought to bear upon the task of deciding cases.

But the suggestion that judges are free to decide as they see fit is also dangerous and misleading. It is dangerous, as it debases the judicial role and undermines an important aspect of the rule of law and the role of the courts in a constitutional democracy. It is misleading, as it invites judges to decide in a manner that would ignore fundamental principles of judicial decision-making.

My aim in writing this book has been to open a window on judicial decision-making and to encourage a healthy conversation between judges, lawyers, and the public at large about the nature of the judicial role.

# Glossary

**apex court** A court at the highest level of the judicial hierarchy, such as the Supreme Court of Canada

**appellate court** A court that hears appeals from judgments of the first instance or trial courts

**as-of-right appeal** An appeal that can be made to a higher court without first having to obtain permission or leave to appeal

**Attorney General** The member of Cabinet who is the senior legal adviser to the government and is responsible for prosecutions and ensuring that the government complies with the law

**bias** A predisposition to decide on an irrelevant or improper ground

**binding authority** Legal authority the judge must follow, relevant provisions of the Constitution, and statutes and governing precedential judicial rulings

**case at bar** The case or issue that is actually before the court

**cause of action** A set of facts that give a person the right to claim a legal remedy

**common law** The body of law, derived from the precedents established by the decisions of the courts, as distinct from statute law passed by the legislature

**consideration** The exchange of something of value to support the enforcement of a contract

**contextual analysis** Assessing legal issues in the light of the relevant prevailing social, cultural, economic, and political factors

**correctness standard** The reviewing or appellate court is entitled to say that the first-instance decision is either right or wrong, and if it is wrong, to substitute its own decision

**damages** A monetary award made to an injured party to compensate for the harm caused by the wrongful act of another

**declaratory theory** The view that judges do not make the law but rather discover something that was always there and declare it

**deductive reasoning** Starting with a general statement or hypothesis and working towards a result that flows logically from that general statement or hypothesis

**defendant** The person sued in a civil proceeding

**deference** The principle that a reviewing or appellate court should respect the first-instance decision and refrain from approaching the case as if they were the first-instance decision-maker

**democratic process model** The view that judicial review advances democracy by protecting the fundamental rights and freedoms that are essential to democratic life

**dialogue theory** The view that judicial review involves an exchange between courts and legislatures in which neither have the final say

***dictum*** *See obiter dictum*

**discretion** The power to choose from a range of possible courses of action

**division of powers** The constitutional allocation of authority between the federal and provincial governments to enact legislation

**dualist tradition** The principle that international commitments are not directly enforceable in domestic courts unless specifically incorporated into domestic law by Parliament

**due process** Principles of procedural fairness that have evolved through the common law

**duty of care** A legal relationship that subjects the actor to liability for harm caused to another

***en banc* sittings** The practice of having all members of an appellate court sit to resolve important issues

**equity** The system of law originating in the English Court of Chancery that enforced duties of trust, honesty, and fair dealing

**hard case** A case in which there is no clear legal rule or principle to determine the outcome

**horizontal precedent** A precedent from a court at the same level in the judicial hierarchy

**impartiality** A state of mind in which the adjudicator is disinterested in the outcome and is open to persuasion by the evidence and submissions

**inductive reasoning** Working towards a result from a specific case or proposition

**injunction** An order of the court requiring a party to perform some act or refrain from some conduct so as to respect the rights of another

**judicial activism** An inclination by the court to be bold about making law or striking down laws and policies that contravene the Constitution

**Judicial Committee of the Privy Council** A tribunal of senior English judges that hears appeals from Commonwealth countries and that served as Canada's final court of appeal until 1949

**judicial restraint** An inclination by the court to be more cautious about overturning government laws and policies

**judicial review** The power of the courts to determine the constitutionality of legislation enacted by the people's elected representatives; also the power of the courts to review administrative decisions

**jurisdiction** The legal authority to decide

**Lord Chancellor** Until recently, the highest judicial officer in England who was a member of Cabinet and speaker in the House of Lords, and presided at appellate judicial proceedings in the House of Lords and the Judicial Committee of the Privy Council

**majoritarianism** The argument that as judicial review involves unelected judges overriding the decisions of democratically elected legislators, it is undemocratic and to be sharply curtailed, if not eliminated

**minimalism** The argument that cases should be decided as narrowly as possible, and broad pronouncements should be avoided

**natural justice** Common law procedural rights that apply when a decision affecting one's legal rights is taken, including the right to be heard by an impartial tribunal

**negligence** Failure to exercise the care of a reasonably prudent person in breach of a legal duty of care, rendering the actor liable for damages for harm caused to the injured party

***obiter dictum*** Something said in a judgment that is not necessary for the decision

**originalism** The argument that the meaning of the Constitution must be determined by the intention of the framers

**palpable and overriding error** The standard that determines when an appellate court can reverse a trial judge's findings of fact: a clear and obvious error that goes to the heart of the case

**persuasive authority** A precedent or legal argument that carries some weight but does not bind the judge

**plaintiff** The person who asserts a claim in a civil proceeding

**precedent** A past judicial decision that is used to determine the outcome of another case

**privity of contract** A direct contractual relationship between the parties

**Privy Council** *See* Judicial Committee of the Privy Council

***ratio*** The essential core of the reasons for decision to which the authority of precedent is attached

**reasonableness standard of review** A deferential standard based on the idea that certain questions do not lend themselves to one specific, particular result and that tribunals are to be accorded a margin of appreciation within the range of acceptable and rational solutions

**social and legislative facts** Facts relating to the impact and effect of legislation, matters of opinion ordinarily proved by expert social science evidence

**standard of review** The standard of review that defines what an appellate or reviewing court can and cannot do in relation to a first-instance decision from an administrative agency or a trial court

***stare decisis*** The principle that prior decisions on the same issue are binding

**strict liability** Liability that does not depend upon proof of negligence or fault

**torts** Non-contractual civil wrongs recognized at common law

**vertical precedent** A decision from a court higher in the judicial hierarchy on the point to be decided

# Notes

## 1 Introduction

1 HLA Hart, *The Concept of Law*, 3d ed (Oxford: Oxford University Press, 2012).

2 Lon L Fuller, *The Morality of Law* (New Haven, CT: Yale University Press, 1963).

3 HLA Hart, "Positivism and the Separation of Law and Morals" (1958) 71 Harv L Rev 593; Lon L Fuller, "Positivism and Fidelity to Law: A Reply to Professor Hart" (1958) 71 Harv L Rev 630.

4 HLA Hart, *Law, Liberty and Morality* (Stanford: Stanford University Press, 1963); Hart, *The Morality of the Criminal Law* (Jerusalem: Hebrew University 1965); Patrick Devlin, *The Enforcement of Morals* (London: Oxford University Press, 1965).

5 Karl Llwellyn, *The Bramble Bush: Our Law and Its Study* (New York: Oceana, 1930).

6 Ronald Dworkin, *Taking Rights Seriously* (London: Duckworth, 1977).

7 Robert J Sharpe, *The Law of Habeas Corpus* (Oxford: Oxford University Press, 1976).

8 Part I of the *Constitution Act, 1982*, being Schedule B to the *Canada Act 1982* (UK), 1982, c 11.

9 A successful challenge to the *Vital Statistics Act* provision that required that children be registered with their father's last name. The case was unreported, as the Attorney General of Ontario conceded the point without argument, and while an order was made, no written reasons were given.

10 *Reference Re Bill 30 (1986), An Act to Amend the Education Act (Ont)* [1987] 1 SCR 1148.

11 *Re Klein and Law Society of Upper Canada; Re Dvorak and Law Society of Upper Canada* (1985) 50 OR (2d) 118 (Div Ct); *Re Ontario Film & Video Appreciation Society and Ontario Film Review Board et al* (1986) 57 OR (2d) 339 (Div Ct); *Zylberberg v Sudbury Board of Education (Director)* (1986) 55 OR (2d) 749 (Div Ct) aff'd (1988) 52 DLR (4th) 577 (Ont CA) and *Canadian Civil Liberties Assn v Ontario (Minister of Education)* (1988) 64 OR (2d) 577 (Div Ct) (1990), 65 DLR (4th) 1 (Ont CA) in the Divisional Court. The cases proceeded before the Court of Appeal after my appointment as Executive Legal Officer at the Supreme Court of Canada. I also represented the CCLA in *Hill v Church of Scientology of Toronto* [1995] 2 SCR 1130.

12 In 2003, Kent Roach and I published a biography of Brian Dickson that traces his life and career and provides a thorough account of his remarkable contribution to Canadian law: *Brian Dickson: A Judge's Journey* (Toronto: University of Toronto Press, 2003).

13 Francis Bacon, *The Advancement of Learning* (1605), quoted in Susan Haack, *Evidence Matters: Science, Proof, and Truth in the Law* (New York: Cambridge University Press, 2014) at 1.

14 The source for this often repeated quotation is uncertain. It has been attributed to various people, including Yogi Berra.

15 See Stephen Waddams, *Dimensions of Private Law: Categories and Concepts in Anglo-American Legal Reasoning* (Cambridge: Cambridge University Press, 2003).

16 Aharon Barak, *The Judge in a Democracy* (Princeton: Princeton University Press, 2006) at 117.

17 Stuart Hampshire, *Justice Is Conflict* (Princeton: Princeton University Press, 2000).

18 See, for example, Jane Stapleton, "Comparative Economic Loss: Lessons from Case-Law Focused 'Middle Theory'" (2002) 50 UCLA L Rev 531.

19 Barak, *supra* note 16 at 114.

20 Stephen Smith, *Contract Theory* (Oxford: Oxford University Press, 2004) ch 1.

21 Stapleton, *supra* note 18 at 532.

22 Guido Calabresi, "Property Rules, Liability Rules and Inalienability: One View of the Cathedral" (1975) 85 Harv L Rev 1089 at note 2.

## 2 A Judge's Work

1 (UK), 30 & 31 Vict, c 3, s 96, reprinted in RSC 1985, Appendix II, No 5.

2 *Ibid*, s 99(2).

3 *Judges Act*, RSC 1985, c J-1, s 42. A judge who has reached 75 and has held judicial office for at least 10 years is also eligible for the judicial pension or to elect supernumerary status.

4 *Ibid*, s 28.

5 *Ibid*, s 3.

6 Two notable examples are Supreme Court Justices Brian Dickson and Bertha Wilson.

7 Three former professors and deans: MacPherson JA (Osgoode), Sharpe JA (University of Toronto), Gillese JA (Western) and four former professors: Trotter JA (Queen's), Huscroft JA and Miller JA (Western), Paciocco JA (Ottawa).

8 A Anne McLellan, "Foreword" (2000) 38 Alta L Rev at 603; Andre S Millar "The 'New' Federal Judicial Appointments Process: The First Ten Years" (2000) 38 Alta L Rev 616.

9 The current application form may be found at http://www.fja-cmf. gc.ca/appointments-nominations/forms-formulaires/ph-fc/phf-fc-law-lois-eng.pdf.

10 In 2007 a representative of the law enforcement community was added, but that requirement was removed in 2016. There is one Judicial Advisory Committee for each province except Ontario, for which there are three, and Quebec, for which there are two.

11 *Supreme Court Act*, RSC 1985, c S-26, s 5. The eligibility of a Federal Court judge for appointment to one of the three Quebec positions was considered in *Reference re Supreme Court Act, ss 5 and 6* 2014 SCC 21, [2014] SCR 433.

12 There was a long tradition of direct appointments from the bar to the Ontario Court of Appeal prior to 2006 when, regrettably, the practice was dropped. Many of the court's strongest members were appointed directly from the bar.

13 *Ibid*, s 6.

14 *Ibid*, s 9(2).

15 *Judges Act*, s 43.1(1).

16 Irwin Cotler, "The Supreme Court Appointment Process: Chronology, Context and Reform" (2007) 58 UNBLJ 131 at 4.

17 *Ibid*.

18 Brent Rathgeber, *Irresponsible Government: The Decline of Parliamentary Democracy in Canada* (Toronto: Dundurn, 2014) at 199–202.

19 AM Dodek, "Reforming the Supreme Court Appointment Process, 2004–14: A 10-Year Democratic Audit" (2014) 67 SCLR (2d) 111.

20 See Office of the Commissioner for Federal Judicial Affairs Canada, "Qualifications and Assessment Criteria," http://www.fja-cmf.gc.ca/scc-csc/qualifications-eng.html. For the Advisory Board's Report for Justice Rowe's appointment, see http://www.fja-cmf.gc.ca/scc-csc/Report-Independent-Advisory-Board-for-the-Supreme-Court-of-Canada-Judicial-Appointments-(November2016)_en.pdf, and for Justice Martin's appointment, see http://www.fja-cmf.gc.ca/scc-csc/smartin-report-rapport-eng.html.

21 See, for example, British Institute of International and Comparative Law, *Cape Town Principles on the Role of Independent Commissions in the Selection and Appointment of Judges,* 2016, https://www.biicl.org/documents/868_cape_town_principles_-_feb_2016.pdf.

22 *Courts of Justice Act,* RSO 1990, c C-43, s 43.

23 The Ontario Judicial Council comprises the Chief Justice of Ontario, the Chief Justice and the Associate Chief Justice of the Ontario Court of Justice, three other judges, two lawyers, and four lay persons. Its mandate is to investigate complaints against provincially appointed judges and deal with judicial education and standards of judicial conduct.

24 *Cape Town Principles, supra* note 21 at para 14.

25 *The Constitutional Reform Act* 2005 (UK) established an independent Judicial Appointments Commission with responsibility for recommending a single candidate for each vacancy that arises. Judicial appointments in Israel are also made on the recommendation of independent committees. See Basic Law: The Judicature, Courts Law [Consolidated Version], 5744-1984, ss 1–24. South Africa also has an independent recommendation committee. See Penelope E Andrews, "The South African Judicial Appointment Process" (2006) 44 Osgoode Hall LJ 568.

26 *Reference re Supreme Court Act,* ss 5 and 6, *supra* note 11 at para 49.

27 Under s 27(8) of the UK's *Constitutional Reform Act 2005*, the selection commission must "ensure that between them the judges will have knowledge of, and experience of practice in, the law of each part of the United Kingdom." The Judicial Appointments Commission has a duty "to have regard to the need to encourage diversity in the range of persons available for selection for appointments" (*ibid,* s 64).

28 *Statute of the International Court of Justice,* art 9, "At every election, the electors shall bear in mind not only that the persons to be elected should individually possess the qualifications required, but also that in the body as a whole the representation of the main forms of civilization and of the principal legal systems of the world should be assured."

29 *Rome Statute of the International Criminal Court,* art 26, s 8(a)(i).

30 "Will Women Judges Really Make a Difference?" (1990) 28 OHLJ 507.

31 *R v S (RD)* [1997] 3 SCR 484 at para 38: "[J]udges in a bilingual, multi-racial and multicultural society will undoubtedly approach the task of judging from their varied perspectives."

32 Lord Clarke MR, "Selecting Judges: Merit, Moral Courage, Judgment and Diversity" (2009) 5 HCQR 49; Baroness Hale, "The Appointment and Removal of Judges: Independence and Diversity," International Association of Women Judges, 8th Biennial Conference, 3–7 May 2006, Sydney, Australia; Chief Justice McLachlin, "Why We Need Women Judges," International Association of Women Judges, 8th Biennial Conference, 3–7 May 2006, Sydney, Australia; Samreen Berg & Lorne Sossin, "Diversity, Transparency and Inclusion in Canada's Judiciary," in Graham Gee & Erika Rackley, eds, *Debating Judicial Appointments in an Age of Diversity* (New York: Routledge, 2017).

33 McLachlin, "Why We Need Women Judges," *supra* note 32.

34 Each province has a superior court, but different labels are used: Queen's Bench (New Brunswick, Manitoba, Saskatchewan, Alberta); Supreme Court (Newfoundland, Prince Edward Island, Nova Scotia, British Columbia); Cour Supérieur (Quebec).

35 The most significant exception to the jurisdiction of provincial superior courts is judicial review of federal administrative agencies, which is assigned to the Federal Court of Canada.

36 Robert Sharpe & Kent Roach, *Brian Dickson: A Judge's Journey* (Toronto: University of Toronto Press, 2003). Although this book was published several years after my appointment, I had started the work while I was still a professor.

37 See *Hyrniak v Maudlin* 2014 SCC 7, [2014] 1 SCR 87, emphasizing the advantages of summary judgment to achieve quicker and more affordable justice.

38 The prime example of a standard instruction that is extremely difficult to follow is the co-conspirators' exception to the hearsay evidence rule: see *R v Carter* [1982] 1 SCR 938.

39 See especially, Lord Woolf, *Access to Justice: Final Report to the Lord Chancellor on the Civil Justice System in England and Wales* (HM Stationery Office, 1996), a report that led to a significant overhaul of English civil procedure incorporating case management as its central feature.

40 Warren K Winkler, "Civil Justice Reform: The Toronto Experience" (2007) 39 Ottawa L Rev 99 at 104–5; Ronit Dinovitzer & Jeffrey S Leon, "When Long Becomes Too Long: Legal Culture and Litigators' Views on Long Civil Trials" (2001) 19 Windsor YB Access to Just 106.

41 See Owen Fiss, "Against Settlement" (1984) 93 Yale LJ 1073.

42 Marc Galanter, "A Settlement Judge, Not a Trial Judge: Judicial Mediation in the United States" (1985) 12 JL & Soc'y 1 at 1–18; Judith Resnik, "Managerial Judges" (1982) 96 Harv L Rev 374; Hugh F Landerkin & Andrew J Pirie, "Judges as Mediators: What's the Problem with Judicial Dispute Resolution in Canada?" (2003) 82 Can Bar Rev 249.

43 As Ian Binnie explained upon his retirement from the Supreme Court of Canada (Jacquie McNish, "The Supreme Court's retired, but hardly retiring, Ian Binnie," *Globe and Mail*, 10 April 2012):

   [T]he law is forever being modified. For that modification to take place, there has to be this stream of nutrients flowing up. When that stream is impaired – as it is by taking work out and giving it to alternative dispute resolution – then the work at the top suffers because the judges are not exposed to the same range of problems, with the same depth and the same frequency.

44 *Criminal Code*, s 691.

45 While a provincial court of appeal and the Federal Court of Appeal have the power to grant leave to appeal: *Supreme Court Act*, ss 37 and 37.1, that power is not exercised in practice, and leave to appeal is dealt with by the Supreme Court itself: *Supreme Court Act* s 40(1).

46 As a general rule, fresh evidence on appeal may be admitted only if it was not available at the time of the trial: see *R v Palmer* [1980] 1 SCR 759.

47 *Ontario Rules of Civil Procedure*, RRO 1990, Reg 194, r 61.04 (3).

48 *Ibid*, s 61.10(1).

49 *Ibid*.

50 Lorne Sossin, "The Sound of Silence: Law Clerks, Policy Making and the Supreme Court of Canada" (1996) 30 UBC L Rev 279; Paul R Baier, "The Law Clerks: Profile of an Institution" 26 Vand L Rev 1125.

51 See *R v Mian* 2014 SCC 54, [2014] 2 SCR 689.

52 The Court of Appeal for Quebec follows this practice. The English Court of Appeal and the UK Supreme Court meet briefly before the oral argument to identify key points with a view to focusing counsel's argument: see Alan Patterson, *Final Judgment: The Last Law Lords and the Supreme Court* (Oxford: Hart Publishing, 2013) at 74–5.

53 I give examples of this in chapters 4 and 9.

54 Erica S Weisgerber, "Unpublished Opinions: A Convenient Means to an Unconstitutional End" (2009) 97 Geo LJ 621. *Federal Rules of Appellate Procedure*, 32.1(a) forbids restricting the citation of federal judicial opinions issued after 1 January 2007, but there remain "unpublished"

decisions that can be cited but that lack precedential value. Richard A Posner, *Divergent Paths: The Academy and the Judiciary* (Cambridge, MA: Harvard University Press, 2016) at 238–40 is critical of this practice.

55 *Courts of Justice Act*, s 123(5); Canadian Judicial Council, *Ethical Principles for Judges* (Ottawa: CJC, 1998), ch 4, states as Principle 3 under the heading *Diligence*: "Judges should endeavour to perform all judicial duties, including the delivery of judgments, with reasonable promptness." Commentary 10 notes that in 1985, the Canadian Judicial Council resolved that reserved judgments should be delivered within six months after hearings, except in special circumstances.

56 I discuss this in greater detail in chapter 6.

57 Richard A Posner, *How Judges Think* (Cambridge, MA: Harvard University Press, 2010) at 221; Posner, *Divergent Paths: The Academy and the Judiciary, supra* note 54 at 223.

58 Emmett Macfarlane, *Governing from the Bench: The Supreme Court of Canada and the Judicial Role* (Vancouver: UBC Press, 2013) at 106–7.

59 See, e.g., *Manitoba Metis Federation Inc v Canada (AG)* 2013 SCC 14, [2013] 1 SCR 623 at para 156, Rothstein J. Compare the majority opinion, at para 84–90, asserting that while the precise point was not argued, it should have been in the contemplation of the parties. See also *R v Jordan* 2016 SCC 27, [2016] 1 SCR 631 at para 274 per Cromwell J. The UK Supreme Court generally accepts the convention that cases should not be decided on points not argued but has, on occasion, departed from that convention: see Patterson, *supra* note 52 at 20–9.

60 For a good review of this area, one that I have significantly relied on, see Peter Hogg & Ravi Amarnath, "Why Should Judges Dissent" (2017) 67 UTLJ 126; Freda Steel, "The Role of Dissents in Appellate Judging" (2017) 67 UTLJ; Robert Richards, "Writing Separately" (2017) 67 UTLJ 149; Marie-Claire Belleau & Rebecca Johnson, "Ten Theses on Dissent" (2017) 67 UTLJ 156.

61 Patterson, *supra* note 52 at 91–4.

62 That practice changed in 1966: Judicial Committee (Dissenting Opinions), Order 1966 (UK) CSI 1966, No 1100.

63 Claire L'Heureux-Dubé J, "The Dissenting Opinion: Voice of the Future?" (2000) 38 Osgoode Hall LJ 495.

64 For a recent example, see *Quebec (AG) v A* 2013 SCC 5, [2013] 1 SCR 6.

65 James Lee, "A Defence of Concurring Speeches" (2009) Pub L 305.

66 Lord Reid, "The Judge as Law-Maker" (1971–2) 12 JSPTL 22 at 29: "The truth is that it is not often possible to reach a final solution of a difficult problem all at once. It is better to put up with some

uncertainty – confusion if you like – for a time than to reach a final solution prematurely."

67 Hogg & Amarnath, *supra* note 60 at 127. The Manitoba Court of Appeal has a similar rate: Steel, *supra* note 60 at 143. The dissent rate in US Federal Circuit Courts varies from 1 to 4.8 per cent; Douglas Ginsburg, "The Behavior of Federal Judges: A View from the D.C. Circuit" (2013) 97 Judicature 109, citing Lee Epstein, William Landes, & Richard Posner, *The Behavior of Federal Judges: A Theoretical and Empirical Study of Rational Choice* (Cambridge, MA: Harvard University Press, 2013).

68 See, e.g., *Halpern v Canada (AG)* (2003) 65 OR (3d) 161 (CA), the same-sex marriage case.

69 I expand on this in chapter 6.

70 That is the view taken by Hogg & Amarnath, *supra* note 60.

71 Posner, *How Judges Think*, *supra* note 57 at 32–3.

72 Learned Hand, *The Bill of Rights* (Cambridge, MA: Harvard University Press, 1958) at 72.

73 Diane P Wood, "When to Hold, and When to Reshuffle: The Art of Decision Making on a Multi-Member Court" (2012) 100 Cal L Rev 1445 at 1476.

74 See, e.g., the same-sex marriage decision, *Obergefell v Hodges*,135 SCt 2584 at 2630: "The opinion is couched in a style that is as pretentious as its content is egotistic ... Of course the opinion's showy profundities are often profoundly incoherent."

75 Ruth Bader Ginsburg, "The Role of Dissenting Opinions" (2010) 95 Minn L Rev 1 at 4.

76 Wood, *supra* note 73 at 1455.

77 Ginsburg, *supra* note 75 at 3.

78 Scalia & Whelan, eds, *Scalia Speaks: Reflections on Law, Faith, and Life Well Lived* (New York: Crown Forum, 2017) at 279.

79 *Criminal Code*, s 691(1).

80 Charles Hughes, *The Supreme Court of the United States* (New York: Columbia University Press, 1928) at 68.

81 William J Brennan, "In Defence of Dissents" (1986) 37 Hastings LJ 427 at 431.

82 Notable examples are Laskin J's dissent in *Murdoch v Murdoch* [1975] 1 SCR 423 effectively adopted in *Rathwell v Rathwell* [1978] 2 SCR 436 and *Pettkus v Becker* [1980] 2 SCR 834, and Dickson J's dissent in *Reference re Public Service Employee Relations Act (Alta)* [1987] 1 SCR 313, adopted in *Saskatchewan Federation of Labour v Saskatchewan* 2015 SCC 4, [2015] 1 SCR 245.

83 See Melvin I Urofsky, *Dissent and the Supreme Court: Its Role in the Court's History and the Nation's Constitutional Dialogue* (New York: Pantheon Books, 2015). Perhaps the most notable example is Justice Harlan's dissent in *Plessy v Ferguson* 163 US 537 (1896) rejecting the separate but equal doctrine, a dissent that became the law in *Brown v Board of Education* 347 US 483 (1954).

### 3 Is the Law Uncertain?

1 Benjamin Cardozo, *The Nature of the Judicial Process* (New Haven, CT: Yale University Press, 1921) at 166.
2 *Ibid* at 143.
3 *Nichomachean Ethics*, 1137 a-b, quoted in Frederick Schauer, *Thinking Like a Lawyer* (Cambridge, MA: Harvard University Press, 2009) at 120.
4 John Morden, "The 'Good' Judge" (2005), 23 Advocate's Soc J 13 at 26, quoting Alfred Tennyson, *Aylmer's Field* (London: Macmillan, 1891) at 14. Generality as an essential attribute of law is discussed by Lon Fuller in his book *The Morality of Law* (New Haven, CT: Yale University Press, 1964) at 46–9.
5 HLA Hart, *The Concept of Law*, 3d ed (Oxford: Oxford University Press, 2012) at 124.
6 *Supra* note 3.
7 HLA Hart, "Positivism, and the Separation of Law and Morals" (1958) 71 Harv LR 630 at 663.
8 *Ringsted v Lady Lanesborough* (1783) 3 Dougl 197 at 203, 99 ER 610 at 613.
9 [1932] AC 562 (HL), also discussed in chapters 4 and 5.
10 *George v Skivington* (1869) LR 5 Ex 1.
11 This test is more fully discussed in chapter 5. A test for a general duty of care was enunciated more than a decade earlier in American law: *MacPherson v Buick Motor Co* 217 NY 382, 111 NE 1050 (1916), (NYCA), Cardozo J.
12 *Donoghue, supra* note 9 at 580.
13 *Cooper v Hobart* 2001 SCC 79, [2001] 3 SCR 537 at para 54, discussed in greater detail in chapter 5.
14 *Hamilton v Mendes* (1761) 2 Burr 1198 at 1214.
15 RE Megarry, *A Second Miscellany-at-Law* (London: Stevens & Sons, 1973) at 134.
16 Ernest Weinrib, *The Idea of Private Law,* rev ed (Oxford: Oxford University Press, 2012) at xiii.
17 I discuss this in chapter 6.

18 Gérard La Forest, "Some Impressions on Judging" (1986) 35 UNBLJ 145 at 148.

19 Aharon Barak, *The Judge in a Democracy* (Princeton: Princeton University Press, 2006) at 3.

20 Paul Weiler, *In the Last Resort: A Critical Study of the Supreme Court of Canada* (Toronto: Carswell/Methuen, 1974) at 117.

21 Brian Tamanaha, *Beyond the Formalist-Realist Divide: The Role of Politics in Judging* (Princeton: Princeton University Press, 2010) at 171.

22 *Edwards v Canada (AG)* [1930] AC 124. In this part I have drawn freely from Robert Sharpe & Patricia McMahon, *The Persons Case: The Origins and Legacy of the Fight for Legal Personhood* (Toronto: University of Toronto Press, 2007).

23 *Interpretation Act* (1850), UK 13–14 Vict, c 21, s 4.

24 *Chorlton v Lings* (1868) LR 4 CP 374 at 386.

25 *Nairn v University of St Andrews* [1909] AC 147 at 160.

26 *Sex Disqualification (Removal) Act, 1919*, UK 9 & 10 Geo V, c 71, s 1.

27 *Viscountess Rhonddha's Claim (Committee for Privileges)* [1922] 2 AC 339 at 365.

28 *Reference re the Meaning of the Word "Persons" in Section 24 of the British North America Act* [1928] SCR 276.

29 Ian Bushnell, *The Captive Court: A Study of the Supreme Court of Canada* (Montreal & Kingston: McGill-Queen's University Press, 1992) at 56.

30 [1928] SCR at 282.

31 *Edwards, supra* note 22 at 128.

32 *Ibid* at 134.

33 *Ibid.*

34 *Ibid* at 138.

35 *Ibid.*

36 *Ibid* at 136.

37 *Ibid.*

38 *The Persons Case, supra* note 22 at 181–2.

39 George Henderson, "Eligibility of Women for the Senate" (1929) 7 Can Bar Rev 617 at 619.

40 *R v Stone* [1999] 2 SCR 290 at para 239.

41 *Bliss v Canada (AG)* [1979] 1 SCR 183.

42 *Brooks v Canada Safeway Ltd* [1989] 1 SCR 1219.

43 *R v Lavallee* [1990] 1 SCR 852.

44 *Rathwell v Rathwell* [1978] 2 SCR 436 at 443.

45 See, e.g., Karl Llewellyn, *The Bramble Bush* (New York: Oceana, 1930); Jerome Frank, "Are Judges Human?: Parts I & II" (1931) 80 U Penn L Rev

17, 233; Underhill Moore & Theodore Hope, "An Institutional Approach to the Law of Commercial Banking" (1929) 38 Yale LJ 703.

46 *Muller v Oregon* 201 US 412 (1908).

47 Henry Hart, Albert Sacks, William Eskridge, & Philip Frickey, eds, *The Legal Process: Basic Problems in the Making and Application of Law* (Westbury, NY: Foundation, 1994). This book remained an unpublished set of teaching materials until after the death of the two authors, Hart and Sacks.

48 Herbert Wechsler, *Toward Neutral Principles of Constitutional Law* (1959) 73 Harv L Rev 1.

49 See, e.g., Duncan Kennedy, "Form and Substance in Private Law Adjudication" (1976) 89 Harv L Rev 1685; Roberto Mangabeira Unger, *The Critical Legal Studies Movement* (Cambridge, MA: Harvard University Press, 1983).

50 See, e.g., Catharine MacKinnon, *Sexual Harassment of Working Women* (New Haven, CT: Yale University Press, 1979); Jennifer Nedelsky, "Reconceiving Autonomy" (1989) 1 Yale JL & Feminism 7; Martha L Minow, *Making All the Difference: Inclusion, Exclusion & American Law* (Ithaca, NY: Cornell University Press, 1990); Richard Delgado, *Critical Race Theory: An Introduction* (New York: New York University Press, 2011).

51 See, e.g., Ronald Coase, "The Problem of Social Cost" (1960) 3 JL & Econ 1; Guido Calabresi, *The Costs of Accidents: A Legal and Economic Analysis* (New Haven, CT: Yale University Press, 1970); Richard A Posner, *Economic Analysis of Law* (New York: Little Brown, 1973); Robert H Mnookin & Lewis Kornhauser, "Bargaining in the Shadow of the Law: The Case of Divorce" (1979) 88 Yale LJ 950.

52 HLA Hart, "American Jurisprudence through English Eyes: The Nightmare and the Noble Dream" in *Essays in Jurisprudence and Philosophy* (Oxford: Oxford University Press,1983) at 123.

53 Richard A Posner, *How Judges Think* (Cambridge, MA: Harvard University Press, 2010). Posner defines pragmatism in law, at 40, as "basing a judicial decision on the effects the decision is likely to have, rather than on the language of a statute or of a case, or more generally on a preexisting rule."

54 *Vetrovec v R* [1982] 1 SCR 811 at 823.

55 "'Judicial Activism'? A Riposte to the Counter Reformation" (2005) 11 Otago L Rev 1 at 27.

56 Tamanaha, *Beyond the Formalist-Realist Divide, supra* note 21 at 197.

57 There are, however, undoubtedly some cases that settle because the law *is* uncertain and the parties decide to avoid the risk of litigation.

58 In the decade between 2007 and 2017, the Supreme Court decided 778 appeals and was unanimous in the result in 538 cases (including cases where there were concurring opinions): graph found on the Supreme Court of Canada website: "Split vs. Unanimous," https://www.scc-csc.ca/case-dossier/stat/cat4-eng.aspx#cat4c. Compare Emmett Macfarlane, "Consensus and Unanimity at the Supreme Court of Canada" (2010) SCLR 52 (2d) 379 pointing out that the Court is often unanimous in the result but not in the reasoning that leads to the result.

59 Cardozo, *supra* note 1 at 128.

60 See George Priest & William Klein, "The Selection of Disputes for Litigation" (1984) 13 J Leg Stud 1, pointing out that as only contentious cases get litigated, they represent a biased sample of all legal events. See also, Schauer, *supra* note 3 at 22.

61 See *White v Chief Constable* [1998] 2 WWR 1509 at 1549, Lord Hoffmann, describing an earlier decision as "one of those cases in which one feels that a slight change in the composition of the Appellate Committee would have set the law on a different course."

62 John Roberts, *Confirmation Hearing on the Nomination of John G Roberts Jr to Be Chief Justice of the United States*, 12 September 2005, Serial No J-109–37 (Washington: US Government Printing Office, 2005).

63 I discuss the need for judicial introspection in greater detail in chapter 12.

64 HLA Hart, *supra* note 5 at 273.

65 In chapter 10, I discuss the challenge to this view posed by the doctrines of deference and discretion, which posit that a decision-maker may choose from a range of reasonable options, none of which are right or wrong.

66 HLA Hart, *supra* note 5 at 201–5.

67 Ronald Dworkin, *Taking Rights Seriously* (London: Duckworth, 1977) at 105.

68 *Ibid* at 81.

69 Ronald Dworkin, *Law's Empire* (Cambridge, MA: Harvard University Press, 1986) at 243.

70 *Ontario Securities Commission v Greymac Credit Corp* (1986) 30 DLR 4th 1 (Ont CA) at 24; aff'd [1988] 2 SCR 172, 173. See also Aharon Barak, *The Judge in a Democracy, supra* note 19 at 107: "In such situations [where the law does not dictate a clear answer], I try to be guided by my North Star, which is justice. I try to make law and justice converge, so that the Justice will do justice."

71 Cardozo, *supra* note 1 at 89. See also Aharon Barak, *Judicial Discretion* (New Haven, CT: Yale University Press, 1987) at 124–9.

72 Lord Hoffmann, "Ronald Dworkin" (2013) Issue 17 Oxford Law News 8.

73 Alan Patterson, *Final Judgment: The Last Law Lords and the Supreme Court* (London: Hart Publishing, 2013) at 268–73.

74 Barak, *The Judge in a Democracy, supra* note 19 at 118.

### 4  Do Judges Make Law?

1 Aharon Barack, *Judicial Discretion* (New Haven, CT: Yale University Press, 1989) at 102.

2 Benjamin Cardozo, *The Nature of the Judicial Process* (New Haven, CT: Yale University Press, 1921) at 21.

3 William Blackstone, *Commentaries on the Laws of England*, vol 1 (Oxford: Clarendon, 1765) at 69, 71.

4 *Kleinwort Benson Ltd v Lincoln City Council* [1999] 2 AC 349 at 377–9.

5 Lord Reid, "The Judge as Law Maker" (1972–3) 12 JSPTL 22.

6 *Southern Pacific Company v Jensen* 244 US 205, 222 (1917) (dissenting).

7 2007 SCC 10, [2007] 1 SCR 429 at para 85.

8 A product of the declaratory theory that we have not yet entirely shed is that changes in the law announced by judicial decision are generally applied retroactively as if the law always existed as pronounced: for discussion, see ML Friedland, "Prospective and Retrospective Judicial Lawmaking" (1974) 24 UTLJ 170; John Lovell, "From Now On: Temporal Issues in Constitutional Adjudication" (2005) 18 Nat'l J Const L 17; Sujit Choudhry & Kent Roach, "Putting the Past Behind Us? Prospective Judicial and Legislative Constitutional Remedies" (2003) 21 SCLR (2d) 205. However, the Supreme Court regularly makes remedies for constitutional wrongs prospective only: see *R v Hislop, supra* note 7 at paras 81–108. See also *R v Jordan* 2016 SCC 27, laying down a new framework for deciding cases involving the right to be tried within a reasonable time under s 11(b) of the *Charter*. For cases already in the system, the Court provided for a "transitional exceptional circumstance" that considers the parties' reasonable reliance on the law as it previously existed. In *National Westminster Bank plc v Spectrum Plus Limited & Ors* [2005] UKHL 41, [2005] 2 AC 680, after a careful review of the issue, Lord Nicholls concluded, at para 41, that a "never say never" approach should be adopted and that if "altogether exceptionally" a court were to engage in prospective overruling, he "would not regard

it as trespassing outside the functions properly to be discharged by the judiciary under this country's constitution."

9 Barak, *Judicial Discretion, supra* note 1, at 229–33, canvassing models to describe judicial law-making, rejects both the declaratory and policy models and adopts the "model of [judicial] legislation as an incident to adjudication."

10 Robert Goff, "The Search for Principle" (1983) Proceedings of the British Academy 169 at 183–4.

11 Roscoe Pound, "A Theory of Judicial Decisions for Today" (1923) 36 Harv LR 940 at 956.

12 This topic is discussed in greater detail in chapter 5.

13 Leslie Green, "Law and the Role of a Judge" in KK Ferzan & SJ Moore, eds, *Legal, Moral, and Metaphysical Truths* (Oxford: Oxford University Press, 2016), 323 at 334.

14 Referring to John Finnis, *Natural Law and Natural Rights* (Oxford: Oxford University Press, 1980) at 270.

15 Green, *supra* note 13 at 334.

16 *Muscutt v Courcelles* (2002) 60 OR (3d) 20 (CA).

17 Robert J Sharpe, *Interprovincial Product Liability Litigation* (Toronto: Butterworths, 1982).

18 *Sinclair v Cracker Barrel Old Country Store Inc* (2002) 60 OR (3d) 76 (CA); *Leufkens v Alba Tours International Inc* (2002) 60 OR (3d) 84 (CA); *Lemmex v Sunflight Holidays Inc* (2002) 60 OR (3d) 54 (CA); *Gajraj v DeBernardo* (2002) 60 OR (3d) 68 (CA).

19 Reviewed in *Van Breda v Village Resorts Limited* 2010 ONCA 84, 98 OR (3d) 721 at paras 55–7.

20 The Uniform Law Conference of Canada's model *Court Jurisdiction and Proceedings Transfer Act.*

21 Vaughan Black & Mat Brechtel, "Revising *Muscutt*: The Ontario Court of Appeal Takes Another Look" (2009) 36 Adv Q 35.

22 Tanya Monestier, "A 'Real and Substantial' Mess: The Law of Jurisdiction in Canada" (2007) 33 Queens LJ 179.

23 See chapter 7.

24 *Van Breda v Village Resorts Limited, supra* note 19.

25 *Club Resorts Ltd v Van Breda* 2012 SCC 17, [2012] 1 SCR 572.

26 Discussed below at notes 48–9.

27 See, e.g., *Hunt v T&N plc* [1993] 2 SCR 289, at para 25, stating that the real and substantial connection test "was not meant to be a rigid test, but was simply intended to capture the idea that there must be some limits on the claims to jurisdiction" and that "the assumption of and

the discretion not to exercise jurisdiction must ultimately be guided by the requirements of order and fairness, not a mechanical counting of contacts or connections."

28 Cass Sunstein, *One Case at a Time: Judicial Minimalism on the Supreme Court* (Cambridge, MA: Harvard University Press, 1990).

29 John Morden, "The 'Good' Judge" (2005) 23 Advocates' Soc'y J 13 at 22.

30 *Ibid.*

31 While I remain a minimalist at heart, I recognize that even the cautious judge will sometimes be confronted with a case that requires a decision that will take the law in a new direction. In chapter 9, I give an example where I concluded that it was time for the law to recognize a claim for violation of certain privacy rights.

32 Peter Cane, "The Common Law, the High Court of Australia and the United States Supreme Court" in Paul Daly ed, *Apex Courts and the Common Law* (Toronto: University of Toronto Press, forthcoming).

33 *Watkins v Olafson* [1989] 2 SCR 750.

34 *Ibid* at 757.

35 *Ibid* at 760–1.

36 *Ibid* at 763.

37 *Pushpanathan v Canada (Minister of Citizenship and Immigration)* [1998] 1 SCR 982 at para 36, citing Peter Cane, *An Introduction to Administrative Law*, 3d ed (Oxford: Oxford University Press, 1996) at 35.

38 *Pushpanathan* at para 36.

39 Lon Fuller, "The Forms and Limits of Adjudication" (1978) 92 Harv L Rev 353. Compare Jeff King, "The Pervasiveness of Polycentricity" [2008] Public Law 101.

40 [1991] 3 SCR 654.

41 *Canada Evidence Act*, RSC 1985, c C-5, s 4.

42 *Salituro, supra* note 40 at 666.

43 *Ibid* at 673.

44 *Ibid* at 678. In 2015, Parliament dealt the final blow to spousal incompetency and provided that a spouse is both competent and compellable to testify for the prosecution: *Canada Evidence Act*, s 4(2).

45 John McCamus, "The Future of the Canadian Common Law of Contract" (2014) 31 J Contract Law 131.

46 I explain what I mean by policy choices in chapter 5.

47 *R v Stone* [1999] 2 SCR 290 at para 239.

48 *Morguard Investments Ltd v De Savoye* [1990] 3 SCR 1077 at 1099.

49 *Ibid* at 1098.

50 *RWDSU, Local 580 v Dolphin Delivery Ltd* [1986] 2 SCR 573 at 603.

51 *Hill v Church of Scientology of Toronto* [1995] 2 SCR 1130 at 1169.
52 *Dagenais v Canadian Broadcasting Corp* [1994] 3 SCR 835.
53 See *Hill, supra* note 51; *WIC Radio Ltd v Simpson* 2008 SCC 40, [2008] SCR 420.
54 2007 ONCA 771, 87 OR (3d) 241.
55 2009 SCC 62, [2009] 3 SCR 712. I had ruled that as the media defendant had raised a different defence and not litigated the responsible journalism defence at trial, it was not entitled to rely on it on appeal. The Supreme Court disagreed with that proposition, ordered a new trial, and dealt with the responsible journalism defence in *Grant v Torstar, infra,* note 56, a case it decided at the same time as *Cusson.*
56 *Grant v Torstar Corp* 2009 SCC 61, [2009] 3 SCR 640.
57 *R v Khan* [1990] 2 SCR 531.
58 *Pettkus v Becker* [1980] 2 SCR 834.
59 *Bhasin v Hrynew* 2014 SCC 71, [2014] 3 SCR 494 at para 40.
60 *Rathwell v Rathwell* [1978] 2 SCR 436 at 453–4.
61 Barak, *Judicial Discretion, supra* note 1 at 106.
62 Cardozo, *supra* note 2 at 141.
63 Tom Bingham, *The Rule of Law* (London: Penguin Books, 2011) at 45–6.
64 Mel Eisenberg, *The Nature of the Common Law* (Cambridge, MA: Harvard University Press, 1988) at 4–5, quoted in McCamus, *supra* note 45. See also Beverley McLachlin, "The Evolution of the Law of Private Obligations: The Influence of Justice La Forest" in Rebecca Johnson & John McElvoy, eds, *Gérard La Forest at the Supreme Court of Canada 1985–1997* (Winnipeg: Canadian Legal History Project, 2000) at 23: "[L]egislatures only rarely intervene to correct anomalies in the law of private obligation … Change in this area, if it is to be made at all, must be made by the courts."
65 In chapter 9, I provide an example of the importance of trial judgments in changing the law.
66 This point is discussed in chapter 7.

## 5 Rules, Principles, and Policies

1 The idea of these categories is borrowed from Ronald Dworkin, *Taking Rights Seriously* (London: Duckworth, 1977) especially at 22–8.
2 Kathleen M Sullivan, "The Justice of Rules and Standards" (1992) 106 Harv L Rev 22 at 58.
3 *Ibid* at 24.

4 American writers use the terminology of "rules" and "standards": see, e.g., Sullivan, *supra* note 2; Duncan Kennedy, "Form and Substance in Private Law Adjudication" (1976) 89 Harv L Rev 1685; Pierre Schlag, "Rules and Standards" (1985) 33 UCLA Rev 379; Adam H Morse, "Rules, Standards and Fractured Courts" (2010) 25 Okla City L Rev 3.

5 See HLA Hart, *The Concept of Law*, 3d ed (Oxford: Oxford University Press, 2012).

6 I am grateful to my research assistant, Scarlett Smith, for suggesting the distinction between operational and background principles.

7 See *Baker v Canada.(Minister of Citizenship and Immigration)* [1999] 2 SCR 817.

8 Benjamin Cardozo, *The Nature of the Judicial Process* (New Haven, CT: Yale University Press, 1921) at 48.

9 Dworkin, *supra* note 1.

10 *Hall v Herbert* [1993] 2 SCR 159. See also *Patel v Merza* [2016] UKSC 42, allowing the claimant to recover money lent to place bets tainted by illegality. The bets were not placed and the claim for restitution of the money was allowed.

11 *Reference Re Secession of Quebec* [1998] 2 SCR 217.

12 *Ibid* at 240.

13 *Ibid*.

14 *Ibid* at 247.

15 *Ibid* at 248.

16 2014 SCC 32 at para 27.

17 Stephen Waddams, *Law of Contracts*, 6th ed (Toronto: Canada Law Book, 2010) at paras 542–4. For an extended discussion of principles and policies in contract law, see Stephen Waddams, *Principle and Policy in Contract Law: Competing or Complimentary Concepts?* (Cambridge, MA: Cambridge University Press, 2011).

18 Robert Sharpe & Kent Roach, *The Charter of Rights and Freedoms*, 6th ed (Toronto: Irwin Law, 2017) at 60.

19 See *Trinity Western University v The Law Society of Upper Canada* 2016 ONCA 518.

20 Dworkin, *supra* note 1 at 22.

21 See James Plunkett, "Principle and Policy in Private Law Reasoning" (2016) 75 Cambridge LJ 366.

22 Waddams, *Principle and Policy*, *supra* note 17; Jane Stapleton, "The Golden Thread at the Heart of Tort Law: Protection of the Vulnerable" (2003) 24 Aust Bar Rev 135.

23  Ernest Weinrib, *The Idea of Private Law*, revised ed (Oxford: Oxford University Press, 2012); Robert Stevens, *Torts and Rights* (Oxford: Oxford University Press, 2007); Alan Beever, *Rediscovering the Law of Negligence* (Oxford: Oxford University Press, 2007).

24  *Bell ExpressVu Partnership v Rex* 2002 SCC 42, [2002] 2 SCR 559, quoting Elmer Driedger, *Construction of Statutes*, 2d ed (Toronto: Butterworths, 1983) at 87.

25  Cardozo, *supra* note 8 at 66, 67.

26  Plunkett, *supra* note 21. See also Andrew Robertson, "Constraints on Policy-Based Reasoning in Private Law" in Andrew Roberson & Tang Hang Wu, *The Goals of Private Law* (Oxford: Hart, 2009).

27  Waddams, *Principle and Policy, supra* note 17 at 14, quoting MacCormick, *Legal Reasoning and Legal Theory* (Oxford: Oxford University Press, 1978) at 263: "'Policy' has become a hideously inexact word in legal discourse, but if we wish to use it with any exactitude at all, we had better use it as denoting those courses of action adopted by Courts as securing or tending to secure states of affairs conceived to be desirable." Aharon Barak, *Judicial Discretion* (New Haven, CT: Yale University Press, 1987) at 183–4 distinguishes "policy" considerations that "are of a type that the judge, with the tools at his disposal, is capable of learning and applying in a reasonable manner" (what I have called principles) from other "policy" considerations that "are of a type that that causes the judge difficulty in formulating a position, given his institutional limitations" and that fall within the preserve of the legislature.

28  For discussion, see Daniella Murynka, "Give Me One Good Reason: The 'Principled Approach' in Canadian Judicial Opinion" (2015) 40 Queen's LJ 609.

29  RSO 1990, c U2, s 2.

30  RSO 1990, c B18, s 2.

31  *Canada Business Corporations Act,* RSC c C-44, s 241; *Business Corporations Act,* RSO 1990, c B16, s 248.

32  RSC 1985, c B-3, s 173.

33  RSC 1985, c C-36.

34  *Securities Act,* RSO 1990, c S5, s 127.

35  For a good discussion of the hearsay rule, see David Paciocco & Lee Stueser, *The Law of Evidence,* 7th ed (Toronto: Irwin Law, 2015) chs 4 and 5.

36  *R v Khan* [1990] 2 SCR 531 at 540.

37  *Ibid.*

38  *Ibid* at 540 (drawing on *Ares v Venner* [1970] SCR 608); *R v Smith* [1992] 2 SCR 915; *R v Khelawon* 2006 SCC 57, [2006] 2 SCR 787.

39 See Peter Maddaugh & John McCamus, *The Law of Restitution* (Toronto: Canada Law Book, looseleaf).

40 *Pettkus v Becker* [1980] 2 SCR 834.

41 *Rathwell v Rathwell* [1978] 2 SCR 436 at 453–4.

42 *Pettkus, supra* note 40 at 847–8.

43 *Bhasin v Hrynew* 2014 SCC 71, [2014] 3 SCR 494.

44 *Ibid* at para 40.

45 *Ibid* at para 42.

46 See John McCamus, "Abuse of Discretion, Failure to Cooperate and Evasion of Duty: Unpacking the Common Law Duty of Good Faith in Contractual Performance" (2004) 29 Advoc Q 72; Stephen Waddams, "Unconscionability in Contracts" (1974) 39 Modern L Rev 369.

47 *Supra* note 43 at para 60.

48 *Ibid* at para 63.

49 *Ibid* at para 67.

50 *Ibid* at para 67, citing *Peel (Regional Municipality) v Canada* [1992] 3 SCR 762 at 788.

51 *Ibid* at para 71.

52 *Ibid* at para 73.

53 *Ibid* at para 92.

54 See DJ Galligan, *Discretionary Powers* (Oxford: Clarendon, 1986) at 43.

55 *Donoghue v Stevenson* [1932] AC 562. The facts of the case were never proven as the case came before the House of Lords on a pleadings motion. The defendant argued that, even if true, the facts alleged by Donoghue did not in law make out a valid claim.

56 *Ibid* at 579.

57 *Ibid* at 580.

58 *Ibid* at 580.

59 *Ibid* at 580.

60 The source for Lord Atkin's good neighbour principle was the parable of the Good Samaritan (Luke 10:25–37) offered by Jesus as an answer to a question from a lawyer who pressed for details when told that the way to eternal life was to love his neighbour as himself.

61 *Supra* note 55 at 580.

62 *Cooper v Hobart* 2001 SCC 79, [2001] 3 SCR 537, applying with some modification *Anns v Merton London Borough Council* [1978] AC 728, [1977] 2 All ER 492 (HL). The UK courts have taken a different path and departed from *Anns*: see *Caparo Industries plc v Dickman* [1990] 2 AC 605; *Murphy v Brentwood District Council* [1991] 1 AC 398.

63 *Cooper, supra* note 62 at paras 30–1.

64 *Ibid* at para 31.
65 *Ibid* at para 35, citing *Canadian National Railway Co v Norsk Pacific Steamship Co* [1992] 1 SCR 1021 at 1151.
66 *Ibid* at para 30.
67 *Ibid* at para 31.
68 I am grateful to Jason Neyers for suggesting this nomenclature.
69 *Supra* note 62 at para 1.
70 *Ibid* at para 30 (emphasis in original).
71 *Ibid* at para 50.
72 *Ibid* at para 54.
73 *Ibid* at para 55.
74 *Ibid* at para 39. In *Deloitte & Touche v Livent Inc (Receiver of)* 2017 SCC 63 at para 41 the majority emphasized that as the residual policy inquiry "would limit liability in the face of findings of both proximity and reasonable foreseeability," it should be relied upon narrowly, and "[o]nly in rare cases – such as those concerning decisions of governmental policy or quasi-judicial bodies, should liability be denied when a defendant's negligence causes reasonably foreseeable injury to a plaintiff with whom he or she shares a close and direct relationship" [citations omitted].
75 EW Thomas, "How Judges Decide Cases: The Eternal Struggle between Discretion and Precedent" (paper given at the National Judicial Institute Civil Law Seminar 2010). The argument is more fully fleshed out in Thomas, *The Judicial Process: Realism, Pragmatism, Practical Reasoning and Principles* (Cambridge: Cambridge University Press, 2005).
76 *Peel (Regional Municipality) v Canada; Peel Regional Municipality v Ontario* [1992] 3 SCR 762 at 802.
77 See the articles cited *supra* notes 2 and 4.
78 *Caparao Industries, supra* note 62 at 618.
79 *Murphy v Brentwood District Council, supra* note 62 at 471.
80 *Council of the Shire of Sutherland v Heyman* (1985) 157 CLR 424 at 481.
81 *Roxborough v Rothmans of Pall Mall Australia Ltd* [2001] HCA 68 at paras 70–4. For a response and defence of the principled approach, see Carmine Conte, "From Only the 'Bottom-Up'? Legitimate Forms of Judicial Reasoning in Private Law" (2015) 35 Oxford Journal of Legal Studies 1
82 *OBG Ltd v Allen* [2007] UKHL 21, [2008] AC 1.
83 *Ibid* at para 31 (references omitted).
84 Lord Goff of Chieveley, "*The Search for Principle*" (1983) 69 Proc Brit Acad 169 at 186.
85 *Criminal Justice Act*, 2003, c 44, ss 114–26.

86  *Principle and Policy, supra* note 17 at xvi.

87  See, for example, art 1457 of the *Civil Code of Quebec* specifying the general conditions for civil liability:

Every person has a duty to abide by the rules of conduct incumbent on him, according to the circumstances, usage or law, so as not to cause injury to another.

Where he is endowed with reason and fails in this duty, he is liable for any injury he causes to another by such fault and is bound to make reparation for the injury, whether it be bodily, moral or material in nature.

He is also bound, in certain cases, to make reparation for injury caused to another by the act, omission or fault of another person or by the act of things in his custody.

88  See Beverley McLachlin, "The Role of the Supreme Court of Canada in Shaping the Common Law" in Paul Daly ed, *Apex Courts and the Common Law* (Toronto: University of Toronto Press, forthcoming).

89  2016 SCC 27, [2016] 1 SCR 631.

90  s 11(b).

91  [1992] 1 SCR 771.

92  *Supra* note 89 at para 40.

93  *Ibid* at para 50.

94  *Ibid* at para 157.

95  *Ibid* at para 151.

96  *Ibid* at para 147.

97  2012 SCC 72, [2012] 3 SCR 726.

98  2010 ONCA 670, 102 OR (3d) 161.

99  *Supra* note 97 at para 31.

100  *Ibid* at para 69.

101  *Ibid.*

102  Frederick Schauer, *Thinking Like a Lawyer* (Cambridge, MA: Harvard University Press, 2009) at 9.

103  Emphasis added.

104  *R v Nova Scotia Pharmaceutical Society* [1992] 2 SCR 606.

105  *Irwin Toy Ltd v Quebec (AG)* [1989] 1 SCR 927.

106  *Ibid* at 983.

107  *Reference re Sections 193 and 195.1(c) of the Criminal Code (Man)* (1990) 56 CCC (3d) 65 at 91.

108  *Supra* note 104.

109  *Ibid* at 638.

110  *Ibid* at 639.

## 6 Disciplined Judicial Decision-Making

1 The classic discussion is Benjamin Cardozo, *The Nature of the Judicial Process* (New Haven, CT: Yale University Press, 1921).

2 For an excellent discussion that has helped me shape my thinking on these issues, see Frederick Schauer, *Thinking Like a Lawyer* (Cambridge, MA: Harvard University Press, 2009).

3 Charles Fried, "The Artificial Reason of the Law or: What Lawyers Should Know" (1981) 60 Tex L Rev 35.

4 Peter Birks, "The Academic and the Practitioner" (1998) 18 Legal Studies 397 at 406.

5 See chapter 7.

6 Schauer, *supra* note 2 at 7.

7 Aristotle's *Politics and Athenian Constitution*, ed by John Warrington (JM Dent, 1959), book III, s 1287 at 97, quoted in Tom Bingham, *The Rule of Law* (London: Penguin Books, 2011) at 3.

8 Australian Chief Justice Owen Dixon is widely regarded as a leading exponent of legal formalism: see Owen Dixon, "Concerning Judicial Method" in *Jesting Pilate* (Melbourne: Law Book, 1965) at 152.

9 *Prohibitions del Roy* (1607) 12 Co Rep 63, quoted by Jerome Bickenbach, "The 'Artificial Reason' of the Law" (1990), 12 Informal Logic 23. See also Fried, *supra* note 3 at 58: "The law's rationality is a rationality apart." Peter Birks writes of the "the specialized rationality" of the law: "Equity in Modern Law: An Exercise in Taxonomy" (1996) 26 West Aust L Rev 3 at 98.

10 Aharon Barak, *The Judge in a Democracy* (Princeton: Princeton University Press, 2006) at 59.

11 *Ibid* at 67.

12 Schauer, *supra* note 2 at 33.

13 *Southern Pacific Company v Jensen* 244 US 205 at 221 (1917) per Holmes J: "A common-law judge could not say, 'I think the doctrine of consideration a bit of historical nonsense and shall not enforce it in my court.'"

14 *Burnet v Colorado Oil & Gas Co* 285 US 393 at 412 (1932).

15 The most notable exception is the Supreme Court of the United Kingdom, formerly the House of Lords, which routinely sits in panels of five or seven judges and only rarely convenes a panel comprising all members of the court.

16 I discuss the procedure followed to establish a five-judge court in chapter 7.

17 28 USC § 46(c) (1982). See also Federal Rule of Appellate Procedure 35(a), which implements subsection 46(c).

18 See, for example, the practice in Alberta, described in *R v Arcand* 2010 ABCA 363 at paras 209–11; Ian Greene, "The Process of Collegial Decision-Making," in *Final Appeal: Decision-Making in Canadian Courts of Appeal* (Toronto: James Lorimer, 1998) at 79.

19 *Murphy v Welsh* [1993] 2 SCR 1069.

20 The current trend is for fewer mandatory minimum sentences to survive constitutional review: *R v Nur* 2015 SCC 2015, [2015] 1 SCR 773; *R v Anderson* 2014 SCC 41, [2014] 2 SCR 167; *R v Lloyd* 2016 SCC 13, [2016] 1 SCR 130.

21 See HT Edwards, "The Effects of Collegiality on Judicial-Decision Making" (2003) 151 Univ of Penn LR 1639.

22 I discuss these issues in greater detail in chapter 2.

23 Jeffery Segal & Harold Speth, *The Supreme Court and the Attitudinal Model Revisited* (New York: Cambridge University Press, 2002) at 53.

24 John Roberts, *Confirmation Hearing on the Nomination of John G Roberts Jr to Be Chief Justice of the United States*, 12 September 2005, Serial No J-109–37 (Washington: US Government Printing Office, 2005).

25 RE Megarry, "Temptations of the Bench" (1978) 16 Alta L Rev 406 at 410.

26 *English v Emery Reimbold & Strick Ltd* [2002] EWCA Civ 605 at para 16.

27 Alfred Denning, *The Road to Justice* (London: Stevens & Sons, 1955) at 29.

28 *R v REM* 2008 SCC 51, [2008] 3 SCR 3 at para 11.

29 Trevor Allan, "Procedural Fairness and the Duty of Respect" (1998) 18 OJLS 497 at 499; Mark Elliot, "Has the Common Law Duty to Give Reasons Come of Age Yet?" [2011] PL 56 at 62–3.

30 Mathilde Cohen, "Reason-Giving in Court Practice: Decision-Makers" (2007–8) 14 Colum J Eur L 257 at 258, 265.

31 *Lawyer and Litigant in England* (London: Stevens & Sons, 1962).

32 *R v Sheppard* 2002 SCC 26, [2002] 1 SCR 869.

33 *R v REM, supra* note 28, quoting Michael Taggart, "Should Canadian Judges Be Legally Required to Give Reasoned Decisions in Civil Cases" (1983) 33 UTLJ 1 at 7.

34 *R v Sussex Justices, Ex parte McCarthy* [1924] 1 KB 256.

35 Hamish Stewart, "The Trial Judge's Duty to Give Reasons for Judgment in Criminal Cases" (2010) 14 Can Crim L Rev 19 at 23.

36 David Dyzenhaus, "The Politics of Deference: Judicial Review and Democracy" in Michael Taggart ed, *The Province of Administrative Law* (Oxford: Hart Publishing, 1997) 279–307.

37 John Rawls, *A Theory of Justice* (Cambridge, MA: Harvard University Press, 1971) at 133.

38 *R v Sheppard, supra* note 32 at para 5.

39 Patricia Wald, "The Rhetoric of Results and the Results of Rhetoric" (1995) 62 U Chi LR 1371 at 1419.

40 EW Thomas, *The Judicial Process: Realism, Pragmatism, Practical Reasoning and Principles* (Cambridge: Cambridge University Press, 2005) at 248.

41 John Rawls, *Political Liberalism* (New York: Columbia University Press, 1993) at 216, 231–40; Frederick Schauer, "Giving Reasons" (1994–5) 47 Stan L Rev 633; Cohen, *supra* note 30 at 263–4.

42 Ronald Dworkin, *Law's Empire* (Cambridge, MA: Harvard University Press, 1986) at 165.

43 *Ibid* at 167.

44 *Ibid* at 219. See also Lon Fuller, *Anatomy of the Law* (New York: Praeger, 1968) at 94 (quoted in Barak, *The Judge in a Democracy, supra* note 10 at 12): "The rules applied to the decision of individual controversies cannot simply be isolated exercises of individual wisdom. They must be brought into, and maintained in, some systemic interrelationship; they must display some coherent internal structure."

45 Jerome Frank, "What the Courts Do in Fact" (1932) 26 Illinois LR 645 at 655.

46 Karl N Llewellyn, "Remarks on the Theory of Appellate Decisions and the Rules or Canons about How Statutes Are to Be Construed" (1949–50), 3 Vand L Rev 395 at 397.

47 JC Hutcheson, "The Judgment Initiative: The Function of 'Hunch' in Judicial Decision" (1929) 14 Cornell LR 274 at 278.

48 Albie Sachs, *The Strange Alchemy of Life and Law* (Oxford: Oxford University Press, 2009) ch 2.

49 *Ibid* at 49–50.

50 *Ibid* at 53.

51 *Ibid*.

52 Robert Sharpe & Kent Roach, *Brian Dickson: A Judge's Journey* (Toronto: University of Toronto Press, 2003) at 352, 391–2, 405, 406; Emmett Macfarlane, *Governing from the Bench: The Supreme Court of Canada and the Judicial Role* (Vancouver: UBC Press, 2013) at 113–14.

53 Sachs, *supra* note 48 at 53.

54 Ruth Bader Ginsburg, "The Obligation to Reason Why" (1985) 37 Univ of Florida L Rev 205 at 207.

55 *United States v Forness* 125 F.2d 928 (2nd Cir 1942) at 942.

56 Daniel Kahneman, *Thinking, Fast and Slow* (London: Allen Lane, 2011); Chris Guthrie, Jefferey J Rachlinski, & Andrew J Wistrich, "Blinking on the Bench: How Judges Decide Cases" (2007) 93 Cornell LR 1; Chris Guthrie, Jeffrey J Rachlinski, & Andrew J Wistrich, "Inside the Judicial Mind" (2000–1) 88 Cornell L Rev 777.

57 John Morden, "The 'Good' Judge" (2005) 23 Advocates' Soc J 13 at 20.

58 Roger Traynor, "Some Open Questions on the Work of State Appellate Courts" (1957) 24 U Chicago L Rev 211 at 224.

59 Jonathan Haidt, "Moral Psychology and the Law: How Intuitions Drive Reasoning, Judgment, and the Search for Evidence" (2013) 64 Alabama L Rev 867.

60 See *Report of the Commission on Proceedings Involving Guy Paul Morin* by the Honourable F Kaufman (Toronto: Ontario Ministry of the Attorney General, 1998); *Inquiry Regarding Thomas Sophonow* by the Honourable Peter de Carteret Cory (Winnipeg: Manitoba Justice, 2001).

61 In addition to the problems discussed here, Guthrie, Rachlinski, & Wistrich *supra* note 56, discuss the "representativeness heuristic," the tendency to undervalue statistical information; "framing," the way people confront risky decisions, by assessing things from the status quo. Most people prefer a certain $100 gain over a 50 per cent chance of winning $200, but prefer a 50 per cent chance of losing $200 over a certain $100 loss.

62 Guthrie, Rachlinski, & Wistrich, *supra* note 56 at 19–20.

63 *Ibid* at 24. For greater elaboration, see Jeffrey J Rachlinski, "A Positive Psychological Theory of Judging in Hindsight" (1998) 65 U Chicago L Rev 571.

64 Sachs, *supra* note 48 at 49.

65 Roscoe Pound, "A Theory of Judicial Decision for Today" (1923) 36 Harv L Rev 940 at 951: "The trained intuition of the judge continually leads him to the right results for which he is puzzled to give unimpeachable reasons." See also Richard A Posner, *Divergent Paths: The Academy and the Judiciary* (Cambridge, MA: Harvard University Press, 2016) at 227: "Intuition honed by experience may be a surer guide to a reasonable decision than analytical power."

66 Guthrie, Rachlinski, & Wistrich, *supra* note 56 at 30. For a more sceptical view of intuition, see Richard A Posner, *How Judges Think* (Cambridge, MA: Harvard University Press, 2010) at 107–17.

67 See, e.g., Segal & Speth, *The Supreme Court and the Attitudinal Model Revisited, supra* note 23; Cass Sunstein et al, *Are Judges Political? An*

*Empirical Analysis of the Federal Judiciary* (Washington DC: Brookings Institute Press, 2006).

68 See, e.g., Benjamin Alarie & Andrew Green, "Charter Decisions in the McLachlin Era: Consensus and Ideology at the Supreme Court of Canada" (2009) 47 Sup Ct L Rev 475; Benjamin Alaire, Andrew Green, & Edward Iacobucci, "Panel Selection on High Courts" (2015) 65 UTLJ 335; CL Ostberg & Matthew Westein, *Attitudinal Decision Making in the Supreme Court of Canada* (Vancouver: UBC Press, 2004); David Songer, *The Transformation of the Supreme Court of Canada: An Empirical Examination* (Toronto: University of Toronto Press, 2008); James Stribopoulos & Moin Yahya, "Does a Judge's Party of Appointment or Gender Matter to Case Outcomes? An Empirical Study of the Court of Appeal for Ontario" (2007) 45 OHLJ 315; Benjamin Alarie & Andrew Green, *Commitment and Cooperation on High Courts: A Cross-Country Examination of Institutional Constraints on Judges* (New York: Oxford University Press, 2017).

69 See Brian Tamanaha, *Beyond the Formalist-Realist Divide: The Role of Politics in Judging* (Princeton: Princeton University Press, 2010) ch 8.

70 Macfarlane, *Governing from the Bench, supra* note 52 at 23, 101, 131.

71 Ostberg & Westein, *supra* note 68.

72 Harry Edwards, "The Judicial Function and the Elusive Goal of Principled Decision Making" (1991) Wis L Rev 837 at 855.

## 7 Working with Precedent

1 *Carter v Canada (AG)* 2015 SCC 5, [2015] 1 SCR 331 at para 44. For similar statements, see Roscoe Pound, *Interpretations of Legal History* (Cambridge, MA: Harvard University Press, 1923) 1: "Law must be stable and yet it cannot stand still"; Aharon Barak, *Judicial Discretion* (New Haven, CT: Yale University Press, 1987) 264: "Stability without change is decline. Change without stability is anarchy."

2 *Quinn v Leathem* [1901] AC 495 (HL) at 506.

3 *Ibid.*

4 2014 SCC 53, [2014] 2 SCR 633.

5 This is discussed in greater detail in chapter 10.

6 2016 SCC 37, [2016] 2 SCR 23.

7 See Neil Duxbury, *The Nature and Authority of Precedent* (Cambridge: Cambridge University Press, 2008) at 67–90.

8 Brian Dickson, "The Role and Function of Judges" (1980) 14 L Soc'y Gaz 138 at 182.

9 Rupert Cross & JW Harris, *Precedent in English Law*, 4th ed (Oxford: Clarendon, 1991) at 77.

10 *Sunbolf v Alford* (1838) 3 M & W 218 at 252, quoted in Cross, *supra* note 9 at 77.

11 [1932] AC 562.

12 See, e.g., *Jetivia SA & Anor v Bilta (UK) Ltd & Ors* [2015] UKSC 23 at para 30, holding with respect to *Stone & Rolls Ltd v Moore Stephens* [2009] UKHL 39, [2009] 1 AC 1391, a decision dealing with a highly contentious issue of the availability of the defence of illegality to a company in liquidation: "[I]t is not in the interests of the future clarity of the law for it to be treated as authoritative or of assistance" except on its specific facts.

13 *Re King* [1963] EWCA Civ 1, [1963] Ch 459 at 483.

14 (1868) LR 3 HL 330.

15 *Knuller v D* [1972] 2 All ER 898 at 903.

16 See William J Brennan, "In Defence of Dissents" (1986) 37 Hastings LJ 427. Justice Brennan routinely and repeatedly dissented on the constitutionality of capital punishment because of his deeply held belief that the death penalty was cruel and unusual.

17 See Dickson CJ concurring in *Professional Institute of the Public Service of Canada v Northwest Territories (Commissioner)* [1990] 2 SCR 367 at 374.

18 For a good discussion of these issues, see Debra Parkes, "Precedent Unbound? Contemporary Approaches to Precedent in Canada" (2007) 32 Man LJ 135.

19 *Sellars v R* [1980] 1 SCR 527 at 529.

20 *R v Henry* 2005 SCC 76, [2005] 3 SCR 609 at para 57.

21 *Ibid.*

22 *R v Prokofiew* 2010 ONCA 423, aff'd 2012 SCC 49, [2012] 2 SCR 639.

23 *Re Hansard Spruce Mills Ltd* [1954] 4 DLR 590 (BCSC) at 592; *Holmes v Jarrett* (1993) 68 OR (3d) 687 (Gen Div) at 673–7.

24 *Re Hansard, supra* note 23 at 592.

25 *Young v Bristol Aeroplane Co Ltd* [1944] KB 718.

26 *Ibid* at 725.

27 *R v Bell* (1977) 15 OR (2d) 425 at 430. See, however, *Douglas v Stan Fergusson Fuels Ltd*, 2018 ONCA 192 at para 79 applying the *per incuriam* exception.

28 *R v Neves* 2005 MBCA 112, [2006] 4 WWR 464 at para 106.

29 *Morelle Ltd v Wakeling* [1955] 1 All ER 708 (CA). See also *R v Neves, supra* note 28 at paras 78–82.

30 *Secretary of State for Trade and Industry v Desai* [1991] EWJ No 176 (CA) at para 34.

31 Parkes, *supra* note 18 at paras 42–3; *Bell v Cessna Aircraft Co* [1983] 6 WWR 178 (BCCA); *Mellway v Mellway* (2004) 187 Man R (2d) 247 (CA); *Thomson v Workers' Compensation Board (Nova Scotia)* 2002 NSCA 58; 2003 NSCA 14; *R v Arcand* 2010 ABCA 363.

32 For example, see chapter 4 at note 23 (assumed jurisdiction).

33 *Thomson Workers'*, *supra* note 31 (Nova Scotia); *R v Arcand*, *supra* note 31 (Alberta); *Skidmore v Blackmore* (1995) 55 BCAC 191, 122 DLR (4th) 330 (British Columbia).

34 *Practice Statement (Judicial Precedent)* [1966] 1 WLR 1234.

35 *Davis v Johnson* [1978] UKHL 1, [1979] AC 264.

36 *David Polowin Real Estate Ltd v Dominion of Canada General Insurance Co* (2005) 76 OR (3d) 161; adopted by the Manitoba Court of appeal in *R v Neves*, *supra* note 28.

37 *Polowin*, *supra* note 36 at para 125.

38 *Ibid* at para 127. See also Aharon Barak, *The Judge in a Democracy* (Princeton: Princeton University Press, 2006) at 159: "The judge must ask himself if the damage from preserving the present law is greater than the damage from changing it judicially."

39 For a similar case, see *Thomson v Workers'*, *supra* note 31.

40 *Polowin*, *supra* note 36 at para 140.

41 *Ibid* at para 143.

42 Here I draw upon Sharpe, "The Doctrine of *Stare Decisis*," in DeLoyd Guth, ed, *Brian Dickson at the Supreme Court of Canada 1973–1990* (Winnipeg: Supreme Court of Canada Historical Society, Faculty of Law, University of Manitoba, 1998).

43 *London Street Tramways Co Ltd v London CC* [1898] UKHL 1, [1898] AC 375.

44 *Stuart v Bank of Montreal* (1909) 41 SCR 516.

45 See chapter 4.

46 *R v Jogee* [2016] UKSC 8. See also *Knauer v Ministry of Justice* [2016] UKSC 9 and *Patel v Mirza* [2016] UKSC 42.

47 *Jogee* at para 85.

48 *Supra* note 34. Practice statements are, as the label suggests, ordinarily used to regulate minor procedural concerns, and the formal legal validity of making such a striking move away from the past in this manner has been questioned: see Duxbury, *supra* note 7 at 131–9.

49 *Reference Re Farm Products Marketing Act* [1957] SCR 198 at 212.

50 *Binus v R* [1967] SCR 594 at 601.

51 See, e.g., *Paquette v R* [1977] 2 SCR 189 at 197.

52 *R v Bernard* [1988] 2 SCR 833.

53　See *R v Chaulk* [1990] 3 SCR 1303; *R v B (KG)* [1993] 1 SCR 740.

54　*Canada v Craig* 2012 SCC 43, [2012] 2 SCR 489 at para 27.

55　*Reference Re ss 193 and 195.1(1)(c) of the Criminal Code (Man)* [1990] 1 SCR 1123.

56　*Canada (AG) v Bedford* 2013 SCC 72, [2013] 3 SCR 1101 at para 42.

57　This reasoning has also been used in England: see, e.g., *Murphy v Brentwood District Council* [1991] 1 AC 398 at 471–2: "There can be no doubt that to depart from the decision [*Anns v Merton London Borough Council* [1978] AC 728] would re-establish a degree of certainty in this field of law which it has done a remarkable amount to upset."

58　*Rathwell v Rathwell* [1978] SCR 436.

59　*Murdoch v Murdoch* [1975] SCR 423, per Laskin CJ.

60　*Rathwell, supra* note 58 at 443.

61　*Minister of Indian Affairs v Ranville* [1982] 2 SCR 518 at 528.

62　*Bernard, supra* note 52 at 55.

63　*R v Cuerrier* [1998] 2 SCR 371, at para 34; *R v DLW* 2016 SCC 22, [2016] 1 SCR 402 at paras 59–62.

64　*Henry, supra* note 20 at para 44.

65　*R v Santeramo* (1976) 32 CCC (2d) 35 (Ont CA) at 46, per Brooke JA: "I do not feel bound by a judgment of this Court where the liberty of the subject is in issue if I am convinced that that judgment is wrong" (cited with approval in *Bernard, supra* note 52 at para 55).

66　*R v R* [1992] 1 AC 599.

67　*R v Salituro* [1991] 3 SCR 654 (narrowing the common law rule making one spouse incompetent to testify against the other); *Henry, supra* note 20 overruling *R v Mannion* [1986] 2 SCR 272 and limiting the reach of the s 13 *Charter* protection against self-incrimination. See also *Arcand, supra* note 31.

68　*Henry, supra* note 20 at para 44. See also *R v Prokofiew* 2012 SCC 49, [2012] 2 SCR 639 at para 66.

69　*R v Nur* 2015 SCC 15, 1 SCR 773 at para 59.

70　In addition to the cases discussed below, see *United States v Burns* 2001 SCC 7, [2001] 1 SCR 283, overruling *Kindler v Canada (Minister of Justice)* [1991] 2 SCR 779, and *Reference re Ng Extradition (Can)* [1991] 2 SCR 858; *Henry, supra* note 20 overruling *R v Mannion* [1986] 2 SCR 272; and, in part, *R v Kuldip* [1990] 3 SCR 618; *Health Services and Support – Facilities Subsector Bargaining Assn v British Columbia* 2007 SCC 27, [2007] 2 SCR 391, overruling *Reference re Public Service Employee Relations Act (Alta)* [1987] 1 SCR 313; *PSAC v Canada* [1987] 1 SCR 424; *RWDSU v Saskatchewan* [1987] 1 SCR 460; *Professional Institute of the Public Service of*

*Canada v Northwest Territories (Commissioner)* [1990] 2 SCR 367; *Mounted Police Association of Ontario v Canada (Attorney General)* 2015 SCC 1, [2015] 1 SCR 3 overruling *Delisle v Canada (Deputy Attorney General)* [1999] 2 SCR 989; *R v Jordan* 2016 SCC 27, [2016] 1 SCR 631 overruling *R v Morin* [1992] 1 SCR 771.

71 In serious criminal cases, there is a right of appeal to the Supreme Court on a question of law where there has been a dissent on a point of law in the provincial court of appeal: *Criminal Code*, s 691(1)(a) or where an acquittal is reversed by the court of appeal and a conviction entered: s 691(2)(b). There is also a right of appeal from a decision of a provincial appellate court on a reference directed by the lieutenant governor: *Supreme Court Act*, RSC 1985, c S-26, s 36.

72 Bora Laskin, "The Role and Function of Final Appellate Courts: The Supreme Court of Canada" (1975) 53 Can Bar Rev 469 at 475.

73 See *Copthorne Holdings Ltd v R* 2011 SCC 63, [2011] 3 SCR 721 at para 57: "Before a Court will entertain reversing a recently decided decision, there must be substantial reason to believe the precedent was wrongly decided"; *R v Nedelcu* 2012 SCC 59, [2012] 3 SCR 311 at para 115; *Nishi v Rascal Trucking Ltd* 2013 SCC 33, [2013] 2 SCR 438 at para 28.

74 *Bedford, supra* note 56 at para 42.

75 *Supra* note 20 at paras 45–6. In *Ontario (Attorney General) v Fraser* 2011 SCC 20, [2011] 2 SCR 3, at para 136, Rothstein J, concurring with the majority but not on this point, referred to the list of factors in *Planned Parenthood of Southeastern Pennsylvania v Casey* 505 US 833 (1992), at 854–5:

1. Has the rule proved to be intolerable because it defies workability?
2. Is the rule subject to a reliance that would lend a special hardship to the consequences of overruling and add inequity to the cost of repudiation?
3. Have related principles of law developed as to have left the old rule no more than a remnant of abandoned doctrine?
4. Have facts so changed, or come to be seen so differently, as to have robbed the old rule of significant application or justification?

76 See chapter 11.

77 *R v Henry, supra* note 20; *Fraser, supra* note 75 at para 58.

78 See chapter 11.

79 *Bedford, supra* note 56.

80 *Carter, supra* note 1.

81 *Reference re ss 193 and 195.1(1)(c) of the Criminal Code (Man)* [1990] 1 SCR 1123; *Rodriguez v British Columbia (AG)* [1993] 3 SCR 519.

82  *Bedford, supra* note 56 at para 38. See also *Carter, supra* note 1 at para 44.

83  *Carter, supra* note 1 at para 42.

84  *Saskatchewan Federation of Labour v Saskatchewan* 2015 SCC 4, [2015] 1 SCR 245.

85  *Reference re Public Service Employee Relations Act (Alta)* [1987] 1 SCR 313.

86  *Saskatchewan Federation, supra* note 84 at para 32.

87  *RJR-MacDonald Inc v Canada (AG)* [1995] 3 SCR 199.

88  See chapter 10 for discussion of this principle.

89  A possibility raised in *RJR-MacDonald, supra* note 87 at para 82 as a reason for rejecting a deferential standard of review. I discuss this issue further in chapter 10.

90  *Canada v Craig* 2011 FCA 22, [2011] 2 FCR 436 considering *Gunn v Canada* [2007] 3 FCR 57, 2006 FCA 281 and *Moldowan v Canada* [1978] 1 SCR 480.

91  2012 SCC 43, [2012] 2 SCR 489.

92  *Ostime v Australian Mutual Provident Society* [1960] AC 459 at 489, per Lord Denning. For a similar statement from a Canadian judge, see *General Brake & Clutch Service Ltd v WA Scott & Sons Ltd* (1975) 59 DLR (3d) 741 (Man CA) at 742 per Freedman CJM: "[I]t is no part of the function of any Court to make error perpetual."

93  Duxbury, *supra* note 7 at 183.

94  BV Harris, "Final Appellate Courts Overruling Their Own 'Wrong' Precedents: The Ongoing Search for Principle" (2002) 118 LQR 408 at 427; Parkes, *supra* note 18.

### 8  Authority: What Counts?

1  For a concrete example of what I have in mind, see chapter 9 discussing my decision in *Jones v Tsige*.

2  Patrick Glenn, "Persuasive Authority" (1987) 32 McGill LJ 261 at 264.

3  This part draws freely upon Robert Sharpe, "The Old Commonwealth: Canada" in Louis Blom-Cooper, Brice Dickson, & Gavin Drewry, eds, *The Judicial House of Lords 1876–2009* (Oxford: Oxford University Press, 2009).

4  Although the list of judges who could and did sit on the Privy Council was long and varied: see Robert Sharpe & Patricia McMahon, *The Persons Case: The Origins and Legacy of the Fight for Legal Personhood* (Toronto: University of Toronto Press, 2007) at 145–6.

5  Bora Laskin, *The British Tradition in Canadian Law* (London: Stevens & Sons, 1969) at 61.

6 Ian Bushnell, *The Captive Court: A Study of the Supreme Court of Canada* (Montreal and Kingston: McGill-Queen's University Press, 1992) at 292.

7 *Stuart v Bank of Montreal* (1909) 41 SCR 516 at 548.

8 Frank Anglin, "Some Differences between the Law of Quebec and the Law as Administered in the other Provinces of Canada" (1923) 1 Can Bar Rev 33 at 38.

9 *Robins v National Trust* [1927] AC 515 at 519.

10 See, e.g., *Village of Granby v Menard* (1900) 31 SCR 14 at 22.

11 Bushnell, *supra* note 6 at 291.

12 Bora Laskin, "The Supreme Court of Canada: A Final Court of and for Canadians" (1951) Can Bar Rev 1038 at 1075.

13 HE Read, "The Judicial Process in Common Law Canada" (1959) 37 Can Bar Rev 265 at 268.

14 Peter McCormick, "The Supreme Court of Canada and American Citations 1945–1994: A Statistical Overview" (1997) 8 Sup Ct LR 527.

15 *Re Board of Commerce Act, 1919, and the Combines and Fair Prices Act 1919* [1922] 1 AC 191.

16 *Toronto Electric Commissioners v Snider* [1925] AC 396.

17 HA Smith, "Residue of Power in Canada" (1926) 4 Can Bar Rev 432 at 434.

18 Vincent MacDonald, "The Canadian Constitution Seventy Years After" (1937) 15 Can Bar Rev 401; WPM Kennedy, "The British North America Act: Past and Future" (1937) 15 Can Bar Rev 393; FR Scott, "The Consequences of the Privy Council's Decisions" (1937) 15 Can Bar Rev 485.

19 [1926] AC 482.

20 Rowell to King, 11 March 1926, quoted in M Prang, *NW Rowell: Ontario Nationalist* (Toronto: University of Toronto Press, 1975) at 441.

21 Quoted in JG Snell & Frederick Vaughan, *The Supreme Court of Canada: History of the Institution* (Toronto: University of Toronto Press, 1985) at 183.

22 Minutes of Convocation of the Law Society of Upper Canada, 1938 including the report of a special committee to review a bill to abolish appeals to the Privy Council.

23 Robert Sharpe & Kent Roach, *Brian Dickson: A Judge's Journey* (Toronto: University of Toronto Press, 2003) at 317–20.

24 *Libman v The Queen* [1985] 2 SCR 178 at para 12.

25 *Geffen v Goodman Estate* [1991] 2 SCR 353 at 374.

26 [1932] AC 562.

27 [1964] AC 465.

28 [1970] AC 1004.

29 [1978] AC 728.

30 [1991] 1 AC 398 at 471.

31 *Canadian National Railway Co v Norsk Pacific Steamship Co* [1992] 1 SCR 1021.

32 *Ibid* at 1149.

33 See also *Hill v Hamilton-Wentworth Regional Police Services Board* 2007 SCC 41, [2007] 3 SCR 129, holding that the police can be liable in tort for negligent investigations, refusing to follow English authority to the contrary: see *Hill v Chief Constable of West Yorkshire* [1988] 2 All ER 238 (HL).

34 JM MacIntyre, "The Use of American Cases in Canadian Courts" (1966) 2 UBC L Rev 478.

35 Sharpe & Roach, *supra* note 23; *Re BC Motor Vehicle Act* [1985] 2 SCR 486; *Hunter et al v Southam Inc* [1984] 2 SCR 145; *R v Keegstra* [1990] 3 SCR 697. The same may be said of cases under the *Canadian Bill of Rights*: see, e.g., *R v Miller* [1977] 2 SCR 680 at 706 per Ritchie J.

36 See, e.g., *Jones v Tsige,* discussed in chapter 9.

37 *R v Appulonappa* 2015 SCC 59, [2015] 3 SCR 754 at para 40.

38 Council of Europe, *European Convention for the Protection of Human Rights and Fundamental Freedoms, as amended by Protocols Nos 11 and 14*, 4 November 1950, ETS 5; UN General Assembly, *Universal Declaration of Human Rights*, 10 December 1948, 217 A (III).

39 *United States v Burns* 2001 SCC 7, [2001] 1 SCR 283 at para 53 (European Court of Human Rights); *R v Morgentaler* [1988] 1 SCR 30 at 46 (Constitutional Court of Germany); *Arsenault-Cameron v Prince Edward Island* [1999] 3 SCR 851 at para 4 (Constitutional Court of South Africa); *R v St Pierre* [1995] 1 SCR 791 at para 84 (Supreme Court of Israel).

40 See Scalia & Whelan, eds, *Scalia Speaks: Reflections on Law, Faith, and Life Well Lived* (New York: Crown Forum, 2017) at 250–9; "The Relevance of Foreign Legal Materials in U.S. Constitutional Cases: A Conversation between Justice Antonin Scalia and Justice Stephen Breyer" (2005) 4 Int J Constitutional Law 519; Stephen Breyer, *The Court and the World: American Law and the New Global Realities* (New York: Alfred A. Knopf, 2015).

41 UN General Assembly, *International Covenant on Civil and Political Rights*, 16 December 1966, United Nations, Treaty Series, vol 999 at 171.

42 UN General Assembly, *International Covenant on Economic, Social and Cultural Rights*, 16 December 1966, United Nations, Treaty Series, vol 993 at 3.

43 *Slaight Communications v Davidson* [1989] 1 SCR 1038 at 1056–7.

44 *Suresh v Minister of Citizenship and Immigration and AG Canada* 2002 SCC 1, [2002] 1 SCR 3 at para 78.

45 *Health Services and Support – Facilities Subsector Bargaining Assn v British Columbia* 2007 SCC 27, [2007] 2 SCR 391 at para 78.

46 *Divito v Canada (Public Safety and Emergency Preparedness)* 2013 SCC 47, [2013] 3 SCR 157 at para 23; *Saskatchewan Federation of Labour v Saskatchewan* 2015 SCC 4, [2015] 1 SCR 245 at para 64.

47 In this part, I have drawn freely on Robert Sharpe & Vincent-Joël Proulx, "The Use of Academic Writing in Appellate Decision-Making" (2011) 50 Can Bus LJ 550.

48 The case in question was *Reference Re the Validity of the Wartime Leasehold Regulations* [1950] SCR 124. See Gordon Bale, "WR Lederman and the Citation of Legal Periodicals by the Supreme Court of Canada" (1993–4) 19 Queen's LJ 36 at 49–50; WF Bowker, "Extra-Judicial Writing" (1980) 18 Alta L Rev 458 at 467; Peter McCormick, "Do Judges Read Books, Too? Academic Citations by the Lamer Court 1991–96" (1998) 9 Sup Ct L Rev (2d) 463 at 465–8.

49 GV Nicholls, "Legal Periodicals and the Supreme Court of Canada" (1950) Can Bar Rev 422.

50 See Paul Weiler, *In the Last Resort: A Critical Study of the Supreme Court of Canada* (Toronto: Carswell/Methuen, 1974).

51 O Hood Phillips, *A First Book of English Law* (London: Sweet & Maxwell, 1948) at 156.

52 See Sharpe & Roach, *supra* note 23 at 213–17.

53 McCormick, *supra* note 48 at 465.

54 *Ibid* at 492.

55 The use of academic writing by appellate courts has attracted considerable attention and empirical analysis: see Vaughan Black & Nicholas Richter, "Did She Mention My Name? Citation of Academic Authority by the Supreme Court of Canada, 1985–1990" (1993) 16 Dal LJ 377; Peter McCormick, "Judicial Authority and the Provincial Courts of Appeal: A Statistical Investigation of Citation Practices" (1993) 22 Man LJ 286.

56 Sharpe & Roach, *The Charter of Rights and Freedoms*, 6th ed (Toronto: Irwin Law, 2017) at 59–60.

57 Benjamin N Cardozo, "Introduction," in *Selected Readings in the Law of Contracts* (New York: Macmillan, 1931) at vii (quoted in Nicholls, *supra* note 49 at 443–4).

58 See, e.g., Mirjan R Damaska, *The Faces of Justice and State Authority: A Comparative Approach to the Legal Process* (New Haven, CT: Yale

University Press, 1991); Claire L'Heureux-Dubé, "By Reason of Authority or by Authority of Reason" (1993) 27 UBC L Rev 1.

59 Roderick A Macdonald, "Understanding Civil Law Scholarship in Quebec" (1985) 23 Osgoode Hall LJ 573 at 577.

60 Sharpe & Roach, *supra* note 23 at 165.

61 Alfred Denning, "Book Review" (1947) 63 LQR 516 (quoted in George W Keeton, *The Elementary Principles of Jurisprudence*, 2d ed (London: Sir Isaac Pitman & Sons, 1949) at 127. See also Frederick Evan Crane: "Why Law School Reviews? A Symposium" (1935) 4 Fordham L Rev 1 at 3.

62 Richard A Posner, *Divergent Paths: The Academy and the Judiciary* (Cambridge, MA: Harvard University Press, 2016) at 43.

63 Black & Richter, *supra* note 55; McCormick, *supra* note 48.

64 Peter W Hogg, *Constitutional Law of Canada*, 5th ed Supp (Toronto: Thomson/Carswell, 2007).

65 Ruth Sullivan, *Sullivan and Driedger on the Construction of Statutes*, 4th ed (Markham, ON: Butterworths, 2002).

66 Pierre-André Côté, *The Interpretation of Legislation in Canada*, 4th ed (Toronto: Carswell, 2011).

67 Sidney Lederman, Alan Bryant et al, *The Law of Evidence in Canada*, 4th ed (Toronto: LexisNexis, 2014).

68 Stephen Waddams, *The Law of Contracts*, 7th ed (Toronto: Canada Law Book, 2017); Angela Swan & Jacob Adamski, *Canadian Contract Law*, 3d ed (Toronto: LexisNexis, 2012); John McCamus, *The Law of Contracts*, 2d ed (Toronto: Irwin Law, 2012).

69 Allen Linden & Bruce Feldthusen, *Canadian Tort Law*, 10th ed (Toronto: LexisNexis, 2015).

70 See, e.g., Lord Cook of Thorndon's reasoning and comments in *Hunter v Canary Wharf Ltd* [1997] 21 WLR 684 at 718–19.

71 Michel Bastarache, "The Role of Academics and Legal Theory in Judicial Decision-Making" (1999) 37 Alta L Rev 739 at 746. See also Judith S Kaye, "One Judge's View of Academic Law Review Writing" (1989) 39 J Legal Educ 313 at 319.

72 Robert Goff, "The Search for Principle" (1983) Proceedings of the British Academy 169 at 184.

73 Bastarache, *supra* note 71 at 739.

74 See, e.g., Harry T Edwards, "The Growing Disjunction between Legal Education and the Legal Profession" (1992) 91 Mich L Rev 34 at 45.

75 See, e.g., *Reference Re Secession of Québec* [1998] 2 SCR 217 at para 84: "Some commentators have suggested that secession could be a change of

such a magnitude that it could not be considered to be merely an amendment to the Constitution. We are not persuaded by this contention."

76 Sharpe & Roach, *supra* note 23 at 167.

77 Black & Richter, *supra* note 55 at 377. See also McCormick *supra* note 48 at 495.

78 *Bhasin v Hyrnew* 2014 SCC 71, [2014] 3 SCR 494.

79 [1989] 1 SCR 641.

80 *Ibid* at 658.

81 *Ibid* at 660.

82 *Pelech v Pelech* [1987] 1 SCR 801; *Richardson v Richardson* [1987] 1 SCR 857; *Caron v Caron* [1987] 1 SCR 892.

83 *G(L) v B(G)* [1995] 3 SCR 370 and *Moge v Moge* [1992] 3 SCR 813.

84 *Van Breda v Village Resorts Ltd* (2010) 98 OR (3d) 721, aff'd *Club Resorts Ltd v Van Breda* 2012 SCC 17, 1 SCR 572.

85 *Muscutt v Courcelles* (2002) 60 OR (3d) 20 (CA).

86 *Van Breda, supra* note 84 at para 55.

87 *Ibid* at para 56.

88 See, e.g., *R v Lavallee* [1990] 1 SCR 852; *M(K) v M(H)* [1992] 3 SCR 6 at 27–32; *Canada (AG) v Mossop* [1993] 1 SCR 554; *Symes v Canada* [1993] 4 SCR 695 at 763; *R v W(R)* [1992] 2 SCR 122 at 133–4; *R v Chartrand* [1994] 2 SCR 864; *Moge, supra* note 83; *R v Daviault* [1994] 3 SCR 63; *R v Seaboyer* [1991] 2 SCR 577; *RJR-MacDonald v Canada* [1995] 3 SCR 199; *R v Finta* [1994] 1 SCR 701.

89 *Keegstra, supra* note 35.

90 *M(K) v M(H), supra* note 88, especially at 35–8.

91 Claire L'Heureux-Dubé, "Re-examining the Doctrine of Judicial Notice in the Family Law Context" (1994) 26 Ottawa L Rev 551 at 562. See also Bastarache, *supra* note 71 at 746: "[M]ost [judges] have not been primary caregivers and do not have any experience with the social and economic costs of being a custodial parent."

92 *R v Lavallee, supra* note 88.

93 (2006) 217 OAC 269.

94 *Charter*, s 24 (1), "Anyone whose rights or freedoms, as guaranteed by this Charter, have been infringed or denied may apply to a court of competent jurisdiction to obtain such remedy as the court considers appropriate and just in the circumstances."

95 Richard F Devlin, "We Can't Go On Together with Suspicious Minds: Judicial Bias and Racialized Perspective in *R v RDS*" (1995) 18 Dal LJ 408 at 419–21.

96  Kent Roach, "Making Progress on Understanding and Remedying Racial Profiling" (2004) 41 Alta L Rev 895 at 896.

97  David M Tanovich, "E-Racing Racial Profiling" (2004) 41 Alta L Rev 905 at 916; David M Tanovich, "Using the *Charter* to Stop Racial Profiling: The Development of an Equality-Based Conception of Arbitrary Detention" (2002) 40 Osgoode Hall LJ 145 at 161–5.

98  *Peart, supra* note 93 at para 95.

99  *Public School Boards' Assn of Alberta v Alberta (AG)* [1999] 3 SCR 845 at para 3; *R v Spence* 2005 SCC 71, [2005] 3 SCR 458 at para 58.

100  *Canada (AG) v Bedford* 2013 SCC 72, [2013] 3 SCR 1101; *Carter v Canada (AG)* 2015 SCC 5, [2015] 1 SCR 331.

101  See Glenn, *supra* note 2 at 298: "The use of persuasive authority is thus essential to law itself and uniformity of law comes not through imposition but persuasion, in the daily world or legal practice."

## 9 Judicial Decision-Making: A Case Study

1  2012 ONCA 32, 108 OR (3d) 241.

2  The parties agreed that as the facts were undisputed, the case could be decided as a summary judgment. The motion judge granted Tsige's motion for summary judgment and dismissed that of Jones: 2011 ONSC 1475 (SCJ).

3  Superior Court judges are entitled to sit as judges of the Court of Appeal on a temporary basis at the invitation of the Chief Justice.

4  *Euteneier v Lee* (2005) 77 OR (3d) 621.

5  *Ibid* at para 63.

6  *Athans v Canadian Adventure Camps Ltd* (1977) 17 OR (2d) 425 (HCJ); *Krouse v Chrysler Canada Ltd* (1973) 1 OR (2d) 225 (CA). Both cases involved commercial entities exploiting the images of star athletes.

7  See the discussion below of the four categories of claims for breach of privacy.

8  *Hunt v Carey Canada Inc* [1990] 2 SCR 959.

9  *Somwar v McDonald's Restaurants of Canada Ltd* (2006) 79 OR (3d) 172 at para 31 (Stinson J).

10  *Motherwell v Motherwell* (1976) 73 DLR (3d) 62 (Alta SC Ap Div); *Dyne Holdings Ltd v Royal Insurance Co of Canada* (1996) 135 DLR (4th) 142 (PEISC Ap Div).

11  See William L Prosser, "Privacy" (1960) 48 Cal L Rev 383 and the discussion of American law below.

12 *Wainwright v Home Office* [2003] UKHL 53. However, the UK Supreme Court has since made reference to the "tort of invasion of privacy": *PJS v News Group Newspapers Ltd* [2016] UKSC 26 at para 32.

13 *Campbell v MGN Ltd* [2004] UKHL 22, [2004] 2 AC 457; *Mosely v News Group Newspapers Ltd* [2008] EWHC 1777.

14 *Lenah Game Meats Pty Ltd v Australian Broadcasting Corp* [2001] HCA 63.

15 *Hosking v Runting* [2004] NZCA 34, [2005] 1 NZLR 1 (CA).

16 See SD Warren & LD Brandeis, "The Right to Privacy" (1890) Harv L Rev 193.

17 See, e.g., Peter Burns, "The Law and Privacy: The Canadian Experience" (1976) 54 Can Bar Rev 1 at 261 warning of "the pressing need to preserve 'privacy' which is being threatened by science and technology to the point of surrender."

18 *Jones, supra* note 1, at para 68.

19 Warren & Brandeis, *supra* note 16.

20 *Ontario (AG) v Dieleman* (1994) 20 OR (3d) 229 (Adams J).

21 *RWDSU, Local 580 v Dolphin Delivery Ltd* [1986] 2 SCR 573, [1986] SCJ No 75.

22 *Ibid* at 603.

23 *Hunter v Southam Inc* [1984] 2 SCR 145 at 158–9.

24 *R v Dyment* [1988] 2 SCR 417 at 427.

25 *R v Tessling* 2004 SCC 67, [2004] 3 SCR 432 at para 23, quoting AF Westin, *Privacy and Freedom* (London: Bodley Head, 1970) at 7.

26 Brian Dickson, "The Role and Function of Judges" (1980) 14 L Soc'y Gaz 138 at 166.

27 Warren & Brandeis, *supra* note 16.

28 *Ibid* at 195.

29 Prosser, *supra* note 11.

30 *Ibid* at 389.

31 §652B.

32 *Jones, supra* note 1 at para 21.

33 *Ibid* at para 47, referring to *Personal Information Protection and Electronic Documents Act, 2000*, SC 2000, c 5 ("PIPEDA"); *Personal Health Information Protection Act, 2004*, SO 2004, c 3 ("PHIPA"); *Freedom of Information and Protection of Privacy Act*, RSO 1990, c F.31; *Municipal Freedom of Information and Protection of Privacy Act*, RSO 1990, c M.56; *Consumer Reporting Act*, RSO 1990, c C.33.

34 PIPEDA, *supra* note 33.

35 *Jones, supra* note 1 at para 49. I had to revisit this issue in relation to PHIPA in *Hopkins v Kay* 2015 ONCA 112, where we held that the scheme created by that Act did not preclude a common law tort claim.

36  British Columbia, *Privacy Act*, RSBC 1996, c 373; Manitoba, *Privacy Act*, RSM 1987, c P125; Saskatchewan, *Privacy Act*, RSS 1978, c P-24; Newfoundland, *Privacy Act*, RSNL, 1990, c P-22; Quebec, *Civil Code of Québec*, SQ 1991, c 64, arts 3 and 35–7, *Charter of Human Rights and Freedoms*, RSQ c C-12, s 5.

37  BC *Privacy Act*. The Newfoundland and Saskatchewan Acts use similar language. See Newfoundland *Privacy* Act, s 3(1): "It is a tort, actionable without proof of damage, for a person, wilfully and without a claim of right, to violate the privacy of an individual"; and s 2 of Saskatchewan, *The Privacy Act*, s 2: "It is a tort, actionable without proof of damage, for a person wilfully and without claim of right, to violate the privacy of another person." The Manitoba *Privacy Act* is somewhat broader but no more precise: "A person who substantially, unreasonably, and without claim of right, violates the privacy of another person, commits a tort against that other person." Quebec's legislation is also cast in very general terms: see *Charter of Human Rights and Freedoms*, CQLR, c C-12, s 5: "Every person has a right to respect for his private life."

38  This would not preclude a plaintiff who suffered actual pecuniary loss from recovering damages to reflect the actual loss.

39  *Jones, supra* note 1 at para 65.

40  Discussed in chapter 4.

41  *Jones, supra* note 1 at para 69.

42  Thomas DC Bennett, "Privacy, Corrective Justice and Incrementalism: Legal Imagination and the Recognition of a Privacy Tort in Ontario" (2013), 50 McGill LJ 49; Robyn Bell, "Tort of Inclusion upon Seclusion: An Incremental Step in Privacy Law" [2015] Ann Rev of Civ Lit 99.

43  Chris DL Hunt, "Privacy in the Common Law: A Critical Appraisal of the Ontario Court of Appeal's Decision in *Jones v Tsige*" (2012) 37 Queen's LJ 665.

## 10  Standard of Review and Discretion

1  Dissenting in *Canadian Broadcasting Corp v SODRAC 2003 Inc* 2015 SCC 57, [2015] 3 SCR 615 at para 185.

2  David Stratas, "The Canadian Law of Judicial Review: A Plea for Doctrinal Coherence and Consistency," 2016 42 Queen's LJ 27 at 28.

3  *Constitution Act, 1867*, ss 96–100; *Crevier v Quebec (AG)* [1981] 2 SCR 220.

4  See, e.g., Gordon Hewart, *The New Despotism* (Edinburgh: R & R Clark, 1929).

5  [1979] 2 SCR 227.

6  *Ibid* at 236.

7 *Ibid.*
8 *Ibid* at 237.
9 David Mullan, "Developments in Administrative Law: The 1978–1979 Term" (1980) 1 Sup Ct L Rev 1 at 22.
10 Robert Sharpe & Kent Roach, *Brian Dickson: A Judge's Journey* (Toronto: University of Toronto Press, 2003) at 171–5.
11 *Dunsmuir v New Brunswick* 2008 SCC 9, [2008] 1 SCR 190.
12 *Ibid* at para 47.
13 *Ibid.*
14 David Dyzenhaus, "The Politics of Deference: Judicial Review and Democracy," in M Taggart, ed, *The Province of Administrative Law* (Oxford: Hart, 1997) 279 at 286, quoted with approval in *Dunsmuir, supra* note 11 at para 48.
15 Inadequacy of reasons is not, however, a stand-alone ground for review, and the reviewing court may determine that, when considered in the light of the record as a whole, the result reached is reasonable: *Newfoundland and Labrador Nurses' Association v Newfoundland and Labrador* 2011 SCC 62, [2011] SCR 708.
16 This is known as a "privative clause." See for example, *Labour Relations Act, 1995*, SO 1995, c 1, Sched A, s 116:
    No decision, order, direction, declaration or ruling of the Board shall be questioned or reviewed in any court, and no order shall be made or process entered, or proceedings taken in any court … to question, review, prohibit or restrain the Board or any of its proceedings.
17 *Edmonton (City) v Edmonton East (Capilano) Shopping Centres Ltd* 2016 SCC 47, [2016] 2 SCR 293.
18 *Dunsmuir, supra* note 11 at para 54.
19 *Ibid.*
20 *Ibid* at para 55, quoting *Toronto (City) v CUPE Local 79* 2003 SCC 63, [2003] 3 SCR 77 at para 62. "Questions of this nature are rare and tend to be limited to situations that are detrimental to 'consistency in the fundamental legal order of our country'": *Commission scolaire de Laval v Syndicat de l'enseignement de la région de Laval* 2016 SCC 8, [2016] 1 SCR 29 citing *Canada (Canadian Human Rights Commission) v Canada (Attorney General)* 2011 SCC 53, [2011] 3 SCR 471 at para 22 and *McLean v British Columbia (Securities Commission)* 2013 SCC 67, [2013] 3 SCR 895 at paras 26–7.
21 For detailed review, see Roger Kerans & Kim Wiley, *Standards of Review Employed by Appellate Courts*, 2d ed (Edmonton: Juriliber, 2006);

Donald Brown, *Civil Appeals* (Toronto: Thomson Rueters, looseleaf) chs 14, 15, 16.

22  *Housen v Nikolaisen* 2002 SCC 33, [2002] 2 SCR 235. In *Benhaim v St-Germain* 2016 SCC 48, [2016] 2 SCR 352 at para 38, the court quoted with approval the description offered by Stratas JA in *South Yukon Forest Corp v R* 2012 FCA 165 at para 46: "When arguing palpable and overriding error, it is not enough to pull at leaves and branches and leave the tree standing. The entire tree must fall." At para 39, the court quoted with approval the observation of Morissette JA in *JG v Nadeau* 2016 QCCA 167 at para 77: "a palpable and overriding error is in the nature not of a needle in a haystack, but of a beam in the eye" (translation).

23  *Waxman v Waxman* 2004 OJ No 1765, 186 OAC 201 (CA) at para 296.

24  *Ibid* at para 297.

25  Roger J Traynor, "Some Open Questions on the Work of State Appellate Courts" (1957) 24 U Chicago L Rev 211 at 222.

26  (2003) 67 OR (3d) 737, leave to appeal to the Supreme Court of Canada refused, 22 April 2004.

27  *Housen, supra* note 22 at para 9.

28  *Schwartz v Canada* [1996] 1 SCR 254 at para 32.

29  RD Gibbens, "Appellate Review of Findings of Fact" (1991–2) 13 Adv Q 445 at 446, cited in *Housen, supra* note 22 at para 14.

30  *Ibid*.

31  Traynor, *supra* note 25 at 221.

32  *Housen, supra* note 22 at paras 16–18, where these reasons are identified but listed in a different order. See also Daniel Jutras, "The Narrowing Scope of Appellate Review: Has the Pendulum Swung Too Far?" (2006) 32 Man LJ 61.

33  *Housen* at para 17.

34  *Equity Waste Management of Canada v Panorama Investment Group Ltd,* (1997) 35 OR (3d) 321 (CA).

35  *Hryniak v Mauldin* 2014 SCC 7, [2014] 1 SCR 87.

36  *Housen, supra* note 22.

37  *Teal Cedar Products Ltd v British Columbia* 2017 SCC 32, [2017] 1 SCR 688 at para 44.

38  *Canada (Director of Investigation and Research) v Southam Inc* [1997] 1 SCR 748 at para 35.

39  *Sattva Capital Corp v Creston Moly Corp* 2014 SCC 53, [2014] 2 SCR 633 at para 43.

40  *Ibid* at para 23.

41 See, e.g., *MacDonald v Chicago Title Insurance Co of Canada* 2015 ONCA 842, 127 OR (3d) 663.

42 2016 SCC 37, [2016] 2 SCR 23.

43 John McCamus, *The Law of Contracts*, 2d ed (Toronto: Irwin Law, 2012), at 185, quoted in *Ledcor, supra* note 42 at para 25.

44 *Ledcor, supra* note 42 at para 51.

45 *Canada (Director of Investigation and Research) v Southam Inc, supra* note 38 at para 37. See Yves-Marie Morisette, "Appellate Standards of Review Then and Now" (2017) 18 Journal of Appellate Practice and Process 55 at 76 arguing that the distinction between questions of law and fact turns on whether the decision "has a normative reach beyond the dispute" being decided.

46 *Canada (AG) v Bedford* 2013 SCC 72, [2013] 3 SCR 1101.

47 *Reference re ss 193 and 195.1(1)(c) of the Criminal Code (Man)* [1990] 1 SCR 1123.

48 *RJR-MacDonald Inc v Canada (AG)* [1995] 3 SCR 199.

49 *Bedford, supra* note 46 at para 51.

50 Jutras, *supra* note 32 at 71.

51 *Northwest Territories (Attorney General) v Association des parents ayants droit de Yellowknife* 2013 NWTCA 2 at para 22, Slatter JA.

52 In this part I have drawn freely on Sharpe, "Application and Impact of Judicial Discretion in Commercial Litigation," in ML Pilkington, JM Spence, & H Dumont, eds, *The Administration of Justice in Commercial Disputes* (Toronto: Edition Themis, 1997). I have also benefited greatly from Stephen M Waddams, "Judicial Discretion" [2001] OJLS 59.

53 Aharon Barak, *Judicial Discretion* (New Haven, CT: Yale University Press, 1987) at 7.

54 Georgina Jackson & Janis Sara, "Selecting the Judicial Tool to Get the Job Done: An Examination of Statutory Interpretation, Discretionary Power and Inherent Jurisdiction in Insolvency Matters" [2007] Ann Rev Insol L at 56.

55 Waddams, *supra* note 52 at 59.

56 See Barak, *supra* note 53 and Waddams *supra* note 52.

57 *R v Wilkes* (1770) 4 Burr 2527 at 2539.

58 "Principled Remedial Discretion" (2004) SCLR (2d) 101.

59 *Hindson v Kersey* (1765) 8 How St Tr 57.

60 [1959] SCR 121.

61 *Ibid* at 140.

62 HM Hart & AM Sacks, *The Legal Process: Basic Problems in the Making and Application of Law* (Cambridge: Tentative Edition, 1958) at 162. Compare

Denis Galligan, *Discretionary Powers: A Legal Study in Official Discretion* (Oxford: Clarendon, 1990) at 8:

According to its etymological origins, the idea of discretion is judgment, in particular good judgment. In its modern legal usage, however, discretion has come to connote, perhaps unfortunately, rather autonomy in judgment and decision.

63 Barak, *supra* note 53 at 12.
64 *Ibid* at 7.
65 Robert Sharpe, *Injunctions and Specific Performance*, 5th ed (Toronto: Canada Law Book, 2017).
66 Roach, *supra* note 58; Kent Roach, *Constitutional Remedies in Canada* (Toronto: Canada Law Book, looseleaf).
67 Roach, *supra* note 58 at 148.
68 Galligan, *supra* note 62 at 7. With reference to equitable remedies, see *Doherty v Allen* (1878) App Cas 709 at 728: "[T]he discretion is not one to be exercised according to the fancy of whoever is to exercise the jurisdiction in Equity, but is a discretion to be exercised according to the rules which have been established by a long series of decisions, and which are now settled to be the proper guide to judges in the Court of Equity."
69 Waddams, *supra* note 52 at 61.
70 *Dunsmuir, supra* note 11.
71 *Criminal Code*, RSC 1985, c C-46, s 718.
72 *R v Shropshire* [1995] 4 SCR 227; *R v Lacasse* 2015 SCC 64, [2015] 3 SCR 1089.
73 Appeal rights are usually restricted for "interlocutory orders." The distinction between final orders, which may be appealed, and interlocutory orders, which may not, has been notoriously difficult to draw.
74 Kerans & Wiley, *supra* note 21 at 261.
75 Waddams, *supra* note 52 at 64.
76 Different umpires may have a tendency to define the strike zone differently. Although there is no appeal, Major League Baseball monitors and disciplines umpires for errant strike zones: see Richard A Posner, *How Judges Think* (Cambridge, MA: Harvard University Press, 2010) at 79.

## 11 Role of the Judge in a Constitutional Democracy

1 This chapter draws freely on Robert Sharpe & Kent Roach, *The Charter of Rights and Freedoms*, 6th ed (Toronto: Irwin Law, 2017).
2 *R v Morgentaler* [1988] 1 SCR 30.

3 *Loyola High School v Quebec (AG)* 2015 SCC 12, [2015] 1 SCR 613.

4 *Carter v Canada (Attorney General)* 2015 SCC 5, [2015] 1 SCR 331.

5 *Reference Re Same-Sex Marriage* 2004 SCC 79, [2004] 3 SCR 698.

6 *R v Hart* 2014 SCC 52, [2014] 2 SCR 544.

7 *Chaoulli v Quebec (AG)* 2005 SCC 35, [2005] 1 SCR 791.

8 *R v Khawaja* 2012 SCC 69, [2012] 3 SCR 555.

9 Supreme Court of Canada, "Statistics 2007 to 2017," https://www.scc-csc.ca/case-dossier/stat/cat3-eng.aspx#cat3b.

10 *PS v Ontario* 2014 ONCA 900, 123 OR (3d) 651; *R v Meads* 2018 ONCA 146. In *Daly v Ontario (AG)* (1997) 38 OR (3d) 37, I held that legislation restricting the rights of Catholic school boards to hire Catholic teachers violated the denomination education rights guaranteed by s 93(1) of the *Constitution Act, 1867*.

11 See the authorities cited *infra* notes 14–15, 18.

12 See, e.g., *Canada (AG) v Bedford* 2013 SCC 72, [2013] 3 SCR 1101.

13 See, e.g., *Vriend v Alberta* [1998] 1 SCR 493.

14 See, e.g., Michael Mandel, *The Charter of Rights and the Legalization of Politics in Canada*, 2d ed (Toronto: Thompson Educational Publishers, 1994); Allan Hutchinson, *Waiting for CORAF: A Critique of Law and Rights* (Toronto: University of Toronto Press, 1995).

15 Rainer Knopff & FL Morton, *Charter Politics* (Scarborough, ON: Nelson Canada, 1992); FL Morton & Rainer Knopff, *The Charter Revolution and the Court Party* (Toronto: Broadview, 2000).

16 Morton & Knopff, *supra* note 15. Although I was an academic who argued *Charter* cases on behalf of special interest groups (see chapter 1), I escaped being labelled as a member of the "court party."

17 Kent Roach, *The Supreme Court on Trial: Judicial Activism or Democratic Dialogue*, 2d ed (Toronto: Irwin Law, 2016) ch 5.

18 Jeremy Waldron, "The Core of the Case against Judicial Review" (2006) 115 Yale LJ 1346; Emmett Macfarlane, *Governing from the Bench: The Supreme Court of Canada and the Judicial Role* (Vancouver: UBC Press, 2012).

19 *McCulloch v Maryland* 17 US 4 Wheat 316 (1819).

20 From the argument of Edward Blake in *St Catherine's Milling and Lumber Co v The Queen* (1888) 14 App Cas 46 at 50, adopted in *Edwards v Canada (AG)* [1930] AC 124 at 137.

21 Benjamin Cardozo, *The Nature of the Judicial Process* (New Haven, CT: Yale University Press, 1921) at 17.

22 *Ibid* at 83.

23 I develop this in greater detail below in the discussion of the Persons Case and the living tree metaphor for constitutional interpretation.

24 The Supreme Court referred to this point in one of its most important early *Charter* decisions: *Reference re s 94(2) of the Motor Vehicle Act (BC)* [1985] 2 SCR 486 at 497.

25 Brian Dickson, "Remarks at the Luncheon with the Judges of the British Columbia Court of Appeal," 8 May 1986, quoted in Robert Sharpe & Kent Roach, *Brian Dickson: A Judge's Journey* (Toronto: University of Toronto Press, 2003) at 380.

26 Bertha Wilson, "We Didn't Volunteer" (April 1999) Policy Options 8.

27 SC 1960, c 44.

28 *Ibid*, s 2.

29 *R v Drybones* [1970] SCR 282.

30 [1974] SCR 1349.

31 *Bliss v Attorney General of Canada* [1979] 1 SCR 183.

32 *Vriend, supra* note 13 at para 56.

33 In particular, the *International Convention on Civil and Political Rights*, the *International Covenant on Economic, Social and Cultural Rights*, and the *Convention on the Elimination of Racial Discrimination*.

34 Britain, the home of parliamentary supremacy, has not entirely succumbed. The *Human Rights Act*, 1998, does not allow the courts to strike down laws enacted by Parliament. However, the *Human Rights Act* does provide that the courts are to declare that laws that violate protected rights and freedoms are incompatible with the *Human Rights Act*.

35 Waldron, *supra* note 18. Lord Sumption had made a similar argument regarding the role of the European Court of Human Rights: see NW Barber, Richard Ekins, & Paul Yowell, eds, *Lord Sumption and the Limits of Law* (Oxford: Hart Publishing, 2016).

36 Peter Russell, "The Political Purposes of the *Canadian Charter of Rights and Freedoms*" (1983) 61 Can Bar Rev 30 at 51–2.

37 See especially *Reference re Secession of Quebec* [1998] 2 SCR 217.

38 John Hart Ely is a strong proponent of this view in *Democracy and Distrust: A Theory of Judicial Review* (Cambridge, MA: Harvard University Press, 1980). Patrick Monahan echoes this view, with his own refinements, in *Politics and the Constitution: The Charter, Federalism and the Supreme Court of Canada* (Toronto: Carswell, 1987). See also Aharon Barak, *The Judge in a Democracy* (Princeton: Princeton University Press, 2006) especially at 24–6, 33–5.

39 *Sauvé v Canada (Chief Electoral Officer)* 2002 SCC 68, [2002] 3 SCR 519 at paras 34 and 13.

40 *R v Big M Drug Mart Ltd* [1985] 1 SCR 295 at 346.

41　*Mouvement laïque québécois v Saguenay (City)* 2015 SCC 16, [2015] 2 SCR 3 at para 75.

42　*Ghaidan v Godin-Mendoza* [2004] UKHL 30 at para 132.

43　Jacob Weinrib, "The Modern Constitutional State: A Defence" (2014) 40 Queen's LJ 165.

44　*Ibid* at 185.

45　*Andrews v Law Society of British Columbia* [1989] 1 SCR 143; *Law v Canada* [1999] 1 SCR 497.

46　*Vriend, supra* note 13 at para 142.

47　Ely, *supra* note 38. For a similar defence of the role of the *Charter* see Roland Penner, "The Canadian Experience with the *Charter of Rights*: Are There Lessons for the United Kingdom?" [1996] Pub L 104 at 113.

48　Scalia & Whelan, eds, *Scalia Speaks: Reflections on Law, Faith, and Life Well Lived* (New York: Crown Forum, 2017) at 188.

49　*Morgentaler, supra* note 2.

50　Robert Bork, *Correcting Virtue: The Worldwide Rule of Judges* (Toronto: Vintage, 2002) at 87.

51　See Antonin Scalia, *A Matter of Interpretation* (Princeton: Princeton University Press, 1998). Compare David Strauss, *The Living Constitution* (Oxford: Oxford University Press, 2010).

52　See, however, Grant Huscroft & Bradley W Miller, eds, *The Challenge of Originalism: Theories of Constitutional Interpretation* (New York: Cambridge University Press, 2011).

53　*Re Motor Vehicle Act, supra* note 24.

54　*Ibid* at para 51.

55　*Ibid* at para 53.

56　*Edwards, supra* note 20.

57　*British North America Act, 1867*, s 24.

58　*Edwards, supra* note 20 at 128.

59　*Ibid* at 136.

60　*Ibid* at 135.

61　*Ibid* at 136.

62　*Hunter et al v Southam Inc* [1984] 2 SCR 145 at 155.

63　*Ibid*.

64　*Big M Drug Mart, supra* note 40 at 344.

65　*Secession Reference, supra* note 37 at para 53; *Quebec (AG) v Canada (AG)* 2015 SCC 14, [2015] 1 SCR 693 at para 18.

66　*Reference re Senate Reform* 2014 SCC 32, [2014] 1 SCR 704.

67　Benjamin Oliphant, "Taking Purposes Seriously: The Purposive Scope and Textual Bounds of Interpretation under the Canadian Charter of Rights and Freedoms" (2015) 65 UTLJ 239 at 246.

68 *Ibid* at 261.

69 *Irwin Toy v Quebec (AG)* [1989] 1 SCR 927.

70 *Edwards, supra* note 20.

71 *Gosselin v Quebec (AG)* 2002 SCC 84, [2002] 4 SCR 429.

72 Ronald Dworkin is a strong proponent of this view. See, for example, *Taking Rights Seriously* (London: Duckworth, 1977).

73 Lorraine Weinrib, "Limitations on Rights in a Constitutional Democracy" (1996) 6 Caribbean L Rev 428 at 439.

74 Cass Sunstein, *Radicals in Robes* (New York: Basic Books, 2005).

75 Subject to section 28, which states that, notwithstanding anything in the *Charter*, "the rights and freedoms referred to in it are guaranteed equally to male and female persons." Section 33 cannot override this guarantee.

76 For an example, see the discussion of the Quebec signs law debate, *infra.*

77 Peter W Hogg & Allison A Bushell, "The *Charter* Dialogue between Courts and Legislatures (Or Perhaps the *Charter of Rights* Isn't Such a Bad Thing After All)" (1997) 35 Osgoode Hall LJ 75; Roach, *supra* note 17. Dialogue is also discussed by Iacobucci J in *Vriend, supra* note 13 at paras 138–9 and by Bastarache J in *M v H* [1999] 2 SCR 3 at 182.

78 Legislative replies are examined in Roach, *supra* note 17, chs 10, 14, and 17; Janet Hiebert, *Charter Conflicts? What Is Parliament's Role?* (Montreal and Kingston: McGill-Queen's University Press, 2002). Hogg & Bushnell, *supra* note 77, argue that there have been legislative replies in about two-thirds of cases; and Christopher Manfredi & James Kelly, "Six Degrees of Dialogue: A Response to Hogg and Bushnell" (1999) 37 Osgoode Hall LJ 513, argue that the number of true replies is closer to a third. See also Peter W Hogg & Allison A Thornton, "Reply to 'Six Degrees of Dialogue'" (1999) 37 Osgoode Hall LJ 529.

79 *RJR-MacDonald Inc v Canada (Attorney General)* [1995] 3 SCR 199.

80 *Canada (Attorney General) v JTI Macdonald Corp* [2007] 2 SCR 610.

81 *Morgentaler, supra* note 2.

82 *Carter, supra* note 4.

83 *Bedford, supra* note 12.

84 Hogg & Bushnell, *supra* note 77.

85 Roach, *supra* note 17 at 308.

86 *R v O'Connor* [1995] 4 SCR 411.

87 *R v Mills* [1999] 3 SCR 668 at para 58.

88 Rosalind Dixon, "The Supreme Court of Canada, Charter Dialogue and Deference" (2009) 47 Osgoode Hall LJ 235.

89 *Sauvé v Canada, supra* note 39.

90  *Ibid* at para 17.
91  *Canada (Attorney General) v JTI Macdonald Corp, supra* note 79 at para 11.
92  *Alliance des professeurs de Montréal v Quebec* (1985) 21 DLR (4th) 354 (Que CA).
93  *Ford v Quebec* [1988] 2 SCR 712.
94  Anglophone merchants who were adversely affected by the override also brought successful international claims about its use, adding an international dimension to the use of the override: *John Ballantyne and Elizabeth Davidson, and Gordon McIntyre v Canada* Communication No 385/1989: Canada 05/05/93. CCPR/C/47/D/385/1989.
95  Tsvi Kahana, "The Notwithstanding Mechanism and Public Discussion: Lessons from the Ignored Practice of Section 33 of the *Charter*" (2001) 44 Can Public Admin 255, cataloguing sixteen uses between 1982 and 2001.
96  *Ford, supra* note 93.
97  Kahana, *supra* note 95.
98  Gregoire Webber, "The Unfulfilled Potential of the Court and Legislative Dialogue" (2009) 43 Can J Pol Sci 443 at 452.
99  Aileen Kavanagh, "The Lure and Limits of Dialogue" (2016) 66 UTLJ 83 at 120.

## 12  A Judicial State of Mind

1  *Therrien (Re)* 2001 SCC 35, [2001] 2 SCR 3 at para 111.
2  Ss 96–9 and the preamble with its reference to a "Constitution Similar in Principle to That of the United Kingdom."
3  Section 11(d) guarantees individuals charged with a criminal offence "a fair and public hearing by an independent and impartial tribunal."
4  The *European Convention of Human Rights, Art 6*: "In the determination of his civil rights and obligations or of any criminal charge against him, everyone is entitled to a fair and public hearing within a reasonable time by an independent and impartial tribunal established by law." The *Universal Declaration of Human Rights, Art 10* provides: "Everyone is entitled in full equality to a fair and public hearing by an independent and impartial tribunal, in the determination of his rights and obligations and of any criminal charge against him." *The United Nations Basic Principles on the Independence of the Judiciary* (1985), *Art 2* provides: "The judiciary shall decide matters before them impartially, on the basis of facts and in accordance with the law, without any restrictions, improper influences, inducements, pressures, threats or interferences, direct or indirect, from any quarter or for any reason."

5 See *Valente v R* [1985] 2 SCR 673.

6 Martin L Friedland, *A Place Apart: Judicial Independence and Accountability in Canada* (Ottawa: Canadian Judicial Council, 1995).

7 *R v Lippé* [1991] 2 SCR 114 at 139.

8 *Beauregard v Canada* [1986] 2 SCR 56 at 70.

9 Aharon Barak, *The Judge in a Democracy* (Princeton: Princeton University Press, 2006) at 77.

10 David M Walker, *Oxford Companion to Law* (Oxford: Oxford University Press, 1980) at 601.

11 *Valente, supra* note 5 at 685, LeDain J.

12 *R v S (RD)* [1997] 3 SCR 484 at 528.

13 *R v Parks* (1993) 15 OR (3d) 324 at 336 (leave to appeal to the SCC dismissed 24 April 1994). In *Wewaykum Indian Band v Canada* 2003 SCC 45, [2003] 2 SCR 259, the Supreme Court of Canada referred to the following definition of bias:

   a leaning, inclination, bent or predisposition towards one side or another or a particular result. In its application to legal proceedings, it represents a predisposition to decide an issue or cause in a certain way which does not leave the judicial mind perfectly open to conviction. Bias is a condition or state of mind which sways judgment and renders a judicial officer unable to exercise his or her functions impartially in a particular case.

14 *R v Parks, supra* note 13; *R v Williams* [1998] 1 SCR 1128.

15 *Dimes v Proprietors of Grand Junction Canal* (1852) 3 HL Cas 759 at 793–4.

16 *R v Bow Street Metropolitan Stipendiary Magistrate, Ex parte Pinochet Ugarte (No 2)* [2000] 1 AC 119.

17 *R v Bow Street Metropolitan Stipendiary Magistrate, Ex parte Pinochet Ugarte (No 3)* [2000] 1 AC 147.

18 *R v Sussex Justices; Ex parte McCarthy* [1924] 1 KB 256 at 259.

19 *Committee for Justice and Liberty v National Energy Board* [1978] 1 SCR 369 at 394–5; *R v S (RD), supra* note 12 at para 31.

20 *Ibid.*

21 *Helow v Secretary of State for the Home Department* [2008] UKHL 62 at paras 2 and 3.

22 *Wewaykum, supra* note 13.

23 *Dimes, supra* note 15 at 793.

24 *Wewaykum, supra* note 13 at para 72.

25 See Grant Hammond, *Judicial Recusal: Principles, Process and Problems* (Oxford: Hart Publishing, 2009); Donald Brown, *Civil Appeals* (Toronto: Thomson Rueters, looseleaf) ch 11; Jula Hughes & Philip Bryden,

"Beyond the Reasonable Apprehension of Bias Test Providing Judges Better Tools for Addressing Judicial Disqualification" (2013) 36 Dal LJ 171; Hughes & Bryden, "From Principles to Rules: The Case for Statutory Rules Governing Aspects of Judicial Qualification" (2016) 53 OHLJ 853; Geoffrey Lester, "Disqualifying Judges for Bias and Reasonable Apprehension of Bias: Some Problems of Practice and Procedure" (2001) 24 Advocates Q 326.

26 William Blackstone, *Commentaries on the Laws of England*, vol 3 (Oxford: Clarendon, 1768) at 361.

27 *Locabail (UK) Ltd v Bayfield Properties Ltd* [2000] QB 451 at para 3.

28 The need to limit judge-shopping has been judicially recognized: see *Re JRL; Ex parte CJL* (1986) 161 CLR 342 at 352: "Although it is important that justice must be seen to be done, it is equally important that judicial officers discharge their duty to sit and do not, by acceding too readily to suggestions of appearance of bias, encourage parties to believe that by seeking the disqualification of a judge, they will have their case tried by someone thought to be more likely to decide the case in their favour."

29 Compare James Goudkamp, "The Rule against Bias and the Doctrine of Waiver" (2007) 26 CJQ 310, arguing against waiver on the ground that the behaviour of a private party should not be allowed to sacrifice the public interest in impartial justice.

30 Hammond, *supra* note 25 at 109–14; *Arsenault-Cameron v Prince Edward Island* [1999] 3 SCR 851. However, there are cases where the challenge has been decided by the full panel: see Lester, *supra* note 25 at 339–40. In *SOS-Save Our St Clair Inc v City of Toronto et al* (2005) 78 OR (3d) 331 (Div Ct), the challenge was presented to the full panel. The judge accused of bias dismissed the challenge, but the other two members of the panel disagreed. They stated that they could not overrule their colleague but stepped down so that the case could be heard by a differently constituted panel.

31 Hammond, *supra* note 25 at 82–4.

32 *Ibid* at 113.

33 *Locabail, supra* note 27; *Jones v DAS* 2003 EWCA 1071.

34 Philip Bryden & Jula Hughes, "The Tip of the Iceberg: A Survey of the Philosophy and Practice of Canadian Provincial and Territorial Judges Concerning Judicial Disqualification" (2011) Alta L Rev 569.

35 *Re JRL, supra* note 28 at 352. See also *Beard Winter LLP v Shekhdar* 2016 ONCA 493 at para 10, per Doherty JA:

[A] judge is best advised to remove himself if there is any air of reality to a bias claim. That said, judges do the administration of justice a disservice by simply yielding to entirely unreasonable and unsubstantiated recusal demands. Litigants are not entitled to pick their judge. They are not entitled to effectively eliminate judges randomly assigned to their case by raising specious partiality claims against those judges. To step aside in the face of a specious bias claim is to give credence to a most objectionable tactic.

36 *President of the Republic of South Africa v South African Rugby Football Union* 1999 (4) SA 147.

37 *Ibid* at para 48.

38 *Ibid.*

39 *Locabail, supra* note 27 at para 25, applied in *Yukon Francophone School Board, Education Area #23 v Yukon (AG)* 2015 SCC 25, [2015] 2 SCR 282 at para 59.

40 Kate Malleson, "Safeguarding Judicial Impartiality" (2002) 22 J Legal Stud 53.

41 John Leubsdorf, "Theories of Judging and Judge Disqualification" (1987) 62 NYULR 237 at 277–8.

42 *R v S(RD), supra* note 12 at para 38.

43 *Locabail, supra* note 27 at 471.

44 E Gerhart, *Quote It! Memorable Legal Quotations* (Buffalo: William S Hein, 1987) at 507, referring to 1 Lab LJ 122, November 1949 at 122.

45 Brian Dickson, "The Role and Function of Judges" (1980) 14 Law Soc'y Gaz 138 at 143, quoted by Maryka Omatsu, "The Fiction of Judicial Impartiality" (1997) 9 Can J Women & L 1 at 8.

46 Lord Justice Scrutton, "The Work of Commercial Courts" (1921) 1 Camb LJ 6 at 8; quoted by Bertha Wilson, "Will Women Judges Really Make a Difference?" (1990) 28 OHLJ 507 at 509.

47 Benjamin Cardozo, *The Nature of the Judicial Process* (New Haven, CT: Yale University Press, 1921) at 12–13.

48 *Yukon Francophone Schoolboard, supra* note 39 at para 33.

49 *South African Commercial Catering and Allied Workers Union v Irvin & Johnson Ltd (Seafoods Division Fish Processing)* 2000 (3) SA 705 at para 13, quoted *Yukon Francophone Schoolboard, supra* note 39 at para 35.

50 Canadian Judicial Council, *Commentaries on Judicial Conduct* (Cowansville: Les Editions Yvon Blais, 1991) at 12–13. See also the judgment of L'Heureux-Dube and McLachlin JJ in *R v S (RD), supra* note 12 at 501:

[W]hile judges can never be neutral, in the sense of purely objective, they can and must strive for impartiality ... [it is recognized] as inevitable and appropriate that the differing experiences of judges assist them in their decision-making process and will be reflected in their judgments, so long as those experiences are relevant to the cases, are not based on inappropriate stereotypes, and do not prevent a fair and just determination of the cases based on the facts in evidence.

Cory J expressed similar views at 533:

Throughout their careers, Canadian judges strive to overcome the personal biases that are common to all humanity in order to provide and clearly appear to provide a fair trial for all who come before them. Their rate of success in this difficult endeavour is high.

51 *Supra* note 12.
52 Quoted at para 6, *ibid.*
53 L'Heureux-Dubé and McLachlin JJ writing with La Forest and Gonthier JJ concurring.
54 *Ibid* at para 48.
55 *Ibid* at para 56.
56 Major J (Lamer CJC and Sopinka J concurring).
57 *Ibid* at para 13.
58 *Ibid* at para 152, Cory J (Iacobucci J concurring).
59 *Yukon Francophone School Board, supra* note 39.
60 *Charter,* s 23.
61 *Yukon Francophone School Board, supra* note 39 at para 61.
62 Compassion is sometimes imbedded in the law itself. For example, as stated in *R v Aravena* 2015 ONCA 250 at para 64, the criminal defence of duress recognizes that "[t]he criminal law cannot demand acts of heroism, but must instead set standards of conduct 'which ordinary men and women are expected to observe if they are to avoid criminal responsibility,'" citing *R v Howe* [1987] AC 417 at 430.
63 John Morden, "The 'Good' Judge" (2005) 23 Advocates' Soc J 13 at 3.
64 Beverley McLachlin, "The Judicial Vision: From Partiality to Impartiality" (Nova Scotia Judicial Education Seminar, 3–8 June 1998) at 2.
65 Claire L'Heureux Dubé, "Making a Difference: The Pursuit of a Compassionate Justice" (1997) 31 UBC L Rev 1 at 9.
66 Brian Dickson, "The Law and Compassion," Convocation Address, University of Toronto, 20 June 1986.
67 Benjamin Zipursky, "*Deshaney* and the Jurisprudence of Compassion" (1990) 65 NYUL Rev 1101, see especially 1129 and 1146.

68  Jennifer Nedelsky, "Embodied Diversity and Changes to the Law"
    (1997) 42 McGill LJ 91. See also Martha Minow, "Beyond Universality"
    (1989) U Chi Legal F 115.

69  Nedelsky, *supra* note 68 at 94.

70  *Ibid* at 107.

71  See e.g. the judgment of Lady Hale in *Rhodes v OPO* [2015] UKSC 32,
    demonstrating a full appreciation and understanding of the situation
    of a child who would likely suffer distress from reading a book written
    by his father, but refusing an injunction to restrain publication on the
    ground that the claim of the mother made on behalf of the child could
    not be made out in law.

72  Morden, *supra* note 63 at 22.

73  *Supra* note 50 at 46.

74  McLachlin, *supra* note 64 at 17–18.

75  Richard F Devlin, "Judging and Diversity: Justice or Just Us?" (1996) 20
    Prov Judges J (no 3) 4.

76  *Ibid* at 16–17.

77  Rupert Ross, *Dancing with a Ghost: Exploring Aboriginal Reality* (Toronto:
    Penguin Canada, 2006) at 3.

78  *Ibid* at 55.

79  See *R v RAH* (1995) 61 BCAC 126. The trial judge disbelieved an Indig-
    enous accused because he gave his evidence in simple "yes" or "no" an-
    swers without elaboration. The Court of Appeal reversed on the ground
    that it was dangerous to draw adverse inferences on this basis where
    the accused and complainant were both young Indigenous people and
    where credibility was the central issue.

80  *R v Lavallee* [1990] 1 SCR 852.

81  *R v Ewanchuk* [1999] 1 SCR 330.

82  *Ibid* at para 95.

83  RSC 1985, c C-46, s 718.2(e): "[A]ll available sanctions, other than
    imprisonment, that are reasonable in the circumstances and consistent
    with the harm done to victims or to the community should be consid-
    ered for all offenders, with particular attention to the circumstances of
    Aboriginal offenders."

84  *R v Gladue* [1999] 1 SCR 688 at para 64; *R v Ipeelee* 2012 SCC 13, [2012] 1
    SCR 433.

85  Art XXIX, Oscar Handlin & Mary Handlin, eds, *The Popular Sources of
    Political Authority: Documents on the Massachusetts Constitution of 1780*
    (Cambridge, MA: Belknap of Harvard University Press, 1966).

## Conclusion

1 For a civilian perspective, see Guy Thuillier, *L'Art de Juger* (Paris: Economica, 2001).
2 OW Holmes, *The Common Law* (Boston: Little Brown, 1891) at 1.

# Index

Abella, Justice Rosalie, 121, 203, 260
abortion. See *Charter of Rights and
  Freedoms*
academic writing, 13, 83–5, 109,
  170, 179–87, 193, 196
administrative law, 27, 31, 36, 37,
  66, 78, 100, 132, 203–8, 216, 223
adversarial system, 81, 84, 93, 133,
  180, 236
alternative dispute resolution, 33–6
American decisions, authority of,
  176–8
American Law Institute
  Restatement of the Law, 177,
  197, 200
Amnesty International, 253
anchoring, 142–3
Anglin, Chief Justice Frank, 4, 62,
  64, 69, 173, 175
*Anns v Merton London Borough
  Council* (1978), 117–18, 176
apex courts, 52, 97, 130, 136, 154,
  157, 159–67, 169, 256
appeal as of right, 37, 163, 226
appeal book, 38
applications, 30–1
Aristotle, 54, 127

artificial reason of the law, 128
assisted suicide. See *Charter of
  Rights and Freedoms*
assumed jurisdiction, 82–5,
  184
Atkin, Lord, 58, 110–13, 151

Bacon, Francis, 13, 118, 255
Barak, Aharon, 14, 60, 92, 128, 216,
  220, 251
Bastarache, Justice Michel, 182
*Bedford*. See *Canada (Attorney
  General) v Bedford*
bench memo, 41
Bentham, Jeremy, 66
best interests of the child, 100, 104
*Bhasin v Hrynew* (2014), 108–10
bias, 20, 90, 142–3, 185–6, 190,
  251–64, 266–9
Bingham, Lord Tom, 93
Binnie, Ian, 8, 21, 153, 164
bipolar dispute, 87, 89, 93
Black, Vaughan, 183
black-letter rules, 14, 98, 99, 106–7,
  143, 191, 193, 266
Blackstone, William, 79, 173, 201,
  254

Bork, Robert, 238–9
Brandeis, Justice Louis, 65–6, 129, 196
Brandeis brief, 65–6
Brennan, Justice William, 52
*British North America Act, 1867*, 61, 174. See also *Constitution Act, 1867*
Brown, Justice Russell, 119–20
Brownlie, Ian, 9
Bryant, Alan, 181
By the Court opinions, 49

Calabresi, Guido, 15
Camden, Lord, 217–18
Cameron, Justice Edwin, 260
*Canada (Attorney General) v Bedford* (2013), 162, 165–8, 214–16
Canadian Civil Liberties Association, 11
Canadian Judicial Council, 22, 261, 266
Cardozo, Justice Benjamin, 53, 71, 74, 78–9, 93, 100, 104, 180, 232, 260
*Carter v Canada (Attorney General)* (2015), 147, 167–8
Cartwright, Chief Justice, 49
case management, 31–4, 133
Cathedral at Rouen, 13, 15, 229, 248
Chancery. *See* equity
*Charter of Rights and Freedoms*:
abortion, 228, 238–9, 245, 257;
academic writing, 185–6; assisted suicide, 147, 165–6, 186, 228, 245;
*Charter* values, 91–2, 195, 201, 245; democratic process model, 229, 236–8, 242, 248; democratic rights, 244; dialogue theory, 230, 244–8; equality, 71, 102, 233–4, 236–8, 240, 242, 244; expression,
freedom of, 71, 91–2, 97, 102, 123, 180, 200, 238, 240, 243, 247; fair trial, right to, 121–2; gays and lesbians, rights of, 102, 228, 231, 234, 237, 247; international law, 178–9; interpretation, 105, 109, 228–48; judicial independence, 250; language rights, 244, 263; life, liberty, and security of the person, right to, 119, 122–3, 214–15, 236–41, 244; majoritarianism, 229–36, 248; national security, 228; notwithstanding clause, 165, 243–4, 246–7; originalism, 229–30, 238–42, 248; philosophers, 180; police powers, 228–9; precedent, 160–8; principles of fundamental justice, 71, 122, 214, 239; property rights, 241; prostitution, 165–6, 214–15; reasonable limits, 104, 122–3, 243; religion, freedom of, 102, 121–2, 228, 236, 238, 243; remedies, 221; right to be tried within a reasonable time, 119–21; rights as trumps, 230, 242–4, 248; social welfare rights, 241; strike, right to, 166; Superior Court jurisdiction, 27; unreasonable search and seizure, 195; vote, right to, 236, 238, 244, 246
Chouinard, Justice Julien, 153
civil law, 49, 109, 118–19
class actions, 31, 223
*Club Resorts Ltd v Van Breda* (2012), 184
cognitive psychology, 141–3
Coke, Sir Edward, 127–8
collegial decision-making, 31, 49–51, 132, 210, 255

commercial law, 19, 27, 31, 35, 36, 37, 58–9, 90, 105, 109, 122, 223

commercial list, 35, 36

common law tradition: judicial law-making, 88, 93–4, 97, 125, 180, 199–200, 231, 272; other jurisdictions, 176; precedent, 78, 150; reasoning, 35, 55–6, 59, 118, 155, 188, 192; remedies, 221

compassion, 12, 259, 264–9, 273

concurring opinions, 48–52, 149

confirmation bias, 142

consideration, 128–9

*Constitution Act, 1867*, 18, 61, 240, 250. See also *British North America Act, 1867*

constitutional interpretation, 63, 64, 71, 102, 166, 174, 228–48. See also *Charter of Rights and Freedoms*

constructive trust, 92, 107

contextual nature of law, 53, 59–65, 71, 81–2, 84, 100, 103, 112, 119–21, 175, 182, 184–6, 259, 261–3, 267–8, 271

contract, freedom of, 102, 110

*Cooper v Hobart* (2001), 112–15

correctness, 203–16, 223, 226

Cory, Justice Peter, 29, 91

Côté, Justice Suzanne, 21

Côté, Pierre-André, 181

*Cottrelle v Gerrard* (2003), 209

credibility of witnesses, 70, 223–5, 252, 257, 262, 267

criminal trials, 32, 36, 252

critical legal studies, 66, 68, 134, 139

critical race theory, 66, 185

Cromwell, Justice Thomas, 109–10, 120

Cunningham, Associate Chief Justice Douglas, 190

*CUPE v New Brunswick Liquor Corporation* (1979), 206–7

*Cusson v Quan* (2007), 92

David Asper Centre for Constitutional Rights, 11

*David Polowin Real Estate Ltd v Dominion of Canada General Insurance Co* (2005), 158–9

declaratory theory, 79–80, 173, 201

deductive method, 55, 116, 189

defamation, 91–2, 194

deference, 133, 148, 166–8, 203–27; to Parliament, 204, 235–6, 246

Denning, Lord, 136, 151, 168

Devlin, Patrick, 4

Devlin, Richard, 186, 267

dialogue theory. See *Charter of Rights and Freedoms*

Dickson, Chief Justice Brian, 3, 11–12, 27, 28, 37, 68, 108, 150, 161–2, 175, 179, 183, 185, 196, 206, 233, 237, 251, 260, 265

disciplined decision-making, 45–7, 71, 73, 92, 100, 112, 115–16, 118, 122–4, 125–45, 168, 217–19, 241, 248, 250, 271–3

discretion, 32, 55, 58, 72, 76, 99–100, 105, 117, 123, 132–3, 216–27, 231

discrimination, 63–4, 81, 217, 228, 233–4, 236–7, 252, 259, 266

disqualification. See recusal

dissents, 38, 48–52, 72, 120, 121, 130, 132, 152, 161, 162, 245, 263

distinguishing, 6, 147–52, 161, 169, 171, 191–2

Divisional Court, 31, 37

Doherty, Justice David, 185–6

*Donoghue v Stevenson* (1932), 56–8, 110–13, 118, 151, 176

Driedger, Elmer, 181
dualist tradition, 178
*Dunsmuir v New Brunswick* (2008), 207
Duplessis, Maurice, 218
duty judge, 39
duty of care, 56–8, 80, 110–15, 151
duty to sit, 255–6
Duxbury, Neil, 169
Dworkin, Ronald, 9, 73, 74, 101, 139

efficiency, 66, 103, 114, 131, 147, 210–12, 215, 226–7, 254–5
Eisenberg, Mel, 94
empirical studies, 144
*en banc* sittings, 44, 130, 154, 256
endorsements, 45
English decisions, authority of, 172–6
equality. See *Charter of Rights and Freedoms*; impartiality; women, rights of
equitable remedies, 221
equity, 101, 116–17
error correction, 45, 50–1, 70, 95–6, 163
*European Convention for the Protection of Human Rights and Fundamental Freedoms*, 178
exceptions, 55–8, 106–7, 156, 160, 169
Executive Legal Officer, Supreme Court of Canada, 11–12, 37
extricable error of law, 213
*ex turpi causa*, 100–1

factum, 10, 31, 38, 41, 42, 47
fair trial, right to, 91, 119, 121, 256
family law, 33–3, 36, 65, 78, 89, 100, 122, 162, 183, 185, 224, 225, 252

Feldthusen, Bruce, 181
feminist legal theory, 66
finality, 219, 225–7
five-judge panel, 39, 44, 51, 83, 130, 157, 184
foreign decisions, authority of, 178–9
foreign judgments, recognition and enforcement, 90–1
formalism, 60, 62, 64, 65–8, 127–9, 170, 173, 175, 187
framers' intent. See under *Charter of Rights and Freedoms*: originalism
France, 6–7
Frank, Judge Jerome, 139, 141
freedom of expression. See *Charter of Rights and Freedoms*
freedom of religion. See *Charter of Rights and Freedoms*
Friedland, Martin, 10
Fuller, Lon, 4

Galligan, Denis, 222
gaps, 55–8, 80, 100, 107, 111, 113, 116–17, 195, 272
Gardiner, Lord Chancellor, 160
generalist judges, 36, 39–40
generality of law, 53–6, 58–9, 66, 84, 99, 105, 118, 122, 217, 219–22, 225, 272
*General Motors of Canada Ltd v City National Leasing* (1989), 183
Ginsburg, Justice Ruth Bader, 52, 140–1
Glenn, Patrick, 172
Goff, Lord Robert, 79–80, 118, 182
Gonthier, Justice Charles, 123, 249

good faith in contract law, 92, 108–10, 115, 183

Green, Leslie, 80–1

*habeas corpus*, 8–9

Hale, Baroness Brenda, 237

Halsbury, Lord Chancellor, 159

hard cases, 54, 68, 71–6, 116, 129–30

Hart, H.L.A., 4, 54, 67, 69, 72

hate speech, 102, 185

hearsay evidence, 92, 106–7, 108, 110, 115, 118

*Hedley Byrne & Co Ltd v Heller & Partners Ltd* (1964), 176

*Henry, R v* (2005), 164–5

Hercules, 73

Herridge, William, 8

hindsight bias, 143

*Hislop, R v* (2007), 79

Hoffmann, Lord, 74, 118, 253

Hogg, Peter, 181, 245

Holmes, Justice Oliver Wendell Jr, 79, 259–60, 270

*Home Office v Dorset Yacht Club Co Ltd* (1970), 176

horizontal precedent, 154–9

*Housen v Nikolaisen* (2002), 212–13

hunch. *See under* judicial: hunch

Iacobucci, Justice Frank, 88–90, 234, 237

impartiality, 13, 26, 251–69

incremental change, 75, 85–9, 91, 93, 95, 109–10, 118, 147, 176, 200

indeterminacy, 65–70

Indigenous people, 231, 233, 251, 267–8

inductive method, 55, 56, 116, 189

intermediate appellate court, 21, 39, 44, 49, 51–2, 70, 76, 85, 96–7,

130, 154, 156–9, 167, 169, 215, 229, 270–1

*International Covenant on Civil and Political Rights*, 178

*International Covenant on Economic, Social and Cultural Rights*, 178

international law, 9, 24, 26, 178–9, 186, 234–5, 250

interpretive theory, 14

interveners, 83–4, 236

intrusion upon seclusion. *See* privacy

*Irwin Toy Ltd v Quebec (AG)* (1989), 123

issues not raised by parties, 42, 47–8, 81–2, 133

*Jogee, R v* (2016), 159

*Jones v Tsige* (2012), 188–202

*Jordan, R v* (2016), 119–22

judge-shopping, 254, 257

judicial: activism, 230–1, 244; appointments, 18–26; education, 23, 261–2; hunch, 139–44, 190–1; independence, 22–3, 90, 250–1; integrity, 50, 249–50, 254, 256, 269; introspection, 72, 182, 256–63, 269; law-making, 65, 66, 75, 77–97, 103–4, 120, 125, 149, 154, 164, 176, 188–202, 230–2, 248, 272–3

jurisdictional review, 205–8

jury charges, 32, 42

jury trials, 28, 32, 42

Jutras, Daniel, 216

*Kahn, R v* (1990), 106–7

Karakatsanis, Justice Andromache, 119–20

*Keegstra, R v* (1990), 185

Kerans, Justice Roger, 226
King, William Lyon Mackenzie, 62, 175
Kirby, Justice Michael, 68
Krever, Justice Horace, 10

La Forest, Justice Gérard, 60, 90, 185
Lamer, Chief Justice Antonio, 27, 123
Laskin, Chief Justice Bora, 164, 173, 174, 179
Laskin, Justice John, 158–9
*Lavallee, R v* (1990), 185
law and economics, 14, 66
law as integrity, 14, 40, 41, 73, 80, 90, 97, 101, 116, 132, 135, 137–9, 156, 165, 172, 204, 207–9
law clerks, 40–1, 47, 180, 181
law reform commissions, 94
leave to appeal, 37, 38, 41, 52, 84, 96, 150, 155, 159, 163–4, 226, 270
Lebel, Justice Louis, 121
*Ledcor Construction Ltd v Northbridge Indemnity Insurance Co* (2016), 148–9, 213–14
Lederman, Sidney, 181
legalism, 60, 71, 128
legal officers, 40–1, 43
legal process school, 66
legal realism, 4, 66–7, 134, 139
legal uncertainty, 5–6, 53–76
legislature, role of, 6, 66, 77–8, 81, 86, 88, 91, 93–4, 97, 103, 131, 159, 165, 198–9, 204, 223, 228–49
L'Heureux-Dubé, Justice Claire, 183, 185, 265
limitation periods, 131
Linden, Allen, 181
living tree, 64–5, 239–42, 248

logic of discovery, 140–1
logic of justification, 140–2

Macdonald, Roderick, 180
MacKinnon, Bert, 7–8
MacKinnon, McTaggart, 3, 7–8, 9–11
MacPherson, Justice James, 37
majoritarianism. See *Charter of Rights and Freedoms*
mandatory minimum sentence, 131
mandatory retirement for judges, 18
Mandela, President Nelson, 256
Mansfield, Lord, 56, 58, 217–18
Martin, Justice Sheila, 22, 23
Mason, Justice Anthony, 255
McCamus, John, 88, 181
McLachlin, Chief Justice Beverley, 86–7, 117, 121, 246, 265, 267
mechanical reasoning, 55, 60, 65, 68, 99, 115, 143, 147, 149, 168, 171, 172, 173, 190, 221, 264, 271
mediation, 33–4
Megarry, Sir Robert, 136
mid-level theory, 14
Mill, John Stuart, 66
minimalism, 50–1, 84–5, 88, 95–6, 131, 197
mixed law and fact, 212–13
*M(K) v M(H)* (1992), 185
Moldaver, Justice Michael, 119–20
Monet, Claude, 15
Morden, Justice John, 73–4, 141
*Morin, R v* (1992), 119
motions, 9, 30–1, 37, 39, 192
Murphy, Emily, 61–2

*Murphy v Brentwood District Council* (1991), 176
*Muscutt v Courcelles* (2002), 82–4, 184

*Nadan, R v* (1926), 174–5
Nadon, Justice Marc, 22
National Judicial Institute, 261–2
Nedelsky, Jennifer, 265
negligence, 56–8, 80, 104, 110–15, 151, 176
*Nova Scotia Pharmaceutical Society, R v* (1992), 123
*NS, R v* (2012), 121–2

oath, judicial, 52, 60, 74, 126, 254, 256, 258
*obiter dicta*, 149–54, 191–2
open court principle, 35, 45, 137
operative theory, 14
oral argument, 42–4
organic evolution, 56, 63–5. *See also* living tree
originalism. See *Charter of Rights and Freedoms*
over-inclusive, 55, 99
overruling, 6, 52, 64, 117, 119, 130, 147, 152, 156–69, 176

palpable and overriding error, 166, 208–9, 213, 215
Parliament. *See* legislature, role of
parliamentary supremacy, 231, 235
patent unreasonableness, 206–7
*Peart v Peel Regional Police Services Board* (2006), 185–6
*Pelech v Pelech* (1987), 183
*per incuriam*, 156
Persons Case (1928), 61–5, 81, 239
persuasive authority, 149–50, 170–9, 186, 193, 196, 201

*Pettkus v Becker* (1980), 107–8
*Pinochet, Ex Parte, R v Bow Street Metropolitan Stipendiary Magistrate, Ugarte (No 2)* (2000), 252–3
policies, 86–9, 93–4, 98, 102–4, 112–17, 159, 184, 197–9, 235, 238
polycentric dispute, 87, 93
positivism, 4, 72
Posner, Judge Richard, 67
Potts, Joe, 8
Pound, Roscoe, 80
practical reasoning, 5, 13, 27, 44, 79, 111, 126, 139, 143, 266, 273
*Practice Statement (Judicial Precedent)* (1966), 160
precedent: discipline of, 129–31; dissents and concurring opinions, 49, 52; doctrine of, 5–6, 146–69; error-correction appeals, 45; gaps and exceptions, 56–7, 113; judicial hierarchy, 94–6, 210; other jurisdictions, 170–4; social context, 60. *See also under* judicial: law-making
presiding in court, 27–9
principled approach, 105–24
principles: background, 100–2, 104, 107–12, 195; coherence, 73–5, 139–40, 272; discipline of, 140, 143–5, 187, 241–2, 271–4; discretion, 216, 221–2; international law, 178; judicial law-making, 193–7, 201; legal theory, 14–15; nature of, 58, 66, 99–124, 232; operational, 99–100, 102, 104, 106, 111–12
principles of procedural fairness, 100, 207
privacy, 71, 75, 188–202
privity, 57–8, 111

proportionality, 104, 211, 243
Prosser, William, 196
prostitution. See *Charter of Rights and Freedoms*
publication bans, 91
public opinion, 90, 138, 236
public policy, 77, 94, 114, 117, 184, 235, 236
public reason, 138

Rachlinski, Jefferey, 143
racial issues, 66, 185–6, 252, 261–2, 265–6, 268
Rand, Justice Ivan, 218
Rathberger, Brent, 22
*ratio decidendi*, 148–51, 153
reasonableness standard of review, 132–3, 148, 166–7, 203–24
reasons, for judgment:
  administrative law, 207–8;
  assignment of, 42, 44–5; discipline of, 92, 125, 132, 134–45, 200–1, 242, 250, 273; discretionary decisions, 218–19, 222; dissenting and concurring, 48–52; error-correction appeals, 45, 70; hard cases, 72–6; law clerks, 40, 42, 47; precedential value, 148–57; preparation of, 30, 46, 45–8, 72–4, 82–4, 132, 201; timeliness, 29–30, 46
recusal, 254–6
*Reference Re Secession of Quebec* (1998), 101–2
*Reference Re Sections 193 and 195.1(c) of the Criminal Code* (1990), 123
*Reference Re Senate Reform* (2014), 102, 241
Reid, Lord, 79, 152
reserved judgments, 46–8

result-oriented decision-making, 47, 84, 142
Richter, Nicholas, 183
right answers, 16, 69, 71–6, 145, 207, 224
Roach, Kent, 185, 217, 221
Roberts, Chief Justice John, 71–2, 134
*Roncarelli v Duplessis* (1959), 218
Rothstein, Justice Marshall, 121, 167
Rowe, Justice Malcolm, 22, 23
Rowell, Newton, 175
rule of law, 81, 101, 122–4, 138, 168, 205, 207, 272, 274
rules: black letter, 14, 98, 99, 106–7, 143, 191, 193, 266; discretionary decisions, 217–22; judicial hunch, 139–44; judicial law-making, 86–94; nature of, 5–6, 14, 53–68, 73–4, 78, 98–124, 191–5, 261–2, 265–6, 268–9, 271–3
Russell, Peter, 235
*Rylands v Fletcher* (1868), 151–2

Sachs, Justice Albie, 139–41
*Salituro, R v* (1991), 87–9
Sankey, Lord, 63–5, 240
*Saskatchewan Federation of Labour v Saskatchewan* (2015), 166–7
*Sattva Capital Corp v Creston Moly Corp* (2015), 148, 213–14
Scalia, Justice Antonin, 51–2, 178, 238
Schauer, Frederick, 122, 127
scholarly writing. See academic writing
Scrutton, Lord Justice, 260
self-defence, 64, 185, 268
self-reflection. See under judicial: introspection

Senate, 61–4, 102, 240, 241
sentencing, 32, 131, 143, 224, 225, 246
settlement conferences, 32–4
Sexton, Edgar, 8
sexual orientation, 102, 228, 231, 234, 237, 257–8
social and legislative facts, 166–8, 186–7, 261, 268
social context: academic writing, 182, 184–6; constitutional interpretation, 61–5, 119–21, 240; impartiality, 259–62, 267–8; judicial law-making, 60–5, 81, 84, 89–90, 97, 161–2, 194, 196, 202; legal interpretation, 67, 71, 100, 112, 271–2
social science, 65, 126, 166, 184–6, 214–15
Sopinka, Justice John, 21, 181
spousal immunity, 87–90
*S(RD)*, *R v* (1997), 262–3
standard of review, 203–16
standards, 54, 55, 56, 128–9, 131, 216, 219, 220–2. *See also* principles
*stare decisis*. *See* precedent
statutory interpretation, 63, 64, 77–8, 103, 181
Stewart, Hamish, 137
Stone, Arthur, 7–8
Stratas, Justice David, 203
Strathy, Chief Justice George, 8
striking claims, 192–3
Sullivan, Ruth, 181
summary judgment, 30, 191, 211–12
Superior Court of Justice, 27
supernumerary judges, 18–19, 37
Supreme Court of Canada: academic writing, 179–80,

183–6; appeal as of right, 38, 52; appointments, 21–4, 26; concurring and dissenting reasons, 49, 52, 68, 72; constitutional role, 226–48; executive legal officer, 11–12; formalism, 60–4, 173–4; international law, 178–9; jurisprudential role, 70, 83–90, 95–6, 270–2; law clerks, 47; leave to appeal, 38, 52; precedent, 130, 147, 153–4, 157–69, 214–16; principled approach, 106–24; reasons, 135–6, 140
Swan, Angela, 181

Tanovich, David, 185
technological change, 194, 196, 201–2
Thomas, Justice E.W., 116, 138
time limits, 31, 41, 43
trial judges: factual findings, 69–70, 132–3, 223–5, 252, 270; law-making, 94–7, 192; precedent, 147, 153–4, 166–8; reasons, 41, 137; standard of review, 50–1, 70, 148, 208–15, 219–20, 223–5; work of, 27–32
trial record, 28, 38, 41, 43, 133

unconscionability, 77, 102, 105, 109
under-inclusive, 55, 99
*Universal Declaration of Human Rights*, 178
universality, principle of, 54–5, 59, 209–10, 265, 271
University of Caen, 6–7
University of Oxford, 3, 8–9
University of Toronto, Faculty of Law, 3–6, 10–11, 12

University of Western Ontario, 4
unjust enrichment, 92, 107–8, 110,
    115, 117–19
unreasonableness, 132, 148, 203–16,
    219, 220, 223, 224
utilitarianism, 66

*Van Breda.* See *Club Resorts Ltd v
    Van Breda* (2012)
vertical precedent, 153–4
vote, right to, 61, 236, 238, 240, 244,
    246

Waddams, Stephen, 118, 181, 222, 226
Wade, William, 8–9
waiver, 254–5
Wald, Judge Patricia, 138

Waldron, Jeremy, 235
*Watkins v Olafson* (1989), 85–9
Weiler, Paul, 60
Weinrib, Ernest, 60
Weinrib, Jacob, 237
Weinrib, Lorraine, 242
Wilson, Justice Bertha, 26, 233
Winkler, Chief Justice Warren, 190
wisdom, 12, 32, 50, 118, 150, 155,
    192, 261, 266
women, rights of, 61–5, 81, 88–90,
    162, 185, 233–4, 240, 252
Women's Legal Action Fund, 11
women's suffrage, 61, 240
won't write, 46, 140
written argument. *See* factum
wrongful conviction, 142